STATE RESPONSIBILITY AND THE INDIVIDUAL
Reparation in Instances of Grave Violations of Human Rights

State Responsibility and the Individual

Reparation in Instances of Grave Violations of Human Rights

Edited by

Albrecht Randelzhofer

Professor of Law at the Free University, Berlin

and

Christian Tomuschat

Professor of Law at the Humboldt University, Berlin
Associated Member, Institut de droit international

MARTINUS NIJHOFF PUBLISHERS
THE HAGUE / LONDON / BOSTON

A C.I.P Catalogue record for this book is available from the Library of Congress.

ISBN 90-411-1147-6

Published by Kluwer Law International,
P.O. Box 85889, 2508 CN The Hague, The Netherlands

Sold and distributed in North, Central and South America
by Kluwer Law International,
675 Massachusetts Avenue, Cambridge, MA 02139, USA

In all other countries, sold and distributed
by Kluwer Law International, Distribution Centre
P.O. Box 322, 3300 AH Dordrecht, The Netherlands

Printed on acid-free paper

Printed and bound in Great Britain by Antony Rowe Ltd.

Table of Contents

Foreword

In July 1996, the International Law Commission (ILC) concluded the first reading of its long-standing project on State responsibility. Hopefully this draft will be adopted on second reading during the current quinquennium of the ILC (1997-2001) notwithstanding the suggestions made by the new Special-Rapporteur, Professor James Crawford, to effect major changes.[1] In fact, the draft articles are the fruit of many political compromises. On one hand, they may be considered too detailed on some issues regarding the origin of international responsibility. On the other hand, they also contain some glaring gaps. In particular, no trace of any rights of individuals can be found in the proposed regime of secondary rules. This reluctance to deal with the individual as a holder of rights under international law contrasts sharply with new tendencies that seem fundamentally to alter traditional concepts of international law, tendencies which the ILC has apparently discarded.

It is a matter of common knowledge that there exist nowadays treaties which provide that individuals suffering injury from unlawful conduct of State authorities may be awarded compensation by international bodies – hence as a matter of international law. Article 50 of the European Convention on Human Rights and Article 63 of the American Convention on Human Rights stand out as the main witnesses of this new configuration of international law according to which the individual appears as an autonomous actor on the international level. Most recently, the Rome Statute of the International Criminal Court[2] has directed the Court to establish principles relating to reparation to victims, including restitution, compensation and rehabilitation (Article 75). Furthermore, it is sometimes assumed that even outside a specific treaty regime private persons may be entitled to claim reparation for harm sustained by them as a consequence of a violation of human rights standards encapsulated in customary law. At the United Nations, draft principles have

---

[1] In particular, he has recommended to separate the special regime of international crimes from the draft articles on State responsibility, see First report on State responsibility, UN doc. A/CN.4/490/Add.3, 11 May 1998, para. 101.
[2] Of 17 July 1998, UN doc. A/CONF.183/9.

A. Randelzhofer and C. Tomuschat (eds.), State Responsibility and the Individual, vii–ix.
© 1999 *Kluwer Law International. Printed in Great Britain.*

been elaborated by the Special-Rapporteur of the Sub-Commission on Prevention of Discrimination and Protection of Minorities, Mr. Theo van Boven, which aim at recognizing the right of any victim of (gross) violations of human rights to obtain redress.[3] To date, these principles have not yet been confirmed by a formal resolution.

It was the objective of an International Colloquium organized in Berlin by the Law Faculties of the Free University and the Humboldt University from 26 to 28 September 1997 to examine these new tendencies and at the same time probe into their legitimacy and usefulness. It is certainly true that human rights are greatly strengthened if any significant breach gives rise to an individual entitlement to reparation. On the other hand, juridical logic sometimes overlooks the simple fact that States cannot be treated in the same way as business corporations. States are organizations of peoples which inevitably are actors in history, but may also become victims of history. Uprisings, revolutions and wars can be constrained by legal norms only to a limited extent. The damage caused by such eruptions of irrationality may be of such magnitude that to impose a burden on the author State to wipe out all of the economically assessable consequences of those events would condemn the human community concerned – also the generations to come – to an existence as eternal debtor. This very basic consideration must lead one to asking with great insistence whether a 'privatized' regime of State responsibility is really a desirable model for the settlement of reparation claims under all circumstances. If agreements are concluded on an inter-State level, the necessary accommodations dictated by political wisdom can be effected. Judges, however, are institutionally prevented from looking beyond the case which they have to decide. Thus, it may be necessary to find flexible solutions, adapted to the specific circumstances of the case at hand. The United Nations Compensation Commission, mandated to resolve Gulf War claims against Iraq, currently constitutes the primary example of a mechanism that combines traditional elements of diplomatic protection with some degree of leeway for individuals to assert their rights on their own account.

The papers of the Conference have been collected in this volume which, furthermore, also reproduces the main features of the discussions held after each block of presentations. It was felt that such a wealth of ideas and suggestions was put forward by the participants that without them the book would be incomplete. The article by Bardo Fassbender was written after the Conference at the request of the organizers. Since the Conference took place in Berlin, it would have looked awkward if the German experience of

---

[3] Basic Principles and Guidelines on the Right to Reparation for Victims of [Gross] Violations of Human Rights and International Humanitarian Law, UN doc. E/CN.4/1997/104, 16 January 1997, infra (annex).

'Vergangenheitsbewältigung' had not been studied. To be sure, it is not easy to retrieve the guiding principles underlying the complicated legal regime enacted after the fall of the Berlin wall to provide reparation to victims of socialist rule. Yet these complexities make clear that according to the opinion of the competent legislative bodies the simplistic formula of full reparation for any human rights violation was not deemed to provide an ideal solution to the injustices of the past.

The book would not have materialized without the assistance of many helping hands. Bardo Fassbender assumed the functions of editorial revisor. Julia Lehmann and Catherine Brady took care of the linguistic correctness of the pieces written by non-native speakers. Other main contributions were made by Oliver Dörr, Georg Reichel and David Meinertz, who were involved in preparing the Conference and revising the footnotes. Colette Baume-Herrmann had the challenging task of reconstructing the discussion from tapes which sometimes were not absolutely reliable. We are grateful to all of the members of our staff for having dedicated their best efforts to making this book possible.

The organizers are deeply indebted to the Fritz Thyssen Stiftung for generously sponsoring the Conference.

Albrecht Randelzhofer
Christian Tomuschat

Contributors

Bardo Fassbender is Assistant Professor at the Institute of International and European Law, Humboldt University, Berlin. His publications on public international law, constitutional law, and legal history include *UN Security Council Reform and the Right of Veto: A Constitutional Perspective* (The Hague etc., 1998) and 'The United Nations Charter as Constitution of the International Community' (*Columbia Journal of Transnational Law* 36 (1998), 529-619).

Lovell Fernandez is Professor of Public and Adjective Law at the University of the Western Cape in Bellville, Republic of South Africa. He is also an Advocate of the High Court of South Africa and an advisor to the South African Ministry of Justice. He specializes in transitional law, access to justice and in issues relating to criminal justice and the State. In 1996 and 1997 he was involved as a fulltime consultant in drawing up the *Justice Vision 2000* document, which is the blueprint for the transformation and restructuring of the justice system under the new democratic government.

Eckart Klein is Professor of Constitutional Law, Public International Law and European Law at the University of Potsdam. From 1981 to 1994, he held the same position at the University of Mainz. From 1974 to 1976, he was a law clerk at the German Federal Constitutional Court, and from 1969 to 1981 a research fellow at the Max Planck Institute for Comparative Public Law and International Law in Heidelberg. He is the author and editor of books and articles on public international law, European Law and German Constitutional law, and on human rights, including *Lehrbuch des Verfassungsprozessrechts* (Law of Constitutional Procedure) (co-author, Heidelberg, 1991), and *Handkommentar zum Vertrag über die Europäische Union* (Commentary on the Treaty Establishing the European Union) (Cologne, since 1991).

Matti Pellonpää is Judge of the European Court of Human Rights and Professor of International Law at the University of Helsinki (presently on leave of absence from the last-mentioned post). Before the constitution of the new court, he was President of the First Chamber of the European Commission of Human Rights. He also served as a Legislative Counsellor in the Finnish Ministry of Justice, as a Judge of the Supreme Administrative Court,

A. Randelzhofer and C. Tomuschat (eds.), State Responsibility and the Individual, xi–xiii.
© 1999 *Kluwer Law International. Printed in Great Britain.*

and in various other non-academic positions in Finland. From 1984 to 1986, he was Legal Assistant at the Iran-United States Claims Tribunal in The Hague, and from 1993 to 1996 member of a panel of the United Nations Compensation Commission in Geneva. He is the author of numerous publications.

Riccardo Pisillo-Mazzeschi is Professor of International Law at the University of Siena. He was previously Professor of Private International Law at the same university (1985-1990) and Professor of International Law at the University of Cagliari (1990-1994). He was a Visiting Professor at Tulane Law School and a Visiting Scholar at University College London. His publications include a book on termination and suspension of treaties, a book on due diligence and State responsibility, and a number of studies and articles on public international law, private international law, and European Community law.

Albrecht Randelzhofer is Professor of Constitutional Law, Administrative Law, Public International Law and European Law at the Free University of Berlin (since 1976). He has been a Visiting Professor in Cambridge (United Kingdom) and Ann Arbor (Michigan, United States). He is a Member of the Permanent Court of Arbitration in The Hague, a Judge of the Constitutional Court of Berlin, and a Member of the Public International Law Advisory Board of the German Ministry of Foreign Affairs. He has served as arbitrator in international cases and counsel in cases before the Federal Constitutional Court of Germany. He was Vice-President of the Berlin Society of Law and a Member of the Executive Board of the German Society of International Law.

W. Michael Reisman is Hohfeld Professor of Jurisprudence at the Yale Law School where he has been on the Faculty since 1965. He has been a visiting professor in Tokyo, Hong Kong, Berlin, Basel, Paris and Geneva. He is a Fellow of the World Academy of Art and Science and a former member of its Executive Council. He is a member of the Advisory Committee on International Law of the Department of State, co-Editor-in-Chief of the American Journal of International Law, the Vice-Chairman of the Policy Sciences Center, Inc., and a member of the Board of The Foreign Policy Association. He has served as arbitrator and counsel in many international cases and was Vice-President and then President of the Inter-American Commission on Human Rights of the Organization of American States and Vice-President and Honorary Vice-President of the American Society of International Law.

Christian Tomuschat is Professor of Public Law and Director of the Institute of International and European Law, Humboldt University, Berlin. He was previously Professor of Public Law and Director of the Institute of International Law, University of Bonn (1972-1995). He was a Member of the Human Rights Committee under the International Covenant on Civil and Political Rights (1977-1986), a Member of the International Law Commission (1985-1996), and Coordinator of the Historical Clarification Commission of Guatemala (February 1997-January 1999). From 1993 to 1997, he held the position of President of the German Society of International Law. In 1993, he gave a course at the Hague Academy on International Law on *Obligations Arising for States without or against Their Will*. He is the author and editor of numerous books and articles on international, European and German constitutional law, including *Modern Law of Self-Determination* (Dordrecht etc., 1993) and *The United Nations at Age Fifty: A Legal Perspective* (The Hague etc., 1995).

Norbert Wühler is Chief of the Legal Service of the United Nations Compensation Commission in Geneva (since 1992). From 1983 to 1991, he was Legal Assistant to the President and, from 1987, Deputy Secretary-General of the Iran-United States Claims Tribunal in The Hague. Prior to that, he worked as a research fellow at the Max Planck Institute for Comparative Public Law and International Law in Heidelberg. He has been a secretary and a member of international arbitral tribunals, and has published books and articles on the settlement of disputes and the international judicial system.

Individual Reparation Claims in Instances of Grave Human Rights Violations: The Position under General International Law

Christian Tomuschat

I. INTRODUCTION

A few years ago, a major diplomatic row was about to develop between Germany and the United States of America. A U.S. citizen had sued the German State for injuries suffered during the Nazi period. This plaintiff, Hugo Princz, a person of Jewish ethnicity, originally lived with his family in Czechoslovakia. After the United States declared war against Germany in 1942, he was arrested and assigned to a concentration camp together with all the members of his family. At the end of the Second World War, he remained as the only survivor, having endured years not only of hardship, but cruelties and horrors of unspeakable dimensions. The new democratic Germany attempted to make good at least a part of what still could be repaired. Extensive programs of compensation were adopted by the legislative bodies and put into operation. Princz, however, had no access to any of these programs.[1] Eventually, through his action initiated in March 1992, he sought an amount of 20 million dollars as compensatory and punitive damages.

Many legal problems arose in connection with this suit. The first one was of course the issue of jurisdiction of the American tribunals seized with the case. According to general rules of international law, reflected also in the U.S. Foreign Sovereign Immunities Act (FSIA),[2] foreign States are generally protected from legal actions brought against them in American courts. Immediately thereafter, however, the question was to be answered whether

---

[1] For the factual details see the first-instance decision of the U.S. District Court for the District of Columbia, 23 December 1992, 813 F. Supp. at 22. It was controversial whether Princz could have benefitted from any of the programs. He had made two applications, the first one in 1955, but was each time advised that he was not eligible for them. Further attempts to obtain an *ex-gratia* payment, undertaken between 1984 and 1987, proved also unsuccessful.

[2] 28 U.S.C. §§ 1330, 1602-1611.

1

A. Randelzhofer and C. Tomuschat (eds.), State Responsibility and the Individual, 1–25.
© 1999 *Kluwer Law International. Printed in Great Britain.*

Princz had a cause of action against Germany. According to our understanding, U.S. law of torts was not applicable to facts occurring between 1942 and 1945 somewhere in Europe. Neither did Princz rely on the law of Czechoslovakia. His contention was that the rights he vindicated derived directly from international law.

It need not be stressed here that the legal underpinnings of the suit as thus conceived of by Princz were clearly inconsistent with traditional thinking about the structure of international law. Before 1945, in any event, the individual hardly existed as a holder of rights under international law. A classical exposition of the prevailing views can be found in Oppenheim's treatise which stated with unmitigated rigor:

> Since the Law of Nations is a law between States only, and since States are the sole exclusive subjects of International Law, individuals are mere objects of International Law, and the latter is unable to confer directly rights and duties upon individuals.[3]

This was by no means an isolated voice. In almost similar terms, Dionisio Anzilotti said on the same issue:

> ...la conduite d'un Etat, toute contraire qu'elle soit au droit international, ne saurait jamais donner naissance à un droit de l'individu à la réparation du dommage souffert.[4]

It is a matter of common knowledge that the classical doctrine of international law had to be reconsidered after the door to the high ground of international law was opened to the individual by the Charter of the United Nations and the chain of juridical events it put into motion. No learned author could today deal with the legal position of the human being in just one sentence as this was considered sufficient at the turn of the century. Hersh Lauterpacht himself, who continued Oppenheim´s treatise, made himself the champion of the new concept of international law in his famous book 'International Law and Human Rights' of 1950, where he wrote:

> The Charter of the United Nations, in recognising the fundamental human rights and freedoms, has to that extent constituted individuals subjects of the law of nations.[5]

II. THE ILC'S DRAFT ARTICLES ON STATE RESPONSIBILITY

Given this development, it is all the more surprising that the International Law Commission (ILC) in its draft articles on State responsibility, adopted in

---

[3] *International Law*, Vol. I, 1905, 200.
[4] 'La responsabilité internationale des Etats à raison des dommages soufferts par des étrangers', *Revue générale de droit international public* 13 (1906), 5, at 5.
[5] *International Law and Human Rights*, 1950, 61.

1996,[6] makes no mention of the individual as an actor in the legal relationship brought into being by a breach of a rule of international law. The entire set of provisions deals only with States as affected subjects of international law. To be sure, the draft contains an already famous article defining the injured State (Article 40), where specific reference is made to the breach by an author State of its obligations in the field of human rights (paragraph 2(e)(iii)). However, even in that connection, according to the ILC the secondary rights originated by a violation accrue solely and exclusively to States – the States entitled to claim performance of the duties breached. Thus, to put it bluntly, the ILC draft could have been drawn up in almost the same terms a century ago, leaving apart the word 'human rights' and the timid excursion of the ILC into the realm of international crimes. Neither Oppenheim nor Anzilotti would have had any great difficulties in understanding the text as it is now pending for comments before the second and final reading.

According to an old Latin adage, all roads lead to Rome. Within the United Nations system, the brain stations focusing all the efforts undertaken are located in New York and/or, as far as legal activities and in particular human rights are concerned, in Geneva. In fact, not only the ILC traditionally held its annual meetings in Geneva, but also the Sub-Commission on Prevention of Discrimination and Protection of Minorities, which for years now has been debating a project concerning the rights of individuals in instances of grave violations of human rights. And yet, despite this proximity in the *Palais des Nations*, the ILC draft articles on State responsibility have taken no account of the work carried forward in the same building a few doors further on. Theo van Boven, the rapporteur on the topic, criticized this unfortunate state of affairs,[7] but to no avail.

We do agree that this criticism is justified insofar as the ILC has failed even to debate the issue. On the other hand, it would certainly have been much too difficult to change the structure of the draft articles after the foundations had been laid in the sixties, more than thirty years ago, by Roberto Ago who was indeed the intellectual leader of the ILC with regard to the topic of State responsibility. In his second report, commenting briefly on the scope of the

---

[6] Report of the International Law Commission on the work of its forty-eighth session, 6 May-26 July 1996, General Assembly Official Records, Fifty-first Session, Supp. No. 10 (A/51/10), 125.

[7] Study concerning the right to restitution, compensation and rehabilitation for victims of gross violations of human rights and fundamental freedoms, Final report, UN doc. E/CN.4/Sub.2/1993/8, 2 July 1993, para. 47. The revised version of the 'Basic Principles and Guidelines on the Right to Reparation for Victims of [Gross] Violations of Human Rights and International Humanitarian Law' is contained in UN doc. E/CN.4/1997/104, 16 January 1997, reprinted in this book as an annex. The proposal was not adopted at the 1997 session of the UN Commission on Human Rights, see resolution 1997/29, 11 April 1997.

ILC's work *ratione personae*, he emphasized that for the time being the work to be carried out would be confined, as far as the passive side of the legal relationship generated by unlawful conduct was concerned, to the responsibility of States.[8] He did not specifically deal with the question of who might derive secondary rights from a breach of an international obligation. Quite obviously, however, he took it for granted that only States could acquire new rights under the law of responsibility[9] to be codified since, in his view, obligations based on international law were primarily owed to States.[10]

Thus, from the very first day, the codification process was geared to States exclusively. Neither were international organizations taken into account nor the individual, whose recognition as a subject of international law also in the field of State responsibility would have constituted an even greater challenge to the ILC, not only in terms of legal rationalization but also in political terms. In fact, to acknowledge the individual as a subject enjoying an autonomous status which is independent of that of his or her home State necessarily means that the State as a system of governance loses some elements of its sovereign powers. Governments are reluctant to accept such a diminished role. It will be the main aim of this paper to study whether it is in the best interest of the individual to be taken forward in such a process of legal emancipation.

In this connection, a complex difficulty can be clearly perceived. The language of the ILC's draft articles is admirable in its generosity with regard to States as far as human rights violations are concerned. According to Article 40(2)(e)(iii), in case of such a violation every other State party to the legal system of protection at stake is to be considered as having suffered legal injury. This means, in other terms, that if a State breaches an obligation predicated on customary law any other State of this globe passes into the category of injured State. This is reconfirmed for human rights violations that may be characterized as international crimes (Article 40 (3)). In the case of treaty systems, the injured States are the other States parties of the agreement concerned. The consequences deriving from this legal arrangement are just overwhelming. Any State thus having suffered injury in a legal sense is vested with all the rights that may come into existence by an internationally wrongful act. It may claim cessation as well as all forms of reparation, namely restitution in kind, compensation, satisfaction and guarantees of non-repetition

---

[8] Second report on State responsibility, UN doc. A/CN.4/233, Yearbook of the ILC (YILC) 1970 II, 177, at 178 para. 5.

[9] A few years earlier, commenting on Sir Humphrey Waldock's draft proposals on the Law of Treaties, Ago said: 'He could not subscribe to an article that took a positive view on the international personality of the individual at that stage in the development of international law', YILC 1964 I, 117 para. 50.

[10] A similar approach can be perceived in Ian Brownlie's book *State Reponsibility*, Part I, 1983. Brownlie does not deem it necessary to discuss who the holder of reparation claims may be.

(Article 42(1)). No distinction is drawn between directly affected and other, 'third' States that have not sustained any material damage. In fact, precisely with regard to human rights violations, it would be difficult to establish and maintain that distinction since in general the victims of such violations are the citizens of the author State itself. Thus, all other States are 'third' States, at least if one uses a yardstick shaped by perceptions of national interest that still dominate political realities.

III. STATE PRACTICE

1) States as Guardians of the Rights of Foreign Peoples

The legal landscape *du meilleur des mondes* does not correspond to what can be empirically observed, and thus one may doubt whether the ILC on this point has merely codified current practices based on *opinio iuris* or whether it has leapt forward in an unconscious effort to reshape the law. It is true that there is ample evidence for governments appealing to other governments to heed their human rights obligations and to desist from conduct inconsistent with their commitments either existing under general international law or deriving from the Charter of the United Nations or other multilateral treaties. As far as the European system for the protection of human rights and fundamental freedoms is concerned, suffice it to refer to the State applications directed against the Greece of the colonel torturers[11] or against Turkey after the military coup of 1980.[12] Relevant in this connection are also the procedures and mechanisms of the UN Commission on Human Rights and the General Assembly. In general, however, the diplomatic representations, recommendations, calls and admonishments emerging from these and other UN bodies are directed towards putting an end to a situation in breach of human rights commitments. In a rare number of instances resolutions of United Nations bodies have referred to the issue of reparation for damage sustained.[13] But for an individual third State to claim reparation to the benefit of the victims is something almost unknown in international practice. In venturing so far ahead a State not directly affected would certainly not feel at ease. Taking a stand to defend the rights and interests of the citizens of a third

---

[11] *Yearbook of the European Convention on Human Rights* 11/II (1969), 691; 12 (1969), 1.

[12] Decisions and Reports 35, 143; 44, 31.

[13] See, for instance, resolutions for the benefit of the victims of ethnic cleansing in the former Yugoslavia, UN GA resolutions 47/147, 18 Dec. 1992, para. 11; 48/153, 20 Dec. 1993, para. 13; 49/196, 23 Dec. 1994, para. 24; 50/193, 22 Dec. 1995, para. 12. The model for these resolutions was UN GA resolution 194 (III) of 11 Dec. 1948, para. 11, on the situation of Palestinian refugees.

country is already a noble gesture which inevitably has its political costs. But no government can really feel motivated to go into the fine work of bringing redress to an afflicted foreign population. Here, the limits of what altruism can achieve are obviously reached. The situation is totally different if a State has been hurt in the person of its citizens. Then its general duty to protect the rights and interests of its national community is activated. Diplomatic protection in the traditional sense has its strong incentives in the accountability of any democratic government towards its electorate as well as in the interest to shield national assets from any harmful interference by other States. To espouse the cause of foreign citizens in a foreign country, however, is always a discretionary decision which even a strong State is normally extremely reluctant to take. In other words, the system for the reparation of human rights violations as conceived of by the ILC is hardly workable. If the aggrieved victim himself had a remedy at its disposal it would gain strength and effectiveness. As it stands, it holds more promise than it can actually deliver.

2) *The Power of States to Dispose of the Rights of Their Citizens*

Granting the victim of a human rights violation autonomous rights vis-à-vis the author State might at the same time dispose of a problem that has not yet found a satisfactory solution, namely the power of States to settle claims of their citizens at a negotiating table where such claims may constitute but one item in a series of others which politically may be deemed to be more important. An example that readily comes to mind is the case of the so-called comfort women used by Japanese soldiers for their sexual pleasure during the Second World War.[14] Most of these women were of Korean and Philippine nationality. For decades, they did not publicly mention their plight, still afflicted by feelings of shame and degradation that undermined their self-esteem. When they finally overcame their inhibitions, they found out that their countries, acting with a view to bringing about peace in the mutual relationship, might have renounced any possible claims against Japan resulting from the war. A similar debate took place in Germany two years ago when the ethnic Germans who had once inhabited the *Sudetenland* objected to a

---

[14] For details see International Commission of Jurists (ed.), *Comfort Women: An Unfinished Ordeal*, 1994; report by Special Rapporteur on violence against women, its causes and consequences, Ms. Radhika Coomaraswamy, on the mission to the Democratic People's Republic of Korea, the Republic of Korea and Japan on the issue of military sexual slavery in wartime, UN doc. E/CN.4/1996/53/Add.1, 4 January 1996. Recently, the South Korean Government decided to pay compensation to 'comfort women' itself, see *International Herald Tribune*, 22 April 1998, 6.

common declaration prepared by Prague and Bonn[15] out of fear that this diplomatic settlement would ignore the claims they believed to enjoy against the Czech Republic on account of the treatment they had been subjected to in connection with their forcible expulsion from their ancestral lands after the end of the Second World War.[16] Although one may be naturally inclined to assist Hugo Princz or the Korean and Philippine comfort women or the *Sudeten* Germans, it is also clear, almost at first glance, that to overturn the traditional legal edifice of how war claims are settled could entail serious legal problems.

Before delving into matters more related to legal policy, however, some reflections on whether the basic requirements for possibly accepting an individual entitlement to reparation for damage resulting from human rights violations may be deemed to exist.

IV. NECESSARY REQUIREMENTS OF POTENTIAL INDIVIDUAL REPARATION CLAIMS

1) Breach of Legal Obligation under International Law

According to the first part of the draft articles of the ILC, an internationally wrongful act presupposes that an obligation under international law has been breached (Article 3(b)). There could be no justification for departing from this requirement with regard to individual claims. This conclusion must above all be drawn from the simple fact that the rights arising from an internationally wrongful acts are secondary rights, deriving from a primary substantive right that has been breached. Hence, if there is no primary right there can be no secondary right. To jump from a position which legally is non-existent to a true legal right would go against all laws of logic. Only if it can be assumed that individuals are true holders of human rights as personal entitlements can the line of reasoning be pursued to its very end.

Again we must refer in this connection to the traditional position that international law constitutes a pattern of mutual relationships among States. If this were still the case today, our investigation would be doomed from the very outset. Therefore, it must be asked how the legal position is to be assessed today. It goes without saying that this question must be answered

---

[15] The Declaration was signed on 21 January 1997 in Prague; German Text: *Bulletin des Presse- und Informationsamts der Bundesregierung* 1997, 61.

[16] For an extensive discussion see C. Tomuschat, 'Die Vertreibung der Sudetendeutschen. Zur Frage des Bestehens von Rechtsansprüchen nach Völkerrecht und deutschem Recht', *Zeitschrift für ausländisches öffentliches Recht und Völkerrecht* 56 (1996), 1 et seqq.

according to 'orthodox' international thinking in consonance with Article 38 of the Statute of the International Court of Justice. What matters here is positive law, although it may be difficult to say with any degree of precision and reliability where the law stands.

Reparation is a comprehensive term that includes many forms of redressing injury caused in violation of rules of international law. According to Article 42 of the draft articles on State responsibility adopted by the ILC,[17] an injured State is entitled to reparation in the form of restitution in kind, compensation, satisfaction and assurances and guarantees of non-repetition, either singly or in combination. The 'Van Boven Principles'[18] very similarly provide for restitution, compensation, rehabilitation (as a special remedy for individuals) and satisfaction and guarantees of non-repetition. In the following, the main focus shall be on restitution and financial compensation, the main forms of reparation which make the dilemmas inherent in establishing a satisfactory regime particularly ostensible.

2) Some Examples

a) The European Communities

There is one primary example of a legal system that has brushed aside almost any distinction between States as the guardians of the collective interests of their peoples, their governments being the only agencies authorized to act on the international level, and individuals, who must accept that their governments act on their behalf, sometimes just as they wish they should do, sometimes, however, against those wishes if the general interest dictates a different solution. Reference is made, of course, to the legal order of the three European Communities. The case which still today stands out as a landmark is the case of *Van Gend & Loos*, decided in 1961,[19] where the Court of Justice of the European Communities ruled that any Community citizen had a right to see the law determining his or her position be respected by Community institutions as well as by member States. In particular, the Court held that the way in which a rule of the Community system was framed was irrelevant; it was not a requirement that the individual be explicitly referred to as the holder of a right. Thus, the way was open for anyone to rely on the provisions directly affecting him or her, trying to enforce them not only through the Court of Justice of the European Communities, but also through national judicial bodies. The ultimate spearhead of this jurisprudence was shaped when

---

[17] Supra note 6.
[18] Supra note 7.
[19] Reports 1963, 1.

the Court ruled in 1991 in the *Francovich* case[20] that an individual who suffers damage as a result of a member State of the Communities not respecting its obligations resulting from Community law enjoys a right to reparation of the damage caused by such unlawful behaviour. Details of this jurisprudence are still controversial,[21] but the principle stands: since the individual is deemed to be placed at the same level as the States which have created the Community legal order, no differentiation seems justifiable, provided that the rules in issue are clearly intended to benefit the Community citizen. What applies to secondary rules (*Francovich*) must also apply to primary rules (*Brasserie du Pêcheur*[22]). Thus, if States have the (theoretical) right to claim compensation for breach of Community law,[23] this right cannot be denied to private citizens.

Only in some areas has the Court of Justice of the European Communities shied away from applying its jurisprudence to its full extent. Until now, in particular, it has maintained its jurisprudence according to which, as a rule, no one may invoke GATT provisions to his or her personal benefit.[24] Thus, the way is also closed for claims seeking compensation for failure to heed the obligations laid down in that agreement. One certainly does not err in assuming that the Court, in relegating the GATT to a secondary rank in the legal hierarchy of the Community system, was influenced by fears that the Community might have to face up to uncalculable financial consequences if any erroneous – or deliberately wrong – application could expose it to reparation suits.

---

[20] Reports 1991, I-5403. In *Francovich*, the specific subject-matter was failure to translate into domestic law the contents of a Community directive. A later case with a similar factual background is *Dillenkofer*, 8 October 1996, Reports 1996, I-4867.

[21] See, for instance, M.R. Deckert, 'Zur Haftung des Mitgliedstaates bei Verstößen seiner Organe gegen europäisches Gemeinschaftsrecht', *Europarecht* 1997, 203 et seqq.; A. Hatje, 'Die Haftung der Mitgliedstaaten bei Verstößen des Gesetzgebers gegen europäisches Gemeinschaftsrecht', *Europarecht* 1997, 297 et seqq.; M. Herdegen & Th. Rensmann, 'Die neuen Konturen der gemeinschaftsrechtlichen Staatshaftung', *Zeitschrift für das gesamte Handelsrecht und Wirtschaftsrecht* 161 (1997), 522 et seqq.; C. Tomuschat, 'Das Francovich-Urteil des EuGH – Ein Lehrstück zum Europarecht', in: *Festschrift für Ulrich Everling*, Vol. II, 1995, 1585 et seqq.; W. van Gerven, 'Bridging the Unbridgeable: Community and National Tort Laws after *Francovich* and *Brasserie*', *International and Comparative Law Quarterly* 45 (1996), 507 et seqq.

[22] Judgment of 5 March 1996, Reports 1996, I-1131, paras. 20-23.

[23] See C. Tomuschat, 'Völkerrechtliche Schadensersatzansprüche vor dem EuGH', in: *Festschrift für Bodo Börner*, 1992, 441 et seqq.

[24] *Schlüter* case, Reports 1972, 1219, at 1228/1229. This judgment has never been overturned. The ECJ has even denied member states the right to invoke the GATT provisions, see judgment in *Germany v. Council*, 5 October 1994, Reports 1994, I-4973. For a vivid criticism of this jurisprudence see Ernst-Ulrich Petersmann, 'Darf die EG das Völkerrecht ignorieren?', *Europäische Zeitschrift für Wirtschaftsrecht* 1997, 325 et seqq.

b) Other Treaty Systems

There are a number of legal systems for the protection of human rights under which the individual, after having endured years of litigation, may finally be granted an award of compensation. It has been the main task of the colloquium whose contributions are assembled in this book to look into these mechanisms, asking whether one can already speak of true rights of the claim- ant/petitioner/applicant or whether the discretion of the competent judicial bodies is too wide to permit such conclusion. In the present context, attention will be confined to examining the legal position under general international law, outside the specific framework of any multilateral treaty for the protec- tion of human rights.

3) Rights under International Law

In order to gain a solid point of departure, we shall start from the premise that a clear distinction must be drawn between rights which the individual enjoys under domestic law and rights which directly accrue to him or her under international law. It is not enough to refer to the existence of human rights treaties in order to draw the conclusion that personality under international law exists. Up to the present time, most legal systems require a national legal act for the conferral of the rights set forth in human rights treaties on individuals. Thus, the legal position of the individual is then governed by domestic law, a legal configuration which was in the past constantly stressed by communist countries in particular but which was and is no specificity of that group of countries alone. It is significant, in this connection, that all of the present-day human rights treaties, inasmuch as they mention compensation to the benefit of an individual who has sustained injury, enjoin the State party concerned to enact national legislation for that purpose. The most telling example in point is provided by Article 13 of the Convention against Torture and Other Cruel, Inhuman or Degrading Treatment or Punishment[25], according to which every State party 'shall ensure in its legal system that the victim of an act of torture obtains redress and has an enforceable right to fair and adequate compensa- tion'. As far as the International Covenant on Civil and Political Rights[26] is concerned, Article 14, para. 6, states that having suffered punishment as a result of miscarriage of justice, an individual 'shall be compensated according to law', i.e. national law. Less explicit is Article 9, para. 5, of the Covenant

---

[25] Adopted by UN General Assembly resolution 39/46, 10 December 1984, Bundesgesetzblatt 1990 II, 247.

[26] Adopted by UN General Assembly resolution 2200 A (XXI), 16 December 1966, UNTS 999, 171.

('Anyone who has been victim of unlawful arrest or detention shall have an enforceable right to compensation'). But it is obvious from the context that here, too, reference is made to a legal proposition under domestic law.

To the extent that substantive law permits no clear answers, one may turn to substantive law in its conjunction with procedural law. Indeed, as from ancient times, since the classical Roman period, these two areas have been closely intertwined. Similarly, the English system has always stressed the importance of a remedy. One can certainly agree with the proposition that where there is a remedy there is a right. If a person is ensured the opportunity to enforce a given rule directly advantageous to him or her the legal system concerned provides the maximum of legal benefits it may ever grant. This position may then be fairly characterized as a right, and its reverse side as a legal obligation.

At the international level there exists no general mechanism that would allow the citizens of a given country to assert their human rights entitlements under general international law against their own government. All the systems that have gained prominence in recent years are designed for the enforcement of the rights set forth in specific treaties. And it is well known, furthermore, that at the universal level the competent bodies have not been vested with powers of binding decision-making.[27] Thus, the attempt to derive individual rights – which would at the same time be State obligations – from actually available remedies fails.

a) Acts Stigmatized as Criminal by the International Community

A substantive conceptual bridge to rights of the individual under general international law has its foundations in two particularly serious classes of breaches of international law, namely on one hand international crimes as defined by the ILC draft articles on State responsibility and, on the other, crimes against the peace and security of mankind as defined in the draft Code which the ILC adopted at the same time at its 1996 session.[28] We do not overlook the fact that crimes against the peace and security of mankind are only indirectly linked to the topic of State responsibility to be dealt with here, since they cope with the issue of individual criminal responsibility. Nonetheless, it is important – albeit trivial – to note that the two categories of unlawful acts run to a large extent parallel to one another. They both designate conduct that is abhorred by the international community. In that sense, crimes against the peace and security of mankind shed light on what is meant by stigmatizing

---

[27] Thus, the Human Rights Committee under the International Covenant on Civil and Political Rights is confined to formulating 'views' when ruling on individual communications (Article 5 (4) of the (First) Optional Protocol to the Covenant).

[28] ILC Report 1996 (supra note 6), 14.

certain acts as international crimes. In fact, at the Nuernberg trial it became abundantly clear for what reason new concepts were found to be necessary. Under the traditional system of State responsibility, the only entity that would have borne responsibility for the atrocities committed by the evil Nazi empire would have been the German State. No one of the criminal leaders of that evil empire would have been personally accountable. Rightly, it was felt that this was an untenable situation. The criminal State was denied the benefit of sovereign immunity as a cloak shielding its agents. This denial was predicated on the premise that certain acts, which shock the conscience of mankind, must be considered unlawful and punishable, irrespective of the domestic law of the State concerned, if humankind is to survive as a civilized community of human beings.

If one takes this philosophy as the starting point, the conclusions to be drawn therefrom are simple. If certain acts of barbarity are unconditionally criminal and unjustifiable, also and even specifically if they are committed by State agents, the inference is that every system of governance must by law abstain from engaging in such acts. In other words, the State – and any other adressee of commands originating from the level of international law – has a legal obligation towards every human being not to practice conduct that violates the core rights of the human person. It certainly requires some effort to identify the different classes of such conduct. One may have to ask, in particular, whether the crimes listed in the Statute of the International Military Tribunal of Nuernberg,[29] the Statute of the Yugoslavia Tribunal[30] and the draft Code of Crimes against the Peace and Security of Mankind adopted by the ILC faithfully reflect the minimum standard of civilization which may under no circumstances be affected. Whatever this necessary research may give birth to, one can be sure from the very outset that genocide in particular belongs to the type of criminal acts which every State is enjoined to abstain from under international law not only by virtue of obligations towards other States, but pursuant to a commitment which it directly owes to the human beings concerned. Genocide figures prominently in all legal acts setting out the most abhorrent breaches of legal rules that can ever be conceived of. It appears in Article 19 of the ILC draft articles on State responsibility as well as in the draft Code of Crimes against the Peace and Security of Mankind (Article 17), it is one of the crimes listed in the statutes of the present-day international criminal tribunals, it is the subject-matter of a specific international agree-

---

[29] Reprinted in: D. Schindler & J. Toman, *The Laws of Armed Conflicts*, 3rd ed. 1988, 913.
[30] UN Security Council resolution 827 (1993), approving the report of the Secretary-General, UN doc. S/25704, 3 May 1993.

ment[31] and it has been condemned by the International Court of Justice as an attack on the basic values of the community of humans.[32] In other words, whatever a domestic legal order may determine to the contrary, under international law genocide is and remains illegal. Nobody can be required *ex lege* to submit to genocidal practices, and this general condemnation must lead to the inference that the individual enjoys a personal right not to be subjected to genocide.

b) Primary and Secondary Rights

As a next step it must be asked what conclusions may be drawn from the assumption that every human being enjoys a direct right under international law not to be treated in violation of the rules setting forth the basic requirements of humanity. As can be learned in particular from the example of the European Communities, a primary right does not necessarily translate into a secondary right as a consequence of its breach. Rather, such a chain reaction marks another – and potentially far-reaching – step in the development of a legal system.

Two major issues come to mind in this connection. First, a right to resistance might be derived from the legal construction developed above[33] although it must be admitted that inferences not or scarcely corroborated by practice might be attacked as purely theoretical inventions. Today, however, we are not discussing a possible right to resistance, our interest is focused on claims of reparation that might accrue to an individual victim of grave violations of human rights directly by virtue of international law.

In trying to find out whether primary rights may be converted into secondary rights, one is almost compelled to look again to the European Communities. Here, that historic step was taken after the legal system had existed for more than thirty years. Additionally, the legal order of the European Communities is rich in institutions. It is endowed not only with policy-making and executive organs, but also with a genuine judicial branch. This judicial branch, furthermore, is made up not only of the Community courts proper, but also of the national tribunals of the member States. Indeed, it is common knowledge that the Court of Justice of the European Communities has devised ways and means to put all the domestic judicial bodies at the service of Community law, enjoining them to discard national law of whatever category inconsistent with

---

[31] Convention on the Prevention and Punishment of the Crime of Genocide, adopted by UN GA resolution 260 A (III) of 9 December 1948.

[32] Advisory opinion on *Reservations to the Convention on Genocide*, ICJ Reports 1951, 15, at 23; *Application of the Convention on the Prevention and Punishment of the Crime of Genocide, Provisional Measures, Order of 8 April 1993*, ICJ Reports 1993, 3, at 23.

[33] See our study: 'The right of resistance and human rights', in: UNESCO (ed.), *Violations of human rights: possible rights of recourse and forms of resistance*, 1984, 13 et seqq.

Community law. Thus, to proclaim that persons victims of a violation of Community law by one of the member States are entitled to seek reparation of the damage suffered from a State that has failed in its duties is not a hollow contention, but a legal proposition that can be translated into hard facts by taking the case to the national tribunals generally competent for compensation claims arising from official misconduct.

4) Legal Remedies for the Enforcement of Individual Claims

a) Remedies under General International Law

Under general international law, no forum exists for such claims. Still today, as a general rule, the individual has no standing before international tribunals. In particular, only States may appear before the International Court of Justice in contentious proceedings. Private persons always need specific arrangements by way of specialized treaties setting up appropriate bodies of adjudication.

b) Domestic Remedies

Given that obvious lack of remedies at the international level, the possibilities offered by national legal systems must be explored. Can domestic tribunals be used as enforcement agencies for reparation claims having their legal basis in international law?

aa) One thing is hardly open to doubt. Any State is entitled to repair the damage which its own citizens have sustained, whatever the legal source of an assumed obligation to provide compensation or other forms of reparation. In such instances, no problems of jurisdiction arise, though it will never be entirely clear whether the claims set forth by national statutes may be additionally linked to some rule of international law. Mostly, such operations are launched if a dictatorial regime has been toppled and the democratic successors then have to deal with heaps of criminal trash as leftovers of the past. If today in South Africa special victims of the *Apartheid* system receive some kind of compensation or if victims of the socialist system in the German Democratic Republic – persons imprisoned on political grounds for long periods of time – are similarly granted some more symbolic payments in recognition of their plight nobody really inquires into the legal background, asking whether such compensatory damages may have been owed to the beneficiaries also on account of a corresponding duty under international law.

bb) It is an entirely different situation when a State is faced with claims of its citizens against foreign States that have been introduced before its own tribunals. Under general rules of international law, such suits are inadmissible for lack of jurisdiction. No State is superior to any other one. The principle of sovereign immunity prevents judges of one country from adjudicating legal actions brought against a foreign State if none of the recognized exceptions applies. It is today almost generally accepted that no State can invoke its sovereign immunity as a defence against being sued if it has engaged in commercial activities (*acta iure gestionis*).[34] But it would be hard to contend that international consensus exists as to possible forfeiture of sovereign immunity in cases of serious human rights violations. The judgment of first instance in the *Princz* case,[35] which applied such a doctrine of forfeiture, was reversed on appeal.[36] We agree with this rejection. Disputes between two sovereign States must in principle be settled according to mechanisms and procedures of international law. Since hierarchically all States are located at the same level, none may issue unilateral orders which any other one would have to obey. Any departure from this normative model would require solid and persuasive justification. Yet the only imaginable ground for denying sovereign immunity would in some way relate to the idea of punishment. At first glance, the argument may sound convincing that a State committing atrocities such as genocide should not be able to defend itself by invoking immunity, a legal device to be reserved to law-abiding States. The argument, however, does not resist closer scrutiny. Punishment may be legitimate at the hands of the organized international community. It should not be a legal tool that can be easily adduced to provide a legal shield for all kinds of actions in departure from the ordinary regime of inter-State relations. It would be extremely hazardous to grant individual States a power to mete out punishment to other States.

Lastly, one cannot avoid facing up to realities. The commercial-activity exception to sovereign immunity does not really hit the political heart of a foreign State. To the extent that a government carries out market activities in foreign countries, it knows perfectly well that it has to accept the laws of the market as any other commercial actor. If, however, actions which a foreign State carries out in the exercise of genuine policy determinations are subjected to judicial scrutiny, the picture changes dramatically. One can hardly believe that such judgments would be recognized and heeded by the defendant. Perhaps the United States as the most powerful actor in the present-day world could hope to impose respect for judgments handed down by its tribunals against foreign countries. But even the United States would hardly appreciate the reverse situation, namely that claims raised against them would be

---

[34] 28 U.S.C. § 1605 (a)(2); Entscheidungen des Bundesverfassungsgerichts (BVerfGE) 16, 27; ILC draft articles on jurisdictional immunities of States and their property, YILC 1991 II, Part Two, 13, Art. 10.

[35] 813 F. Supp. at 22, 26 s.

[36] 26 F. 3d 1166 (D.C. Cir. 1994).

entertained by tribunals in other countries. To create here an opening in the wall of sovereign immunity would be a fruitless exercise, benefitting international lawyers but hardly their clients.

cc) Similar considerations apply to a different configuration where a State would make its judicial system available to foreigners pressing reparation claims against third States. In the United States, a debate has taken place on the question whether the Alien Tort Statute may allow for actions against foreign States in disregard of the provisions of the Foreign Sovereign Immunities Act. According to the Alien Tort Statute,

> the district courts shall have original jurisdiction of any civil action by an alien for a tort only, committed in violation of the law of nations or a treaty of the United States.[37]

In a limited number of cases, U.S. courts have relied on the Alien Tort Statute and other legal arguments in order to entertain such reparation claims. In *Von Dardel v. USSR* the U.S. District Court for the district of Columbia held that sovereign immunity must be discarded 'where the foreign state defendant has acted in clear violation of international law'.[38] Accordingly, it entered a default judgment against the USSR. No appeal was brought by the defendant. The USSR preferred simply to ignore the judgment. Shortly afterwards in *Amerada Hess v. Argentine Republic,* the U.S. Court of Appeals for the Second Circuit, speaking through Chief Judge Feinberg, stated in analogous terms that according to 'the modern view' of international law, for which two not too prominent American authors were cited,[39] 'sovereigns are not immune from suit for their violations of international law'.[40] This decision, however, was appealed by Argentina.[41] The U.S. Supreme Court reversed the judgment

---

[37] 28 U.S.C. § 1350 (1988). For some comments on the recent practice relating to the Statute see W. R. Casto, 'The Federal Courts' Protective Jurisdiction over Torts Committed in Violation of the Law of Nations', *Connecticut Law Review* 18 (1986), 467 et seqq.; C.H. Crocket, 'The Role of Federal Common Law in Alien Tort Statute Cases', *Boston College International & Comparative Law Review* 14 (1991), 29 et seqq.; K.C. Randall, 'Further Inquiries into the Alien Tort Statute and a Recommendation', *International Law and Politics* 18 (1986), 473 et seqq.

[38] 623 F. Supp. at 246, 253 (1985) = 77 I.L.R. 258, at 265.

[39] The legal reasoning advanced by J. J. Paust, 'Federal Jurisdiction over Extraterritorial Acts of Terrorism and Nonimmunity for Foreign Violators of International Law under the FSIA and the Act of State Doctrine', *Virginia Journal of International Law* 23 (1983), 193 et seqq., at 220-232, can hardly be called a persuasive treatment of the issue.

[40] 26 ILM 1375, at 1380 (1987). Concurring A. Bianchi, 'Denying State Immunity to Violators of Human Rights', *Austrian Journal of Public and International Law* 46 (1994), 195 et seqq., at 223-224; the same opinion can already be found in an earlier article: 'Violazioni del diritto internazionale ed immunità degli Stati dalla giurisdizione civile negli Stati Uniti: il caso *Hercules*', *Rivista Italiana di Diritto Internazionale* 72 (1989), 546 et seqq., at 589.

[41] In legal doctrine, the judgment was overwhelmingly criticized, see F.L. Kirgis, 'Alien Tort Claims, Sovereign Immunity and International Law in the United States', *AJIL* 82 (1988), 323 et seqq.; T. M. O'Toole, '*Amerada Hess Shipping Corp. v. Argentine Republic*: An Alien Tort

of the Court of Appeals, basing its reasoning on an interpretation of the Foreign Sovereign Immunities Act as the only statute providing jurisdiction over foreign States.[42] It did not specifically address the plaintiff's argument that a State that breaches its international obligations forfeits its immunity. Indeed, given the doctrine of precedence of any statute over general rules of international law,[43] the Supreme Court simply had to apply the Foreign Sovereign Immunities Act. Under that doctrine, it was irrelevant whether general international law had developed along different lines. However that may be, there exists now an established jurisprudence that the exceptions to sovereign immunity as provided for in the Foreign Sovereign Immunities Act[44] are of an exclusive nature and do not permit of any extension *ratione materiae*.[45]

Although the Supreme Court did not predicate its reasoning on any argument drawn from international law, its interpretation of the Foreign Sovereign Immunities Act would appear to be in full conformity with what would have had to be inferred from an analysis of the relevant rules of customary international law. As already said, any departure from the model of immunity would require a persuasive rationale. But to introduce a legal device according to which any country in the world should be competent to adjudicate claims brought by any private person against any third State would be utterly unreasonable. A model of universal jurisdiction may be adequate for cases of criminal prosecution where the defendant has in fact been apprehended and can be physically put on trial. However, a foreign State is never

---

Statute Exception to Foreign Sovereign Immunity', *Minnesota Law Review* 72 (1988), 829 et seqq.; K.E. Stitcher, '*Amerada Hess* and Foreign Sovereign Immunity', *Stanford Journal of International Law* 24 (1987-88), 585 et seqq.; D.L. Zimic, Comment, *Virginia Journal of International Law* 28 (1987), 221 et seqq., at 244.

[42] 102 L. Ed. 2d 818 (1989) = 81 I.L.R. 658.

[43] See *Restatement of the Law, Foreign Relations Law of the United States*, Vol. 1, 1987, 63, § 115(1).

[44] Obviously, immunity only protects States and not an entity like the PLO, unless such protection is specifically provided for under treaty law. Consequently, in the case of *Tel-Oren v. Libyan Arab Republic*, 726 F.2d 774 (1984), where essentially a concurrent action against the PLO was discussed, the discussion centered on whether the Alien Tort Statute did not only provide subject-matter jurisdiction, but created at the same time a right of action. Issues of sovereign immunity were not touched upon.

[45] It is on this basis that the *Princz* case was dismissed by the Court of Appeals for the District of Columbia, 26 F.3d 1166, 1176 (D.C. Cir. 1994). In a dissenting opinion, Judge Wald held that 'Germany waived its sovereign immunity by violating the *jus cogens* norms of international law condemning enslavement and genocide (ibid., at 1179), proceeding from the assumption that 'a state waives its right to sovereign immunity when it transgresses a *jus cogens* norm' (ibid., at 1183). Similarly, in *Siderman v. Republic of Argentina*, the Court of Appeals for the Ninth Circuit held that even an alleged violation of *jus cogens* by a foreign State does not confer jurisdiction on U.S. courts. See 965 F.2d 699 (9th Cir. 1992), at 718-719. *Cert. denied*, 507 U.S. 1017 (1993).

present in a civil suit brought against it in a tribunal of a third country. Thus, a judgment entered against it can have no direct effect.[46] Finally, the foreign observer is compelled to note that American authors in their yearning to create legal remedies hitherto unavailable invariably view the United States tribunals as the arbitrators passing judgment on human rights violations perpetrated in other countries.[47] It does not seem to occur to them that the United States could easily slide into the role of the defendant. But who would really want Guatemalan judges evaluate claims brought against the United States on account of the occurrences during the invasion of Panama or Mexican judges doing the same on account of the American involvement in the armed conflict in Guatemala? A world full of self-appointed human rights vigilantes is certainly more a trauma than a vision of paradise.[48]

V. COLLECTIVE SETTLEMENT OF REPARATION CLAIMS – OR CASE-BY-CASE APPROACH?

Lastly, a general issue must be addressed. It can be stated in very simple terms. Providing the aggrieved individual with a personal right to reparation means in fact to individualize the process of reparation of harm done. This does not raise any big problems where isolated cases of governmental misconduct are in issue. In a stable democracy governed by the rule of law grave human rights violations causing injury to the victims will always be a rare exception. It is on this assumption that the regional treaty systems for the protection of human rights operate. Our reflection on a general regime of reparation must, however, take into consideration those situations where massive violations have occurred. Genocide never happens as an incident that appears and disappears over night. As a rule, it is the offspring of a general breakdown of law, leaving thousands of victims. Another situation of mass violations of human rights was constituted by the *Apartheid* regime in South Africa. It is these situations, which go much beyond the famous 'consistent

---

[46] Judge Wald, loc. cit. (note 45) consistently failed to acknowledge that denying immunity for purposes of criminal prosecution is subject to other considerations than denying immunity to a foreign State in a civil suit.

[47] See, for instance, comment by M. Leigh on *Saudi Arabia v. Nelson*, 113 S.Ct. 1471, *AJIL* 87 (1993), 442, at 444: '...observers, especially those interested in the expansion of human rights law, will be even more disappointed that the Court failed to use this case as a vehicle for providing a remedy in U.S. courts for intentional torts committed by foreign states in their own territory'.

[48] See also skepticism shown by C. Schreuer, *State Immunity: Some Recent Developments*, 1988, 60.

pattern of gross and reliably attested violations of human rights',[49] that deserve close attention if one is seriously concerned with finding the right answers.

Two situations of massive human rights violations must be distinguished. On one hand, a criminal regime may have killed, maimed or suppressed its own people. Unfortunately, there is no lack of examples. Suffice it again to refer to the South Africa of the *Apartheid* period, to Germany under the Nazi regime, or to Guatemala, a country which has become familiar to the present writer, at the time when counter-insurgency strategies were applied to fight a guerilla force that had won large strongholds in the countryside. Totally different are situations where the citizens of another country become the victims of criminal foreign policies resorting to aggressive war, ethnic cleansing and, again, genocide. In the first place, Nazi Germany may be mentioned in this connection. But there is, unfortunately, no lack of other examples.

1) Patterns of National Self-Destruction

a) Material Reparation

As far as patterns of national self-destruction are concerned, the sad reality is that a national community succeeding to liberate itself from a group of criminals that had usurped and maintained political power will have no one else to redress the evil acts committed than itself. Rebuilding a decent societal environment requires a collective effort by all members of the community. The necessary decisions will have to be made in the exercise of the right of self-determination inasmuch as everyone will have to bear the burdens of the past. In the case of the *Apartheid* regime it would be even absurd to contend that, since every member of the black population group had been a victim of the policies of the preceding regime, he or she was holder of a reparation claim against the Republic of South Africa under its new democratic leadership. *Grosso modo*, the beneficiaries of these reparation claims would have to pay themselves for the monies granted to them since public money is invariably levied from the tax-payer. After a democratic regime has been established, the distinction between 'them' and 'us' does not work any more. The debts of the State are debts affecting everyone.

The conclusion from the preceding considerations is that in such instances there can be no hard and fast rules to be inferred from general principles of international law. How a nation should face up to its past, a challenge for

---

[49] ECOSOC resolution 1503 (XLVIII), 27 May 1970.

which Germans have coined the concept of *Vergangenheitsbewaeltigung*,[50] must be left to that nation itself. At the most, some clues may be gleaned from modern treaties for the protection of human rights although none of these treaties was framed with a view to situations of mass violations of human rights. The International Covenant on Civil and Political Rights, for instance, sets forth a provision calling for a national regime of compensation in case a person was unlawfully arrested or detained (Article 9 (5)) and a second one (Article 14 (6)) enjoining States to grant compensation to persons victims of miscarriage of penal justice, but no similar rule exists as far as unlawful killings are concerned. Obviously, it lay far beyond the imagination of the framers that a governmental apparatus might degenerate into a killing machine. Otherwise, compensation would also have been prescribed for the most egregious one of all possible breaches of human rights standards.

Inevitably, in addressing the consequences of a past characterized by State crime, new regimes will have to make bitter choices. The requirements of justice will have to be weighed against the needs of the present and the future. Additionally, a paradox arises. The more persons a criminal government drove into death and destruction, the lesser is the chance of the individual victim to obtain reparation commensurate with the injury suffered. The available national wealth is a natural limit to any revendications. Thus, in the Federal Republic of Germany persons unjustifiably detained in the former German Democratic Republic on political grounds received extremely limited amounts of compensation for each day or month spent in prison,[51] and in Guatemala the surviving family members of the more than 100,000 civilians who were killed or disappeared during the armed conflict can hardly hope to be granted pensions that could be regarded at least as a financial reflection of the losses they sustained. There can be no realistic expectations that other nations will assume the financial burden of providing the funds necessary for making good the harm done. Facing up to the hard consequences of its past is a task that every nation must primarily discharge by its own efforts.

It is the weakness of the 'Van Boven principles',[52] which at first glance are immensely appealing, that they seek to establish a uniform regime for all kinds of human rights violations, starting from the premise that, in principle,

---

[50] For a comparative analysis of the European experience in particular see T. Garton Ash, 'The Truth about Dictatorship', *The New York Review of Books*, 19 February 1998, 35 et seqq.

[51] Gesetz über die Rehabilitierung und Entschädigung von Opfern rechtsstaatswidriger Strafverfolgungsmaßnahmen im Beitrittsgebiet, 29 October 1992, Bundesgesetzblatt 1992 I, 1814, § 17: D-Mark 300 per month of detention contrary to basic principles of justice. See the contribution by B. Fassbender to this book, infra at 251.

[52] Basic Principles and Guidelines (supra note 7).

individuals should enjoy an individual right to reparation.[53] The Principles do not distinguish between different factual situations, or else, they follow the seemingly persuasive logic that 'reparations shall be proportionate to the gravity of the violations' (paragraph 7). All this is well-intentioned and, we repeat it again, may be perfectly workable within the framework of a system of governance adhering to the rule of law which, exceptionally, in derogation from its general policy objectives, gets involved in human rights violations through unlawful conduct of individual agents. But it provides no solution to national catastrophes which have left the entire nation deeply wounded. What can be attained in such circumstances must be assessed in the light of requirements of justice, which demand indeed that the injury suffered should be wiped out, and the actual capabilities of the national community concerned, on the other hand. If the number of victims is relatively small, like in Chile under the Pinochet regime, it may be possible to grant everyone some basic pension benefits.[54] The bigger the number of persons killed and disappeared, on the other hand, the greater the difficulty to lend a generous hand to everyone who was adversely affected.

b) Moral Reparation
The factual obstacles just referred to do not stand in the way of moral reparation. Such reparation, which does not impose an (excessive) economic burden on the nation concerned, can mainly take two forms.

   On the one hand, in order to prevent the reoccurrence of the disaster just gone through, a decision may be taken to investigate the past and to lay down the traumatic experiences of a period of lawlessness and lack of respect for human life in a comprehensive report. As a mechanism for discharging that task, truth commissions have in recent years appeared in many parts of the world, the most prominent ones being those established in Argentina, Chile, El Salvador, South Africa and Guatemala.[55] These commissions certainly constitute State practice. However, one may doubt whether this practice is already widespread enough, and whether it is sufficiently supported by *opinio juris*, to generate a rule of customary international law obligating States to

---

[53] But see paragraph 6 of the Basic Principles (note 7): 'Reparation may be claimed individually and where appropriate collectively, by the direct victim ...'.

[54] See M. Quiroga, 'The Experience of Chile', in: Netherlands Institute of Human Rights (ed.), *Seminar on the Right to Restitution, Compensation and Rehabilitation for Victims of Gross Violations of Human Rights and Fundamental Freedoms*, SIM Special No. 12, 1992, 101 et seqq., at 111.

[55] See, in particular, T. Buergenthal, 'The United Nations Truth Commission for El Salvador', *Vanderbilt Journal of Transnational Law* 27 (1994), 498 et seqq., 510 et seqq.; P.B. Hayner, 'Fifteen Truth Commissions- 1974 to 1994: A Comparative Study', *Human Rights Quarterly* 16 (1994), 600 et seqq.; C. Tomuschat, 'Between National and International Law: Guatemala's Historical Clarification Commission', in: *Festschrift für Günther Jaenicke*, 1999 (forthcoming).

clean their house after a major breakdown of law and order by detailing formally in writing what went wrong.

In a similar fashion, a government may acknowledge the crimes of the past and present its apologies to the victims. This also has become a current practice in recent years, even in relations between nations where sometimes such apologies have been expressed decades after the fateful events.[56]

Yet, no matter how important these forms of moral reparation may be, they normally do not occur in the specific relationship between an aggrieved individual and the responsible government, but are conceived of as mechanisms of collective settlement of a dark chapter of the national history. The claim of a nation fully to know the truth[57] should remain on the agenda as a project of legal policy,[58] but it is certainly not an individual right.

2) Injury Inflicted upon Other Nations

A second group of cases is much more akin to the traditional categories of international law. We are referring to instances where citizens of another country were injured by acts which may be classified both as international crimes and crimes against the peace and security of mankind. War of aggression, genocide or ethnic cleansing are to be considered in this connection. The idea to grant an individual reparation claim to every single victim of any such acts is fascinating at first glance. In particular, through such a compensation scheme it could be ensured that indeed payments made reach the affected persons and do not disappear somewhere in the bureaucracy of the

---

[56] In traditional inter-State law, this is nothing new, see, for instance, Article 45, paragraph 2(a) of the ILC's draft articles on State responsibility (supra note 6).

[57] See Oslo Agreement of 23 June 1994 between the parties to the armed conflict in Guatemala on the establishment of the Historical Clarification Commission, Preamble, paragraph 2: 'Considerando el derecho del pueblo de Guatemala a conocer plenamente la verdad sobre estos acontecimientos ...', reprinted in: Procuraduría de Derechos Humanos (ed.), *Los Acuerdos de Paz*, Guatemala 1997, 41; see also the Chilean Decreto Supremo No. 355 of 25 April 1990, Preamble, paragraph 1: 'Que la conciencia moral de la Nación requiere el esclarecimiento de la verdad sobre las graves violaciones a los derechos humanos cometidas en el país ...', reprinted in: Informe de la Comisión Nacional de Verdad y Reconciliación, Vol. I, Tomo 1, reprint 1996, xi; Annex to the Salvadoran Peace Agreements of 27 April 1991, relating to the Truth Commission, Preamble, paragraph 2: 'Reconociendo la necesidad de esclarecer con prontitud aquellos hechos de violencia de singular trascendencia, cuyas características y repercusión, así como la conmoción social que originaron, reclaman con mayor urgencia el conocimiento de la verdad ...', reprinted in: Naciones Unidas, Informe de la Comisión de la Verdad para el Salvador, De la Locura a la Esperanza. La guerra de 12 años en El Salvador, 1992-1993, 201.

[58] See 'Van Boven Principles' (supra note 7), paragraph 15 (b): 'Verification of the facts and full and public disclosure of the truth'.

beneficiary State, a fate which is not uncommon to payments based on lump sum settlements. On the other hand, the *Hugo Princz* case, where originally 20 million dollars were in issue, makes it quite clear that a process of individual settlement of claims deriving from human rights violations during a war or other historical catastrophes would run into dimensions almost beyond human imagination. During the Second World War, approximately 60 million people died. The Soviet Union alone suffered 20 million deaths. If Germany had had to cover the full range of the material losses entailed by this horrendous toll of human lives it would never have been able to stand up again as a nation. On the other hand, for instance, after the end of the Second World War roughly 3 million *Sudeten* Germans were expelled from their ancestral homes, and at least 225,000 of them were killed through official and private acts of revenge, clearly in violation of applicable human rights standards. However, the German Government did not even try to raise the legal problems connected with these sad occurrences in an attempt to endorse the claims of the victims.

Thus, the issue to be squarely faced is quite clear. A system of reparation based on individual claims may be workable and effective during fair weather periods in countries which, by and large, respect the rule of law. It does not provide the ideal legal framework for dealing with responsibility issues of large scale. If millions of people have suffered injury as a consequence of an armed conflict between two States, a pattern of collective settlement is much to be preferred.

First of all, individual suits would not reach their goal. Debtor countries would simply refuse to honour the judgments handed down against them in foreign countries. As yet, the doctrine of sovereign immunity stands. And it must be admitted that invoking immunity cannot be regarded as a simple pretext for evading responsibility. After a historical disaster, it will generally be impossible to treat each and every case individually. The expenditure of human resources for that purpose would be out of proportion to the need again to establish peaceful relations between the nations concerned. If thousands of lawyers could as of right participate in bringing about settlements, there would be no chance of ever closing a chapter of collective guilt of a nation. Lastly, the crucial point is again that the economic potential of a nation must be taken into account. In 1996, the ILC included a provision in its draft articles on State responsibility pursuant to which a people may never be deprived of its essential means of subsistence (Article 42 (3)). This rule, approved by a majority of members but heatedly attacked by others, draws its justification from three considerations. On one hand, States are not abstract entities, but organizations of peoples, who certainly bear a responsibility for their own fate, but who may also have been driven down the path of crime by their leaders, the individual member of the society concerned often being as helpless as any victim in a foreign country. Second, to impose an unrealistic burden on a people simply means laying the seeds of new conflict. No people accepts to be treated as a pariah forever. Third, it can hardly be justified to compromise the lives of a younger generation which had no more influence on the decisions taken by their fathers and mothers than any citizen of a third country.[59]

All these elements are not susceptible of being taken into consideration if a flood of individual claims is unleashed. They require to be dealt with at a conference table where a comprehensive framework for a global settlement may be established. It should not be forgotten that nations having fought a war have generally exhausted their resources. A country which, in addition to having to rebuild its society and its economy, would have to make good without any exception all the damage it has caused to others would find itself in a situation of bankruptcy. Under international law, there exists no legal regime of bankruptcy. But peace settlements in the past have regularly tried to establish a fair balance that makes it possible for a defeated debtor country to join again the community of civilized nations. In the Potsdam Agreement, an instrument of not only world-wide, but also local importance, it was expressly stated that the German people should make good the harm done by the Nazi regime 'to the greatest possible extent'[60]. Likewise, the peace settlement imposed on Iraq by Security Council resolution 687 abstains from requiring 'adequate, effective and prompt' payment – we are using the Hull rule[61] in an unusual context – for all the damages caused by the aggression against Kuwait. Wisely, it was determined that Iraq should be required to transfer to the Compensation Fund no more than 30 percent of its oil revenues.[62] Thus, even in modern times we find actual examples of an awareness that after historical catastrophes the simple rule that the author State is liable to make full reparation cannot apply without major modifications.[63] As a

---

[59] See our comments 'How to Make Peace after War: The Potsdam Agreement of 1945 Revisited', *Die Friedens-Warte* 72 (1997), 11 et seqq. For a similar assessment see B. Graefrath, 'Reponsibility and Damages Caused: Relationship between Responsibility and Damage', *Recueil des Cours* 185 (1984-I), 9 et seqq., at 92; B. Graefrath & M. Mohr, 'Legal Consequences of an Act of Aggression: The Case of the Iraqi Invasion and Occupation of Kuwait', *Austrian Journal of Public and International Law* 43 (1992), 109 et seqq., at 136.

[60] Potsdam Agreement, 2 August 1945, reprinted in: I. v. Münch (ed.), *Dokumente des geteilten Deutschland*, 1968, 32, Section IV: Reparations from Germany.

[61] Note from U.S. Secretary of State Cordell Hull to the Mexican Government of 22 August 1938, reprinted in: G.H. Hackworth, *Digest of International Law*, Vol. III, 1942, 658.

[62] UN Security Council resolution 705(1991), para. 2.

[63] See also E. Benvenisti & E. Zamir, 'Private Claims to Property Rights in the Future Israeli-Palestinian Settlement', *AJIL* 89 (1995), 295 et seqq., at 331, who advocate a standard of 'adequate' instead of full compensation.

consequence therefrom, it must be inferred that an individualized responsibility regime is unsuitable for such instances.

And yet, after a specific historical pattern of international wrong-doing has been overcome and peaceful conditions have been restored again, it may be possible to assess the amount of damage caused and then to permit at least in some fields individual reparation of the losses suffered by the victims of the wrongful actions in issue. Thus, it was agreed between the victorious Western Powers of the Second World War and Germany that property unlawfully confiscated should be restored to its rightful owners.[64] With a view to settling patrimonial claims between the United States and Iran, a Claims Tribunal was set up before which individuals have been allowed to vindicate compensation for the damage sustained by them. And for the settlement of the injurious consequences resulting from Iraq's aggression against Kuwait, an intermediate solution was found that takes account of the aggrieved individual, whose claims have to be channelled, in principle, by his home State. The diversity of the mechanisms established in such circumstances shows once again that no rigid system of reparation is ever conceivable. The 'Van Boven Principles' may certainly serve as a first blueprint which, however, must at a second stage be modified and adapted to prevailing circumstances that cannot be discarded as irrelevant.

VI. CONCLUSION

We have come to the end of our fragmentary considerations. Many doubts have been raised. Our provisional conclusion is that there is much room for individual reparation claims within the framework of specific treaty regimes. Even parts of a global peace settlement can be left to individual proceedings. Under general international law, however, it would be unwise to suggest that the traditional system of State responsibility should be replaced by a system where the holder of the new rights deriving from an internationally wrongful act would be, as a rule, the individual having directly sustained the damage in issue.

---

[64] Convention on the Settlement of Matters Arising out of the War and the Occupation as amended by the Protocol on the Termination of the Occupation Regime in the Federal Republic of Germany, 23 October 1954, Bundesgesetzblatt 1955 II, 405, at 418, Chapter III: Internal Restitution. For a short explanation, see K. J. Partsch, 'The Federal Republic of Germany', in: *Seminar* (supra note 54), 130 et seqq., at 135-136. See also information provided by E. Khiddu-Makubuya, 'Uganda', ibid., 86-100, at 90, on restitution of property to Asians expelled from Uganda by a former regime.

Individual Reparation Claims under the International Covenant on Civil and Political Rights: The Practice of the Human Rights Committee

Eckart Klein

I. Some Preliminary Remarks

1. Let me start by saying how grateful I am to have the opportunity to share with you some thoughts on a topic that goes to the *very heart of human rights protection*. Although the idea of human rights as such is not dependent on the existence of individual reparation claims, there is no doubt that the recognition of such claims considerably strengthens the whole concept and presents a major step forward in enhancing the effective protection of human rights.[1] However, as jurists we must not have illusions but have to look for a legally sound basis for claims, whatever they are.

2. The issue I have to deal with today is part of the area of *State responsibility*,[2] but in a special, I would like to say, in a progressive way. Our starting point is a violation of human rights as provided for by treaties such as the International Covenant on Civil and Political Rights or by general public international law. Any disregard for such rights by a State constitutes a breach of an international obligation, is an internationally wrongful act entailing the international responsibility of that State. According to a generally accepted principle and to a famous dictum of the Permanent International Court of Justice, 'the breach of an engagement involves an obligation to make reparation in an adequate form'[3]. But to whom?

The traditional law of State responsibility only envisages entitlements of the injured State or States,[4] and even the draft of the International Law Commis-

---

[1] A.H. Robertson, 'Implementation System: International Measures', in: L. Henkin (ed.) *The International Bill of Rights*, 1981, 357.
[2] See also T. van Boven, 'Study concerning the right to restitution, compensation and rehabilitation for victims of gross violations of human rights and fundamental freedoms', Final Report, UN Doc. E/CN.4/Sub.2/1993, para. 40 et seq.
[3] P.C.I.J., Series A No.9 (1927), 21.
[4] A. Verdross & B. Simma, *Universelles Völkerrecht*, 3rd ed. 1984, 873 et seq.

A. Randelzhofer and C. Tomuschat (eds.), State Responsibility and the Individual, 27–41.
© 1999 Kluwer Law International. Printed in Great Britain.

sion maintains this attitude.[5] This limited approach has rightly been criticized because it does not take into account at all a whole category of international treaties, namely that of human rights treaties, thus neglecting important modern developments.[6]

It is of course true that States do not lose their legal position, as members of the international community or as parties to a human rights treaty, if another State has violated its international obligations. In so far as they are injured they retain their rights. They are always entitled to ask for compliance with the legal obligations and to draw the generally accepted consequences from a violation of those obligations.[7] But this understanding alone does not meet the particular features of human rights commitments. They oblige States to respect and ensure these rights not only vis-à-vis other States[8] but also vis-à-vis all individuals within their territory and subject to their jurisdiction.[9] The individuals receive a legal position of their own. They are not only objects of international commitments but they are co-actors endowed with a substantive right of their own on the international plane.[10] They may claim respect for and protection under the rights which have been guaranteed.[11] This legal status is derived from the very nature of human rights.

Further possible conclusions are not excluded but require specific legal reasoning. Since the foundation of the United Nations in 1945, we have witnessed a gradual development in human rights law characterized by four steps[12]:

First, the acceptance of human rights by States entails their international responsibility in case of violation.[13]

Second, the commitments following from human rights obligations confer rights not only on States but also on human beings themselves.[14] They are the

---

[5] See UN Doc. A/CN.4/L.528/Add.2; C. Tomuschat, *Gegenwartsprobleme der Staatenverantwortlichkeit in der Arbeit der Völkerrechtskommission der Vereinten Nationen*, 1994, 17.

[6] A. H. Robertson (note 1), 358 et seq.

[7] For the connection with diplomatic protection see J. Kokott, 'Zum Spannungsverhältnis zwischen nationality rule und Menschenrechtsschutz bei der Ausübung diplomatischer Protektion', in: G. Ress & T. Stein, *Der diplomatische Schutz im Völker- und Europarecht*, 1996, 45 et seqq.

[8] W. K. Geck, 'Die Ausweitung von Individualrechten durch völkerrechtliche Verträge und der Diplomatische Schutz', in: *Einigkeit und Recht und Freiheit – Festschrift für Karl Carstens*, 1984, 339 et seqq.

[9] See Art. 2, para.1, CCPR, Art.1 ECHR.

[10] van Boven (note 2), para. 42.

[11] van Boven (note 2), paras. 45 and 137.

[12] E. Klein, *Menschenrechte. Stille Revolution des Völkerrechts und Auswirkungen auf die innerstaatliche Rechtsanwendung*, 1997, 23 et seqq.

[13] See supra note 3.

[14] M. Trassl, *Die Wiedergutmachung von Menschenrechtsverletzungen im Völkerrecht*, 1994, 107.

immediate beneficiaries of human rights and therefore the real victims of violations.

Third, an individual's right to standing before an international body cannot be taken for granted. There is no generally recognized international authority to which an individual could address him- or herself, claiming to be a victim of a human rights violation, and which could decide such a complaint. Rather, standing to claim respect of human rights must be established by conventional provisions.

Lastly, the entitlement of the individual victim of a human rights violation to reparation and, if so, to what kind of reparation remains to be explained. What is the legal basis for such a claim? Can it be found in the general rules of public international law, particularly the rules concerning the responsibility of States, or do we need also a conventional basis? In any event, a procedural right to ask an international body for assistance in determining the existence and content of a reparation claim must again be found in the relevant treaty.

It is this fourth and last point on which I shall now focus, with special regard to the International Covenant on Civil and Political Rights. But before doing so, the notion of reparation that I will use should be clarified.

3. The term *reparation* should here be understood as comprising all measures which have to be taken by a violating State in order to remedy the consequences of the breach of its human rights commitments. Reparation for human rights violations has, in the words of Theo van Boven, 'the purpose of relieving the suffering of and affording justice to victims by removing or redressing to the extent possible the consequences of the wrongful acts ... Reparation should respond to the needs and wishes of the victim.'[15]

Cessation of wrongful conduct and non-repetition of the breach of the obligation should be distinguished from reparation since they directly reflect or, more exactly, constitute part of the treaty obligations themselves: i.e. the obligation to respect and ensure the rights recognized by the treaty concerned. If there is, however, a claim or decision by a competent body to assure and guarantee in a certain and specific way the non-repetition of the violation, then we may subsume this under the term of reparation because this determination would go beyond the normal performance of the treaty. Therefore, on the whole, the term reparation covers a broad range of possibilities for redress. Some examples taken from the practice of the Human Rights Committee will demonstrate this in more detail.

---

[15] van Boven (note 2), para.137 nos. 3 and 4.

II. THE PRACTICE OF THE HUMAN RIGHTS COMMITTEE AND ITS LEGAL BASIS

1. Turning now to the Covenant on Civil and Political Rights it should be noted what the Covenant understands by *human rights protection*. Article 2, para. 1, contains the general statement which is developed by the human rights enshrined in Part III of the Covenant. The Human Rights Committee, in its General Comment No. 3 of 1981, has sought to define the extent of the obligations under the Covenant by stating that they are 'not confined to the respect of human rights, but that States parties have also undertaken to ensure the enjoyment of these rights to all individuals under their jurisdiction.'[16] The definition of the scope of protection is important as it mirrors the area of possible violation and reparation.

From the very beginning, the Human Rights Committee, acting under the Optional Protocol, has not only delivered its views on violations of Covenant articles by a State party, but has also drawn conclusions from this finding and asked the State for *redress.*[17] The way the Committee has expressed itself on this issue is very diverse, and of course dependent on the facts in each case. Some examples will illustrate this diversity.

In a case (1996) where the Committee found a violation of Articles 7 and 10, para. 1, the author was said to be 'entitled to an effective remedy for the violations suffered. The Committee considers that this should entail adequate compensation for the ill-treatment and lack of medical attention he suffered. The State party is under an obligation to ensure that similar violations do not occur in the future.'[18]

In another case (1996), the Committee found a violation of Articles 9(3), 10(1) and Article 14(3(c)) and (5) (undue delay and review by higher tribunal). According to the Committee the author 'is entitled to an effective remedy. The Committee has noted that the State party has commuted the author's death penalty to life imprisonment. In view of the fact that the author spent over ten years in prison, of which five and a half years on death row, the Committee considers that the appropriate remedy would be the author's early release, and, pending release, the immediate improvement of the circumstances of Mr. Neptune's detention. Moreover, in order to avoid similar violations in the future, the Committee recommends to the State party to improve the general conditions of detention.'[19]

---

[16] HRC, General Comment No. 3, 28 July 1981, UN Doc. A/36/40.
[17] First case: *Hernández Valentini de Bazzano v. Uruguay*, Communication No. 5/1977. For further examples, see D. McGoldrick, *The Human Rights Committee*, 1994, 188.
[18] *Sterling v. Jamaica*, Communication No. 598/1994, para. 10.
[19] *Neptune v. Trinidad and Tobago*, Communication No. 523/1992, para. 11.

In a third case (1996), the Committee found a violation of Articles 6 and 14, para. 3 (b) and (d). It therefore expressed the view that the author was entitled to a remedy. 'However, the State party has commuted Mr. Graham's death sentence to life imprisonment. The Committee considers that commutation of the death sentence constitutes an adequate remedy ... for the violation of Article 6. As regards the violation of Article 14, para. 3 (b) and (d), the State party should provide an appropriate remedy. The Committee stresses the duty of the State party to ensure that similar violations do not occur in the future.'[20]

In a torture case (1994) the Committee urged 'the State party to take effective measures (a) to carry out an official investigation into the author's allegations of torture, in order to identify the persons responsible for torture and ill-treatment and to enable the author to seek civil redress; (b) to grant appropriate compensation to Mr. Rodriguez, and (c) to ensure that similar violations do not occur in the future.'[21]

In another case (1996), Article 26 was found to have been violated. According to the Committee, 'the State party is under an obligation to provide the author ... with an effective remedy, which may be compensation if the property in question cannot be returned. The Committee further encourages the State party to review its relevant legislation to ensure that neither the law itself nor its application is discriminatory.'[22]

In a Canadian case (1994), the Committee was of the view that a violation of Article 19, para. 2, had taken place. It continued: 'The Committee notes that the contested provisions of the Quebec Charter of the French language were amended by Bill No. 86 in June 1993, and that under the current legislation Mr. Singer has the right, albeit under special conditions and with two exceptions, to display commercial advertisements outside his store in English. The Committee observes that it has not been called upon to consider whether the Charter of the French language in its current version is compatible with the provisions of the Covenant. In the circumstances it concludes that the State has provided Mr. Singer with an effective remedy.'[23]

The last example that I will give again concerns Canada (1993). That State was found to have violated Article 7 (not Article 6) because it had extradited the author of the communication to the U.S. where he faced the death penalty which would be executed by cyanide gas asphyxiation. Aware of the fact that the author was already in the U.S., the Committee concluded by requesting the State party 'to make such re-presentations as might still be possible to avoid

---

[20] *Graham and Morrisson v. Jamaica*, Communication No. 461/1991, para. 12.
[21] *Rodriguez v. Uruguay*, Communication No. 322/1988, para. 14.
[22] *Adams v. The Czech Republic*, Communication No. 586/1994, para. 13.2.
[23] *Singer v. Canada*, Communication No. 455/1991, para. 13.

the imposition of the death penalty and appeals to the State party to ensure that a similar situation does not arise in the future.'[24]

The cases just outlined raise the question, on what basis are the conclusions of the Committee founded? We must address this problem in terms of jurisdiction and substantive law.

2. As far as the *jurisdictional competence* of the Human Rights Committee is concerned, the wording of the Optional Protocol, Article 5 *in juncto* Article 1, might suggest that the Committee has to confine itself to a finding as to whether the author of a communication is the victim of a violation of a right set forth in the Covenant.[25] However, the quoted articles are far from clear.[26] They do not state that the Committee is prevented from also expressing its view on the conclusions which should be drawn from the violation. Starting from its first 'view' in 1981, the Committee has always interpreted Article 5, para. 4, of the Optional Protocol as an implicit authorization to advise the parties to a conflict on how redress should be achieved.[27] This is a sound interpretation because a view stating only the fact of the violation would in many cases rather deepen the author's sense of being a victim than restore legal peace. Seen from this angle, the Optional Protocol would otherwise lose much of its importance. This is still more true if one takes into account that there is also a material legal basis for reparation claims by the victim of a Covenant rights violation. If this is correct then even fewer arguments can be raised against the scope of jurisdiction claimed by the Committee.

3. a) The *substantive legal basis* of individual reparation claims, upon which the Committee relies in substance, is Article 2, para. 3(a), of the Covenant.[28] While the first views have drawn their conclusions from the human rights violations without referring to any provision, the following views quote Article 2, para. 3,[29] and later on, still more precisely, Article 2, para. 3(a). This is, today, a persistent pattern.[30] The Committee develops from this provision the individual claims for reparation in all their variety.

There are some more specific articles in the Covenant dealing with the right to release (Article 9, para. 3) or to compensation (Articles 9, para. 5, and 10, para. 6). The difference is that these articles themselves specify, under certain circumstances, the consequences which the violating State necessarily has to

---

[24] *Ng v. Canada*, Communication No. 469/1991, para. 18.
[25] B. Graefrath, *Menschenrechte und internationale Kooperation*, 1988, 167 et seq.
[26] Trassl (note 14), 35 et seq.
[27] See C. Tomuschat, 'Anmerkungen des Bearbeiters', *EuGRZ* 6 (1979), 502.
[28] Approving van Boven (note 2), para. 50.
[29] See *Celiberti v. Uruguay*, Communication No. 56/1979, para. 12.
[30] Incorrect therefore Trassl (note 14), 39 note 8.

draw from the violation.[31] With regard to Article 9, para. 3, release is the only legal alternative to a trial within a reasonable time; release in this case is part of the conventional guarantee itself, not a measure possibly to be taken by way of reparation. In my following remarks I shall only deal with Article 2, para. 3(a).

b) The qualification of this provision to be a suitable basis for reparation claims is not undisputed. The main counter-argument relates to the term *remedy* or *recours*. While the English legal term *remedy* would cover not only the procedural right but also redress or reparation, a similarly broad meaning could not be given to the French term *recours*.[32] According to this opinion, the substantive basis can only be found in the rules of general public international law which provide for redress after an internationally wrongful act has occurred.[33]

It might be that the Human Rights Committee is not sufficiently exact in this respect. The importance of Article 2, para. 3(a), lies in the understanding of it as obliging States parties which have violated the Covenant to provide the injured individual with legal opportunities to claim reparation.[34] But Article 2, para. 3(a), does not merely have a procedural meaning. It should be interpreted as incorporating into the Covenant the substantive consequences of a violation of an international human rights obligation by providing the victims with the necessary effective remedy. Therefore, it is not the term *remedy* or *recours* that is crucial, but the *rationale* according to which the provision is framed. When a violation has occurred a remedy is not effective if there is no substantive claim.[35] This interpretation transfers the rule of general public international law into a conventional norm which stands on its own. There is therefore no need still to resort to general rules in order to find a legal basis for reparation claims entailed by violations of the Covenant.

c) The reparation claim is directed *against the State party* having violated one of the rights enshrined by the Covenant. Certainly, the victim has no international claim against another individual.[36] It is a different question as to

---

[31] van Boven (note 2), para. 28.

[32] Cf. Raymond, 'A Contribution to the Interpretation of Article 13 of the European Convention on Human Rights', *HRR* 5 (1980), 161, 165 et seq.

[33] Trassl (note 14), 53 et seq.

[34] *Mbenge v. Zaire*, Communication No. 16/1977, para. 18.

[35] M. Nowak, *U.N. Covenant on Civil and Political Rights: CCPR Commentary*, 1993, Article 2, para. 56.

[36] For this problem, see G. Fischer, 'Schadensersatzansprüche wegen Menschenrechtsverletzungen im internationalem Privat-und Prozeßrecht', in: *Festschrift für W. Remmers*, 1995, 447, 463.

whether the State, under Article 2, para. 3(a), may be obliged, for example in disappearance cases, 'to open a proper investigation' and 'to bring to justice those responsible for (the victim's) disappearance, notwithstanding any domestic amnesty legislation to the contrary.'[37] The problem of what the State may be obliged to do relates to the content of the claim.

It is by no means entirely absurd to speculate that there might develop an international claim against the wrongdoing State to provide the victim with an immediate claim (or remedy) against the person who, acting in an official capacity, has performed the human rights violation attributable to the State. Already today one could argue that the violation of human rights belonging to the international *ordre public* must not remain without any effect on the interpretation and application of private law rules within a State.[38] Since the Human Rights Committee has to my knowledge never contemplated this idea I should leave it for further consideration elsewhere.

d) It is the *victim* of the human rights violation – that is, usually the author him- or herself – who is entitled to reparation. The term 'victim' may, however, also include family members or close relatives, perhaps even other persons who are in a specific way connected with the violation.[39] Several proposals have been made to reach a comprehensive definition of the term, for example by the UN General Assembly's Declaration of Basic Principles of Justice for Victims of Crime and Abuse of Power in 1985 or the Conclusions of the Maastricht Conference on the Right to Restitution, Compensation and Rehabilitation for Victims of Gross Violations of Human Rights and Funda- mental Freedoms of 1992. In several cases, especially concerning forced disappearance, the Committee has urged the State party 'to provide for appropriate compensation to the victim and her family'[40], thus implicitly acknowledging the family as a victim.

e) Turning now to the problem of whether the individual reparation claim is a *legal title*, we must first ascertain from which authority the legal entitlement can derive. As it is the Committee which spells out for the State and the victim what it regards as an effective remedy, one might assume that it is the view of the Committee itself that gives legal force to the reparation claim. However, we have to bear in mind that the Committee does not deliver a 'judgment', but

---

[37] *Atachahua v. Peru*, Communication No. 540/1993, para. 10.
[38] Fischer (note 36), 462.
[39] van Boven (note 2), para.15 (quoting from paras.1 and 2 of the UN Declaration of Basic Principles of Justice for Victims of Crime and Abuse of Power, UN Doc. A/RES/40/34 of 29 November 1985).
[40] *Almeida de Quinteros v. Uruguay*, Communication No. 107/1981, para. 14.

a 'view', that it does not make binding decisions[41] (as does, for example, the European Court of Human Rights). The Committee itself has defined its views on the merits 'as non-binding recommendations'[42], and this is also the unanimous understanding in literature.[43] It would be difficult to argue that the Committee's finding on the reparation claim would have a higher legal value than its finding on the violation of the Covenant.

Notwithstanding this assessment, it would be wrong to conclude that the views of the Human Rights Committee do not have any legal meaning at all. Since the States parties to the Optional Protocol have recognized the competence of the Human Rights Committee to receive and consider communications from individuals who claim to be victims of a human rights violation by a State party, it would not correspond with the requirements of good faith just to disregard the recommendations contained in the view.[44] Rather, they must be taken into account by the government of the State party concerned. However, if the State party does not abide by the recommendation, this fact, taken alone, would not amount to a breach of an international obligation and would not entitle the victim to submit a communication. On the other hand, a repetition of human rights violations can be regarded as a new violation and, accordingly, a new communication may be submitted.

The fact that non-compliance with the Committee's recommendation is not, as such, an internationally wrongful act does not exclude the Committee's competence in trying to convince the State again and again to follow its proposals. I shall deal with the follow-up procedure at a later stage. In this context it might be interesting to refer to a case where the author came before the Committee for a second time claiming to be a victim of a violation of Articles 10, para. 1, and 17, para. 1. The Committee found a violation and expressed its view that 'Mr. Pinto is entitled, under Article 2 paragraph 3(a), of the Covenant, to an effective remedy. This should include measures that will prevent a recurrence of treatment such as the author has been subjected to'.[45] But then the Committee continued:

> The Committee notes that the State party has not thus far given effect to the Committee's View of 20 July 1990 in respect of Mr. Pinto's initial communication, in which the Committee decided that he was entitled to a remedy entailing his release. While the death sentence imposed on the author has been commuted to life imprisonment, the fact re-

---

[41] See A. de Zayas, J. Th. Möller & T. Opsahl, *Application of the International Covenant on Civil and Political Rights under the Optional Protocol by the Human Rights Committee*, Center of Human Rights Geneva, 1989, 3.

[42] Annual Report 1988, para. 645.

[43] Cf. McGoldrick (note 17), 151 et seq.

[44] C. Tomuschat, 'Making Individual Communications a Tool for Protection of Human Rights', in: U. Beyerlin et al. (eds.), *Festschrift für Rudolf Bernhardt*, 1995, 623.

[45] *Pinto v. Trinidad and Tobago*, Communication No. 512/1992, para. 10.

mains that he has not been released. The Committee notes its previous finding that the author did not have a fair trial. The continued detention of a person sentenced after an unfair trial may raise issues under the Covenant. The Committee therefore calls upon the State party to remedy the violations of the Covenant established in the Views of 20 July 1990 by releasing the author and to inform the Committee of any action taken in this regard as soon as possible.[46]

If the legal force of the reparation claim cannot be derived from the Committee's view, it may be found in Article 2, para. 3(a), of the Covenant itself. This provision, as I pointed out, has implicitly incorporated the general rule that reparation follows violation,[47] thus enabling individual victims of human rights violations to claim reparation. There is no reason why this claim embodied in a treaty norm should not have legal force.

However, one has to take into consideration that the basic requirement of the claim is an infringement of a right protected under the Covenant. In most cases this requirement will be disputed; the State party will deny any violation of its obligations. As we have seen there is no institution which is authorized to make a legally binding decision on this issue. Therefore, if the State does not accept the finding of the Committee that a violation has occurred, the question is – legally speaking – still open and the same is true, of course, for the reparation claim. As a matter of fact, many States parties refuse to implement the Committee's recommendations on reparation because they object to any allegations of human rights violation. While we may say that the reparation claim is legally founded *in abstracto*, we come, in assessing the claim *in concreto*, across the limits of public international law which is characterized by a lack of binding dispute settlement mechanisms. In practice, the reparation claim is solely backed by the moral, perhaps even quasi-judicial, authority of the Committee.[48] As we shall see this is not a very far-reaching basis.

f) Coming back now to the substance of the recommendations regarding reparation claims, I have to emphasize once more the huge variety of possibilities that have evolved from the Committee's jurisprudence. I have already given some examples; let me now add some more systematic remarks.

aa) In that part of its view where the Committee deals with the reparation issue, rather different elements can be found which, for the sake of clarity, should be distinguished. Some recommendations just ask for compliance with the rights guaranteed by the Covenant, for example, when release is requested for an author who has been tried with undue delay or when the State party is

---

[46] Id., para. 12.
[47] Verdross & Simma (note 4), 873 et seq.
[48] Nowak (note 35), para. 72.

asked to ensure that similar violations do not occur in the future.[49] One could probably argue that both aspects, the claim for regular compliance with the commitments and the claim for reparation, are tied together by Article 2, para. 3(a), of the Covenant. Nevertheless, at least in theory, one should distinguish these two aspects.

bb) The term most used in the current practice of the Committee is that the author is entitled to an 'effective' remedy, and this is of course the term used in Article 2, para. 3(a) itself. However, the Committee sometimes speaks of an 'appropriate' or an 'effective and appropriate' remedy. Very often this entitlement is qualified by further explanations. They include request for early release, further measures of clemency after commutation of the death sentence, medical care, improvement of the detention situation, compensation, prosecution of wrongdoers and even change or amendment of laws.[50]

There is no doubt that the Committee has a hard time dealing with the appropriate qualification. Very often the Committee lacks clarity about what the appropriate action is, with the result that the recommendation is confined to a request for an effective remedy which grants even to a willing State a broad margin of discretion for performance. This, of course, is not very satisfactory. However, one has to bear in mind that the Committee does not wish to undermine its authority by asking for measures which will, for whatever reasons, not be acceptable to the State.

Let me give an example. As you know, capital punishment is not prohibited as such by the Covenant; the Second Optional Protocol has been ratified by only 31 States. However, according to the permanent jurisprudence of the Committee, Article 6 (right to life) is violated if a trial is unfair for reasons set out in Article 10 or Article 14. In such cases the violation of Article 10 or Article 14 leads, at the same time, to a violation of Article 6 if a death sentence has been passed.[51] In former views, the effective remedy requested by the Committee very often included early release; commutation alone was not seen as a sufficient remedy.[52] There is good reason for this request since, as the whole trial was judged to be unfair, life imprisonment would suffer from the same legal deficiency.

---

[49] See, e.g. *Neptune v. Trinidad and Tobago*, Communication No. 523/1992, para. 11; van Boven (note 2), para. 58.

[50] T. van Boven, 'The right to restitution, compensation and rehabilitation for victims of gross violations of human rights and fundamental freedoms', in: G. Alfredsson & P. Macalister-Smith (eds.), *The Living Law of Nations*, 1996, 339, 344 et seq.

[51] *Lewenhoff and Bleier v. Uruguay*, Communication No. 30/1978, para. 14; *Kelly v. Jamaica*, Communication No. 253/1987, paras. 5.6-7.

[52] *Lubuto v. Zambia*, Communication No. 390/1990, paras. 7.2 and 9.

On the other hand, one has to bear in mind the conditions in the respective States and societies in which the recommendation will take effect. Speaking of Jamaica and Trinidad and Tobago (from which most communications concerning capital cases have come before the Committee), one has to recognize that these are very violent societies where the murder rate is very high indeed. The Committee is not in a position, vis-à-vis a State which has not ratified the Second Optional Protocol, to take a different view from that State with regard to the appropriate method of combating criminality. Of course the right to a fair trial is another matter, but to request a State to release a person who, very probably, is a murderer because some conventional safeguards have been disregarded will most likely be, and has indeed been, met by very unfavourable reaction.

There is strong pressure from the population to create safer living conditions, and the governments of the States concerned cannot and will not go in another direction. Under the circumstances, the Committee has perhaps become a bit more modest in this regard, being more or less satisfied if the execution of the death penalty can be averted and the judgement commuted. I understand any criticism which may be raised against such a policy but it is very difficult to take, in practice, another stand.

In cases where the effective remedy includes compensation, the Committee does not specify the amount of money due to the victim. This again leaves to the State party a big margin of discretion. The necessary guidance may be taken from the general principles; the compensation should be prompt, adequate, and effective.[53]

On the other hand, a request to change the existing law in order to provide an effective remedy goes rather far. The Committee asks for this measure only if the law of the State party does not permit an application that does not violate the Covenant. But where the law prevents the State from complying with the Covenant, it is reasonable to demand a change.[54]

4. The *follow-up procedure* that the Committee has established and strengthened over the years is part of our topic because it is a remarkable attempt to make the State accept the Committee's views on violation and reparation, despite its lack of binding force.[55] The competence of the Committee to monitor implementation may be based on an implied power or, alternatively,

---

[53] Verdross & Simma (note 4), 807 et seq. There is no reason not to use the Hull formula in this context, too.

[54] Trassl (note 14), 60 et seq.

[55] M. Schmidt, 'Follow-Up Mechanisms Before UN Human Rights Treaty Bodies and the UN Mechanism Beyond', Paper delivered to the Conference 'Enforcing International Human Rights Law: The Treaty System in the 21st Century', Center for Refugee Studies, York University, Toronto, Canada, June 1997, 12 (on file with author).

directly on Article 1 of the Optional Protocol.[56] It is reasonable to interpret the competence to 'consider' communications as encompassing a mandate to consider the measures adopted by a State party to remedy Covenant violations found in the course of examining a communication. The following procedure evolved gradually.

The first step, made only in 1989, eight years after the first view was taken, was to ask the State party at the very end of the view to inform the Committee on any relevant measures taken in respect of the Committee's views.[57] During the next year (1990), a general statement on follow-up procedure was adopted.[58] The Committee set a deadline for the receipt of such information; while the time limit is to be determined based on the circumstances of each case, it shall not exceed 180 days. In practice, the Committee now regularly fixes a time limit of 90 days, but departure from the rule is possible.[59]

It may be of interest to know how the Committee asks for this information. Since October 1994 the Committee has used the following formula, combining its request for information with an appeal to the State to implement in good faith the Committee's recommendation:

> Bearing in mind that by becoming a State party to the Optional Protocol the State party has recognized the competence of the Committee to determine whether there has been a violation of the Covenant or not and that pursuant to Article 2 of the Covenant the State party has undertaken to assure to all individuals within its territory and subject to its jurisdiction the rights recognized in the Covenant to provide an effective and enforceable remedy in case a violation has been established. The Committee wishes to receive from the State party within 90 days information about the measures taken to give effect to its Views or taken in connection with the Committee's View.[60]

The general statement of 1989 introduced a further element. It created the new function of the 'Special Rapporteur for Follow-Up on Views'.[61] Since 1990 the third Committee member has performed this function. His task is to get in touch with the States parties held to have violated the Covenant and from which reparation was sought, and to inform the Committee about the measures taken.[62] The Special Rapporteur uses formal and informal ways to influence the governments concerned. Usually, during the Committee sessions, some meetings with representatives of non-willing States take place. In one case a special mission was sent to the country in question to ask the State for a more co-operative attitude (Jamaica). The role of the Special

---

[56] Id. at 3.
[57] *Birindwa and Tshisekedi v. Zaire*, Communication No. 241 &242/1989, para. 14.
[58] HRC Annual Report 1990, Vol.I, 144 et seq., Vol.II, Appendix XI, UN Doc. A/45/40.
[59] Tomuschat (note 44), 622.
[60] *Adams v. Jamaica*, Communication No. 607/1994, para. 11.
[61] See supra note 58.
[62] Schmidt (note 55), 4 et seq.

Rapporteur is formally recognized by the Committee's rules of procedure (rule 95). Information on follow-up activities has been included in the Annual Report since 1995.[63]

In its July 1994 session the Committee adopted an even clearer stance. The chapter in question shall clearly convey which States parties have co-operated with the Special Rapporteur and which have failed to do so. The same information will be released through press communiqués. The Committee welcomes further information from NGOs on the subject. Now, following an amendment of the rules of procedure in April 1997, the follow-up progress report of the Special Rapporteur will be made public *in toto*.[64]

However, despite all endeavours the success rate is rather low. Accordingly, the follow-up progress report submitted by the Special Rapporteur at least once a year is becoming a considerable volume; as a matter of fact it informs less on progress than on failure. The last report, adopted during July 1997, enumerates 91 cases from 21 countries dating back to 1982 where no or only incomplete follow-up information has been received.[65] This is a very big figure compared with the total number of 190 views delivered until May 1997 disclosing a violation. Not incorporated in the report are cases where the authors have failed to claim compensation within the statutory time limits of the respective State.

The report draws attention to two interesting views where appropriate compensation had been included in the Committee's request for an effective remedy. In the first case concerning a violation of Article 9, para. 3, by Senegal, the author was offered compensation of 300,000 Senegal Francs;[66] he refused, however, to accept the lump-sum and requested one billion Senegal Francs and asked the Committee to determine the level of compensation to which he is entitled. In the second and similar case Zambia, which was held to have violated Articles 9(2) and (3), 10(1), 12(1) and 19, was also asked to grant appropriate compensation to the author.[67] The State offered 14,5 million of the local currency, whereas the author had claimed 129 million. In both cases the Committee decided to inform the author that it would not interfere with a State party's award, and that the case would be struck from the next follow-up progress report.

---

[63] HRC Annual Report 1995, Follow-Up Activities Under the Optional Protocol, 544 et seq., UN Doc. A/50/40.

[64] HCR Annual Report 1996, 84, UN Doc. A/51/40.

[65] Follow-Up Progress Report, July 1997, CCPR/C/60/R1.

[66] *Koné v. Senegal*, Communication No. 386/1989.

[67] *Kalenga v. Zambia*, Communication No. 390/1990.

III. Final Remarks

In concluding, one can say that the individual communication procedure established by the Optional Protocol is a major achievement in the protection of human rights at the international level. Ninety-two States have ratified the Protocol.[68] The main deficiency is still the lack of binding jurisdiction of the Human Rights Committee. The main success is the recognition of individuals as holders of international claims to respect the Covenant rights and for reparation if they are victims of a violation of these rights. Human rights law has changed and, one may say, rediscovered the international status of the individual. Public international law has, as with any law, a serving function for the individual. This understanding alone does justice to the pledge of the Preamble of the United Nations Charter that the peoples of the United Nations are determined to reaffirm faith in fundamental human rights, in the dignity and worth of the human person.

---

[68] Jamaica now has denounced the Optional Protocol. See N. Schiffrin, 'Jamaica Withdraws the Right of Individual Petition under the International Covenant on Civil and Political Rights', *American Journal of International Law* 92 (1998), 563-568.

Discussion (Part 1)

Zemanek: My remarks or my comments are mainly addressed to Professor Tomuschat's report but they apply to a large extent also to what Mr. Klein has said. We face in my opinion a classical case of a gap between social necessity and political viability. If I start with the draft of the International Law Commission, the question is: If it were to constitute the individual a claimant party under the future convention, could one reasonably expect that States would ratify the convention? We have heard from Professor Klein that even in cases in which some international machinery exists the rate of success is rather low. If we have a new situation in which States have to ratify or to accede to a new convention the chances that they will do so are even smaller. Already now States are extremely reluctant to accept the present draft. And James Crawford, who is the new rapporteur, told me only a short while ago that he feels the necessity of redrafting it completely which would mean that to the 40 years during which the project is already under consideration (it started in the fifties) another ten years, if you consider it realistically, will have to be added. Let me give one example which Professor Tomuschat has already mentioned, but on which I want to elaborate upon: *erga omnes* obligations. The draft says in its present form (article 40) simply that if an obligation exists *erga omnes* each contracting party, if we talk about a treaty, or each party that is bound by a norm of customary international law is to be considered an injured party in case of its violation. What does that mean? May each party make claims? What about the cumulation of claims? What happens if one party puts forward a claim and comes to an understanding with the author State: Is that binding upon the other claimants? Or consider proportionality. If a claimant State is not satisfied and resorts to countermeasures, do we have to measure the proportionality of the countermeasures individually or collectively, in case other States apply countermeasures, too? The Commission has not addressed these questions and although I am in favour of making *erga omnes* obligations internationally enforceable, I recognize that these questions have to be settled before one can hope for the concept to be accepted.

43

A. Randelzhofer and C. Tomuschat (eds.), State Responsibility and the Individual, 43–61.
© 1999 *Kluwer Law International. Printed in Great Britain.*

A very short remark about procedure. May I point out that the International Court of Arbitration has made available model rules for proceedings between a State and a non-State party. So in theory the possibility of an individual claiming exists, but until now no State has been willing to accept the model rules of the International Court of Arbitration. Finally, there is the question of claims under national law. One of my assistants is working on the issue of punitive damages. The fact is that this concept works among common law countries which are familiar with the notion. But even if you have a judgment which grants punitive damages and a convention that obliges to enforce that judgement in a foreign country, the foreign country which does not recognize punitive damages may refuse to execute that part of the judgment, on the ground that it is against its own *ordre public*. So, I mean, there are limits, and things which may work among certain countries which share their belonging to the same legal culture may not work with countries which belong to a different legal culture.

And a final remark to Professor Tomuschat's examples. He mentioned Mexican courts. But what would the result be if a Vietnamese court entertained a claim by a Vietnamese against the United States of America? Do you really believe that the Americans would execute that judgment? In my opinion the answer is quite clear. Thank you very much.

Ress: I would rather raise some questions than give answers to the problems we are facing here. My first problem concerns access to courts which was addressed by Professors Tomuschat and Klein. It may be possible, for instance, to interpret the guarantee in the European Convention on Human Rights regarding access to courts (Article 6) as implying waiver to State immunity. If States in a general convention grant access to courts to every individual on the basis of an arguable claim, then the question arises whether States may still have recourse to State immunity if such a claim comes under the heading of a right under the Convention.

The second point worth mentioning is that many States in their domestic statutes on sovereign immunity have accepted some exceptions even to the *iure imperii* element. The American FSIA accepts exceptions as to expropriations, which are of course sovereign State acts, and there are exceptions to tort claims where the tort is done in the territory of a foreign State against an American citizen. Furthermore, if State A acts in violation of human rights with effect within the territory of the U.S., it cannot claim sovereign immunity when a tort action by an individual victim is brought before the courts of the U.S. So there are already in the existing statutes exceptions precluding immunity with regard to *acta iure imperii*, and I wonder whether there is not an underlying tendency to restrict sovereign immunity in relation to human rights violations. The question then arises, and this is of course a crucial problem, whether in cases of mass violations which were the consequences of wars or major atrocities during the war, there is no room for an individual claimant and not any more room for the concept of State immunity? If you accept such a general approach, you then face the difficult problem: what is the specific criterion? When is a mass violation genocide, or from which point onwards is it mass violation in the field of human rights, and when do you still have individual cases which could be dealt with within the existing machinery? I must admit that I have not yet found a convincing answer to these questions. You must have recourse to other circumstances of the situation, to specific categories, if you do not wish to end up with injustice.

Kooijmans: At this moment I would like to make a preliminary remark. The subtitle of this symposium is 'The legal position of the individual under international law', whereas its main title is 'Individual reparation claims entailed by human rights violations'. The full title therefore links the concept of being a subject of law to the capacity to bring a claim. I have come to wonder whether this linkage is a correct one under all circumstances, whether indeed being a subject of law entails the capacity to bring a claim.

In most textbooks the concept of being a subject of international law or that of legal personality – two concepts which are often used interchangeably although it may be questioned whether that is correct – are defined as the capacity to acquire rights and obligations under international law and to bring claims in case of violation of these rights. That may partly be due to the fact that in the famous *Reparation for Injuries* case[1] the concept of international legal personality and the right to bring a claim were very closely linked. I wonder, however, whether this is always the case, in particular in the field of human rights. In the *East Timor* case the International Court of Justice explicitly said that the people of East Timor are indisputedly entitled to the right of self-determination as a right *erga omnes*.[2] Actually the Court says here that entities which themselves have no right to bring a claim, like the people of East Timor, are entitled to rights which must be respected by everyone; such entities – whether collectivities or individuals – must be seen as enjoying rights under international law and therefore as subjects of international law since logically only subjects of law can enjoy legal rights. If one has the primary right, however, one has also the secondary right to compensation if this primary right is not respected; this does not coincide, however, with the right to bring a claim as is clear from the *East Timor* case. If for argument's sake we assume that international legal personality (e.g. of a state or an

[1] ICJ Reports 1949, 174.
[2] ICJ Reports 1995, 90, at 102.

international organization, like in the *Reparation* case) entails the capacity to bring a claim, then the lesson of the *East Timor* case is that the concepts of international legal personality and that of being a subject of international law are not by necessity identical or interchangeable.

Cassese: I should start by apologizing because I need to make three remarks so I hope I will not be too lengthy. Most of them concern the excellent paper by Christian Tomuschat.

My first remark relates to what he said about the ILC system being hardly workable. I fully agree and I would like to point out that in a way, here again, we witness a phenomenon which is quite common in international law, namely the huge gap between the legal potential offered by the international legal order and the actual behaviour of States or other institutions. In a way international law offers a sort of panoply of legal means which are not used by States or other international actors because they are still living according to an old system. A system in which they are motivated not by a real concern for human rights but actually by their own interests. I think we come across this huge gap many times and also in this area. May I then give you an example of what I also regard as a gap. As you know, the four Geneva Conventions on the victims of war of 1949 did offer to State courts the authority to prosecute and try or extradite people who have allegedly committed war crimes. However, those provisions have never been used until very recently, a few years ago. So again States and governments but also domestic courts are absolutely reluctant to take advantage of so many legal instruments offered by international law. Another example relates to what has happened in Italy, Spain and France with regard to atrocities committed in Argentina, in a period we very well know, in the 70ies, by Argentinian authorities against people living in Argentina. These are cases where criminal proceedings have been instituted in France, in Spain and in Italy. They are therefore different from what has happened in the American cases (*Filartiga*[3] and so on): these are civil suits, as we know, whereas here we are in the area of criminal proceedings. However, and here I would like to draw your attention to what is really indicative of the present trend of States and courts, courts in these countries have instituted proceedings only at the request of and on behalf of people having <u>dual</u> nationality. So in Italy, it was because the Argentinians were also Italians, in Spain because they had dual nationality, and in France, in the *Astiz* case[4], it was because the victims were one or two French nuns. So again States, in these cases, fall back on the old view of international law

---

[3]   630 F.2d 876 (2d Cir. 1980).
[4]   Cour D'Assises de Paris, 16 Mar. 1990, summarized in Revue Générale de Droit International Public 94 (1990), 767.

whereby you can take action only because you protect your own *nationals*. However, it is significant that in the case of Spain, the Spanish investigating judge requested the Swiss authorities to see whether there were Swiss bank accounts owned by about 27 defendants, and the Swiss authorities froze accounts belonging to four of them. Hence, you face some sort of defect. It is a pity that they only acted because the victims were also of Spanish national-ity. It is a real pity.

My second point relates to the question of sovereign immunity or what we can also call the act of State doctrine, as it was mentioned in the *Eichmann* case by the Supreme Court of Israel.[5] My point is as follows, I will try to be as clear as possible: Why do we need, again, to rely upon this question of state sovereignty in the case of gross violations of human rights? I'm not referring to individual, sporadic, isolated breaches of human rights. In case of gross, systematic, large-scale violations of human rights, say committed in country X, I wonder whether in country Y a court could institute proceedings, I mean civil law or criminal proceedings, without necessarily asking itself whether or not the issue of State sovereignty or sovereign immunity or act of State doctrine is involved. To my mind, what applies to war crimes and crimes against humanity should also apply to gross breaches of human rights. I wonder whether we can push international law in this direction. Probably it is not yet *lex lata*. But if you are a general and you commit genocide or war crimes or crimes against humanity you cannot rely upon the act of State doctrine, you cannot invoke immunity as a State organ: you may be brought to court. You can be prosecuted by a criminal court and possibly this could also apply to a civil suit. Actually in the *Filartiga* case Peña Irala was a police captain, he was acting in his official capacity as a Paraguayan policeman and the court rightly disregarded the theory of sovereign immunity, or immunity of organs, or the act of State doctrine. So my query is as follows: should we try to expand this doctrine, so as to encompass also gross, large-scale breaches of human rights, with the consequence that somebody who is brought to court after a civil suit or criminal proceedings cannot say: Look, I was acting in my capacity as, say, an official of the Italian government. I would say: Sorry, the shield of State sovereignty no longer protects you. This is just a query, but if we could move in that direction, imagine large-scale torture or large-scale rape, why should the act of State doctrine cover and protect people who engage in these horrible deeds?

My third point is aimed at drawing your attention to something which I consider a flaw in two resolutions of the Security Council, the ones which set up the Yugoslavia and the Rwanda tribunals. If you read those statutes, which are resolutions of the Security Council as you know, you will find a provision

---

[5]   36 I.L.R. 277 (1968).

which is identical in both statutes whereby, in addition to emprisonment after a trial, the trial chambers may order the return of any property and proceeds acquired by criminal conduct, including by means of duress, to their rightful owners. So here provision is made for the return of property or the proceeds of crime but no provision is made for compensation. I remember when we discussed this and we had to, in a way, spell out and flesh out these provisions in our rules of procedure and evidence some judges were really outraged. I went so far as to say this is a sort of capitalist approach: if somebody has been tortured or raped, no right to compensation, so the poor victim has no rights whatsoever, only to see that the author, the culprit, is brought to trial and duly punished, but cannot claim any compensation for the huge damage he or she may have suffered. However, if you have a wonderful building or if you have, say, paintings or you have money in the bank or in your house and this is taken away, stolen by the enemies and so on, then you are entitled to get back this money. I think this is really strange, a very strange attitude taken by the Security Council. Probably the explanation can be found in what Christian Tomuschat said before, and which is probably right. In mass atrocities committed during wars or war-like situations the way out is probably not to consider compensation to the individual, the thousands of individual victims, the solution is probably a different one. This might be the explanation for this really strange, odd and to my mind highly questionable provision in the statutes adopted by the Security Council. We decided in our rules of procedure to move forward and not to legislate, because we could not do so, but to provide for compensation to victims. We decided to adopt provisions in Rule 106 of our Rules of procedure, whereby the Tribunal has the right to transmit the judgment to the relevant national authorities deciding that somebody, say, has been raped or has been the victim of physical or psychological atrocities, and then we also go on to say that under the national legislation the victim, or persons claiming through the victim, may bring an action in a national court. This is a sort of hint to the victim: please go to the national court and try to get some sort of vindication of your rights. Then, and this is probably crucial, we decided to say that the judgment of the International Tribunal shall be final and binding upon the national court as to the criminal responsibility of the convicted person for such injury. So you see, again, an attempt to remove this shield of State sovereignty, which Italians and dualists like so much because you have two different sets of law. In this case we said, no, we can decide by way of an international provision that judgments may be directly binding upon a national court and therefore the national court has to act accordingly.

Let me just add two points. If you look up the draft statute of the ICC, the International Criminal Court, prepared by the International Law Commission, again you may be puzzled, because there is a provision (article 47) saying that people found guilty, convicted by the court, may be imprisoned or may have to pay a fine, and the fine may be paid to a trust-fund established by the UN Secretary-General for the benefit of victims of crime: therefore, not for the specific benefit of that particular victim. Again I don't understand why, as I say, people who are the victims of huge atrocities should not claim compensation. This compensation can be symbolic, this can be say one dollar or one penny. We all know cases in international law where some States or a particular State was once found guilty and was asked to pay 1.- FF just as a symbolic gesture. Let me remind you, and there I will stop, that back in 1944 in that wonderful booklet he published in America, 'Peace through Law', Hans Kelsen proposed a sort of draft statute for an international criminal court where he provided for the possibility for victims to do what we call in Europe 'constitution de partie civile', namely to be a party as a victim before the court. I think Kelsen was much more forward-looking than all these people in the Security Council or now in Geneva who are drafting those provisions. I think this is important, the more so because otherwise in international criminal proceedings victims never appear in court, except as witnesses. They can testify but they don't have their own interest to push forward. I think we judges from civil law countries feel that this Anglo-American procedure, the adversarial system, in a way tends to neglect the victim. In America you have the civil proceedings after the criminal proceedings, whereas in Europe they can be combined with this 'constitution de partie civile' and this lends a role, a major role, and a voice to the victim.

Meron: I have a number of comments, I apologize for already now saying that I might exceed my time limit, but I will try to speak telegraphese. These are terribly disjointed comments, and let me start by commenting on one of the points made by President Cassese regarding the problems of the Statute and the very enlightened statement in your rules regarding some kind of compensation. It is interesting to reflect on whether there is some inherent power of judicial tribunals to develop rules on compensation. In the United States, in the federal sentencing guidelines we have recently seen some movement in the context of criminal proceedings to give those proceedings some kind of an economic significance, primarily by restitution, but there is some movement in the direction of compensation, so I think that you ought to be saluted for this initiative of including something on that in your rules.

Judge Kooijmans mentioned the question of the standing of an individual. Just one word on that. I think that we should be aware of the fact that there are certain developments taking place which we have not mentioned, and which in the long run can be extremely significant. For example in the World Bank, the Inspection Panel has very broad powers in the context of World Bank policies of lending to governments and supporting various projects. The Inspection Panel has given an extensive standing to individuals to make comments on those projects and that in itself has some significant impact on Bank's policy. I realize that this may not be relevant to individual reparation claims, but it is relevant to the legal position of the individual.

A word about the Tomuschat statement which was extremely comprehensive and interesting. I would like to come back to what Karl Zemanek said, the whole problematique of *erga omnes*. We have the *Barcelona Traction*[6] which is not very well defined or very specific. We have the rules on injured States of the ILC which take the subject a little bit forward. We also have a declaration or a resolution of the Institute of International Law which is not very helpful because it defines *erga omnes* primarily in terms of diplomatic representations. So the main problem we have here is how to translate this emerging principle of international law into something which will have some kind of a component of practice. The practice of the Strasbourg tribunal is really not helpful because those proceedings, although based on the public order of Europe etc., have a very strong grounding in the European Convention on Human Rights. It would be extremely interesting and enlightening if a government would be willing one day on the basis of declarations of acceptance of compulsory jurisdiction of the International Court of Justice, which have been made without any reservations, to bring a case based on *erga omnes* before the International Court of Justice at The Hague and see how far the Court would be prepared at this stage in time to move forward from its previous statements on the subject and apply those in one specific context. Thus, the Court would translate those abstract principles into some kind of a practice.

Turning to Professor Klein's statement, which I found very interesting, the question is how we can develop by common law the principles of the Covenant which are admittedly fairly weak and not comprehensive. With regard to judicial guarantees and due process, the Human Rights Committee has in a very enlightened way in fact expanded Article 6 of the Covenant on capital punishment by being ready to state that certain violations of due process which bear on the question of capital punishment, would constitute a violation of Article 6 which, as we know, is non-derogable. So this is very important. Now when it comes to compensation, which was the principal subject that you have mentioned, the *dispositif* of the Human Rights Committee's views is fairly problematic. Why is that? Well, realizing the dangers and the weaknesses of the Covenant, if you can say that State X should compensate the victim, would it be a tremendous step to ask the victim, before you reach your final position, to give you some more information about the

---

[6]   ICJ Reports 1970, 3, at 33.

damage or the expenses for the lawyers and to try and spell it out? As long as you have not been ready to move the principle from the abstract and to state a figure of specific dollars and cents, we have not moved as far as I would have liked you to move. And, finally, and I will just mention this as my conclusion, when you mention the obligation to ensure, not only to respect, i.e. horizontal obligations, how far would you expand the financial consequences of finding a violation? And finally you have been willing in the case of Article 26 of the Covenant to say that you have competence also for social security when some measures implicate discrimination. I think you have made some very important views on that. Again, how far would you expand the notion of reparation and compensation to those additional issues?

Stein: I can be very brief, because I wanted to make a remark on the cumulation of reparation claims which was already mentioned by Professor Zemanek, and there is nothing to add. I have only two other small remarks in that respect: If the message behind article 40 of the ILC draft is for massive violations of human rights a message of deterrence, telling the responsible State: If you commit massive violations the whole world might be after you, under this aspect article 40 might even be acceptable. The problem is that article 40 is not limited to massive violations, that it could refer to any right guaranteed, for example to those in the 1966 Conventions, and that it is not limited to *erga omnes* violations.

My second remark: Are these rules designed to override the rules on diplomatic protection? If we take a case in which not the own population but foreigners are the victims of those violations, do we do away with the rules of diplomatic protection which are strictly based on nationality, and where we would have – under the acceptable portion of the *Nottebohm* doctrine[7] – a very clear selection of those who could claim reparation? Has this been given up? This is a question to a former member of the ILC.

Malanczuk: I have a question concerning the conceptual framework under which we are discussing the topic 'individual reparation claims entailed by human rights violations'. This requires in my view to have a clear concept of what kind of human rights we are talking of, and what kind of concept of reparation we are talking of. All of us are aware that the human rights concept has become rather confused. We have moved away from the liberal one, the classical concept of negative rights vis-à-vis the State, to social and economic, cultural rights, plus so-called third generation rights: collective rights, self-determination, clean environment and what have you, including the controversial debate on the right to development. Now these are rights of quite a

---

[7] ICJ Reports 1955, 4, at 23.

different nature and I think the convenors of the colloquium have quite rightly limited themselves from the perspective of the rights of the individual as an individual, to the classical liberal concept, except with regard to the last topic UNCC, and we shall talk about that tomorrow. Nevertheless, a problem remains, because also within the framework of the liberal rights, property is the central concept. Therefore it would be advisable also to take into consideration settlement mechanisms such as the International Centre for the Settlement of Investment Disputes, where individuals can have access in the field of state contracts, or to take into consideration the standing of nationals directly against the State within the framework of the Iran-U.S. Claims Tribunal that is based upon a treaty. This tribunal has a hybrid nature, but that is beyond the current discussion. But in many cases it deals with a classical right in a liberal sense: property, which can also be found in the Universal Declaration of Human Rights although the status of that right is not quite clear under customary international law. The UNCC poses a quite different set of problems and my friend Norbert Wühler and I will discuss that again tomorrow.

Second point on the reparation issue. The concept of reparation is also far from clear in my view, and it is not sufficient, with due respect, just to put it into the words of the Hull doctrine: 'prompt, adequate and effective' compensation. The whole doctrine emerges from expropriation cases. 'Prompt' means without delay, 'adequate' means in terms of compensation fair market value, and 'effective' means in a viable currency, not in bonds or in a currency which is not transferable. This all doesn't work if it comes to personal injury cases or to individual rights where an individual has to be released from prison or to mental anguish cases and family restitution. So we are talking about a quite different set of concepts where we have to ask ourselves what are the legal consequences precisely in relation to the specific right that has been violated. That is the appropriate framework I submit to you with respect.

As to the ILC draft articles, Professor Tomuschat has given a very clear statement enlightening me on the fact that the draft is actually not relevant for the topic we are discussing. Even if we were to look at the elements of diplomatic protection which are there, we know that the draft operates on an inter-state level, and not in a sense that it could be relevant for the position of the individual under international law. However, we have to make a qualification there, and maybe that can be extended in a way into the area of progressive development, and that is the point that I also wanted to make, namely one has to distinguish what in this draft is customary international law and what is progressive development. Thus, it has to be made clear whether we are talking *de lege lata* or whether we are talking *de lege ferenda*. Furthermore, with respect to diplomatic protection, it is not quite so that the individual is totally left out, because two aspects at least need to be mentioned. The inter-state claim situation has to take account of the individual, although the State can waive the claim or not pursue it or not give the money to the individual. First, the individual has to exhaust local remedies. That is stated in the draft articles (article 22). So the individual is taken into account, it is the individual which has to exhaust local remedies. And second, the amount of compensation is determined by the loss suffered by the individual. Whether the whole amount is claimed is another matter. But that is the standard to which reference is made.

Two further remarks on the role of national law. Professor Tomuschat has quite rightly said: One has to make a clear distinction between the international level and the national level. I do not want to enter into the old discussion of the relationship between municipal law and international law, monist, dualist theories and so forth – but what is the role of national courts in this respect? I would like to ask my American colleagues, what is the situation of the *Siderman* case[8] now, where a torture claim was brought under the Aliens Tort Act, in 1982 I believe, by the family of an Argentinian citizen against Argentina? That was upheld by the lower California district court for $2.7 mio, but was overturned by the US Court of Appeals with reference to the fact that Argentina might have waived its sovereign immunity because it participated in the proceedings. Now what are the effects of such judgments on the national level stating that a norm of *ius cogens* was violated? Professor Meron just tells me that the case was settled.

And a final remark. I agree with Judge Kooijmans that the important thing is the issue of legal personality. I think it is of no use to discuss in the abstract whether an entity is a subject of international law or not. It is clear that only States are full subjects capable of having all rights and duties of international law, the others are derivative and can have only certain rights and duties. International organizations are created by treaty. Their legal personality is derivative from the treaties and so forth. What matters is international legal personality as a concept and where does international legal personality come up with regard to the standing of individuals. There I would agree that one has to separate it from the issue of bringing claims. Personality means the capacity to have certain rights and duties within the international system and that is not necessarily a question of standing before international courts and tribunals.

Reisman: I thank the speakers and I look forward to reading the papers. I want to make some observations about Christian Tomuschat's approach and some of the policy recommendations that he derives from his approach. In the infantry, there is a rule of thumb: if you have a map and the terrain departs

---

[8] *Siderman de Blake v. Republic of Argentina,* 965 F.2d 699, 717 (9th Cir. 1992).

from the map, go with the terrain! We often start with the map, a set of general principles and try to derive a set of propositions about the rights of individuals in contemporary international law. But if we look at the terrain, we see something quite different. A set of principles reserves for the State certain monopolistic rights over this process, while an extraordinarily dynamic social and political process operates with individuals playing larger and larger roles, operating on courts, on legislatures, on legal advisors, in every democratic country. They communicate by internet and they are very, very effective. What we are seeing is a process in which many of these individual groups, using all of the institutions I just mentioned, are trying to 'privatize', that is to take away from the State, from the Foreign Office or the Department of State, the competence to make claims and to take it into their own hands. They try to exercise that competence in the legislatures, on the executive branch, and in courts in the United States. I submit to you that this phenomenon will spread to many other countries. This is the way international law is being formed.

Now part of this process has established that human rights are matters of international concern. In this respect, I think the policy recommendation that Christian made that compensation and internal rearrangement after systematic human rights violations is a matter for the State itself and not for outsiders, does not work. Ultimately, *'Vergangenheitsbewältigung'* in Germany or in Japan, or in the United States dealing with the detention of Japanese, is a matter that will have to be taken up in the first instance by the State that did it. But these are international events, ignited because outsiders complain about them. Their ultimate resolution will be appraised by the international system. Christian shows how problematic this can be. He is right. It is disruptive of the conduct of international relations if individuals, using their own timing, can start matters in courts or in legislatures and undo agreements that may be in the works or may already have been accomplished. But from the human rights perspective, we must recall that this is done because individuals now have no alternative. They have no access to an international tribunal. We must weigh diplomatic disruption against providing human rights remedies. In the *Princz* case,[9] if Germany had said early on that it was prepared to establish an international tribunal of, say, two or three professors who would have sat and liquidated damages for Princz, the case would, I surmise, have been dismissed immediately in a district court. The moral imperative in United States courts, and now in New Zealand and UK courts, to take up these cases is that there is no alternative forum.

---

[9]   26 F. 3d 1166 (D. C. Cir. 1994).

Thürer: May I address a question to Christian Tomuschat? I wonder if you left out on purpose the law of war in your highly impressive analysis. I think that the law of armed conflicts would be quite interesting to consider as well. First of all, Article 3 of the Hague Convention No. IV respecting the laws of armed conflicts seems to be relevant. Article 3 states two sorts of responsibility. One is the responsibility of one State vis-à-vis another State; the other is that the belligerent party which violates the provisions of the Hague Regulations shall, if the case demands, be liable to pay compensation. We are here confronted with a norm possibly constituting, so it seems to me, a legal basis for a claim to compensation. Of course this provision, which is similar to the one in Art. 91 of the First Additional Protocol of 1977 to the Geneva Conventions, needs interpretation. It is not clear whether or not this provision is self-executive but I think this would be a very rewarding question for further research.

Verhoeven: I will be very short, since I generally agree to a large extent with the comments that have been previously made by Messrs. Cassese and Reisman. My remarks are mainly concerned with the report of Mr. Tomuschat. I probably disagree with the starting point of this report, i.e. that international law does not necessarily require that breaches of its rules must be repaired, compensated. In the *Francovich* case,[10] the Court ruled that Community law requires that breaches of its provisions be compensated under Community law. Why? Because, if it were not the case, its credibility would be endangered. In my view, this is also relevant for international law. If it is accepted that States might violate international rules without being punished or forced to repair, the whole system would collapse, especially when basic rules, like the prohibition of resorting to armed force or the safeguard of human rights are at stake. It would be nonsense to suggest that breaches do not give rise to compensation when basic rules are concerned. Quite the contrary. It does not matter in this respect that the violation may be massive. It can be difficult in such a case to determine the appropriate form of reparation or to have the compensation paid. But the principle of responsibility goes unaltered.

It is another issue to decide on the procedural aspects of reparation. The question here is: who is entitled to claim and before which forum? As our colleague Reisman told us, two possibilities exist: an international or a national body. For the time being, international bodies (tribunals, commissions, ...) are very few and access is restricted to States. Generally, the results are most disappointing. Changes are needed to improve access of victims to reparation. Does it help, as mentioned in the draft, that 'third' States be given

---

[10] Court of Justice of the European Communities, Judgment of 19 November 1991, Reports 1991, I – 5403.

access in such a case? I seriously doubt it. The fact that an obligation is said to be, under international law, *erga omnes*, does not mean that everybody is entitled to claim compensation. Nor does it under national law. It would be strange to accept that States could get profit from the massive violation of human rights elsewhere! In order to either permit or collect and distribute reparation, some kind of collective or central authority should be established. There is no such mention in the present draft, the practicability of which is highly questionable. Failing effective international fora, we are left with national bodies. It is a fact that international relations could become more difficult if claims for massive violations of human rights – or other basic rules of international law – were brought before them. Still, I do not see how an individual could be reproached for doing that, when his national State remains passive or when there is no 'national' State at all. This could be effective to some extent. For instance, claims for attachments, even pre-judgment attachments, on certain assets of the State concerned could be introduced. This is not difficult – provided assets exist! – and, in many cases, judges have proved not to oppose systematically such measures. Sure, this could have disruptive effects on international economic relations. Still, it could be the only possibility to get effective compensation, or at least to induce States not to overlook their normal duty to compensate. As pointed out by our colleague Cassese, no immunity should be admitted in such a context. Never indeed was immunity conceived as a device permitting States to elude responsibility for gross violations of basic international law rules. And if it were, it should not be admitted any more.

Fleck: This debate shows very clearly that international principles and custom are developing less progressively than facts. Yet it is important to see that the wrongful acts as defined in the draft articles on State responsibility do not only relate to human rights violations. In this respect I would share Professor Kooijmans' concern with the title of this seminar: Definitely, the subtitle is broader than the first line, and I would like to develop this a little bit further. Referring to the commercial activity exception mentioned by Professor Tomuschat, I think there are also other areas of wrongful acts committed by States which ought to be addressed in this respect. I am referring to the temporary stay of foreign forces in foreign countries as part of the present Partnership of Peace Program of the North Atlantic Alliance, also of other peace-time activities, and of military operations during crisis situations, performed by UN or other military forces. There are no strict rules on how to deal with claims. There is no clear definition between in-duty and off-duty acts committed by the members of those forces and the principle of State immunity always prevails. Considering the practical solution to be proposed, the best way, of course, would be to settle all these claims by way of negotiations. This would sometimes be at the expense of those people who were injured. They are private citizens and not always properly protected in their interests by the State. The question of jurisdiction is totally open, too. I just want to pose this as a question.

Hilger: Mr. Chairman you will not be surprised to hear that, as a legal advisor to my Government, I naturally agree with Professor Tomuschat when he said that the established rules regarding State immunity should as far as possible be left intact. These rules of State immunity naturally also have a function in the relationships between States and the maintenance of peace and so on. But I readily agree with Professor Reisman that there is in today's world a tendency by individuals and non-governmental organizations to privatize all these issues, and therefore in the political context things become difficult. I would like to support very strongly a remark made by Christian Tomuschat yet again that, where a change has occurred to the better, to a democratic society, the new society cannot be expected to compensate fully all the wrongdoings and the crimes which have being committed by the old regime. That was certainly true for Germany in 1945 and for Germany in 1990. That is certainly true for South Africa, as it was true for Argentina and so on.

A second set of short remarks regarding what President Cassese said on the Fourth Geneva Convention. Yes, certainly every State is entitled to prosecute these crimes under the Geneva Conventions. But from a practitioner's point of view you have to see that a State must be in a position to build a valid case. I recall the case of a military officer from Rwanda, a captain, some five or six years ago. He was an exchange officer at the *Führungsakademie der Bundeswehr,* the military staff college in Hamburg. Then appeared a report in a Hamburg newspaper, the 'Stern', where it was quite convincingly indicated that this officer as captain of one of the platoons of the presidential guard had been involved in atrocities in his homeland against his countrymen. A great uproar ensued. The officer was naturally at once dismissed from the German military academy. His residence permit was cancelled. Over the weekend the Hamburg prosecutor looked into the case to find out whether he had enough evidence to build a case against this man and to bring him to court in Hamburg. Unfortunately, this was not possible although the journalists from the 'Stern' were trying to be helpful. The man could enter an airplane and fly home.

The first case where the principle of universal jurisdiction really worked was the *Tadic* case[11], but that case, against the background of former Yugosla-

---

[11] *The Prosecutor v. Dusko Tadic,* 2 Oct. 1995, Judgment of the ICTY Appeals Chamber, Case No. IT-94-1-AR72, ILR 105, 419 (453).

via, the same people who had been in one soccer club over many years found themselves on different sides. The ones were the torturers, the others were the victims. And once all that had happened they found themselves again at the cash register at a supermarket in Munich and all of a sudden the victim said: Ah, isn't that he who tortured me and so on, and it was only therefore that the prosecutor in Munich and the tribunal in Munich could build a valid case, could pursue the case during the first year in Germany until it was possible to hand over Tadic to the Yugoslavia tribunal at the Hague. Regarding the question of whether all these complicated issues of criminal prosecution should have been complemented by material compensation, I recall that the issue was discussed in 1992/93, before the tribunal was set up by the Security Council. This wasn't just a decision of the Council, it was preceded by many contacts and conferences among governments. It was felt at the time that the task was difficult enough and that one should leave it on the criminal side of the matter. But it is certainly debatable whether this was the right decision.

Klein: Ladies and gentlemen, you were kind enough not to put too many questions to me. I take this as evidence that I have completely convinced you, and this of course is not a bad result of our discussion. But let me make some remarks and answer a few questions.

First I would like to agree entirely with the statement made by Professor Zemanek that we need a procedure to deal with claims resulting from violations of *erga omnes* norms. I think it is a real improvement that the draft on State responsibility has recognized this category of claims, and I clearly support this decision, but it is not workable as long as it is not amended by procedural rules. I also agree with President Cassese. Since individuals are the real victims of any human rights violations they must have the chance to be a party to any relevant dispute. Otherwise their substantive rights will be imperfect, and will stay on this imperfect stage of law. This brings me to the remark made by Judge Kooijmans and taken up by several other speakers. Of course, we cannot infer from the legal capacity to be a subject of law the capacity to raise claims. We have to go the other way round. But concerning human rights I would say individuals are the holders of these rights, otherwise the whole idea does not make sense, and so far human beings have to be seen as subjects of law, of public international law. This of course will not automatically entitle them to claim reparation. I tried to express this in my paper. With regard to this point, we have to look for another legal basis, and up to now this basis can only be found in conventional rules.

Now I would like to turn to two questions which I would like to answer in greater detail. I think Professor Stein asked a very valuable question. What is the relationship between diplomatic protection and human rights? I don't think that the concept of human rights can make it in practice without the concept of diplomatic protection, which is a very useful instrument for many – of course not all – cases of human rights violations. The exhaustion of domestic remedies is a requirement for both, for asserting human rights violations before an international body and for diplomatic protection. But if local remedies have been exhausted, in principle both roads are open. Certainly we have to distinguish between some configurations. First, if the home State is a party to a certain human rights treaty, this will or should be understood to the effect that the State has waived its right to exert diplomatic protection as long as the procedure before this international body is pending. But it is another question if the home State is not a party to a convention or to a body to which the individual might apply, while the violating State has accepted the jurisdiction of that body. Difficult questions may arise in this context. For example, the International Covenant on Civil and Political Rights does not provide for any time limits for a victim's claim. Thus, the victim might apply to the Human Rights Committee after years. But, perhaps, in the meantime, the home State has raised the claim of diplomatic protection and has got at least a partly favourable answer from the violating State in favour of its national. What would the Human Rights Committee do in this case? Perhaps it would say, there is no longer a victim, he has already got a remedy. Thus, there might be some procedural possibilites to get out of this trouble, but it is a real problem. So I do appreciate the question.

Professor Meron has asked some questions concerning the Human Rights Committee's practice with regard to compensation and I think the main issue was: Why is the Committee not bold enough to fix a certain amount of money in cases where it thinks that compensation would be the effective remedy? I think there are two answers to this. First, the Human Rights Committee already finds itself rather bold. Very often it calls for compensation, but there are many cases where even a modest request for compensation, even in a symbolic way, does not receive a favourable answer by the States concerned. So I feel the Committee would think it to be perhaps preposterous to fix a definite amount of money, although in most cases no compensation is paid at all. The other answer to our question would be that probably the Committee does not dispose of information detailed enough to assess the issue. Of course, one could ask for more information, but taking into account the length of proceedings already now–it is for years that cases are pending before the Human Rights Committee, of course after the exhaustion of all domestic remedies–, I think this would prolong the proceedings still for at least one more year. You have to consider that the Human Rights Committee, as you are well aware, is not a permanent body but meets for three sessions a year each lasting three weeks, and a lot of other things have to be done during this time.

Well, I think these are the two reasons why the Committee has not followed your proposal so far.

Tomuschat: I shall be very brief because I spoke at length when I made my presentation. I took into account borderline cases, but borderline cases which are part of the terrain which has to be explored. In many minds there exist only *Filartiga* and *Letelier*[12] and some other individual cases, but instances of mass violations: wars, other catastrophes, the *apartheid* regime, what happened in the GDR, what happened in Nazi Germany – all this must be taken into account as well. I regret that during the deliberations of the ILC on the draft articles on State responsibility these situations did not play a prominent role. Attention was largely focused on individual cases, mainly drawn from arbitral awards of the 19th and the beginning of the 20th century. Other situations which are more important, the relationship between Germany and Poland, for instance, were not considered. Consequently, the draft articles are essentially tailored for dealing with individual cases.

A second observation. A distinction must be drawn between individual authors and States as tort feasors. Sometimes in the discussion things were mixed up. Of course individual and collective responsibility are closely interrelated. But think for instance of Adolf Hitler. To deny him immunity against civil suits seems persuasive at first glance. But would it truly make sense to allow 100,000 or 20 million suits to be brought against him if he had survived? You could do that, but it would not really be a big contribution to the development of international law.

Talking now about individuals as subjects of international law, I know perfectly well that the existence of a remedy, that standing before international tribunals is not the test for personality under international law. I said in my presentation no more than if there is a remedy, there is certainly a right and the individual qualifies as a legal subject. But there are other instances as well. It is indeed my conviction that the crimes listed in the draft Code of Crimes and in Article 19 of the draft articles on State responsibility – you could call them also crimes or *erga omnes* violations – prove that the individual can be considered a holder of rights under international law if he or she is protected by such basic rules.

Now as far as immunity is concerned, it should be clear that we are not talking about immunity as a main topic, but it came to the foreground. The paradox is that in cases of massive violations the victims cannot really expect full compensation. Joe Verhoeven did not want to accept this paradox. But it is a paradox, and we must face up to it. During the Second World War, 60 million people, according to reliable statistics, lost their lives. 60 million

---

[12]   630 F.2d 876 (2d Cir. 1980) and 748 F.2d 790 (2d Cir. 1984).

people. Now, if you insist on full reparation, this means that Germans during their lifetime would have had to live in slave-like conditions, in order to make reparation for the harm done, also a new generation of people who had nothing to do with the Second World War and with the Nazi dictatorship. The principle of full reparation simply cannot be enforced in a way which permits of no modifications or reservations.

The last point which I would like to mention is the paradox of restitution of property and compensation for other losses. Antonio Cassese mentioned it. He felt that the discrepancy was truly intriguing as far as the former Yugoslavia is concerned. There exists a big debate also in Germany. Many people claim restitution of the property that was taken from them in the former GDR during the period of 1945 to 1949. But persons who suffered other losses, for instance children of the former bourgeois elite who were not able to attend a grammar school and finally a university, had to confine their lives to becoming farm labourers. Because they were explicitly denied the right to go to university all their professional chances were compromised. Now for that kind of loss sustained under a dictatorial regime ridiculous amounts are being provided for; on the other hand, people who would be successful in their claims for restitution would get everything. To endorse this divergency would be a clear capitalist approach to how the injustices of the past should be repaired. All these paradoxes come up and it is very difficult to resolve them.

Compensation for Human Rights Violations:
The Practice of the Past Decade in the Americas

*W. Michael Reisman**

> No hay camino, el camino se hace al andar.
> *Machado*

I. INTRODUCTION

Compensation practice for human rights violations in the Americas has developed rapidly in the past ten years. Since 1987, the Inter-American Court of Human Rights has handed down a series of compensation decisions. Everyone who participated in the first of them, the *Velásquez-Rodriguez* case, and its companion decision in the *Godinez-Cruz* case, was acutely aware that the hemispheric human rights system was moving into a new, uncharted area. In introducing the case for the Inter-American Human Rights Commission, which had initiated the action before the Court, Edmundo Vargas Carreño, then the Executive Secretary of the Commission, remarked to the Court that

> it is a difficult and delicate matter, because there is no precise conventional base, jurisprudence is sparse and there is no adequate doctrine.

In the same ten year period, the Chilean-U.S. 'Bryan Commission', operating under a Chilean-U.S. treaty, liquidated damages for the murder, in Washington, by Chilean agents, of Orlando Letelier, a former Chilean Foreign Minister, then in exile in the U.S. and Bonnie Moffit, a U.S. national. In the same period, a number of national commissions in Latin America set compensation for individual human rights violations committed by their respective governments against their own nationals. In the United States, the injustice done to Americans of Japanese extraction during the Second World War was finally repaired, if only symbolically, by payment of compensation to

* The author gratefully acknowledges that Ralph Wilde assembled the record on the Civil Liberties Act of 1987, Felipe Irarrazabal assembled the documents on Chilean compensation, Serge Martinez, J.D. 1999 checked the citations and Cheryl A. DeFilippo supervised the preparation of the manuscript.

A. Randelzhofer and C. Tomuschat (eds.), State Responsibility and the Individual, 63–108.
© 1999 Kluwer Law International. Printed in Great Britain.

individuals. Within the past month, the Argentine Government has issued a series of bonds, under the supervision of the IMF, to compensate victims of human rights violations during the military dictatorship. At the same time, some national courts have awarded compensation for human rights violations.

Thus, the Americas, in this past decade, provide a rather rich, temporally concentrated and as yet relatively untapped body of legal experience on the subject of individual compensation for human rights violations. As with all cross-cultural comparisons, one cannot say, with any confidence, that the American experience will be instructive for students of other systems, especially the European system, where both the problems and the contexts may be very different. The political and legal universe in the Americas is, as I will explain, unique, in no small part because of its rich diversity, and a case-by-case formation of a theory and practice of compensation for human rights violations is inevitably influenced by cultural values and pressing political concerns that are, often, quite different from those in other regions.

In this paper, I propose to review, first, the practice of the Inter-American Human Rights Commission and the Inter-American Court of Human Rights, then the Bryan Commission, and finally a number of examples of national practice in North and South America. As the work of national courts in this area is treated elsewhere, it will not be taken up here. I will conclude with some more general observations about the special problems that the issue of compensation for human rights violations poses to scholars, government officials and practitioners.

II. THE ESSENTIAL PROBLEM IN COMPENSATION FOR HUMAN RIGHTS VIOLATIONS

The notion of compensation for injuries – for *lucrum cessans* and *damnum emergens* – has ancient roots in law. Every modern legal system has evolved detailed procedures and valuations for injuries. There is, thus, no shortage of municipal models for compensation for injuries. Each legal civilization and municipal system has its own ways of defining what has been injured, determining the cumulative value, over time, of the actual loss, determining who is entitled to compensation, and applying diverse methods for discounting for current payment. Some systems allow for the pain and suffering of the injured party and some allow for the assessment of 'punitive damages' in addition to actual losses. In systems, such as the United States, where questions may be submitted to a jury, the quantum of awards can be quite labile, though in the United States massive awards are often tempered by subsequent judicial *remitur* at the trial level or by appeal. In systems in which the determination of these matters is reserved to judges and/or assessors, there is likely to be a greater predictability in awards for damages. In systems in which the tariff of damages is set by the legislature, predictability may be greater. In all of these systems, however, determinations of compensation are nominally matters of private law and the essential objective of the law is to arrange a compensation for an injured individual that, excluding the victim's own contribution to the injury, will 'make him or her whole'. Even in circumstances in which a very high award of damages is allowed in order to deter the actions of others who may be similarly situated in the future, i.e., setting compensation for prescriptive purposes, the targets, who may be both *actors* or particular types of *actions* or both, are likely to be in the private sector.

In the sphere of the international protection of human rights, in contrast, compensation uneasily straddles public and private law. The claimant is an individual but the defendant is always a State. While the objective of compensating the injured individual precipitated the process, it shares center stage, in contrast to a domestic injury case, with the concern for reinforcing the aggregate of human rights norms, indeed, more generally, with the maintenance and improvement of the public order of the community. These concerns influence virtually every aspect of international human rights decisions, but have a particular impact on compensation. For one thing, the potential economic and political consequences of compensation awards for the national economy may sometimes be a critical consideration when a State is obliged to make payment. More generally, human rights compensation must always be looked at in terms of the aggregate sanctioning goals of a community while private compensation cases are, first and foremost, about compensation. Public sanctioning goals include *preventing* and *suspending* discrete public order violations that are about to occur; *deterring*, in general, potential public order violations in the future; *restoring* public order after it has been violated; *correcting* the behavior that generates public order violations; *rehabilitating* victims who have suffered the brunt of public order violations; and *reconstructing* in a larger social sense, to remove conditions that appear likely to generate public order violations.[1]

Related to these considerations is the general 'human-rights-predisposition' of the defendant State. Of the three regional human rights systems, the European, alone, has, at least until now, confined subscription to its institutions and processes to States that demonstrated that they were effective *Rechtsstaaten*. States may not join the system until they have met this prerequisite. That fact has major implications for the types of violations that

---

[1] See generally, W.M. Reisman, 'Institutions and Practices for Restoring and Maintaining Public Order', *Duke J. Comp. & Int'l L.* 6 (1995), 175, 176.

are likely to occur and, more important from a systemic standpoint, major implications for the ways that defendant governments are likely to respond to decisions that hold them in violation of prescribed human rights and that then liquidate and order compensation. At the time of the entry into force of the American Convention on Human Rights, many of the States of the Americas were neither democratic nor *Rechtsstaaten*, though most had constitutions that presented a mythic image of constitutional democracy. Many of the States parties were, in effect, what the late Ernst Fränkel of the Free University of Berlin called *Doppelstaaten*,[2] i.e., their constitutional governments were formalistic and ineffective with effective power exercised by a military beyond the control of the civil authorities. In these sorts of States, violations of human rights are often systemic, in that they are the essential techniques for the maintenance of power by the incumbent elite. This is an important distinction. Many of the human rights violations in the European regional system were assimilable to torts and the defendant governments to the status of tortfeasors. In the Americas, until recently, many of the human rights violations were parts of a systematic effort by one group to maintain political power and its perquisites. The implications for compensation questions are obvious.

Other States that became party to the American Convention on Human Rights had serious ongoing insurrections, if not bitter civil wars, in which the insurrectionists employed the methods of guerilla warfare. In others, the Cold War was replicated, in microcosm, in bitter, sometimes covert, and usually 'dirty' wars. Hence the Inter-American Commission and Court had to apply a code of human rights that presupposed a civil society, with the characteristic fundamental political compromises that make such a society possible, in circumstances in which those critical preconditions did not obtain. In still others, organized narcotics traffickers have either corrupted the State apparatus or overwhelmed the judiciary. Hence the receptivity of the governments of defendant States in the Americas to human rights condemnations by a treaty body and the corresponding willingness to pay the reparations that have been indicated may vary widely. In some States, it is a situation of *non possumus*, i.e., the government is simply unable to secure the necessary internal consensus to make the payment. In some circumstances, the actual perpetrators of the human rights violation may feel a sense of justification for their acts, in a belligerent situation, and insofar as they have the power, will simply block compliance.

There is also the economic issue. Savigny remarked that in matters of civil damages, there is always money. Municipal law does not concern itself with alleged inability on the part of a judgment debtor to pay. In international law,

---

[2] See E. Fraenkel, *The Dual State*, 1941.

the situation is more complex. Certainly in the period examined here, full payment for massive human rights violations could well have exceeded the economic capacity of certain States. While the cases examined here make no reference to the actual economic capacity of a defendant State to pay for human rights violations, it is difficult to imagine that responsible judges, especially those installed on a human rights court, could ignore this dimension of the problem. After all, aggravating the economic difficulties of the State could itself have grave human rights consequences for many of the other citizens and leave the human rights situation in the State concerned net worse off.

Authoritative decisions about human rights compensation repeat, in almost mantra-like fashion, a dictum from *Chorzow Factory*, in which the object of reparation is expressed as a *restitutio in integrum*. If restoration of the status quo ante is not possible, compensation is to be paid. This formula provides meaningful guidelines for the case in which a factory has been unlawfully taken from its owners, but tells us relatively little about reparations of human rights violation. A factory may be physically returned: *restitutio in integrum* or specific performance, or its value may be calculated, based on the book value or on an estimation of the flow of revenue to be generated by the enterprise during its economic life, with an appropriate discount for current payment. In human rights violations, particularly those that involve the death of a victim, there is no possibility of a restitution. The victim may be treated as a factory, with a projection of probable income over the course of his or her life, discounted for current payments. But, in fact, the human being is much more than a wealth producer. Many people in the community look to the victim as a source of affection, as a parent, or child, or spouse, or lover, or friend or sibling. Very often it is those deprivations which hurt more intensely and longer than the economic deprivation. In addition, a human rights deprivation in many circumstances is a form of terror, in that many others who are similarly situated, perceive themselves as potential victims and share vicariously in the trauma of the violence. Human rights compensation decisions struggle with this problem by using very elastic terms like 'moral damages', 'ethical damages', or 'pain and suffering'. But in none of them is there a recurring and predictable method by which compensation is liquidated. For many of these reasons, compensation, when paid, seems unsatisfactory and, ironically, inconsistent with the fundamental notion of the humanity of the victim. As we will see, in the practice of the Americas, the legal term, 'just or fair compensation', is, in fact, a complex legal construct which takes account of a wide range of factors, far beyond the loss suffered by the beneficiaries of a victim.

A recurring theoretical problem for human rights compensation is whether a deprivation is to be viewed as an ordinary calamity, for which decision makers may turn to the routine techniques of the *lex loci*, or whether these deprivations are to be viewed as deprivations requiring some measure of punitive damages; or indeed, whether these deprivations are to be viewed as injuries to the community at large, in which case they may require a sanctions program that goes beyond repairing the particular injury suffered. Severe human rights violations, particularly those that are part of a systematic pattern, understandably arouse demands for more than simply compensation.

One of the functions of punitive damages in democratic systems is as a safety-valve for popular indignation at human rights violations and a clear signal to potential violators that violations will henceforth not be facultative obligations, but will always incur substantial additional costs. Rational economic maximizers may be expected to act upon such communications. But governments do not have resources of their own. When punitive damages are ordered for a human rights violation, they are paid for by the population at large. When large strata of the population have been the victims or, in a State terror practice, individuals are randomly selected from those strata as targets of violence with the expectation that other members will be cowed, the imposition of punitive damages involves a second deprivation imposed upon the victims and their families. Lamentably, this was the situation in many parts of the Americas during the time immediately preceding the period under consideration. The Inter-American Court did consider a feasible alternative to this dilemma: the imposition of personal responsibility on the human rights violators.[3] But even if the Court had been bolder, many of the actual violators would not have had the wherewithal to pay.

This particular aspect of compensation for human rights is one of the most frustrating for human rights lawyers. Because the 'State' is identified as the responsible party, it is often innocent people who, in effect, pay the compensation for the human rights violations that have been effected by others, who are violating their human rights. Consider Iraq: Saddam Hussein and the elite of the Baath party have victimized the people of Iraq no less than the people of Kuwait. The compensation scheme that has been established is one which, ironically, continues to enrich the same Iraqi elite, while imposing the real burden of compensation on the people of Iraq.

To be sure, there have been circumstances in which massive, systematic violations were supported by and enured to the benefit of the rest of the population. One thinks, in this regard, of the incarceration of Japanese by the United States during the Second World War, an action which was ostensibly

---

[3]   International Responsibility for the Promulgation and Enforcement of Laws in Violation of the Convention, Advisory Opinion OC-14/94, 9 Dec. 1994.

undertaken for the security of the United States and reviewed by the highest court[4] and was tolerated if not enthusiastically accepted, by the majority of its citizens. Another example may be found in Nazi actions against Jews during the Second World War, especially if one accepts the historical gloss of Professor Goldhagen.[5] But, for the most part in the Americas, a practice of punitive damages for massive human rights violations would have simply imposed an additional deprivation on the strata that themselves were targets of the violation. In this respect, it would not recommend itself as a compensatory or deterrent technique.

III. THE INTER-AMERICAN SYSTEM

The OAS Charter of 1948 incorporates the 'fundamental rights of the individual' as one of the Organization's founding principles.[6] The American Declaration of the Rights and Duties of Man (American Declaration), prepared by the Inter-American Juridical Committee in 1947, was adopted by the OAS in Bogota, Colombia, in 1948 to elaborate upon the Charter's general commitment to human rights.[7]

The Inter-American Commission of Human Rights (Commission) was created in 1959 to serve as a mechanism for overseeing national implementation of such human rights commitments.[8] Composed of seven members elected in their individual capacity, the Commission started operating in 1960 with a vague mandate. In 1965, its competence was expanded to accept communications, request information from governments, and make recommendations 'with the objective of bringing about more effective observance of human rights'.[9] In 1967, the OAS Charter was amended, and the Commission became a principal organ of the OAS. The American Convention of Human Rights (American Convention), signed in 1969, incorporated the Commission and assigned it specified conventional competences.[10] It also created the Inter-American Court of Human Rights (Inter-American Court).

---

[4]   *Korematsu v. U.S.*, 323 U.S. 214 (1944).
[5]   D. Goldhagen, *Hitler's Willing Executioners: Ordinary Germans and the Holocaust,* 1996.
[6]   Charter of the Organization of American States, 30 April 1948, 2 U.S.T. 2394, art. 3. 1995.
[7]   'American Declaration of the Rights and Duties of Man', in: Organization of American States, *Handbook of Existing Rules Pertaining to Human Rights in the Inter-American System*, OEA/Ser.L/V/II.60 Doc. 28, rev. 1 (1983), 21.
[8]   Id.
[9]   Id. at 10.
[10] American Convention on Human Rights, 22 Nov. 1969, ILM 9 (1969), 673 [hereinafter American Convention]. Unless otherwise specified, all references to articles refer to the American Convention.

The American Convention entered into force in 1978. Currently there are twenty-five parties to the Convention.

The Commission has three forms of jurisdiction. Its conventional jurisdiction applies to the twenty-five States that have, to date, become parties to the American Convention. Its judicial invocative jurisdiction provides the competence to invoke the Inter-American Court; it applies to the State-parties to the American Convention that have accepted the Inter-American Court's jurisdiction. While these two forms of jurisdiction depend upon adherence to the American Convention, the Commission's declaration jurisdiction applies to all parties to the OAS Charter, indeed, to all States in the Americas. Hence, every independent State in the Western Hemisphere, even those which have not yet become party to the American Convention, is subject, in some form, to the Commission's jurisdiction.

The Commission's jurisdiction may be invoked by citizens and organizations within the hemisphere. On its own initiative, the Commission may also prepare country reports. To facilitate both of these activities, the Commission conducts on-site visits to individual countries. The Commission also plays a role in regional codification and progressive development. It has drafted a number of important human rights instruments for the OAS, provided technical assistance to State-parties in matters concerning the American Convention, and litigated cases before the Inter-American Court.

Article 44 of the Convention states:

> Any person or group of persons, or any nongovernmental entity legally recognized in one or more member states of the Organization, may lodge petitions with the Commission containing denunciations or complaints of violation of this Convention by a State Party.[11]

A case begins on receipt of a petition alleging a violation of human rights. Petitions about the same event often come from a number of different sources. The Commission examines each petition in terms of the basic requirements of Articles 46 and 47: whether the petition contains names and signatures, whether it states facts that tend to establish a violation of the American Convention or whether it is manifestly groundless, whether domestic remedies have been exhausted, whether the petition has been lodged within specified time limits, and whether the petition is pending in another international proceeding or has already been before the Commission.

If the petition satisfies these threshold requirements, it is relayed to the named government for the latter's information and views. The information supplied by the government may lay the matter to rest, in which case the Commission is required by Article 48(b) to order that the record be closed. It is also possible that the information provided may establish that the petition

---

[11] Id. at Art. 44.

is inadmissible, which also terminates the procedure. If neither occurs, the Commission, with the knowledge of the parties, must proceed to investigate the matter, asking for information it deems necessary, hearing oral arguments, and receiving written statements. It also puts itself at the disposal of the parties with the objective of reaching an amicable settlement.

If an amicable settlement can be arranged, the Commission issues a short report to that effect to the Secretary-General of the OAS. If there is no settlement, the Commission draws up a report stating the facts, its conclusions, and its recommendations. The report is then sent only to the State concerned, which may not publicize it. If, within three months, the matter has not been settled, the Commission has two options: the provisions of Article 50 state that it may issue a final report, which becomes part of the Annual Report to the General Assembly of the OAS; or according to Article 51, the Commission may refer the matter to the Inter-American Court, if the State concerned has accepted the Inter-American Court's jurisdiction.

There is no reason why the Inter-American Human Rights Commission could not specify a measure of damages as compensation. In practice, it has not, confining itself in its Reports issued under Article 51 of the American Convention on Human Rights to a general recommendation that the defendant State pay compensation. In sporadic but unreported Commission efforts, of which this writer is aware, to secure compensation from States that had been ordered in Article 51 Reports, the Commission seemed inclined to incorporate the compensation rules of the State concerned, despite the fact, as we will see, that the Court later indicated that international standards are to govern the liquidation of compensation claims. To my knowledge, no compensation has ever been paid by a State in accord with a recommendation in a Report issued under Article 51 of the American Convention. On occasion, the Commission has informally discussed with governments the possibility of a change in internal legislation which would render the recommendations of the Commission binding on that State. Had this been accomplished, the Commission might have had an incentive to specify damages in its reports under Article 51 of the Convention. In the *Caballero-Delgado* and *Santana* case,[12] the Commission sought to enlist the Court's support in transforming into legally binding obligations the reports it was issuing under Article 51 of the Convention. In that case, the Commission pleaded for the Court to

> declare that based on the principle of *pacta sunt servanda* in accordance with Article 26 of the Vienna Convention on the Law of Treaties, the Government has violated Articles 51(2) and 44 of the American Convention read in conjunction with Article 1(1) by delib-

---

[12] Judgment of 8 Dec. 1995, Series C, No. 22.

erately failing to comply with the recommendation made by the Inter-American Commission.[13]

But the Court elected to interpret the term 'recommendation' in the American Convention as non-binding. Consequently, as the Court said, 'A State does not incur international responsibility by not complying with a recommendation which is not obligatory'.[14] In these circumstances, the Commission has not liquidated damages in its reports.

The failure to take account of the Commission's recommendations meant that a number of States against whom many reports were issued accumulated a large number of inchoate and uncertain 'obligations' to pay reparations. Needless to say, condemnations by the Commission irritated the governments of these defendant States, while the defendant States' obduracy with respect to the recommendations to pay compensation hardly endeared those States to the Commission or to the non-governmental community that was initiating most of the claims. In the early 1990s, as many of these same States began to shed their military dictatorships and return to constitutional rule, the accumulation of claims created an especially awkward situation for these new democratic governments. Many of the governments that now came to power had campaigned on a human rights platform and had criticized their predecessors precisely for the gross violation of human rights that the Commission had condemned. Now these same governments found themselves obliged to defend their predecessors' actions whose unlawfulness they themselves had already acknowledged and publicly announced.

To deal with this problem, the Commission explored the possibility of some sort of lump-sum settlement. This is a common technique in international law, whose economy and speed recommends it. But while its reduction of the transaction costs of the claims process may be significant, its corresponding reduction of the value of the individual claim causes problems from a human rights perspective. While an argument can be made that the Commission could find authority to arrange lump-sum settlements under Articles 48 and 49 of the Convention, the Commission ultimately did not pursue this matter. It did, as mentioned, explore with a number of governments the possibility of an adjustment in internal legislation which would have rendered recommendations for compensation by the Commission binding under national law.

It is only when the Inter-American Human Rights Commission brings a case to the Inter-American Court of Human Rights under Article 51 of the American Convention, that it specifies the theory and measure of damages it is urging. Hence this aspect of the Commission's compensation practice may

---

[13] Id. at para. 67.
[14] Id. at para. 67.

be considered most usefully in our discussion of the role of the Inter-American Court of Human Rights in this regard.

IV. THE INTER-AMERICAN COURT OF HUMAN RIGHTS

1. The Convention

Article 63(1) of the American Convention provides, in relevant part, that

> [i]f the Court finds that there has been a violation of a right or freedom protected by this Convention, the Court shall rule that the injured party be ensured the enjoyment of his right or freedom that was violated. It shall also rule, if appropriate, that the consequences of the measure or situation that constituted the breach of such right or freedom be remedied and that fair compensation be paid to the injured party.

Three categories of remedy and possibly two categories of beneficiary are referred to: (1) injunctive relief; (2) adjustments in the social and legal structures that gave rise to or allowed the breach to occur; and (3) fair compensation which is to be paid to the injured party. The reference to the second category of remedies is not formulated felicitously, but its intention appears clear. The reference to the third category of remedies is a more conventional formula, although there are some conflicts between the English and Spanish versions of the provision. Article 45(3) of the Rules of Procedure of the Court provides

> If the Court is informed that an agreement has been reached between the victim of the violation and the State Party concerned, it shall verify the equitable nature of such agreement (*que el acuerdo sea justo*).

The adjectives 'fair' in Article 63 and the adjective 'equitable' in Rule Article 45(3) are inconsistent renditions of the Spanish 'justa' in the legal formula 'justa indemnización'. 'Justa' in Spanish may mean, depending on the context, just, correct, exact, strict, lawful, equitable and so on. It would probably be most accurate to treat the formula 'justa indemnización' as a hendiadys, translated into English as 'compensation', in the sense that the French term 'cour de justice' should be translated into English as 'court' and not 'court of justice', since modern English does not need the qualifier 'of justice' in order to indicate that the reference is to a judicial institution. Be that as it may, it is not clear why the word 'justa' in the rule of procedure corresponding to Article 63 of the Convention has been translated 'equitable'. It may simply be the result of carelessness. One would think that the better understanding of the compensation to be paid under Article 63 is that it is the *lawful* measure, with respect to which international and appropriate national standards may be examined, rather than an equitable measure. Plainly, however, the interpretation dispute here – like most important interpretation disputes – involves fundamental policy choices with respect both to measure of damages and the degree of discretion to be assigned to the Court. As we will see, the Inter-American Court of Human Rights, too, has not always been precise in its language in this regard.

2. Case Law

a) Velásquez-Rodriguez and Godinez-Cruz

The first cases in which the Court reached a compensation stage arose out of disappearances in Honduras. The matter had been brought to the Commission, which in due course issued a Report. Because Honduras had accepted the jurisdiction of the Court, the Commission then elected to refer the matter to the Court. In the companion cases of *Velásquez-Rodriguez* and *Godinez Cruz*, the Court faced, for the first time, the issue of compensation.

The merits of *Velásquez-Rodriguez* were decided by the Court on July 29, 1988. Honduras was found responsible for the disappearance of Manfredo Velásquez by agents who had operated under cover of public authority.[15] In so doing, Honduras had violated his rights under Articles 7, 1(1), 5 and 4 of the Convention. The Court proceeded to quote Article 63(1), then lamented that it could not, in the nature of the case, order that the victim be guaranteed his rights. It then said

> The Court, however, can rule that the consequences of the breach of the rights be remedied and that just compensation (*justa indemnización*) be paid.[16]

Thereafter, however, the Court only addressed compensation or indemnity and ignored the other potentially applicable form of remedy in Article 63(1). In its dispositive, the Court unanimously decided that Honduras was required to pay a 'justa indemnización compensatoria' to the victim's 'familiares', which the English translation rendered 'next-of-kin', a difference in translation which is potentially significant and part of a concern that recurred in later cases. The authentic Spanish version uses a term that is essentially cultural, whose content may vary depending upon the empirical details of particular cultures or sub-cultures. The English translation adopts a term that imports consanguineous relationships and would, for example, exclude homosexual partners, mistresses or concubines, even in societies or social strata where they might be common or accepted stations.

---

[15] Series C, No. 4 at 158.
[16] Id. at para. 189.

> By six votes to one, the Court decided that the form and amount of such compensation, failing agreement between Honduras and the Commission with six months of the date of this judgment, shall be settled by the Court and for that purpose retains jurisdiction of the case.[17]

Velásquez incorporated two constitutional decisions. First, the Court, consistent with the rules that it had already promulgated, confirmed that, in the first instance, compensation was to be agreed upon by the parties themselves, subject to approval by the Court:

> The Court believes that the parties can agree on the damages (indemnización). If an agreement cannot be reached, the Court shall award an amount. The case shall, therefore, remain open for that purpose. The Court reserves the right to approve the agreement and in the event no agreement is reached, to set the amount and order the manner of payment.[18]

Only if the parties failed to reach agreement within the time limits set by the Court would the matter of compensation be decided in judicial procedures. The Court did not always follow this practice in later cases.

One would think that, as a practical matter, this review function would be rather formal and empty. In case of a negotiated settlement, there would be no controversy between the parties as to whether the settlement was lawful and, in the absence of an adversarial process, the Court would ordinarily have no information on which to test whether the agreement between the parties was *justa*. In fact, in *Velásquez*, the Court did, as we will see, subsequently disallow several items, explicitly and implicitly, that had been the subject of agreement between Honduras and the Commission and in every subsequent case in which the parties were given the first opportunity to arrange compensation, the Court explicitly reserved its right to review the settlement.

The second constitutional decision addressed the question of who was entitled to participate in the settlement process. A majority of the Court held that only the Commission, the defendant State and the Court could participate in the settlement proceeding.[19] Judge Rodolfo Piza dissented on this point, contending that the Convention's exclusion of the injured party from submitting a case to the Court should be interpreted restrictively and should not bar the injured party from participating fully in the compensation phase, after responsibility had been established.[20] The difference between majority and dissent seems vast. In practice, however, it was probably non-existent. It would be difficult to imagine the Commission excluding either the injured party or its counsel; indeed, many of the issues that any liquidation of damages controversy raises can only be addressed with the participation of the

---

[17] Id. at para. 194, sub-para. 6.
[18] Id. at para. 191.
[19] Id. at para. 192.

putative beneficiaries. In any case, the practice of the Commission has been actively to incorporate victims and their counsel. In effect, Judge Piza wished to make the *locus standi* of the individual explicit; the majority preferred to leave it operational but officially unacknowledged.

This second constitutional ruling of the Court failed to make provision for the contingency that the first constitutional ruling had identified, viz., the failure of the parties to agree on damages. In that case, the Court would reactivate the jurisdiction it had reserved and would have found it difficult not to consult the victim and/or putative beneficiaries. As we will see, this is what, in fact, occurred in the earlier cases. In later cases, a routinization of procedures may have reduced the importance of this issue.

Confidentiality is a relative term in OAS practice. It was no secret that the negotiations for damages were encountering difficulties. Shortly before the lapse of the six months period, the Court contingently authorized the President to consult experts, the Commission, the Government of Honduras *and* the victim's family, for their respective views, and if necessary to set a date for hearings. Four days later, the parties submitted to the Court a document (acta), which recorded two points of agreement and one of partial agreement. Honduras and the Commission and those 'familiares' with whom the Commission was acting agreed that Honduras would implement fully the Court's judgment; that only the wife and children of the victim would be beneficiaries; and that the children would be entitled to benefit as soon as they had fulfilled the prerequisites of Honduran law. With respect to measure of damages, however, Honduras proposed 'the most favorable benefits that Honduran legislation provides ... in cases of accidental death', while the Commission also wanted Honduras

> to create for the benefit of the heirs a fund whose amount and form of payment should be determined by the Inter-American Court of Human Rights, taking into account the requirements of international law and those of Honduran legislation.[21]

As the Court had also indicated in its authorization to the President that the views of the victim's family should be sought, the victim's widow submitted a document in which she requested the Court to order Honduras to comply with twelve points. Only three related to the broad meaning of compensation in the second sense of Article 63(1): an education fund for the children of all the disappeared, guaranteed employment for them and a pension fund for their parents. As for the other requests, the first four related to ending the epidemic of forced disappearances, investigation, trial and punishment of the perpetrators and a complete public reporting. Two others related to demobilization of

---

[20] Id. at paras. 6 and 7.

[21] Series C, No. 7, *Velásquez Rodriguez Case*, Compensatory Damages, Judgment of 21 July 1989, para. 5.

the armed bands engaged in effecting the disappearances and the end of pressure on the families of the disappeared. Another request was for a public act, such as naming a park or street for the disappeared.

Shortly afterwards, the Commission submitted its views, which addressed only one of the remedial options offered by Article 63(1) of the Convention. The Commission asked for rigorous investigation, punishment and condemnation of the disappearance of Velásquez. With respect to compensation, the Commission followed the terms of the partial agreement that it had concluded with Honduras. It asked for payment to the widow of the victim of the highest pension recognized by Honduran law[22] and payment to the children of a subsidy until they completed their education. It also asked for title to a house appropriate for a middle-class professional and a cash payment to the wife and children of the victim for 'damages, loss of earnings and emotional harm'.[23]

There were, thus, a few points of agreement between the Commission and Honduras. In its judgment, however, the Court concluded that a comprehensive package of agreements was required. Noting that 'the parties agreed only on the recognition of the beneficiaries of the compensation' and that '[t]he remaining points [of the meeting between the Commission and Honduras] are simple declarations which establish no criteria for fixing the amount of the compensation and, even less, for payment', the Court held that no agreement had been reached.[24] In effect, it had already indicated that it would ignore certain items of agreement when it submitted a list of factual questions to Honduras.

Ten days after the Commission had submitted its views, the attorneys for the victim's family presented the family's views. The document, in effect, a pleading, was prepared by a Washington-based non-governmental organization, Human Rights Watch, and developed an elaborate legal theory with respect to compensation, based on the objects and purposes of the American Convention. Some parts of the theory were not entirely thought through. The essential thrust of the legal argument was that:

> the correct interpretation of the term 'justa indemnización' to which Article 63 refers is that the compensation ... must repair *all* the damage caused, ethical as well as monetary, which includes both *damnum emergens* and *lucrum cessans*. Beyond that, treating, as it does, a crime against humanity (*crimen de lesa humanidad*), the compensation must in-

---

[22] This point of apparent agreement between the Government and the Commission turned out to be the subject of much disagreement when different interpretations of its meaning came into conflict. The Government interpreted it to mean the highest pension available to a teacher, and only for a limited time. The Commission intended the pension to last indefinitely and to be the pension which was awarded to the highest military officials, whose pensions were the 'highest' awarded in Honduras.

[23] Id. at para. 8.

[24] Id. at para. 22.

clude the imposition of punitive damages, because the object is to impede the repetition of such acts and in this manner to protect the international community from the violation of fundamental rights.[25]

The family wished ethical damages ('reparación ética') which were to include public condemnations and affirmations, and exhaustive investigation and prosecution.[26]

With respect to a cash indemnity, the family asked for payment for *damnum emergens* to 'compensate the family for all the expenses and losses suffered as a direct or indirect consequence of the sequestration and eventual assassination'.[27] These included all expenses connected with judicial, non-judicial and media efforts to secure Velásquez' release and medical and psychological expenses for illness incurred or aggravated by the disappearance, including future expenses. The family asked for the *lucrum cessans* to include all the income that Velásquez would have earned for his life expectancy – figuring in increases in salary paralleling his anticipated career change and subsequent promotions until retirement at 65 – and the pension he would have received for the remainder of his natural life expectancy, an estimated ten years. The total was 2,422,420 lempiras. The calculation did not adjust, as is usually done, for the share that Velásquez would have spent on himself nor did it deduct for tax, nor did it discount for current payment. The Court's judgment did not review the methodology of the family, but simply recorded – in terms of the bottom line – the amount that it claimed.

With respect to *damnum emergens*, the family contended that it was a sum, to be determined in the discretion of the Court, to address the emotional injury suffered and to be suffered in the future by the family. The family simply doubled the *lucrum cessans* and asked for a sum of 4,845,000 lempiras. Curiously, the family did not ask for compensation for the suffering that the victim had suffered, a demand common in United States torts practice, which was later adopted by the Court.

The family did, however, ask for punitive damages to deter such future acts, but it mixed two theories in support of its claim. One was that punitive damages were appropriate when the precipitating act was 'particularly vile and abject'.[28] The second was that the precipitating act, as a crime against humanity, did not only affect the victim, but also 'the conscience of the hemisphere'.[29] Velásquez was its sole immediate victim, but the act was a *jus cogens* violation. Hence, this demand for reparations was *erga omnes*: some

---

[25] Letter at 4.

[26] Id. at para. 9.

[27] Letter of Human Rights Watch to the President of the Court, 10 March 1989 (in Spanish; translations by the author), 6.

[28] Id. at 8.

[29] RES/666 of the OAS General Assembly.

reparation was due to 'everybody'. According to the family's theory, this payment had to be made in addition to any damages awarded to Velásquez' family for their *specific* harm. In the absence of some credible international recipient, the family designated itself as the appropriate recipient for this payment, indicating that it would be 'conscious of its responsibility of becoming the trustee of a credit that would be set aside, in part, to benefit the community in general'.[30] The liquidated punitive damages sought were 2,422,000 lempiras.

For its part, the Commission submitted a clinical report prepared by a team of psychiatrists that confirmed a post-traumatic stress disorder, a classification of the World Health Organization for illnesses, accidents and causes of death.[31]

The Government of Honduras proposed the application of the Honduran law of the National Social Security Institute for Teachers which it considered the most favorable or generous Honduran law available. It would have yielded 37,080 lempiras and 4120 lempiras as a severance benefit. In addition, the Government offered to raise this amount to 150,000 lempiras.

The Court asked the government to supply the birth dates of the victims; their civil status under Honduran law; the positions they held and their salaries; their social security status; their academic or professional qualifications; the names of wives and concubines registered in government documents and their community property; names and ages of children in out of wedlock and whether they had any handicaps; names and civil status of parents and other possible claimants and their independent income, if any; life insurance, if any, and the names of beneficiaries; actuarial tables used in Honduras at the time of the disappearance; and relevant Honduran legislation.[32]

The Government submitted most of the documents requested, but maintained its position that the Court had been 'very clear and precise regarding the obligation of Honduras to pay damages, which is to pay *just compensation to the family of the victim, and nothing more*' (underlined in original). Measure of damages, in the Government's view, was to be determined by the system to which the victim was affiliated. As for the clauses for *damnum emergens*, the Government objected that they were designed 'not merely to compensate the Velásquez Rodriguez family, but ... to pay the expenses of the intense media campaign waged against Honduras', as well as to pay legal and other fees.

The strut of the Court's judgment was that compensation, which was required by international law, was to be determined by the American Conven-

---

[30] Human Rights Watch brief, at 9.
[31] Id. at 11.
[32] Id. at para. 13.

tion and applicable principles of international law,[33] and was not limited by, but was independent of the national law of the victim. Elaborating *Chorzow*,[34] the Court held:

> Reparation of harm brought about by the violation of an international obligation consists in full restitution (*restitutio in integrum*), which includes the restoration of the prior situation, the reparation of the consequences of the violation, and indemnification for patrimonial and non-patrimonial damages, including emotional harm.

Chorzow has become a mantra which is evocative but imprecise. With respect to emotional damages, the Court said:

> As to emotional harm, the Court holds that indemnity may be awarded under international law and, in particular, in the case of human rights violations, indemnification must be based upon the principles of equity.[35]

Thus, the Court did not exclude compensation for emotional harm ('daño moral'), which would be based on equity, but the Court excluded punitive damages:

> [t]he expression 'fair compensation', used in Article 63(1) of the Convention to refer to a part of the reparation and to the 'injured party', is compensatory and not punitive.[36]

The Court did not appear at all anxious to take up the social reconstructive competence that Article 63(1) accorded it. The Commission and the victims' families had, as will be recalled, asked the Court to order a number of specific actions and structural changes. Rather the Court held that it had essentially already ordered these measures,[37] though it made no effort to determine if the defendant government had complied. It was perfectly clear that compliance would have required major governmental changes that would not be forthcoming, whatever the Court's writ, so the Court contented itself with saying that

> the judgment on the merits of July 29, 1988, is in itself a type of reparation and moral satisfaction of significance and importance for the families of the victims.[38]

> In sum, then, for the Court the fair compensation, described as 'compensatory' in the judgment on the merits ... includes reparation to the family of the victim of the material and moral damages they suffered because of the involuntary disappearance of Manfredo Velásquez.[39]

The claims for costs incurred in searching for the victim and bringing the case were not rejected on principle, for 'it is theoretically correct that those

---

[33] Id. at para. 31.
[34] PCIJ Series A, No. 9, at 21; PCIJ Series A, No. 17, at 29.
[35] Id. at paras. 26 and 27.
[36] Id. at para. 38.
[37] Id. at paras. 34 and 35.
[38] Id. at para. 36.
[39] Id. at para. 39.

expenses come within the definition of damages', but they were rejected because 'they were not pleaded or proven opportunely'. As 'no estimate or proof of expenses' had been adduced at trial, they could not be awarded. The Court went on to point out that it had already denied litigation costs in its original opinion.[40]

The Commission and the Government were rather close in their legal standard for compensation. The Court, however, took an approach closer to that of the lawyers' for the victims' families. This was not a case of accidental death, the Court reasoned, for which insurance guidelines might have been appropriate. Rather, compensation 'must be calculated as a loss of earning based upon the income the victim would have received up to the time of his possible natural death'.[41] If the victim had survived, he would be entitled to it, or at least to the difference between what he could earn after the calamity and what he would have earned but for it. But, rather inconsistently, the Court added that if the victim did not survive, an adjustment downward might have to be made to take account of the possibility of surviving family members working or otherwise having an income of their own. While this formula could call for and be implemented by precise figures, the Court signaled that it was eschewing a rigorous approach: '[i]t is not correct, then, to adhere to rigid criteria ... but rather to arrive at a prudent estimate of the damages, given the circumstances of each case'.[42] Immediately after this, the Court set compensation at 500,000 lempiras, on the assumption that the sum was only for the benefit of the family identified at trial.[43]

The Court vouchsafes no other basis for its calculation, but we can tease out some of the Court's calculations. The Court's judgment indicated that it took, 'as a point of departure', the monthly salary that Velásquez was receiving at the time of his disappearance, which was 1,030 lempiras. The family had assumed that Velásquez would have worked for 30 more years. The Court assumed 25 years, in accord with Honduran law. Both the Court and the family assumed a pension, but the Court indicated no figures on which it was basing its projection of this part of the compensation. The family, as will be recalled, had projected that the victim would have earned more than 1.6 million lempiras, to which they added a retirement income, bringing it up to

---

[40] Id. at para. 42.

[41] Id. at para. 46.

[42] Id. at para. 48.

[43] Id. at para. 49. It is interesting to note that the Court seemed concerned that there might be other offspring of *Velásquez*, in which case the sum allotted would have been insufficient. However, the Court makes no provision for award of additional compensation should other offspring surface; rather it merely rules that in such a case the portion of the money set aside for the three known children would be divided to give any newly 'discovered' offspring an equal share of the award.

more than 2.4 million lempiras. The Court's figures for Velásquez' working life were 1030 lempiras, for 13 months each year, for 25 years or 334,750. But the family had not allowed for a deduction for that share of the victim's income which would have been consumed by him, nor did they allow for subsequent employment by members of the family. If various values are assigned to each of these factors, of which the Court but not the family had taken account, one may find a movement toward, if not a complete convergence between the methods and even numbers of the Court and the victims' families.

In the view of the Court, moral damages were 'primarily the result of the psychological impact suffered by the family ... because of the violations of the rights' of the Convention. While the attorneys for the family had related these damages to the need for continuing treatment, the Court simply confirmed the injuries and liquidated a sum of 250,000 lempiras to be paid to the family.

Payment was to be made in 90 days of notification of judgment; the sum might be taxable, but no tax could be withheld at source. If the Government elected to pay in six equal monthly instalments, interest would accrue at the rates then current in Honduras. One fourth of the sum was to be paid to the widow of the victim, the remaining three fourths, for the children, was to be put in a trust fund (un fideicomiso) in the Central Bank of Honduras 'under the most favorable conditions permitted by Honduran banking practice'.[44] Monthly payments were to be made until the children reached the age of 25 at which time there was to be a distribution. The Court concluded its judgment by indicating that it would supervise the implementation of the indemnification and would only close the file when compensation was paid.

Honduras did not comply with the ninety day limit for payment. In the meanwhile, the Commission returned to Court some two months later requesting an interpretation and, in effect, an addition to the judgment on compensation, with respect to the trust fund to be established for the children:

> The judgment does not contemplate any protective mechanism to preserve the current purchasing power of the award in the face of inflation or possible devaluations of the lempira. As the Court is aware ... that loss of purchasing power by units of currency has historically been high throughout Latin America, in some countries reaching catastrophic proportions.[45]

The Commission contended that in even the relatively mild inflationary conditions of Honduras, a projection over the life of the trust fund could see its value reduced by 75%.[46] Indeed, in the oral argument it was established to the Court's satisfaction that the lempira had already begun to fluctuate against

---

[44] Id. at para. 58.
[45] Id. at para. 18.
[46] Id. at para. 18.

strong currencies, though the official rate of exchange had remained constant.[47] Hence, in the Commission's view, the need for a protective mechanism: 'a suitable adjustment mechanism would be to estimate the real value of the capital placed in trust in United States dollars of October 20, 1989, and maintain it at that same value throughout the life of the trust'.[48]

The Government opposed the admissibility of the request. In the meanwhile, the Government devalued the lempira by some 30%. In a subsequent brief, the Commission sought to amend its petition by amplifying it and asking the Court to order 'a retroactive adjustment of the purchasing power of the compensation ... to make up for the lempira's devaluation ...'[49]

Honduras opposed this amplification. For Honduras, the judgment was final and it alleged that it was already in the process of complying with it.[50]

The Court held that

> [t]he fact that the damages fixed comprise loss of earnings, calculated on the basis of probable life-span, indicates that the *restitutio in integrum* concept is linked to the possibility of maintaining the real value of the damages stable over a relatively long period of time. One way of meeting this goal is so-called 'indexing', which makes it possible to make periodic adjustments to the sums payable in order to keep the real value constant.[51]

The Court referred to its language in the Compensation phase 'under the most favorable conditions', as meaning

> that any act or measure by the trustee must ensure that the amount assigned maintains its purchasing power and generates sufficient earnings or dividends to increase it; the phrase *permitted by Honduran banking practice* indicates that the trustee must faithfully perform his task as would a good head of family [un buen padre de familia] and that he has the power and the obligation to select diverse types of investment, whether through deposits in strong currencies, such as the United States dollar ... precisely as ordered by the Court.[52]

As for the Commission's request that the Government be obliged to supplement the trust fund periodically to maintain its value, the Court rejected it as imposing something not in the judgment and going beyond interpretation. But in an indirect way, the Court awarded a part of what the Commission sought here.

The Commission had also requested the Court to impose interest for late payment and adjust the amount due under the judgment to take account of the loss of its value in the interim. The Court ordered the payment of interest on the entire amount of the capital due at the regular banking rate in effect in

---

[47] Id. at para. 25.
[48] Id. at para. 20.
[49] Id. at para. 23.
[50] Id. at para. 24.
[51] Id. at para. 29.
[52] Id. at para. 31.

Honduras on the date of payment. By not paying on time, Honduras had impaired the right of the beneficiaries of the compensation or their trustee to take steps to preserve the real value of the sum ordered,[53] e.g., by conversion into a hard currency.[54] The Court ordered that

> [t]his real loss must be compensated by the Government, in addition to the current bank interest payable, by adding to the latter the value of the loss between the date on which the Government should have paid the damages by setting up the trust but neglected to do so, and the date on which it actually complies with its obligations.[55]

Honduras did not pay the judgment creditors until 1995. In the interim, the Commission reported the non-compliance with the judgment to the General Assembly in each of its subsequent Annual Reports. Despite the continuing jurisdiction of the Court, there is no indication that the Court undertook additional measures to secure compliance

The contrast between the compensation approach of the European Court of Human Rights and the American Court is thus quite striking. On the issue of monetary damages, the Inter-American Court of Human Rights in *Velásquez* and *Godinez* concluded with an amount that, though scantily reasoned, was not inconsistent with European practice. On the issue of social reconstructive remedies, however, the Inter-American Court has been much more timid. The European Court has indicated remedies requiring structural changes, as has the European Commission when it settles cases. Comparing what U.S. federal courts would do with the social reconstructive competence of Article 63, the timidity of the American Court is quite striking and may be attributed to its assessment of the larger political context and, inter alia, to the realization that such judgments would have virtually no chance of implementation.

The *Godinez* case was substantially identical to the *Velásquez* case in virtually every respect. There are, however, a few small differences worth noting. *Godinez* was decided almost exactly six months after *Velásquez*, and the Court had witnessed the inability of the Commission and the Government of Honduras to come to an agreement. Where the Court in *Velásquez* originally gave the various parties six months to reach a negotiated settlement between themselves, it gave the parties in *Godinez* no such option, deciding instead that 'compensation [would] be fixed by the Court'.[56] The decision to forgo the possibility of a negotiated settlement in *Godinez* may have been due to a realization that, with essentially the same parties involved in both cases, it was unlikely that a second round of negotiations would prove any more fruitful than the *Velásquez* discussions.

---

[53] Id. at para. 41.
[54] Id. at para. 42.
[55] Id. at para. 42.
[56] *Godinez* judgment, para. 203.

The Court, in dividing the damages among the beneficiaries in *Godinez*, maintained the same split between spouse and offspring that it had in *Velásquez*. Señor Godinez left behind only a single daughter, who was awarded 3/4 of the damages. Her mother received the other 1/4. In *Velásquez*, in contrast, each beneficiary (the wife and three (known) children) received an equal share. *Godinez* suggests that such an equitable distribution was mere fortuity, due to the number of beneficiaries. The Court may have thought it was making an easy rule for division of damages awards. Whatever its intent may have been, the Court itself departed from this approach almost immediately.

b) The Aloeboetoe Case

The *Aloeboetoe* case was brought to the Inter-American Commission in 1988 on behalf of a group of Bushnegroes or Maroons, as they are also known in Suriname, who were beaten and murdered by a jungle commando of the Surinamese Army. In May, 1990, the Commission issued a report under Article 50 of the Convention that largely confirmed the facts alleged by the Petitioners and declared that the Government of Suriname had

> failed to fulfill its obligations to respect the rights and freedoms contained in the American Convention on Human Rights and to assure their enjoyment as provided for in Articles 1 and 2 ....[57]

The Commission also specified that the Government of Suriname had violated the human rights of the subjects as provided for by Articles 1, 2, 4(1), 5(1), 5(2), 7(1), 7(2), 7(3), 25(1) and 25(2) of the American Convention. The Commission called upon the Government to investigate the violations, take measures to avoid their reoccurrence and pay a just compensation to the victims' next of kin. At the same time, the Commission decided to submit the case to the Inter-American Court of Human Rights should Suriname fail to implement its recommendations.

The Government did not comply with the Commission's recommendations and in August, 1990, the Commission brought the case to the Court. In addition to a confirmation of the Commission's factual and legal findings, the Commission prayed

> that the Court find that Suriname must pay adequate reparation to the victims' next of kin (*los familiares*) and, consequently, order the following: payment of indemnization for indirect damages and loss of earnings (*daño emergente y lucro cesante*); reparation for moral damages, including the payment of compensation and adoption of measures to restore the good name of the victims; ... .[58]

---

[57] *Aloeboetoe et al. Case*, Reparations, Judgment of 10 Sep. 1993.
[58] *Aloeboetoe* case at para. 9.

Initially, the Government of Suriname rejected all of the Commission's submissions, but at a public hearing on December 2, 1991, Suriname accepted responsibility. As a result, the case before the Court centered on the issue of compensation. The case presented a number of first impression problems, as the victims all came from a tribe in which the family structure was not nuclear but extensive and affiliations of responsibility, claim and duty were demanded and owed to tribe members beyond the boundaries of a Western nuclear affection unit.

The Court had already adopted the *Chorzow* standard in *Velásquez* and *Godinez*. The Commission argued before the Court that this required a compensation sufficient to remedy *all* the consequences of the violations that took place.[59] The Court, in a general statement that largely determined the outcome of the case, significantly reduced the scope of the reparation obligation of the State that had caused the violation:

> Every human act produces diverse consequences, some proximate and others remote. An old adage puts it as follows: *causa causae est causa causati*. Imagine the effect of a stone cast into a lake; it will cause concentric circles to ripple over the water, moving further and further away and becoming ever more imperceptible. Thus it is that all human actions cause remote and distant effects.

> To compel the perpetrator of an illicit act to erase all the consequences produced by his action is completely impossible, since that action caused effects that multiplied to a degree that cannot be measured.

> . . .

> The solution provided by law in this regard consists of demanding that the responsible party make reparation for the immediate effects of such unlawful acts, but only to the degree that has been *legally* recognized.[60]

The Commission had argued that the social structure of the Saramakas, the tribe in which the victims were members, had characteristics that should influence both the quantum of compensation and its pattern of distribution. But the Commission was inconsistent in its argument. It assembled anthropological data that established a familial configuration in which polygamy frequently occurs and in which the authority system was essentially matrilineal, in that the principal group of relatives, the Bêê, which was composed of all the descendants of one single woman, assumed responsibility for the actions of any of its members. Each member, in turn, was responsible to the group as a whole.[61] The Commission contended that 'this means that the compensation payable to one person would be given to the Bêê, whose

---

[59] Id. at para. 47.
[60] Id. at paras. 47 and 48 (italics in the original).
[61] Id. at para. 59.

representatives would distribute it among its members'.[62] In fact, the Commission, despite its efforts to make this point, did not suggest implementing that approach. Rather, it took what the Court characterized as a 'pragmatic approach' towards identifying the beneficiaries. As for determining the amount of the compensation requested, the Commission took the following factors into account: the age of the victim, his actual and potential income, the number of his dependents and the customs and practices of the Bushnegroes.[63]

The Government contended that the applicable law was Surinamese law, which required that birth certificates or wedding certificates be presented to prove the kinds of legal relationships for which compensation would be awarded. This would have presented a great hardship for the Saramakas, as few of their intra-tribal relationships were officially recorded, due in part to the dearth of official facilities in the interior of Suriname. The Court rejected the government claim, pointing out that 'the situation in which the Saramakas find themselves is due in great measure to the fact that the State does not provide sufficient registry offices in the region; ... Suriname cannot, therefore, demand proof of the relationship and identity of persons through means that are not available to all inhabitants in that region'.

The Court, in determining applicable law, refused to reach the question of whether the Saramaka enjoyed their own international jurisdiction-generating status, a venerable treaty notwithstanding. Rather, it said, 'the only question of importance here is whether the laws of Suriname in the area of family law apply to the Saramaka tribe'. The Court's answer to that question was 'that Surinamese family law is not effective insofar as the Saramakas are concerned. The members of the tribe are unaware of it and adhere to their own rules'. Interestingly, the Court refused to apply this same logic to whether to apply 'rules, generally accepted by the community of nations', of which the Saramakas were most likely unaware as well, and which also do not coincide with Saramaka rules of succession and dependents.

The Court was unwilling to explore the anthropological reality of the Saramakas or adopt the pragmatic construct the Commission proposed. It noted that ILO Convention No. 169 concerning indigenous and tribal peoples in independent countries had not been accepted by Suriname and concluded that it had no alternative but to apply the relevant part of general principles of law,[64] which it identified as a norm that 'a person's successors are his or her children'.[65] But the content of legal terms such as 'children' or 'spouse' or 'ascendants' had to be interpreted according to local law, which required the

---

[62] Id. at para. 59.
[63] Id. at para. 60.
[64] Id. at para. 61.
[65] Id. at para. 62.

Court to 'take Saramaka custom into account',[66] rather than apply Surinamese law. As a practical matter, implementing this approach presented formidable obstacles, as the Saramakas live in the jungle, speak only their own language, marriages and births are, in most cases, not registered and polygamy is practiced.[67] Nonetheless, the Court established a list of the successors of the victims which included polygamous wives as well as their children.[68]

There were limits, however, to just how much weight the Saramaka customs were to be given. As will be recalled, the Commission had pointed to what it asserted was the unique nature of Saramaka society when it asked the Court to award moral damages under a theory of community suffering. The Court rejected the proposition:

> [people] generally belong to intermediate communities. In practice, the obligation to pay moral compensation does not extend to such communities, nor to the State in which the victim participated ... If in some exceptional case such compensation has ever been granted, it would have been to a community that suffered direct damages.

With respect to the other members of the Saramaka social organization whom the Commission had urged be considered as beneficiaries, the Court prescribed for itself, '[c]ertain conditions that must be met for a claim of compensatory damages filed by a third party to be admitted'. There were three such conditions:

- a pattern of payments that was regular and periodic, whether in cash, in kind or in services, by the victim to the claimant had to be established;
- while a legal obligation was not specified as a prerequisite, the nature of the relationship between the victim and the claimant had to sustain the assumption that the payment would have continued if the victim had not been killed; and
- the claimant had to have a financial need that was periodically met by the contributions that had been or would have been made by the victim.

The burden of proof for demonstrating that these third-party claimants were entitled to compensation rested on the Commission, while the corresponding burden of proof for successors or dependents rested on the defendant government. In the instant case, the Court concluded that the Commission failed to meet the three-part test it established.

Aloeboetoe introduced some innovations with respect to moral damages. In *Velásquez* and *Godínez*, it will be recalled, moral damages were 'primarily the result of the psychological impact suffered by the family ... because of the violations of the rights' of the Convention. In *Aloeboetoe*, moral damages related more to the subjective anguish of the victims. Thus the Court said:

---

[66] Id. at para. 62.
[67] Id. at para. 63.
[68] Id. at para. 66.

In the instant case, the victims who died at Tjongalangapassi suffered moral damages when they were abused by an armed band which deprived them of their liberty and later killed them. The beatings received, the pain of knowing they were condemned to die for no reason whatsoever, the torture of having to dig their own graves are all part of the moral damages suffered by the victims. In addition, the person who did not die outright had to bear the pain of his wounds being infested by maggots and of seeing the bodies of his companions being devoured by vultures.

In the Court's opinion, it is clear that the victims suffered moral damages, for it is characteristic of human nature that anybody subjected to the aggression and abuse described above will experience moral suffering. The Court considers that no evidence is required to arrive at this conclusion; the acknowledgment of responsibility by Suriname suffices.[69]

This 'pain and suffering' conception of moral damages extended to the parents of the victims for, as the Court put it,

It can be presumed that the parents have suffered morally as a result of the cruel death of their offspring, for it is essentially human for all persons to feel pain at the torment of their child.

For these reasons, the Court deems it only appropriate that those victims' parents who have not been declared successors also participate in the distribution of the compensation for moral damages.[70]

In this dimension of moral damages, it is the subjective pain of the dependents, caused by the human rights violation, that generates a claim for compensation. With respect to parents, the entitlement to such damages is based on a presumption *juris et de jure*. With respect to others, the burden of proof is on the claimant. It was not established in the case under discussion.

The Court also reserved its earlier understanding of the concept of moral damages. The Commission had asked the Court to order Suriname to pay compensation because it alleged that the killings were racially motivated;[71] in this sense, the Commission was contending that it was the attitude of the defendant government which had motivated the actual violation of the human rights that might give rise to additional damages. The Court did not question the legal formula here, but held that, as a factual matter, the Commission had not established that the violations were racially motivated. The violations had taken place in the course of an insurrection and it seemed plausible to the Court (if not to a student of the record) that the soldiers had acted on the suspicion that the Saramakas were members of the insurrectionist Jungle Commando.

Thus the Court developed several dimensions to the concept of moral damages: such damages could be awarded to compensate the pain and

---

[69] Id. at paras. 51 and 52.
[70] Id. at paras. 76 and 77.
[71] Id. at paras. 81 and 82.

suffering of the victims, which would be assumed irrebuttably in certain types of violations. It could also be established with respect to dependents, but with the exception of parents, the burden of proof that such suffering had actually occurred would rest on the claimants or the Commission. Moral damages could also be awarded for punitive purposes, if the *intention* of the violation was also unlawful under the Convention.

With respect to the method used to liquidate reparations for actual damages for the victims' successors, the Court followed the usual system of determining the income that the victims would have earned throughout their working lives had they not been killed. Interest was added to the sum obtained for the period from the violation until judgment and that amount was then increased by the current net value of the expected income during the rest of the working life of each of the victims. Given the unique characteristics of the indigenous economy of which the victims were members, the Court dispatched its Deputy Secretary to conduct an *in situ* verification of the figures that served as the basis for its calculations.[72] Following *Velásquez* and *Godinez*, the Court reiterated a rather flexible methodology:

> It is not correct, then, in these cases, to adhere to rigid criteria ... but rather to arrive at a prudent estimate of the damages, given the circumstances of each case.[73]

While a systematic methodology was deployed for actual damages, with respect to the liquidation of moral damages, the Court reiterated that 'indemnification must be based upon the principles of equity'.[74] The Court was quick to point out, however, that '[t]he phrases "prudent estimate of the damages" and "principles of equity" do not mean that the Court has discretion in setting the amounts of compensation'. It then referred to the methodology which it had employed in determining damages.

With respect to moral damages, the Court said:

> Bearing in mind the economic and social position of the beneficiaries, such reparations should take the form of a lump-sum payment in the same amount for all the victims, with the exception of Richenel Voola, who was assigned reparation that exceeded that of the others by one-third. As has already been stated, Richenel Voola was subjected to greater suffering as a result of his agony. There is nothing to indicate that there were any differences in the injuries and ill-treatment suffered by the other victims.[75]

The Court accepted the total amount claimed by the Commission for moral damages,[76] which were set at about US $29,000 for each of the victims and an extra 1/3, or about US $10,000, for Richenel Voola.

---

[72] Id. at para. 87.
[73] *Velásquez*, id. at para. 48; *Godinez*, id. at para. 46.
[74] Id. at paras. 25 and 27.
[75] Id. at para. 91.
[76] Id. at para. 92.

As in *Velásquez* and *Godinez*, the Court determined how the compensation awards were to be divided. The Court took judicial notice of the existence of the Saramaka customary practice of multiple wives, and allowed for them in its division of compensation. One third of the material damages were awarded to the wife or wives of each man and two thirds to the children. This was quite a change from *Velásquez*, where the Court and especially the Commission seemed unwilling to discuss the (possible) second companion of the victim in determining the recipients of compensation.

The moral damages were to be split as well, with awards of one quarter to the parents, one quarter to the wives, and one half to the children. All parties fitting into one of these categories for a single victim would share equally in that category's share in the compensation award. The division of the compensation differed slightly from that in *Velásquez* and *Godinez*.

The compensation the Court fixed included an amount to enable the minor children to continue their education. This required the Court to hold Suriname under an obligation to reopen a school and staff it with teaching and administrative personnel and to reopen a medical dispensary as well. The families were also awarded the costs that they had incurred in seeking justice from the defendant government, but the Commission, in keeping with prior cases, was not awarded the costs it had incurred in pursuing the case. The Court, as it had done in the previous cases, ordered the establishment of a trust fund in Suriname and prescribed a timetable for withdrawals. The Court also ordered the establishment of a Foundation 'to act as trustee of the funds'.[77] That measure appears to have been taken because of the character of the Saramaka tribe, its lack of development and familiarity with the complexities of a modern cash economy.

As it had done in previous cases, the Court denied (and in fact here failed entirely to address) the Commission's requests for non-pecuniary damages, which included, among other things, a public apology, memorials named for the victims, and exhumation and return of the bodies.

c) The Gangaram Panday Case

Asok Gangaram Panday, a Surinamese, was detained by the Military Police of Suriname at the airport in Paramaribo on November 5, 1988 upon his arrival from The Netherlands. Family members made repeated inquires about him without any result. They were informed on November 8 that Gangaram Panday had hanged himself in jail. When the body was examined by the family in the morgue and videotaped, many bruises were found and Gangaram's testicles had been crushed. A petition was filed with the Commission on December 17 of the same year. On May 15, 1990, the Commission drew

---

[77] Id. at para. 105.

up its Report in which it concluded that the Government of Suriname had violated Gangaram Panday's rights and recommended an investigation, preventive measures against similar acts in the future and just compensation. If Suriname did not comply within 90 days, the Commission indicated it would refer the matter to the Court. The case came before the Court on August 27, 1990 and the Court issued its judgment on January 21, 1994.

The Court's judgment is puzzling in many respects. The Court had ordered the government to provide information it deemed necessary. The government did not produce the material nor did it give any explanation.[78] Because of this, the Court 'inferred', as it put it, that the victim had been illegally detained by members of the Military Police of Suriname.[79] But despite the fact that the critical evidence was held by the government, the Court refused to make a comparable inference about the victim's injury which could only have occurred during his detention. The Court found no conclusive or convincing indications that the victim had been subjected to torture during his detention.[80] Nor did the Court find convincing proof that Suriname was responsible for the victim's death.[81] In *Velásquez* and *Godinez*, the Court had inferred violations of rights when it was clear that the government in question had allowed certain acts to take place without measures to prevent them or punish those responsible.[82] In *Gangaram Panday*, the Court retreated from this position to a very legalistic, indeed factitious distinction:

> The circumstances surrounding this case make it impossible to establish the responsibility of the State in the terms described above because, among other things, the Court is fixing responsibility for illegal detention by inference but not because it has been proved that the detention was indeed illegal or arbitrary or that the detainee was tortured.[83]

Thus the Court was faced only with a compensation issue with respect to the illegal detention of the victim, for which it held that fair compensation was in order. But '[s]ince Suriname's responsibility has been inferred, the Court decides to set a nominal amount as compensation'.[84] That amount was US $10,000.00

The judgment in *Gangaram Panday* with respect to reparation thus remains opaque. Many aspects of the case, in addition to the reparations component, are problematic and troubling.

---

[78] Id. at para. 50.
[79] Id. at para. 51.
[80] Id. at para. 56.
[81] Id. at para. 61.
[82] *Velásquez*, id. at para. 173; *Godinez*, id. at para. 183.
[83] Id. at para. 62.
[84] Id. at para. 70.

d) *The* Neira-Alegria *Case*

This case arose from a riot at the 'Frontón' prison in Lima, Peru. Control of the prison was delegated to the armed forces who quelled the disturbances. Neira-Alegria and the others had been prisoners at El Frontón and disappeared after the military restored order. They were the subject of a petition to the Commission on August 31, 1987. Despite repeated requests by the Commission, the Peruvian Government continued to refuse to provide information as to the whereabouts or fate of the prisoners. On June 7, 1990, the Commission issued a report, finding that Peru had violated the rights of the subjects of the petition and referred the matter to the Court.

The Court concluded that Neira-Alegria and the other two subjects of the petition had lost their lives due to the effects of the crushing of the uprising by the military forces of the government and as a consequence of the disproportionate use of force by them.[85] As a result, the Court concluded that Peru had violated the right to life as recognized in the American Convention of the subjects of the petition and had violated the right to *habeas corpus*. Peru was, accordingly, obliged to pay fair compensation to the next of kin of the victims and to reimburse the expenditures that they had incurred in the petitions before the national authorities. Reimbursement for expenses was set at US $2100 for each family even though no proof of any kind that the expenses had been incurred was presented. This was quite a change from the *Velásquez* and *Godinez* cases, where reimbursement was actually denied because costs had not been pleaded originally or ever proven.

The Court allowed Peru and the Commission six months to arrange, by mutual agreement, for the form and extent of the compensation; if they could not agree, the Court would make the determination.[86] The parties were not able to negotiate an arrangement for compensation and on September 19, 1996 the Court issued a judgment in the compensation phase.

The Court held:

> The Court considers that the compensation for each of the families of the victims must base itself in both the age of the victims at the moment of their death and the additional years until their life expectancy was fulfilled as well as the income they would have received calculated on their actual salary or in the absence of that information on the minimum monthly salary effective in the country.[87]

While the Court accepted the life expectancy in Peru proposed by the Commission as 77 years, it was not persuaded of the minimum monthly salary figures the Commission adduced. Neither was it convinced by the Govern-

---

[85] *Neira-Alegria et al.* case, Judgment of 19 Jan. 1995, Series C, No. 20, para. 72.

[86] Id. at para. 91.

[87] *Neira Alegria et al.* case: Reparations, Judgment of 19 Sept. 1996 at para. 49; The Court cites in that paragraph its own judgments in *Velásquez, Godinez* and *Aloeboetoe.*

ment's argument that the men had no income whatsoever, due to their incarcerated status and the fact that they were unlikely to be released and earn a living anytime soon. Instead, the Court said

> Taking into account reasons of equity and the actual economic and social situation in Latin America, [the Court] fixes the quantity of probable income per month at [US] $125.00 as the monthly basis to calculate the respective calculation.[88]

It is unclear how the Court made its determination of the probable monthly income or the weight it assigned to the various theories concerning the 'actual' occupations and potential incomes of the victims. The Court indicated that it would deduct 25% from this figure for personal expenses. Finally, an adjustment for present value was made.

With respect to moral damages, the Court refused to be bound by its prior caselaw, but decided that each case had to be analyzed in its own terms. In effect, however, the Court, citing its own holding in *Aloeboetoe*, liquidated moral damages at US $20,000.00 per victim. As to the distribution, the material damages were divided with one-third going to the wife of each of the victims and two-thirds to be divided equally among the children. Moral damages were to be divided with one-half to the children, one-quarter to the surviving spouse and one-quarter to the parents of the victim.

e) The Caballero-Delgado and Santana case

On February 7, 1989, Isidro Caballero-Delgado, a leader of the Santander Teacher's Union, was detained by a military patrol of the Colombian Army. Maria del Carmen Santana, who had worked with Caballero, was detained about the same time. In April of that year, the Commission began an inquiry into the case, which concluded, on September 25, 1992, with the approval of a final Report, including a decision to refer the case to the Court. The case was submitted to the Court on December 24, 1992 and judgment was rendered on December 8, 1995.

The Court found that the municipality in which the events under consideration occurred was a zone of intense army, paramilitary and guerilla activity. It also found that

> there exists sufficient evidence to infer the reasonable conclusion that the detention and the disappearance of Isidro Caballero-Delgado and Maria del Carmen Santana were carried out by persons who belonged to the Colombian Army and by several civilians who collaborated with them... . The fact that more than six years have passed and there has been no news of Isidro Caballero-Delgado and Maria del Carmen Santana permits the reasonable conclusion that they are dead.

. . .

---

[88] Id. at para. 50.

> Conversely, this Tribunal does not find sufficient evidence to demonstrate that Isidro Caballero-Delgado and Maria del Carmen Santana had been subjected to torture or inhumane treatment during their detention... .[89]

The Court also found that Colombia had not remedied the consequences of the violations carried out by its agents, but that given the short time that had transpired between the capture of the victims and their presumed death, there would not have been opportunity for the application of the judicial guarantees contained in Article 8 of the Convention; hence, Colombia had not violated it.

With respect to compensation, the Court did not, as in previous cases, provide the parties with an opportunity to negotiate a settlement. Rather it indicated that it would decide compensation in a subsequent phase.[90]

The compensation judgment was rendered on January 29, 1997. The Court followed the formula it had elaborated in the *Neira Alegría* case: The sum of the income which the victims could have received in the course of a probable lifetime, based on a projection of an average monthly salary less an amount that would have been incurred by the victim for personal expenses, which the Court set at 25% of the income. Then the amount that had been so derived was discounted for present value. Interest was added for the period from the violation until judgment. In the specific case, the Court also added supplementary salary under Colombian law, the so-called *auxilio de cesantía*, which increased the annual salary to 14 months. When the computation was concluded, this part of the award was for US $59,500.00. Because the identity of Maria del Carmen Santana had not been established to the Court's satisfaction and her age was indeterminate, the Court found that it could not order payment for material injuries. Under the circumstances, the Court might have created a statistical construct of a hypothetical Colombian woman in that district, but elected instead to order no payment. This was rather inconsistent with the Court's award of moral damages. Its disbursement was assigned to Colombian courts until such a time as the identity of the beneficiaries of the missing woman became known. The Court seemed especially concerned with the question of who would get the compensation award for Carmen Santana, but gave no reason for dispensing with a wage compensation award while retaining an award for moral damages.

With respect to moral damages, the Court simply fixed a sum of US $20,000.00 for Caballero-Delgado and US $10,000.00 for Carmen Santana. No explanation is given for the different amounts. The Court earlier assumed that they had received the same treatment. With respect to payment of the

---

[89] *Caballero-Delgado* and *Santana* case, Judgment of 8 Dec. 1995, Series C, No. 22 at para. 53.
[90] Id. at para. 72(7).

expenses incurred by the claimants in securing justice in Colombia, the Court took a rather narrow view of the means necessary to press a government to apply its law. For example, telephone calls outside of Colombia and the preparation of signs for political agitation were not deemed reimbursable. In theory, only those funds that were used in direct dealings with the Colombian authorities were to be reimbursed. In actuality, the Court somewhat arbitrarily awarded reimbursement in the amount of US $2000.

With respect to the distribution of the amounts, three equal portions were established, one for Caballero's son, one for his daughter, and one for his permanent companion. The moral damage award for Carmen Santana was to be distributed according to Colombian law. With respect to funds owing to minors, the now familiar technique of establishing a trust fund was also followed.[91] In keeping with its custom, the Court refused to order any non-pecuniary measures (with the exception of the directive to continue to try to locate the remains of the victims and return them to their families). As in previous cases, it declared that the finding of guilt was itself adequate punishment.

f) The Amparo case

The *Amparo* case concerned 16 men from the town of El Amparo who were on a fishing outing, traveling on board a boat in the direction of the Colorada Canal on the Arauca River when they were stopped by members of the Military and the Police of the José Antonio Páez Specific Command who were then conducting a military operation known as Anguila III. The Military and the Police killed 14 of the 16 fishermen. Two of the fishermen escaped and made their way to the police station in El Amparo, where the Commandant resisted pressure from the Páez Specific Command to surrender them. The original petition was lodged against Venezuela on August 10, 1990, and the Commission's final report was issued on October 12, 1993.[92] The case was initiated before the Court on January 14, 1994. On January 11, 1995, the Venezuelan Government informed the President of the Court that Venezuela

does not contest the facts referred to in the complaint and accepts the international responsibility of the State.[93]

In that same note, Venezuela requested the Court to ask the Commission to collaborate with Venezuela in determining in friendly fashion the reparations applicable. The Court, in its judgment of January 18, 1995, confirmed that Venezuela was liable for the payment of damages and established a six-month

---

[91] Id. at para. 61.
[92] Report No. 29/93, 12 Oct. 1993.
[93] *El Amparo* Case, Judgment of 18 Jan. 1995, Series C, No. 19.

period for the Government of Venezuela and the Commission to negotiate a settlement. The Court reserved the right, however, to review and approve an agreement, should one ensue, or to determine itself the scope of reparations and indemnities if a negotiated settlement proved unattainable.

The Commission and Venezuela were unable to reach an accord and the Court took the matter up at the termination of the six-month period, denying an extension which both sides wanted. Hearings were held and on September 14, 1996, the Court issued its judgment on compensation. With respect to material damages, the Court appointed an accountant to assist it in processing the various figures proposed. The Court calculated that the compensation for each of the 14 victims who had been murdered was to be based on their age at the time of death and the years remaining to them during which they would, under actuarial projections, have continued to work in Venezuela. With respect to the two survivors who had been injured, the Court calculated the working life that would otherwise have been available to them. Projected salary was based on cost of living and salaries calculated for rural work at that time less a deduction of 25% for personal expenses, but with the addition of interest calculated for the period from the date of the violation until the date of judgment. These calculations produced awards for material damages ranging between US $23,000.00 and US $28,500.00 for the victims who had suffered death and approximately US $4,500.00 for each of the survivors, who had lost worktime as a result of the violation.

With respect to moral damages, the Court focused on the subjectivity of victim test that it had applied in *Aloeboetoe*, which, as will be recalled, was a presumption *juris et de jure*. Another factor taken into account was the fact that, in contrast to *Velásquez* and *Godínez*, the government had admitted guilt. Moral damages of US $20,000.00 for each of the victims were assessed.[94] The *El Amparo* judgment established seven general principles with respect to distribution. The basic principle was that material damage would be divided with one-third assigned to a surviving wife and the other two-thirds divided equally between surviving children, whereas moral damages were to be divided with one-half to the children, one-quarter to a surviving wife, and one-quarter to surviving parents.[95] Although the guidelines established by the Court indicate cognizance of the possible existence of extramarital companions, they make provision for them only in the case of absence of an actual spouse. Here, however, one of the victims, who had a wife and a mistress, with children by each, had the portion assigned to his estate divided equally between the two conjugal companions. As in previous cases, the Court established a trust fund for beneficiaries who were still minors.

---

[94] Id. at para. 37.
[95] Id. at para. 41.

As in previous cases, the Court held that non-pecuniary damages were not necessary due to the consequences of a declaration of culpability from the Court.

g) The Genie-Lacayo Case

On October 28, 1990, Jean Paul Genie-Lacayo, a 16 year-old resident of Managua, was traveling by car to his home in one of the suburbs of the city. He came upon a convoy of military vehicles transporting military personnel. When he tried to pass them, they fired their weapons at him. Genie did not die immediately, but was abandoned on the highway where he bled to death. Fifty-one AK-47 cartridge were found at the scene. Nineteen bullets had hit Genie's car. Three shots, taken at a short distance, hit the car after it had already stopped.

As Nicaragua's adherence to the jurisdiction of the Court under the American Convention had occurred after the events in question transpired, the Commission could not apply the Convention to the taking of Genie's life by military personnel. Instead, the Commission's report was framed in terms of denial of justice, a continuing delict which may have commenced before the entry into force of Nicaragua's jurisdictional declaration, but continued thereafter and was, in the view of the Commission, subject to its and the Court's jurisdiction. In the next phase of the case, which was decided on January 29, 1997, the Court found that the Government of Nicaragua had impeded the authorities in the judicial investigation of the killing of young Genie and that there had been an unreasonable delay in the process. The Court fixed a compensation of US $20,000.00 to be paid to the father of Genie as a matter of equity. It did not order a reparation of the considerable expenses Genie's father had expended in Nicaragua in order to secure an investigation of the killing of his son.

3. The Bryan Commission: U.S. v. Chile

In 1976, Orlando Letelier, a former Foreign Minister of the Allende Government in Chile, in exile in Washington, D.C. and his assistant, Bonnie Moffitt, a U.S. national, were murdered by a bomb planted under their vehicle. The Chilean Secret Police were suspected in the murder and a suit was brought in a federal district court in the United States. In 1990, the United States and a Chilean constitutional Government that had succeeded the military dictatorship agreed that Chile would make an *ex gratia* payment to the Government of the United States on behalf of the families of the victims. The amount of the compensation was to be determined by an international commission established under the 1914 Treaty for the Settlement of Disputes Between the United States and Chile.[96] The only question for the Commission was the liquidation of compensation.

The Commission met in 1991 and decided unanimously to award a total of US $2,611,892. The principle which the Commission established was based on the now familiar judgment of the Permanent Court of International Justice in *Chorzow*:[97] 'reparation must, as far as possible, wipe out all the consequences of the illegal act and re-establish the situation which would, in all probability, have existed if that act had not been committed'. The Commission was concerned, in its own words, with '[t]he loss of financial support and services and the material and moral damages suffered by each of the claimant family members'. The Commission did not provide for interest.

Projecting, as best it could, the probable income of Letelier after the end of the military dictatorship in Chile, the Commission awarded US $1,200,000.00 to Mrs. Letelier and her sons. It also awarded US $160,000 in moral damages to Mrs. Letelier and US $80,000 to each of the couple's four children. The Commission said that its determination of moral damages was based on the amounts awarded by the jurisdictional organs of the Inter-American system and by arbitration or judicial tribunals; but the Commission did not cite to any particular cases.

The Commission also awarded Mrs. Letelier a reimbursement for medical expenses incurred as a result of the attack. The Commission awarded considerably less for the death of Mrs. Moffitt. Her husband was awarded US $233,000.00, a figure based on, in the words of the Commission, 'Mrs. Bonnie Moffitt's youth and brief working experience'. Because Mr. Moffitt had remarried, the Commission concluded that he could not be presumed to have suffered a loss from the share of his deceased wife's contribution to household expenses after the date of remarriage. In general, the Commission's treatment of the Moffitt claims lacked the clarity of those for Letelier's. For example, the Commission noted that Mr. Moffitt had also been injured in the bomb attack, but added that though a distinction could be drawn between his injuries and the damage caused by the loss of his wife, 'it was virtually impossible to assign a separate value to one or the other'. The Commission agreed instead on a total of US $250,000.00 which it did not try to disaggregate.

The moral damages for the parents of Mrs. Moffitt were set at US $300,000.00. The function of moral damages in the Bryan Commission's theory of reparations seemed related to the degree to which the Chilean government acknowledged responsibility and tried to investigate and itself compensate for the violation. In paragraph 41, the Commission said:

---

[96] 24 July 1914, 39 S.T.A.T. 1645, T.S. No. 621.
[97] PCIJ Ser. A. No. 17.

In considering the compensation for moral damages, the Commission has taken into account the significant steps undertaken by the Chilean Government and Congress to remedy human rights problems as well as the efforts undertaken towards financial reparation
at the domestic level for families of victims.

Thus, the Bryan Commission's award presents a curious contrast in its
treatment of Letelier and Mrs. Moffitt. The Letelier award is rather rigorous
and corresponds to general usage with respect to reparations. The Commission
seemed to struggle with reparations for Mrs. Moffitt's survivors.

V. NATIONAL PRACTICE

While human rights violations are usually considered in individual terms,
there are mass violations which, as a practical matter, must be treated in
collective fashion, lest the transaction costs of processing each claim preclude
worthy individuals from establishing their case or, on balance, impose even
higher transaction costs on the violator than would a system of mass payments. In this respect, international practice has adopted many of the techniques of mass tort compensation in advanced industrial legal systems. This
has been the procedure of the United Nations Claims Commission and has
been adopted at the national level for compensation for mass human rights
violations, especially when the moment of reparation was long after the
violation and the evidentiary problems for the victims or the survivors in
making their case would have been formidable.

1. United States' Compensation of Japanese-Americans for Relocation and Detention During World War II

On February 19, 1942, President Franklin D. Roosevelt signed Executive
Order 9066. American citizens of Japanese ancestry and resident aliens who
were barred from becoming American citizens by discriminatory laws then in
force, were moved from the West Coast to camps in remote parts of the
western United States and were detained there for two and one-half years. A
total of 120,000 people were detained. There had been no cases of sabotage
on the West Coast prior to the relocation order, but the military feared an
invasion by Japan on the West Coast and apparently assumed that Japanese-
Americans, by virtue of their ethnicity, would assist the invader. The Government's assumption was that the West coast Japanese were *per se* disloyal. It
is striking that no comparable programs were initiated against Americans of

German or Italian descent on the East Coast of the country. The constitutionality of the action was ultimately upheld by the Supreme Court.[98]

In 1948, the Japanese-American Evacuation Act awarded compensation for property losses on an individual basis according to the losses suffered. Twenty-six thousand, five hundred sixty-eight claims were settled, with US $37 million paid out. In 1980, Congress established the Commission on Wartime Relocation and Internment of Civilians to examine the actions by the U.S. against Japanese-Americans and the Aleuts, who along with the residents of Pribilof Island, had been evacuated in anticipation of an invasion by Japan. (Japan did, in fact, bomb targets in the Aleutians). While the circumstances of the Aleutian evacuation appeared to have been justified, the conditions under which the Aleuts and Pribilovians were kept in Alaska were atrocious. The Commission held 20 hearings, 3 in Alaska, and took the testimony of more than 750 witnesses. Its final report, entitled, 'Personal Justice Denied', was published in 1982 and formed the basis for the subsequent legislation.

The Civil Liberties Act of 1987 was signed by the President on August 10, 1988. In brief, the Act established a 'Civil Liberties Public Education Fund', administered by the Attorney-General, from which tax-free US $20,000 restitution payments (equal to US $3,000 in 1945 dollars), would be paid to those who were eligible. Payments were to be made over a 10-year period and eligible individuals would have 18 months to decide whether or not to accept the payment. Total appropriations to the trust fund were to be US $1.25 billion with no more than US $500 million being appropriated in any given year.

Plainly, the losses of those who suffered the detention would have varied depending on their age, their life circumstances at the time of detention, their health and so on. While the indignity suffered would have been the same for all, the losses of a minor, who had not yet begun his or her career, would have been considerably less than those of a professional in mid-career. Yet the Commission proposed and Congress accepted the fixed-amount approach for all members of the class. Although most of the discussion in Congress was over the question of whether *any* compensation should be paid, both the Commission and Congress did address the issue of single or individualized reparations.

> The Commission considered such a system at length but ultimately found it flawed.... Ultimately, a claims procedure was not likely to be fair, equitable, speedy or conducive to healing the wartime wounds.[99]

The four flaws in an individualized approach to reparations identified by the Commission were as follows:

---

[98] *Korematsu v. U.S.*, 323 U.S. 214 (1944).
[99] A. Macbeth (former Special Counsel to the Commission on Wartime Relocation and Internment of Civilians), testimony before the Hearing, at 218.

1. It would be unfair because of a lack of evidence.

[W]e know not only from daily experience but from the operation of the Evacuation Claims Act after the war that, 45 years after Executive Order 9066 was issued, only a very small number of claimants could convincingly show through documents or witnesses exactly what their losses were.[100]

2. It would be inequitable because of the arbitrary nature of the tort.

[A] major aspect of any compensation would be for the loss of liberty and the stigma that resulted from the exclusion and detention. Recognizing that awards for losses of this sort inevitably have an arbitrary aspect to them, there appeared to be little merit in requiring 60,000 people to be individually put to the proof of what the effect of the exclusion and detention had on their lives. [101]

If I were interned, I would consider [US] $20,000 as being too little. How do you compensate a child who had just lost his mother, who committed suicide because of depression and anguish? How do you compensate those families who lost their fathers and husbands, who stood up and voiced objection and were shot down by the troops in the camps? They were not violating the laws of the United States. They were just exercising their first amendment rights to speak up, petition the Government. They were not armed. It was a peaceful demonstration. How do you compensate the families of those men? How do you compensate a fellow American for the stigma of being branded disloyal? $20,000, Mr. President, is just token.[102]

3. It would be inappropriate because of time considerations.

[A] claims process would be very time-consuming. We are now at a point where the evacuees are all over forty years old and a great many are in their 70s and 80s. It does not seem the appropriate time to begin the inevitably lengthy process of adjudicating claims.[103]

4. It would be likely to reopen wartime wounds.

... any claims process would automatically be adversarial in nature; this would result in the government's attorneys working to keep awards low by opposing Japanese American claims and contesting the nature of the hardships and the pain and suffering experienced. This would reopen the wartime wounds and work directly against the spirit of healing and magnanimity which a compensatory award should foster.

As to the injuries the fixed amount covered, a calculation was initially prepared for the Commission based on income and property losses (see footnote 18) and this amount was then used by the Commission as the figure for compensation for the personal effects of internment that it recommended to Congress.

... this compensation was primarily aimed at the loss of liberty and the stigma which attended the exclusion...personal issues and losses unlike the loss of tangible property ...[104]

---

[100] Macbeth, id. at 218.

[101] Macbeth, id. at 218.

[102] Senator Inouye, CR-S at 7543.

[103] Macbeth (supra note 99), at 218.

[104] Macbeth (supra note 99), at 219.

... this amount is designed to provide in one action a tangible form of redress for the variety of damages and injury which the Japanese-Americans suffered as a result of Executive Order 9066 and the events which followed from it ...[105]

Although the fixed amount was adopted by Congress, it is nevertheless not clear whether Congress intended to follow the eventual approach that the Commission took as to the losses the amount covers. Although the Senate bill states that the payments 'shall be treated for purposes of the Internal Revenue Laws of the United States as damages for human suffering',[106] the final Act does not make any direct indication in this regard.[107] Some members of Congress clearly viewed the losses in the same manner as the Commission,

... The individual payments acknowledge the unjust deprivation of liberty, the infliction of mental and physical suffering, and the stigma of being branded disloyal, losses not compensable under the Japanese Evacuation Claims Act of 1948 ...[108]

... Those payments would be compensation for the loss of civil and constitutional rights, not for the loss of property ...[109]

Other Senators, however, saw the losses in a different sense,

...the suffering and the property loss involved...[110]

...considering the degree of economic, social, and emotional injury incurred to the internees during their 3-year confinement[111]

...it is clear from the language of this legislation, and from the accompanying committee report, that the authorized funds are intended as compensation for economic loss ... not ... as a symbol but, rather, as economic redress ...[112]

... it is difficult, if not impossible, to make whole by compensation those who suffered the losses ... However, ... there were losses that involved property ...[113]

The amount chosen was related to the injuries it covered in several ways:

- By comparing the amount with that recoverable for false imprisonment and false arrest.

---

[105] Macbeth (supra note 99), at 220-221.
[106] Senate bill, Sec. 205(f)(1).
[107] Sec. 2(a) of the Act states that 'the excluded individuals of Japanese ancestry suffered enormous damages, both material and intangible, and there were incalculable losses in education and job training, all of which resulted in significant human suffering for which appropriate compensation has not been made', but does not connect this directly to the any or all of the remedies that follow (compensation being only one of several remedies in the bill).
[108] Senator Daniel Inouye, Hawaii CR-S at 7543.
[109] Representative Mineta, California, testimony before the Hearing, at 99.
[110] Senator Stevens, at 7545.
[111] Senator Matsunaga, CR-S at 7251.
[112] Senator Chafee, CR-S at 7555.
[113] Senator Stevens, CR-S at 7545.

... it is fairly said on that basis that an award for $20,000 for exclusion and detention for a period of two and a half years is, in fact, quite modest ...[114]

- By comparing the amount with calculations for income and property losses.[115]

   ... It's my understanding that the Commission ... used our range of losses [which focused solely on income and property loss] in the aggregate to develop what they thought was the appropriate amount of restitution per claimant ...[116]

   ... Viewed in these terms [the amount for income and property loss], the monetary remedy urged by the Commission may be adequate but it cannot be claimed to be excessively generous ...[117]

- As an arbitrary, symbolic amount.

   ... an amount that is meaningful and not trivial ... There is no esoteric magic to the exact number chosen by the Commission ...[118]

   ... as a just and fair redress[119]

---

[114] Macbeth (supra note 99), at 195.

[115] In 1983, the Commission asked ICF, Inc. to estimate the value of the losses. The methodology adopted was described by Michael C. Barth, the president of the company, in testimony to the House Judiciary Subcommittee on Administrative Law and Governmental Relations on April 28, 1987, related in CR-S at 7250. ICF, Inc. focused on *income* and *property* losses. *Human capital losses* (in education, training and experience during exclusion and detention) were not covered because they were 'unable to come up with any estimate of these'. *Pain and suffering* was also not included. *Income losses* were defined as the 'amount of income that might have been earned by excludees had they not been in the detention camps during the period 1942-6'. 'These were adjusted for the actual income that was earned by excludees – by detainees while they were in the camps since modest amounts of pay was paid.' The amount was adjusted to take into account both inflation, and the fact that some of the income may have been invested. *Property* losses were calculated by looking at the claims files for the 1947 Japanese-American Evacuation Claims Act and the private files of some citizens involved in litigation at that time. 'Based on this information, we estimated ranges of the amounts of losses per claimant. Now it's possible that not all persons who had property losses filed under the 1947 Evacuation Claims Act. Accordingly, then, in order to ensure that we were not grossly underestimating claims, we conducted various analyses of the amounts of claims that might have been claimed for had people not been ignorant or unaware or otherwise unable to make claims for which they could not provide adequate justification. We also then adjusted our estimates for the fact that 437 million was in fact paid by the US Government to claimants, and between 1947 and 1956 when the final claim was paid (sic). These estimates, because of the substantial data problems, resulted in a large range, but putting together the income and the property loss estimates and adjusting that for inflation to 1983 yielded a range of $810 million to $2 billion. Adjusting for the foregone interest that might have been earned yielded a range of $1.2 - $3.1 billion.'

[116] Barth, previous note.

[117] Macbeth (supra note 99), at 221.

[118] Macbeth (supra note 99), at 222.

[119] Senator Cranston, CR-S at 7260.

... in order to make this apology adequately ...[120]

... It is argued that it is an indication of the significance, of the symbol, of the sincerity of our action ...[121]

- ## As a small proportion of the full entitlement.

  ... When one considers the fact that most of the internees were detained for 3 years or more, the $20,000 lump-sum payments simply cannot be considered excessive .... a very small amount of compensation.[122]

  ... There is no one that suggests that $20,000 is adequate compensation for the time one spent away from home and in a relocation center ...[123]

  ... It is not anywhere near the amount that the Commission found would be necessary to fully compensate these people ... [124]

As to beneficiaries, all those of Japanese ancestry affected by the exclusion orders (estimated at 60,000) were eligible, without distinction.

  ... the Commission concluded that no distinctions should be made among those who were affected by the exclusion orders ... any attempt at such distinctions would be divisive and very difficult to carry out and simply was not justified in terms of the kind of large ... and serious gesture which the Commission thought was appropriate here ...[125]

Distinctions explicitly stated as having been considered and rejected by the Committee included nationality (internees included both Japanese-Americans and Japanese); [126] whether or not the offer of voluntary relocation had been accepted;[127] and the length of detention.[128]

---

[120] Senator Wilson, CR-S at 7546.

[121] Senator Helms, CR-S at 7634.

[122] Senator Matsunaga, CR-S at 7251.

[123] Senator Helms, supra note 121.

[124] Senator Stevens, CR-S at 7549.

[125] Macbeth (supra note 99), at 195.

[126] '... many of those excluded were Japanese rather than American citizens, a few thousand voluntarily left the West Coast before the exclusion orders became effective, many evacuees in their late teens or twenties were able to leave the camps to go to college or jobs in the East or into the army ... While it is undeniably true that the legal status of aliens of enemy nationality in time of war is quite different from that of American citizens, it is willful blindness to treat the Issei as if they were enemy aliens. Immigration to this country from Japan was prohibited in 1924 but Japanese nationals were also prohibited from becoming American citizens. Thus, the Issei had lived here for at least 17 years during a period of rising tensions, and, unlike German and Italian immigrants for whom citizenship procedures were accelerated at the beginning of the war or the immigrant Chinese for whom naturalized citizenship became available during the war, the Issei had no option of becoming American citizens. This was the technical non-citizenship which Congress recognized as not indicative of lack of loyalty in 1942 ...' Macbeth (supra note 99), at 220.

[127] '"Voluntary" relocation was voluntary in name only; people of Japanese descent were not leaving the West coast in 1942 because they believed there were shining opportunities in the

Although the Commission made an effort to estimate, on a generalized basis, the losses incurred by the internees, it is plain, as a number of Senators acknowledged, that the compensation in many cases was far less than that actually suffered. Moreover, no interest was added. The compensation would appear to have been an essentially symbolic acknowledgment on the part of the United States of the injury it had done.

It is noteworthy that in the entire legislative record, no reference is made to an international law standard with respect to compensation. It is not unusual for the United States to rely on its own law, but in the instant case, an additional reason for not using international law might have been the undesirable implication of such a usage, i.e., that this was an international matter between 'Japanese' and 'Americans', and not an internal matter which had to be repaired under United States Law.

2. Chilean Compensation for Human Rights Victims Under the Military Dictatorship

The military coup against the elected government of Salvador Allende in 1972 commenced a period of systematic human rights violations by the military government, in which Chilean nationals were tortured, imprisoned or murdered. After the restoration of constitutional government, Law 19.123 of February 8, 1992 established a Corporación Nacional de Reparación y Reconciliación to administer the reparations. The reparations law applied only to victims of disappearance or death. Torture was not to be compensated. The victims had been mentioned in the Rettig Report of 1991, the famous 'Truth Commission Report'. Four categories of beneficiaries were created: (1) the spouse of the victim if still alive; (2) the mother of a victim or the father if the mother were no longer alive; (3) the mother of an illegitimate child or the father if the mother were no longer alive; and (4) sons and daughters of a victim younger than 25 or without regard to age if disabled. The figures available until December, 1996 show that 4,886 relatives of victims received benefits. From 1992 to 1995, the Chilean Government paid out $80.2 million (in US dollars) to beneficiaries.

Five categories of benefits were created by the law. The first is a pension for life and proportionate health insurance. It currently works out to approxi-

---

interior. In fact, more did not leave precisely because of the demonstrated animosity to Japanese Americans in the interior States...' Macbeth (supra note 99), at 220.

[128] '... [T]he Commission decided against making distinctions in compensation based on the length of detention because it recognized that any compensation voted by Congress would remain an expression of the wartime losses but would not be full compensation for the events of 1942 to 1945 ...' Macbeth (supra note 99), at 220.

mately US $550.00 per month, which is divided up among the various beneficiaries of a single victim. If there is only one beneficiary, the cap is US $340.00. The pension is significantly higher than pensions offered by State and private pension systems in Chile.

The second benefit is a single 'compensatory bonus' of 12 times the amount of a single monthly pension benefit. The third benefit is an educational grant for children of the victim under 35 years of age. The government pays the fees and tuition of higher education and also a monthly stipend of US $70.00 for children in high school.

The fourth benefit relates to health services. A favorable access is given to either the public or private health system. The final benefit is an option available to the children of victims to avoid compulsory military service.

Chile is a party to the American Convention on Human Rights and, hence, subject to the conventional jurisdiction of the Inter-American Commission. Applications were received by the Commission seeking to test the lawfulness of the Chilean reparations regimes against the standards established in the Convention. To my knowledge, those cases are still pending.

VI. APPRAISAL

Given the epidemic of human rights violations that occurred in the Americas in the period preceding the decade of practice surveyed here, relatively few human rights violations were compensated. Nevertheless, it is clear that, at the normative level, there is a regional acknowledgment of an obligation to compensate for human rights violations. The Inter-American Commission and Court, in their symbiotic relationship, seem to have moved into a rather routinized treatment of individual compensation. The Court has adopted the general international practice with respect to material damages. Moral damages have acquired three different meanings in the Court's practice, but the more recent cases relate it to the suffering of the victims, for which a flat sum is given for certain violations without requirement of any additional proof. The Court has not taken the opportunities presented to it to transform the Commission into a more effective international decision-maker with respect to compensation. The *Aloeboetoe* case is probably the only current international decision that has tried to take account of indigenous social structures in fashioning a compensation regime. But the vacillation of the Commission and the uncertainty of the Court produced a rather timid and conventional response to a social structure which is plainly radically different from the model with which the two juridical institutions were familiar.

The Bryan Commission, sitting as an *ad hoc* compensation tribunal, produced a relatively detailed set of reasons for the award it rendered. Unfortunately – for scholars and for subsequent practice – the pleadings in this case have been sealed and, without them, it is difficult to tease out the more detailed reasoning of the Commission.

There are some striking similarities in the two national practices that are surveyed here and which it must be emphasized, do not exhaust the national practice in the hemisphere in the decade under review. All use relatively standardized rather than individualized approaches to compensation. Nonetheless, all acknowledged the community's obligation to provide compensation. In this respect, the Americas at least in this decade, manifested greater sensitivity to an international standard than has been manifested recently in Germany and Japan, where highly legalistic objections were made to compensation of serious and incontestable yet still unresolved human rights violations that had been inherited from an earlier unhappy period.

Individual Reparation Claims under the European Convention on Human Rights

Matti Pellonpää

I. GENERAL REMARKS CONCERNING THE SCOPE OF INDIVIDUAL REPARATION CLAIMS UNDER THE EUROPEAN CONVENTION ON HUMAN RIGHTS

Under the present system established by the European Convention on Human Rights individual reparation claims can, depending on the circumstances, be decided by both the Committee of Ministers of the Council of Europe acting upon the advice of the European Commission of Human Rights, and the European Court of Human Rights. Since the legal principles have mainly been developed by the latter body, the focus in the following presentation is on the practice of the Court. Its power to order reparation in the form of 'just satisfaction' is based on Article 50 of the Convention.[1] It reads as follows:

> If the Court finds that a decision or a measure taken by a legal authority or any other authority of a High Contracting Party is completely or partially in conflict with the obligations arising from the present Convention on Human Rights, and if the internal law of the said party allows only partial reparation to be made for the consequences of this decision or measure, the decision of the Court shall, if necessary, afford just satisfaction to the injured party.

---

[1] On Article 50 see, e.g., M. Enrich Mas, 'Right to Compensation under Article 50', in: R. St. J. Macdonald, F. Matscher & H. Petzold (eds.), *The European System for the Protection of Human Rights* 1993, 775-790; J. Abr. Frowein & W. Peukert, *Europäische Menschenrechtskonvention,* 2nd ed., 1996, 667-722; J.L. Sharpe, 'Article 50', in: L.-E. Pettiti, E. Decaux & P.-H. Imbert, *La Convention européenne des droits de l'homme: Commentaire article par article,* 1995, 809-842. Generally on 'just satisfaction' under the Convention, see also J.-F. Flauss, 'La satisfaction équitable dans le cadre de la Convention européenne des droits de l'homme – Perspectives d'actualité', Universität des Saarlandes, Vorträge, Reden und Berichte aus dem Europa-Institut Nr. 332, 1995; H.C. Krüger, 'Reflections on Some Aspects of Just Satisfaction under the European Convention on Human Rights', in: *Liber Amicorum Marc-André Eissen,* 1995, 255-269. As to the effects of the 11th Protocol, due to enter into force on 1 November 1998, see infra, Sec. VI.

A. Randelzhofer and C. Tomuschat (eds.), State Responsibility and the Individual, 109–129.

This article was inspired by certain clauses to be found in arbitration treaties concluded in the first decades of this century. While it is of importance to recall this connection between the 'reparation regime' of the European Convention and that of general international law, some basic differences should be pointed out at the outset.

Thus, unlike the situation in traditional international law, the violating State's duty to provide reparation for the breach is not owed primarily to other Contracting States but to the injured individual. Although the possibility of a State being awarded reparation in connection with so-called inter-State cases (Article 24 of the Convention) is not excluded, the 'injured party' in Article 50 refers above all to the individual victim of a violation who can address his or her claims directly to the Court in connection with a procedure introduced by him or herself (Article 25).

While the Convention-based 'reparation regime' is broader than that of general international law in the above sense, it is narrower in another respect. In general international law of State responsibility, 'reparation' (in a broad sense) may be said

> to refer to all measures which a plaintiff may expect to be taken by a defendant state: payment of compensation (or restitution), an apology, the punishment of the individuals responsible, the taking of steps to prevent a recurrence of the breach of duty, and any other forms of satisfaction.[2]

Not all such forms of reparation are available under Article 50 of the Convention. The European Court has on many occasions been faced with requests that the violating State be ordered to amend its laws, see to it that a judgment be quashed and so on. The Court, however, has consistently held that it is not empowered to give such directions.[3] The Court's position is in conformity with the intentions of the drafters of the Convention and can also be regarded as one expression of its conception of the 'subsidiary' nature of the European system for the protection of human rights: under this system, the European Court does not play the role of a 'fourth instance' court empowered to quash national judgments but of an organ competent to ensure that the minimum standards guaranteed by the Convention are not violated.[4]

---

[2]   I. Brownlie, *Principles of Public International Law*, 4th ed., 1990, 458.

[3]   See, e.g., the *Hauschildt* judgment of 24 May 1989, Series A no. 154, para. 54 (request that the applicant's 'conviction be quashed and any disqualifications or restrictions placed on him removed' rejected); *Meheni v. France*, Judgment of 26 Sep. 1997, Reports 1997-VI no. 51 paras. 42-43 (no jurisdiction to order the French Government to allow the applicant to return to France). See also infra note 68 and the text preceding it.

[4]   The system may 'indirectly' entail consequences such as changes of legislation and quashing of judgments at the domestic level, but the Court never orders them by virtue of Article 50. Yet where a law, as distinct from an isolated application of it, is the cause of a violation, the State may have to resort to general measures (such as an amendment of the law) to comply with its

The Court has – to cite a case concerning unlawful deprivation of property – emphasized that:

> It follows that a judgment in which the Court finds a breach imposes on the respondent State a legal obligation to put an end to the breach and make reparation for its consequences in such a way as to restore as far as possible the situation existing before the breach.[5]

Even so, the Court cannot itself effect such restitution,[6] although – interestingly enough – in its Article 50 Judgment in the *Papamichalopoulos* case it did order the return of the unlawfully taken property as the primary reparation.[7] Normally, however, the Court at the most indicates that a measure of restitution is recommendable and adjourns the application of Article 50 pending possible measures to be taken at the domestic level.

If it is at the outset sufficiently clear that domestic law does not allow restitution or restitution is impossible because of the nature of the breach in question, or where reserving the application of Article 50 has not led to a solution at the domestic level, the Court itself orders 'just satisfaction'.[8]

---

obligation to abide by the Court's decision (Article 53). The Committee of Ministers, moreover, ensures under Article 54 that such measures are taken. See P. Leuprecht, 'The Execution of Judgments and Decisions', in: *The European System for the Protection of Human Rights* (supra note 1), 791-800. The European Court of Human Rights may also contribute to *restitutio in integrum* in the form of a quashing of a judgment by reserving the application of Article 50 pending reopening proceedings at the domestic level. See, for example, *Barberà, Messegué and Jabardo v. Spain*, Judgment of 13 June 1994 (Article 50), Series A no. 285-C. On the effects of judgments in domestic law, see G. Ress, 'The Effects of Judgments and Decisions in Domestic Law', in: *The European System for the Protection of Human Rights* (supra note 1), 801-851. 'Friendly settlements' may also entail consequences going beyond the confines of the particular case. See C.A. Norgaard & H.K. Krüger, 'Article 28 §§ 1b et 2', in: *La Convention européenne des droits de l'homme: Commentaire article par article* (supra note 1), 661-679; V. Berger, 'Le règlement amiable devant la Cour', ibid., 783-792.

[5] *Papamichalopoulos and Others v. Greece*, Judgment of 31 Oct. 1995 (Article 50), Series A no. 330-B, para. 34.

[6] In *Hentrich v. France*, Judgment of 22 Sep. 1994, Series A no. 296-A, involving pre-emption of real property by tax authorities in violation of Article 1 of the First Protocol the Court stated that 'the best form of redress would in principle be for the State to return the land.' Para. 71. In its above-mentioned Article 50 Judgment in *Papamichalopoulos and Others*, the Court stated that where 'the nature of the breach allows a *restitutio in integrum*, it is for the respondent State to effect it, the Court having neither the power nor the practical possibility of doing so itself.' Para. 34.

[7] In the operative part of the Judgment the Court held '2. ... that the respondent State is to return to the applicants, within six months, the land in issue ..., including the buildings on it', and only '3. ... failing such restitution' was the State to pay compensation equally defined in the judgment.

[8] Although the wording of Article 50 ('if the internal law ... allows only partial reparation') might be understood differently, application of Article 50 does not presuppose that compensation be sought first at the domestic level. The reference to internal law is not a condition of 'admissibility' concerning claims for just satisfaction. See Enrich Mas, supra note 1, 780-781.

This 'satisfaction' principally takes the form of pecuniary compensation.[9] The Court may also hold that a mere finding of a violation – i.e., its declaratory judgment – suffices as just satisfaction. These are the two main forms of reparation granted to an individual victim of a violation of the Convention by virtue of Article 50.

In the next section, the general conditions for the granting of compensation in accordance with Article 50 are dealt with. At the same time, some light is cast on the borderline between the cases justifying compensation and those where the judgment alone is enough.

II. CONDITIONS FOR THE GRANTING OF PECUNIARY COMPENSATION

Violation of a substantive Convention article is a necessary, but not a sufficient, condition for the granting of reparation. First, compensation is not awarded by the Court of its own motion but must be claimed by the applicant.[10] Secondly, even where a claim is made and a violation of a substantive Convention provision found, the Court, according to Article 50, shall afford just satisfaction, only 'if necessary'. Article 50 is based on the relatively wide discretionary power of the European Court of Human Rights as regards just satisfaction. This discretion is apparent not only in the amounts of compensation but also in other respects. In *McCann and Others v. the United Kingdom*, the Court on the one hand found a violation of Article 2 (right to life) on the basis of the killing of three IRA members in Gibraltar but, on the other, denied compensation to the relatives who had introduced the case before the Convention organs. Noting first that it was not clear whether financial compensation was claimed for pecuniary or non-pecuniary damages, the Court went on to say:

> In any event, having regard to the fact that the three terrorist suspects who were killed had been intending to plant a bomb in Gibraltar, the Court does not consider it appropriate to make an award under this head. It therefore dismisses the applicant's claim for damages.[11]

---

[9]   Especially where compensation for material damage is granted as 'just satisfaction', the word 'satisfaction' as a term of the European Convention on Human Rights has a meaning different from 'satisfaction' in general international law where it usually denotes reparation, such as an apology, for moral damage suffered by a State. See C. Gray, *Judicial Remedies in International Law*, 1987, 41-48, 153.

[10]   See, e.g., *Francesco Lombardo v. Italy*, Judgment of 26 Nov. 1992, Series A no. 249-B, para. 25 ('The applicant did not claim any just satisfaction under Article 50 and this is not a matter for the Court to examine of its own motion.').

[11]   *McCann and Others v. the United Kingdom*, Judgment of 27 Sep. 1995, Series A no. 324, para. 219.

This case illustrates that the discretion available to the Court may sometimes be used to reach a compromise between the need to uphold a very high standard of protection of a fundamental right, on the one hand, and a certain reluctance to afford pecuniary reparation in circumstances where the victim of the violation, due to his or her own behaviour, is not regarded as deserving it.[12] On the other hand, the Court's wide discretion may also have contributed to the fact that its reasoning in regard to Article 50 is often meagre and the case-law therefore not easily presented in a systematic fashion.

Be that as it may, the discretion referred to does not of course mean arbitrariness. Upon the fulfillment of certain conditions, a private claimant has a very strong expectation to be awarded compensation. This is true especially as regards claims for *pecuniary* damage, whereas discretion is likely to play a stronger role when the question of compensation for *non-pecuniary* damage is being considered.

In order to justify his or her claim for pecuniary damage, the applicant must, first, prove the existence of the pecuniary loss and, second, establish the causal link between the loss and the violation found by the Court.

In many cases the existence of these two conditions can be established without any particular difficulties. This is the case, for example, where a journalist has been convicted and fined for defamation of a politician in what turns out to be a breach of Article 10 (freedom of speech). The amount of the fines imposed, i.e. the loss, can be easily established, and the causal link between the loss and the violation is no more difficult.[13] In a case such as *Young, James and Webster*, in which the applicants' right to freedom of association (Article 11) had been violated due to their dismissal on the ground that they refused to join a union, the causal link between the violation and the loss – loss of income – is also clear, although quantification of the loss may

---

[12] The wording adopted could be understood to mean that the Court's refusal was based on 'moral' considerations, i.e. the 'unworthiness' of the victims. Another possible and – it is submitted – a better interpretation would appear to be one based on legal considerations, namely 'contributory negligence' (or 'assumption of risk') on the part of the victims who, by embarking on the mission in question, had taken upon themselves the risk of the fatal loss in question.

[13] See e.g. the *Lingens* Judgment of 8 July 1986, Series A no. 103, *Oberschlick v. Austria*, Judgment of 23 May 1991, Series A no. 204 and *Oberschlick v. Austria (no. 2),* Judgment of 1 July 1997, Reports 1997-IV no. 42. In the last-mentioned case the applicant, who had been convicted for having insulted a politician (Mr. Haider), claimed as pecuniary damage the reimbursement of the fine and the politician's costs for court fees and legal representation which the applicant had also been ordered to pay by the domestic court. The European Court held: 'As payment by the applicant of the sums in question was a direct consequence of his wrongful conviction, the Court considers the claim justified.' Judgment, para. 39. See also, e.g., the *Darby* judgment of 23 Oct. 1990, Series A no. 187 (church tax imposed in violation of the Convention ordered to be reimbursed).

be more difficult than in the Article 10 cases just mentioned.[14] In this kind of case, as well as, for example, in cases involving property losses, valuation of the damages may pose difficulties, but the causal link between the losses incurred and the violation is easy to establish.

However, there is a whole category of cases in which the causal link between losses which the applicant may have incurred and the violation poses problems. A most typical case brought before the European human rights organs concerns procedural guarantees under Article 6 (right to a 'fair trial'). Especially where the finding of a violation is based on a procedural irregularity of a somewhat 'formal' nature – say, lack of oral hearing in a criminal case before a Court of Appeal in circumstances in which such a hearing would have been required by Article 6 – the Court of Human Rights typically refuses to speculate as to whether the holding of a hearing would have changed the outcome of the national proceedings. Consequently, a possible claim for loss of earnings due to serving a prison sentence (or otherwise as a consequence of the domestic proceeding's material outcome) is dismissed for lack of a causal link between the losses and the violation of Article 6, since the Court cannot speculate whether the holding of a hearing, or a different composition of the domestic Court etc., would have led to the acquittal of the applicant or to a different outcome in a civil case.[15]

The Court's refusal to speculate about the outcome of the domestic proceedings can be understood as another expression of the 'subsidiarity principle' governing the relationship between national courts and the European Court of Human Rights. The last-mentioned Court is not 'a fourth instance' competent, for example, to substitute its own assessment of evidence for that of the national court. This is illustrated by the case of *Dombo Beheer B.V. v. the Netherlands* in which the Court found a violation of the right to 'equality of arms' (Article 6) on the ground that the applicant company's managing director had not been allowed to testify as a witness on certain negations, whereas the other party had been able to call its negotiator as a witness. With regard to the applicant's claim for damages the Human Rights Court had this to say:

---

[14] The applicants were granted for pecuniary damage, including loss of earnings, amounts between 8,076 and 45,215 pounds. The amounts were less than those claimed but equalled to what the Government had offered in settlement negotiations. The Court based its decision on the Government's offer, noting that 'in any event, claims in respect of future earnings must be based on assumptions and are to that extent uncertain.' See Judgment of 18 Oct. 1982 (Article 50), Series A no. 55, paras. 10-11 (quotation from para. 11).

[15] See, e.g., the *Ekbatani* judgment of 26 May 1988, Series A no. 134 (lack of oral hearing before a Swedish court of appeal in a criminal case) and *Van de Hurk v. the Netherlands*, Judgment of 19 April 1994, Series A no. 288 (the Industrial Appeals Tribunal lacked some characteristics of an 'independent tribunal').

The applicant company's various claims for compensation for pecuniary and non-pecuniary damage ... are based on the assumption that it would have won its case if the national courts had allowed Mr van Reijendam to testify. The Court could not accept this assumption without itself assessing the evidence. The testimony of Mr van Reijendam before the Arnhem Court of Appeal could have resulted in the existence of two opposing statements, one of which would have to be accepted against the other on the basis of supporting evidence. It is not for the European Court of Human Rights to say which should be accepted. This part of the claim for just satisfaction must accordingly be dismissed.[16]

A very strict refusal to speculate about the material outcome of the domestic case may sometimes lead to the denial of compensation even in cases where the violation of the Convention may in fact have resulted in material losses for the applicant. This consequence is to some extent mitigated by the practice of the Court to award compensation for 'loss of opportunities' due to the violation of the right to a fair trial. Compensation on this ground is typically granted where the violation of the right to a fair trial can be said to have been of a somewhat more substantive nature.[17] The 'loss of opportunities' theory has served as a basis for compensation in cases concerning other rights, for example the right of property or the right to education.[18]

Theoretical classification of 'loss of opportunities' as a basis for monetary compensation is difficult.[19] It can be regarded as a sub-heading of compensation for pecuniary damage, but it seems that considerations similar to those favouring compensation for non-pecuniary damage often play a role when an award of compensation for 'loss of opportunities' is being considered. This is also illustrated by the fact that a violation of a certain guarantee under Article 6, such as the right to a hearing within a 'reasonable time', may in some cases give rise to compensation for 'loss of opportunities', in others for 'stress' or 'uncertainty' or other forms of non-pecuniary damage.[20]

---

[16] Judgment of 27 Oct. 1993, Series A no. 274, para. 40

[17] The borderline between cases in which compensation for loss of opportunities is granted and those in which it is not may be tenuous. Compare the *Bönisch* judgment (Article 50) of 2 June 1986, Series A no. 103, para. 11 (violation based on unequal treatment of defence and prosecution experts justified compensation for loss of opportunities) with the above-mentioned (supra note 16 and the preceding text) *Dombo Beheer* judgment (no compensation). Explanation for the difference is possibly to be found in the fact that one case concerned criminal, the other civil proceedings.

[18] See Enrich Mas, supra note 1, 785-86.

[19] D.J. Harris, M. O'Boyle & C. Warbrick, *Law of the European Convention on Human Rights*, 1995, 686-87, deal with it under 'pecuniary damage'. Sharpe, supra note 1, 821, qualifies this item as *sui generis*.

[20] Sometimes the Court, recognizing the difficulty in distinguishing between loss of opportunities and non-pecuniary damage, has awarded a lump-sum covering both elements. See Enrich Mas, supra note 1, 785-86. See also Frowein & Peukert, supra note 1, 677.

As indicated, in addition to pecuniary damage, compensation may also be awarded for non-pecuniary damage (stress, moral or physical pain or suffering, feelings of uncertainty). Compensation under this head can be granted in addition to compensation for pecuniary damage but also in cases where no pecuniary loss can be shown. To be awarded compensation for non-pecuniary damage the applicant must also, in principle, show the existence of such damage and the causal link between it and the violation found.

Compensation for non-pecuniary damage can be awarded, for example, in so-called 'length of proceedings cases'; that is, in cases in which the right to a hearing 'within a reasonable time' as guaranteed by Article 6 has been violated. Compensation is frequently awarded in lengthy civil cases,[21] as well as in criminal cases which have lasted unreasonably long and resulted in the acquittal of the accused.[22]

X v. France can be mentioned as an example of a case in which compensation was granted for non-pecuniary damage caused by the length of proceedings. The civil claim against the State by the applicant – a haemophiliac who had been infected with AIDS by a blood transfusion and who died before the Strasbourg judgment – lasted somewhat in excess of two years. This was regarded as excessive in the exceptional circumstances of the case. The applicant claimed, *inter alia*, 150, 000 francs for non-pecuniary damage on the ground that the 'length of the proceedings had prevented him from obtaining the compensation he had hoped for, and thus from being able to live independently and in better psychological conditions for the remaining period of his life ...'[23]. The Court found:

> ... that the applicant undeniably sustained non-pecuniary damage. Taking into account the various relevant factors and making an assessment on an equitable basis in accordance with Article 50, it award[ed] to his parents the entire 150,000 francs sought.[24]

To take another example, compensation for non-pecuniary damage was also granted in *Beaumartin v. France* where the length and fairness requirements were found to have been violated in a case in which the *Conseil d'Etat* considered itself bound by the Foreign Ministry's interpretation of a so-called

---

[21] See, e.g., *Terranova v. Italy*, Judgment of 4 Dec. 1995, Series A no. 337-B, paras. 25-26 (the Court, dismissing further claims, awarded the applicant ITL 20,000,000 'on an equitable basis' for non-pecuniary damage sustained due to proceedings in the Court of Audit which took over eight years).

[22] See Frowein & Peukert, supra note 1, 705-6.

[23] Judgment of 31 March 1992, Series A no. 234-C, para. 54.

[24] Para. 54. On the question of the successors' right to compensation where the applicant has died, see Krüger, supra note 1, 258-60.

lump-sum agreement. Instead of the claimed total amount of 320,000 francs the Court awarded 100, 000.[25]

López Ostra v. Spain can be mentioned as an example of a case involving a Convention provision other than Article 6. The applicant's right to respect for her home and her private and family life as guaranteed by Article 8 was violated through the State's failure to take sufficient measures against nuisance caused by a waste-treatment plant close to the applicant's home. The Court accepted that the applicant had suffered both pecuniary damage (depreciation of the value of her flat, moving expenses) and non-pecuniary damage, including distress and anxiety due to the deterioration of her daughter's health. Making a global assessment comprising both pecuniary and non-pecuniary damage, the Court awarded ESP 4,000,000.[26]

In many cases the Court denies monetary compensation for non-pecuniary damage, although the existence of such damage and the necessary causal link are accepted. In *Goodwin v. the United Kingdom*, an order requiring a journalist to disclose his source and the fine imposed upon him for having refused to do so violated Article 10 (freedom of expression). The Court accepted 'that there was a causal link between the anxiety and distress suffered and the breach found of the Convention.' Yet it held that 'in the circumstances of the case, ... this finding [of violation] constitutes adequate just satisfaction in respect of the damage claimed under this head.'[27]

---

[25] See Judgment of 24 Nov. 1994, Series A no. 296-B, para. 44 ('The Court cannot speculate as to the conclusions which the *Conseil d'Etat* would have reached if it had not sought the minister's interpretation of the Protocol. It considers, however, that the applicants must have suffered non-pecuniary damage, for which the findings of violations in this judgment do not constitute sufficient reparation. Taking its decision on an equitable basis, as required by Article 50, it awards them FRF 100, 000 under this head.').

[26] See Judgment of 9 Dec. 1994, Series A no. 303-C, para. 65.

[27] Judgment of 27 March 1996, Reports 1996-II no. 7, para. 50. One may only speculate about the nature of the 'circumstances' making the finding of the violation sufficient. The fact that the finding of a violation was largely based on the fundamental importance of the freedom of press in a democratic society – i.e. a general 'policy' consideration as distinct from the individual circumstances of the applicant – may have played a role in this case as well as in cases (see infra) in which the violation results from the mere existence of a certain law. In other words, the applicant may have been regarded as 'representing' a general interest, the importance of which overrides his personal interest in the case. Cf. also Enrich Mas, supra note 1, 787. Sharpe, supra note 1, 814, refers to certain criticism made against the practice of regarding the mere judgment as just satisfaction on the ground that 'la condition de l'application de l'article 50 (un constat de violation) ne peut être en même temps la conséquence juridique découlant de cette disposition'.

In some cases the Court has even denied that the violation has caused any non-pecuniary damage or prejudice at all. In those circumstances, of course, no compensation is granted.[28]

The finding of violation is also typically regarded as sufficient just satisfaction in cases where the violation results from the mere existence of a certain law and the application is in reality aimed at having the law changed. In *Modinos v. Cyprus*, a prohibition on homosexual relations between consenting adults in the Criminal Code was regarded as a violation of the applicant's private life notwithstanding the fact that the applicant had never been prosecuted for his activities or his sexual orientation. The Court refused compensation for 'mental stress and suffering' and other alleged damage, considering that, 'in the circumstances of the case, the finding of a breach of Article 8 constitutes sufficient just satisfaction under this head for the purposes of Article 50.'[29]

Whether or not compensation for non-pecuniary damage is awarded depends not only on the nature of the violation but also on the 'procedural attitude' of the applicant. A specific amount of compensation has to be claimed. As noted by a well-informed writer, 'the absence of adequate specification gives the impression that monetary compensation is not the main purpose of the applicant's action before the Convention institutions.'[30] Where no specific amount is requested, the Court usually regards the finding of a violation in itself as sufficient just satisfaction.[31] The judgment rendered in *Papageorgiou v. Greece* in 1997, however, can be seen to support the

---

[28] In *Kerojärvi v. Finland*, Judgment of 19 July 1995, Series A no. 322, Article 6 was found to have been violated due to non-communication of certain documents to the applicant in domestic proceedings. The Court held that it had 'not been shown that the non-communication caused him any non-pecuniary prejudice' and was therefore 'of the view that the finding of a violation of Article 6 § 1 itself constitutes adequate just satisfaction.' Para. 46. This presumably has to be seen against the background of the somewhat 'technical' nature of the violation.

[29] Judgment of 22 April 1993, Series A no. 259, para. 30. See also Enrich Mas, supra note 1, 787; Frowein & Peukert, supra note 1, 688 and the other cases mentioned therein. The possibility cannot be excluded that fear of an influx of cases based on the law found to be in violation of the Convention may have played some role in formulating the policy of not granting compensation. This possibility was raised by Judge Kooijmanns at the seminar.

[30] Enrich Mas, supra note 1, 787.

[31] See, e.g., *John Murray v. the United Kingdom*, Judgment of 8 Feb. 1996, Reports 1996-I no. 1 paras. 74-76 (claim for compensation for pecuniary and non-pecuniary damage 'in such an amount as the Court might consider equitable' rejected in a case in which a violation of Article 6 was found on the basis of lack of access to a solicitor). Cf., however, *Young, James and Webster*, supra note 14, in which compensation for non-pecuniary damage was granted notwithstanding the fact that no specific amount was claimed. In this case the Government had, in settlement negotiations, offered certain sums under this head, and these sums served as guidance for the determination of compensation by the Court. See Judgment (Article 50), paras. 12-13.

proposition that, in the case of a flagrant violation, compensation for non-pecuniary damage may be granted even in the absence of a specification of the amount claimed.[32] The Court never grants symbolic compensation, such as 'one franc'.[33]

It should also be noted that costs and expenses incurred by a successful applicant are granted as one item of 'just satisfaction' under Article 50. A somewhat technical subject matter of its own, the question of costs and expenses is not dealt with here at any length. Let it be mentioned, however, that upon the fulfilment of other relevant conditions, costs are also granted in cases where the mere judgment is regarded as sufficient satisfaction for any damage.[34]

The Court has never explicitly granted punitive damages but it may be that, within its wide discretion to determine the amount of compensation, it sometimes takes into account considerations (punishment and deterrence) coming close to the idea of punitive or exemplary damages. In *Aksoy v. Turkey*, in which the Court for the first time classified a violation of Article 3 as 'torture',[35] the applicant sought 25,000 pounds for non-pecuniary damage which, it was contended, should be increased by a further 25,000 in the event that the Court found 'an aggravated violation of the Convention' on the grounds of so-called administrative practice. The Court did not address this issue, since it did not find sufficient evidence of the administrative practice, but '[i]n view of the extremely serious violations'it 'decided to award the full amounts of compensation sought as regards pecuniary and non-pecuniary

---

[32] The Court granted 2,500,000 drachmas for the violation of the applicant's right to a fair hearing, although the applicant had left the amount of the reparation sought for non-pecuniary damage to be determined by the Court. See Judgment of 22 Oct. 1997, Reports 1997-VI no. 54 paras. 53-56. The finding of the violation was based on legislative intervention which, when viewed against the background of its timing and method, was decisive in ensuring that the outcome of proceedings between the applicant and the State was favourable to the latter, whereas without the intervention the result would inevitably have been the contrary. See paras. 34-40.

[33] Enrich Mas, supra note 1, 787. A symbolic sum may, however, be awarded by the Committee of Ministers in those cases which (under the system in force pending the entry into force of the 11th Protocol on 1 Nov. 1998) are not brought before the Court. It is worth noting that the Committee (whose decision is not regarded as giving moral satisfaction in the same way as does a judgment of the Court) normally awards pecuniary compensation even in cases where the Court might consider the mere judgment to constitute sufficient satisfaction. See Krüger, supra note 1, 267.

[34] Generally see N. Sansonetis, 'Costs and Expenses', in: *The European System for the Protection of Human Rights* (supra note 1), 755-773.

[35] Article 3: 'No one shall be subjected to torture or to inhuman or degrading treatment or punishment.'

damage.'[36] This reasoning can be understood as indicating that it was the seriousness of the violation from the point of view of the victim rather than any wish to 'punish' the State that determined the high level of the compensation.[37] Both considerations, however, may play a role.

III. QUESTIONS RELATING TO THE LEVEL AND ASSESSMENT OF COMPENSATION

The starting point for assessing the amount of compensation is the full amount of the loss, provided a claim has been made for the full loss. Examples have been given where the valuation of compensation for pecuniary damage does not present any particular problems. If the amount of the fines or tax imposed is the amount of the material loss, no specific valuation problems arise.[38]

Full compensation is also, at least as a rule, the standard of compensation in cases involving property losses incurred due to a violation of Article 1 of the First Protocol. Only rarely is the amount of loss in these cases as easily determinable as in the case of *Stran Greek Refineries v. Greece*, in which arbitrary annulment of an arbitral award constituted the breach. The amount of the award could be taken as the basis for the compensation.[39]

The valuation of tangible property, on the other hand, may pose problems. Two cases involving deprivation of real property in violation of the basic conditions defined in Article 1 of the Protocol are discussed below. They are also of interest from the point of view of the general international law of expropriation.

In the case of *Papamichalopoulos v. Greece* the Court found a violation on the basis of a *de facto* expropriation (occupation of land by the Greek Navy since 1967) which had lasted more than 25 years by the date of the principal judgment of 24 June 1993. The question of the application of Article 50 was

---

[36] Judgment of 18 Dec. 1996, Reports 1996-VI no. 26 para. 113. Awarding the full amount sought is exceptional. See also Lawson & Schermers, *Leading Cases of the European Court of Human Rights,* 1997, 667; Frowein & Peukert, supra note 1, 672-73; Krüger, supra note 1, 268-69.

[37] This would appear to be even clearer in the light of *Aydin v. Turkey,* Judgment of 25 Sep. 1997, Reports 1997-VI no. 50. See infra note 51 and the text preceding it.

[38] See supra note 13 and the cases mentioned therein. Of course, the matters may be more complicated if, in addition to the fine (or tax), compensation is also claimed for other elements of damage.

[39] See Judgment of 9 Dec. 1994, Series A no. 301-B, para. 81 ('... the operative part of the arbitration award declared Stran's claims against the State unfounded in so far as they exceeded 116,273,442 drachmas, 16,054,165 US dollars and 614,627 French francs. Having regard to its finding [of violation of Article 1 of the Protocol] at paragraph 75, the Court concludes that the applicants are entitled to reimbursement of these sums.').

not found to be ready for decision and was therefore reserved. In its Article 50 judgment, the Court emphasized that:

> The act of the Greek Government which the Court held to be contrary to the Convention was not an expropriation that would have been legitimate but for the failure to pay compensation; it was a taking by the State of land belonging to private individuals, which has lasted twenty-eight years, the authorities ignoring the decisions of national courts and their own promises to the applicants to redress the injustice committed in 1967 by the dictatorial regime.

> The unlawfulness of such dispossession inevitably affects the criteria to be used for determining the reparation owed by the respondent State ...[40]

In those circumstances and in the absence of restitution within six months of the judgment, the Court ordered the Greek Government to pay the applicants 'for damage and loss of enjoyment since the authorities took the possession of the land in 1967, the current value of the land, increased by the appreciation brought about by the existence' of certain buildings which had been erected on the land since the occupation, as well as the construction costs of those buildings.[41] In addition, the applicants were granted compensation for 'non-pecuniary damage arising from the feeling of helplessness and frustration'.[42]

The case of *Hentrich v. France* concerned pre-emption of real property by tax authorities found by the Court to have violated the requirement of lawfulness and the principle of proportionality. The Court determined that 'the calculation of pecuniary damage must be based on the current market value of the land'.[43] As in *Papamichalopoulos and Others*, it held that any increase in the value of the property between the violation and the date of the judgment was to benefit the applicant.

The approach adopted in these two cases bears close resemblance to the classical *Case Concerning the Factory at Chorzów*,[44] in which the Permanent Court of International Justice held that one method 'to wipe out' all the concequences of an unlawful taking could consist of an estimation of the (higher) value of the property at the time of the judgment, rather than the time of dispossession. By also granting compensation for non-pecuniary damage in *Papamichalopoulos and Others*, the European Court of Human Rights has included an item which, although not punitive in nature, may in its practical effect come close to 'such punitive or exemplary' damages as are sometimes

---

[40] Judgment (Article 50), supra note 5, para. 36. The principal judgment has been published as no. 260-B in Series A.

[41] Judgment (Article 50), para. 39.

[42] Para. 43. In all, the just satisfaction awarded amounted to more than 5,500 million drachmas.

[43] Judgment of 22 Sep. 1994, supra note 6, para. 71.

[44] *Germany v. Poland*, 1928 PCIJ, Ser. A No. 17 (Judgment of 13 Sep. 1928). This case was relied on by the Court in *Papamichalopoulos*. See Judgment (Article 50), para. 36.

argued to constitute a specific, additional, remedy for unlawful expropriation under general international law.[45]

As to the actual methods applied to determine the current value of the property, the two cases just discussed differed radically. In *Papamichalopoulos and Others*, the Court appointed experts whose report it accepted as a basis for the assessment of damages.[46] This method has not been applied since. The experience may in some respects have been slightly discouraging, and cost/benefit calculations may in any event favour the appointment of experts only in cases involving exceptionally valuable property.

In the *Hentrich* case the Court, instead of appointing experts, resorted to a rather rough estimation of the current value of the land. 'Making its assessment of the damage flowing from the loss of the property and of the enjoyment of it on an equitable basis, as required by Article 50', the Court ended up with a figure of 800,000 francs under this head.[47]

While in cases of deprivation of possessions an approximation of the value of the land may not be an entirely satisfactory solution[48] – property such as real estate has a value which, in principle, is possible to determine – estimation may be inevitable in cases of lesser interferences (qualifying, for example, as a violation of the right to 'peaceful enjoyment of property' within the meaning of the first sentence of Article 1 of the First Protocol). If the ownership remains intact, just satisfaction cannot be such as to reflect the current value of the property.

The *locus classicus* example of such interference is the case of *Sporrong and Lönnroth* concerning expropriation permits (for eight and twenty-three years, respectively) and building prohibitions which, without amounting to *de facto* expropriation, impeded the full enjoyment of the applicants' property rights for a long time. In its Article 50 judgment the Court first defined the criteria which should be taken into account, then proceeded to an estimation of the amount of compensation payable in the light of those criteria.

The Court accepted that a municipality should, after obtaining an expropriation permit, be given some time for planning before the final decision on expropriation. As four years could be regarded as sufficient in this

---

[45] In the *Hentrich* case no compensation was granted for non-pecuniary damage, possibly because no specific amount was claimed under this head. See Judgment of 22 Sep. 1994, paras. 68 and 71. Cf. supra note 30 and the text preceding it.

[46] See Judgment (Article 50), especially para. 39.

[47] Judgment of 3 July 1995 (Article 50), Series A no. 320-A, para. 11.

[48] It should be pointed out, however, that approximation of the value of the property taken is by no means a method resorted to only by the European Court of Human Rights. See M. Pellonpää, 'Valuation of Expropriated or Nationalized Property in International Arbitral Practice of Recent Years', *Essays in International Law* (Publications of the Finnish Branch of the International Law Association), 1987, 145-168.

case, the periods of damage were taken to be four and nineteen years. Elements of damages within these periods included factors such as limitations on the utilisation of the properties, as well as difficulties in obtaining loans secured by mortgage. To these could be added prolonged periods of uncertainty and the non-pecuniary damage caused by a violation of Article 6 which had also been established by the Court.[49] The Court concluded that

> The damage is made up of a number of elements which cannot be severed and none of which lends itself to a process of precise calculation. The Court has taken these elements together on an equitable basis, as is required by Article 50. For this purpose, it has had regard, firstly, to the differences in value [between the two estates in question] and, secondly, to the difference between the two periods of damage.

> The Court thus finds that the applicants should be afforded satisfaction assessed at 800,000 SEK for the Sporrong Estate and at 200,000 SEK for Mrs. Lönnroth.[50]

As the examples cited show, the Court frequently emphasizes its duty to proceed to an assessment of compensation on an equitable basis. While in cases concerning violation of property rights it may be possible to identify factors which must be taken into account in such an assessment, in situations concerning compensation for non-pecuniary damage this may not be as easy. The gravity of the violation is an important element in this regard, as shown by recent cases in which Turkey has been found to have violated the prohibition against torture (Article 3). Thus the relatively high compensation of 25,000 pounds awarded in *Aydin v. Turkey* was explained by the Court 'having regard to the seriousness of the violation suffered by the applicant while in custody and the enduring psychological harm which she may be considered to have suffered on account of being raped'.[51]

The cases of *Aksoy* and *Aydin* (25,000 pounds in both) indicate that there is a foreseeable level of compensation in torture cases. Recent case-law also gives some guidance about the level of compensation in, for example, cases concerning unlawful deprivation of liberty.[52] On the other hand, the amount of compensation – if any – for non-pecuniary damage caused by a violation

---

[49] See Judgment of 18 Dec. 1984 (Article 50), Series A no. 88, paras. 22-25.

[50] Para. 32.

[51] Judgment (supra note 37), para. 131. Cf. also the *Aksoy* case, supra note 36.

[52] Compare the following cases: *K.-F. v. Germany*, Judgment of 27 Nov. 1997, Reports 1997-VII no. 58 (the finding of a violation sufficient in a case where lawful detention had been exceeded by 45 minutes); *Raninen v. Finland*, Judgment of 16 Dec. 1997, Reports 1997-VIII no. 60 (FIM 10,000 awarded for an unlawful deprivation of liberty of some two hours; the fact that the applicant was kept handcuffed without special justification may have been relevant); *Sakik and Others v. Turkey*, Judgment of 26 Nov. 1997, Reports 1997-VII no. 58 (FF 25,000 for a deprivation of liberty lasting 12 days; FF 30,000 for 14 days).

of Article 6 ('fair trial') varies greatly, reflecting the great variety of factual circumstances which may constitute such a violation.[53]

In assessing the amount of compensation for non-pecuniary damage, the Court does not consider itself bound by domestic practices, 'although it may derive some assistance from them.'[54]

IV. INTEREST

Article 50 does not contain any reference to interest. This is also the case with many international claims conventions; yet the ordering of interest is customary in international claims practice even without a specific clause in the relevant treaty.[55] As stated by the Iran-United States Claims Tribunal, 'claims for interest are part of the compensation sought and do not constitute a separate cause of action requiring their own independent jurisdictional grant.'[56]

Although certainly empowered to award interest as a part of just satisfaction under Article 50, the Court was for a long time reluctant to do so. It did occasionally include the interest factor as an element of compensation ('compensatory' interest, as distinct from 'default' or 'moratory' interest). For example, in *Stran Greek Refineries* the Court granted simple interest of 6 per cent calculated from the day of the violation until the day of the award, since

---

[53] To mention a recent case, in *Zana v. Turkey*, Judgment of 25 Nov. 1997, Reports 1997-VII no. 57, the Court awarded the applicant FF 40,000 (to be converted into Turkish liras at the rate applicable at the date of the payment) for non-pecuniary damage on the basis of a breach of Article 6 in connection with which both the 'fairness' and 'length' requirements of the provision had been violated. Compare the cases of *X v. France* (supra note 23: FF 150,000) and *Beaumartin v. France* (supra note 25: FF 100,000).

[54] *Z. v. Finland*, Judgment of 25 Feb. 1997, Reports 1997-I no. 31 para. 122. In this case the applicant's right to private life (Article 8) had been violated in that information about her HIV infection had been made known in connection with criminal proceedings against her husband X (who was also HIV positive). The husband was ultimately convicted of violent sexual offences. The Government argued that compensation, if any, for non-pecuniary damage 'should not reach the level of the awards made in respect of the four victims of the offences committed by X, the highest of which had been FIM 70,000.' Para. 120. The Court, deciding 'on an equitable basis', awarded FIM 100,000 under this head. Para. 112. The claim for non-pecuniary damage was FIM 2 million. Note that the same amount (FIM 100,000) had earlier been awarded as compensation for non-pecuniary damage in another case against Finland in which a violation of Article 8 had also been established. See *Hokkanen v. Finland*, Judgment of 23 September 1994, Series A no. 299-A (violation of the right to family life on the basis of non-enforcement of certain decisions concerning the applicant's right of access to his child). On the question of amounts awarded as non-pecuniary compensation, see Krüger, supra note 1, 264-69.

[55] Generally, see R.B. Lillich, 'Interest in the Law of International Claims', in: *Essays in Honour of Voitto Saario and Toivo Sainio*, 1983, 51-60.

[56] *The Islamic Republic of Iran v. The United States of America*, Decision No. DEC 65-A19-FT, 16 Iran-United States Claims Tribunal Reports, 285, at para. 12.

'the adequacy of the compensation would be diminished if it were to be paid without reference to various circumstances liable to reduce its value, such as the fact that ten years have elapsed since the arbitration decision was rendered.'[57]

For years, however, no default interest (interest from the day of the judgment until the payment) was granted. When faced with a request made in this respect in the first *Sunday Times* case, the Court dismissed it by saying that 'it may be assumed that the United Kingdom will comply promptly with the obligation incumbent on it under Article 53 of the Convention.'[58] Previously the Court did not even indicate any time limit by which the payment obligation arising from Article 53 should be fulfilled.[59]

Apparently as a reaction to certain delays noticed in the payment of compensation granted,[60] the practice changed gradually. As a first step the Court introduced, as from August 1991, a special clause in the operative provisions of its judgments to the effect that the payment of compensation should be made within three months. It was only a logical further step that, as from the beginning of 1996, the Court started ordering default interest, applying the statutory rate applicable in the respondent State as at the date of the adoption of the judgment.[61] The interest is payable from the expiry of the above-mentioned three months until settlement and is awarded even in the absence of any specific request made in this regard.

V. QUESTIONS CONCERNING THE EXECUTION OF COMPENSATION JUDGMENTS

Under the European Convention on Human Rights it is up to the Committee of Ministers of the Council of Europe to supervise the execution of the

---

[57] Judgment, supra note 39, para. 82. See also the *Darby* judgment, supra note 11, para. 38 ('The Court awards Dr. Darby 8,000 kronor under this head [of pecuniary damage], comprising the amount of tax unduly paid in 1979-1981 (3,065 kronor) and interest assessed in the light of the interest rate in Sweden at the time.').

[58] Judgment of 6 Nov. 1980, Series A no. 38, para. 44.

[59] Article 53: 'The High Contracting parties undertake to abide by the decision of the Court in any case to which they are parties.'

[60] Cf. C. Tomuschat, 'Quo Vadis, Argentoratum? The Success Story of the European Convention on Human Rights – and a Few Dark Stains', 12 HRLJ 1992, 401-406, at 404-5.

[61] The judgments of the Court nowadays contain, in the section on 'Application of Article 50 of the Convention', a heading (C) entitled 'Default interest' with, for example, the following contents: 'According to the information available to the Court, the statutory rate of interest applicable in Denmark at the date of adoption of the present judgment is 9.25% per annum.' *A and Others v. Denmark*, Judgment of 8 Feb. 1996, Reports 1996-I no. 2 para. 90. In the operative part of the Judgment, the Court ordered 'that simple interest at an annual rate of 9.25% shall be payable from the expiry of the above-mentioned three months until settlement.'

judgments rendered by the Court. The Committee will retain this task, presently based on Article 54 of the Convention ('The judgment of the Court shall be trasmitted to the Committee of Ministers which shall supervise its execution.'), even under the new system to be established upon the entry into force of Proctocol no. 11.

Where the Court has awarded 'just satisfaction' in the form of compensation, the Committee of Ministers requests from the State party information about the measures taken with a view to executing the judgment. Once the Committee is satisfied that the compensation has been paid (and any possible general measures necessitated by the violation taken), it issues a resolution stating that it has completed its tasks under Article 54.

The system has functioned relatively well in that such payment delays as have occurred have usually been rather insignificant. In the two Greek cases of recent years with very high compensation awards, *Papamichalopoulos and Others* and *Stran Greek Refineries*, however, the applicants have faced serious difficulties. In the latter case, in which the judgment was rendered in December 1994, the Committee of Ministers in May 1996 urged 'the Government of Greece to proceed without delay to the payment of the amount corresponding to the value of the just satisfaction at 9 March 1995' (i.e. the end of the three-month period within which the compensation should have been paid).[62] Finally, on 20 March 1997 the Committee was able to adopt its final resolution noting that the compensation, increased so as to take account of the delay, had been paid.[63]

Occasionally difficulties have arisen not only due to delayed payment by the State but also as a consequence of intervening events in the form of seizure of the sums awarded by the applicant's creditors. The permissibility of such interventions may depend on the circumstances. Thus it is accepted that Governments may set off gainst the Court's cost award their claims for costs owed by the applicants due to domestic proceedings.[64]

The question is not as clear as regards the right of creditors to seize sums awarded by the Court for material or non-material damage. The Court was first invited to express its view of the permissibility of such measures in connection with the *Ringeisen* case.[65] In the light of the 'Interpretation Judgment' rendered in that case in 1973, it seemed (as concluded by one author) 'clear that compensation awarded by the Court under the head of non-pecuniary damages should be paid to the injured party free from any

---

[62] Res. (Int.) DH (96) 251.
[63] Res. DH (97) 184.
[64] See Flauss, supra note 1, 15-16; Krüger, supra note 1, 263-64.
[65] Judgments of 16 July 1971, 22 June 1972 (Article 50) and 23 June 1973 (Interpretation of the Judgment of 22 June 1972), Series A nos. 13, 15 and 16.

attachment or seizure under national law.'[66] As to compensation for material damage, the seizure could be considered possible.

In applying the principles just mentioned, problems may arise in cases in which the Court has awarded a 'lump sum' without indicating which part of the sum is attributable to the material loss, which part to 'moral' loss.

In *Allenet de Ribemont v. France*, the applicant was awarded damages, both pecuniary and non-pecuniary, in the amount 2,000,000 FF for violation of the presumption of innocence and requirements regarding the length of procee-dings. In the main proceedings the applicant had 'asked the Court to hold that the State should guarantee him against any application for enforcement of the judgment delivered by the Paris *tribunal de grande instance* on 14 March 1979 or, failing that, to give him leave to seek an increase in the amount of just satisfaction at a later date.'[67] In accordance with its traditional approach concerning requests for specific orders, however, the Court held 'that under Article 50 it does not have jurisdiction to issue such an order to a Contracting State ...'[68]

Mr. Allenet de Ribemont in fact never received the sum in question, since an attachment based on the above-mentioned domestic judgment was effected on 3 March 1995 at the request of his private creditors. This led the European Commission of Human Rights to request interpretation of the Court's main judgment with the following questions:

Firstly: Is it to be understood that Article 50 ... means that any sum awarded under this head must be paid to the injured party personally and be exempt from attachment?

Secondly: In respect of sums subject to legal claims under French law, should a dis-tinction be made between the part of the sum awarded under the head of pecuniary damage and the part awarded under the head of non-pecuniary damage?

Thirdly: If so, what were the sums which the Court intended to grant the applicant in res-pect of pecuniary damage and non-pecuniary damage respectively?[69]

In its 'Interpretation Judgment' of 7 August 1995 the Court held that it lacked jurisdiction regarding the first question which it understood 'as an invitation to interpret Article 50 in a general, abstract way'[70]. Regarding the two other questions, it considered the operative provisions of the judgment so clear as not to need interpretation.[71]

---

[66] Krüger, supra note 1, p. 262.
[67] Judgment of 10 February 1995, Series A no. 308, para. 63.
[68] Para. 65. See supra note 3 and the text preceding it.
[69] Quoted from the Judgment of 7 August 1996 (Interpretation), Reports 1996-III no. 12, para. 12.
[70] Para. 19.
[71] Para. 23.

Although the Court's decision was based on lack of jurisdiction and lack of need for interpretation, rather than on an examination of the merits of the questions put by the Commission, the conclusion seems inevitable that Contracting parties are free, subject to their own laws, to allow attachment by private creditors.[72]

VI. CONCLUDING REMARKS

The supervision system created by the European Convention on Human Rights will undergo a profound change upon the entry into force of Protocol no. 11 on 1 November 1998. By virtue of this reform a new full-time European Court of Human Rights will be created to replace the present Commission and Court. Substantive obligations under the Convention and its additional Protocols will remain intact, with some modifications of a technical nature.[73]

Although no radical changes are envisaged, the entry into force of the new supervision system may nevertheless provide an opportunity to reconsider certain practices and interpretations concerning the substantive obligations under the Convention, including the question of 'just satisfaction'.

Thus the new Court could, without breaking with the past, increase transparency by elaborating, for example, why in certain cases the mere judgment constitutes sufficient just satisfaction for non-pecuniary damage, whereas in others it does not.[74] The tendency, already discernible in some judgments, of giving reasons for the amount of compensation for non-pecuniary damage (instead of a mere reference to equitable considerations) could be enhanced.[75] It would also appear to be possible to be specific as concerns the distinction between pecuniary and non-pecuniary damage and to

---

[72] Frowein & Peukert, supra note 1, 720: 'Daraus [i.e. from the Judgment of 7 August 1996] kann gefolgert werden, dass Pfändung durch private Gläubiger zulässig ist.'

[73] This applies also to the provision on just satisfaction. In the revised Convention the present Article 50 will be replaced by the following Article 41:

If the Court finds that there has been a violation of the Convention or the protocols thereto, and if the internal law of the High Contracting Party allows only partial reparation to be made, the Court shall, if necessary, afford just satisfaction to the injured party.

[74] Cf. Krüger, supra note 1, 265-69. The *McCann and Others* judgment shows that it is not impossible to give reasons for not awarding compensation (although the reasoning in that particular case may still leave something to be desired). See supra notes 11 and 12 and the related text.

[75] Cf. the *Aydin* judgment, supra note 51 and the text preceding it. See also *Johnson v. the United Kingdom*, Judgment of 24 Oct. 1997, Reports 1997-VII no. 55, para. 77 (some elaboration of factors justifying the compensation of 10,000 pounds for non-pecuniary damage caused by a violation of Article 5, para. 1(e)).

avoid lump sum awards which make it impossible to make this distinction. In so doing the new Court might, on a proper occasion, be able to reconsider the question at issue in the *Ringeisen* and *Allenet de Ribemont* cases.

Under the new system, the 'subsidiarity principle' and the relationship between national courts and the European Court will remain as they are now. Even so, closer interplay between the European and national level courts might be contemplated with a view to coming as close as possible to the ideal of reparation, i.e. the restoration of the situation existing before the breach. To achieve this, increased resort to adjourning proceedings under Article 50 and referring cases to domestic courts for the possible re-opening of proceedings (or for the determination of very complex compensation questions[76]) could be envisaged in proper cases. Such changes cannot, however, be effected by the new Court acting alone and may necessitate also reforms at the level of national systems. Thus, increased co-operation between Strasbourg and national jurisdictions may be needed in order to guarantee the effective functioning of the 'reparation regime' of the European Convention on Human Rights in the new challenges facing it.[77]

---

[76] Cf. *Case of Pressos Compania Naviera S.A. and Others v. Belgium*, Judgment of 3 July 1997, Reports 1997-IV no. 42 (Article 50).

[77] The manuscript was completed in January 1998. A few remarks concerning subsequent developments which took place by the end of 1998 are made below.

As to the question of punitive damages (see supra notes 35-37 and the related text), in *Akdivar and Others v. Turkey*, Judgment of 1 April 1998 (Article 50), Reports 1998-II no. 69, para. 38, the Court explicitly rejected a claim for such damages. In *Tekin v. Turkey*, Judgment of 9 June 1998, to be published in Reports 1998, the Court awarded compensation for inhuman treatment not qualified as torture in the amount of 10,000 pounds (cf. supra note 51 and the preceding and following text). A high amount of compensation (over 300,000 Cyprus pounds), was awarded in *Loizidou v. Turkey*, Judgment of 28 July 1998 (Article 50), to be published in Reports 1998. The compensation was not paid within the prescribed time-limit of three months and had not been paid by the end of the year (cf. supra notes 62 and 63 and the related text). The reform brought about by the 11th Protocol entered into force on 1 November 1998. The first judgments of the new European Court of Human Rights were expected for January 1999.

Discussion (Part 2)

Pisillo Mazzeschi: I would like to raise two brief points.

The first point concerns the report of Professor Pellonpää and the relationship between Article 5, para. 5, and Article 50 of the European Convention on Human Rights. Professor Pellonpää said that Article 5 is a primary rule and so he probably implied that Article 50 is a secondary rule. Now I am not sure I understood this. I think there is a more simple and more important difference between these two articles. Article 5 deals with the right to compensation that the individual has under the domestic law of a State. There is, in other words, an obligation of the State to grant the individual compensation in its domestic courts and under its domestic law. I would call it a compensation of domestic law or a national compensation. Article 50 seems to me a rather different rule, because here one could speak of an international reparation (I will try to develop this concept tomorrow). In fact, under Article 50, an international court, the European Court of Human Rights, awards reparation, usually monetary compensation, in favour of the individual. Then, one has to discuss whether Article 50 contemplates a real international reparation for the benefit of the individual or only an inter-State reparation, an inter-State responsibility. Once there was the idea that the obligation of the wrongdoing State to grant reparation, under Article 50, was not an obligation towards the individual, but rather towards the other States parties. That was the traditional perspective of international law. Now I think that Article 50 can be interpreted more and more as giving a right to the individual, a right to have a satisfaction or a compensation, and this right is implemented by an international court. So, this is a very important example, together with Article 63 of the American Convention, of something new in international law. On the contrary, there are many rules similar to Article 5 of the European Convention, which provide a domestic compensation to individuals for unlawful arrest or a miscarriage of justice. So, I think this is the main difference between Article 50 and Article 5. Maybe this difference could also be described in terms of primary and secondary rules; but it is not entirely clear what it means when one speaks of primary rules for domestic reparation and of secondary rules for international

A. Randelzhofer and C. Tomuschat (eds.), State Responsibility and the Individual, 131–147.
© 1999 *Kluwer Law International. Printed in Great Britain.*

reparation. I just wanted to make this clear to myself and maybe I will receive an answer from Professor Pellonpää.

The other point I wanted to raise is a more general one. I think, if I may interpret the thoughts of the organizers of this meeting, that they had the idea, which was very attractive to me, of linking a particular topic, that of individual reparation claims, to a more general and theoretical problem, namely the legal position of the individual under international law. Now I think that in the discussion we should come back to this topic, maybe tomorrow, but also now, because I think that we have lost sight of that problem, especially in the afternoon. This does not mean that we should stay here to develop theoretical discussions about the international personality in general or the dualistic or monistic conception of international law or things like that. But I think that the goal of this meeting was to start from one precise area of international law, that is human rights, and to link it to the general problem of the position of the individual. The novelty of our topic is that, while in the field of human rights the international personality of individuals is usually dealt with from the point of view of the primary rules or the procedural mechanisms provided for in the human rights treaties, here we make an attempt at starting from the secondary rules, from the rules on responsibility. I think that this is interesting. So the problem is: Does an individual have a right to reparation for breach of human rights? And does this right derive from domestic law or from international law or from an obligation of international law which is enforceable only through domestic law? And is the obligation of international law a self-executing, or a non self-executing obligation? I believe that we should try not to lose sight of these problems.

Danilenko: I really enjoyed the presentation of Professor Pellonpää. I think that when you consider the European system, it displays serious contradictions. On the one hand, it claims to be the most effective system of human rights enforcement on this planet. The European Court of Human Rights actually functions as a kind of Pan-European constitutional court. On the other hand, we have Article 50 of the European Convention which is extremely restricted. Under Article 50, in cases where the internal law of the party violating the Convention allows only partial reparation to be made for the consequences of a breach, the European Court may, 'if necessary, afford just satisfaction to the injured party'. Only if 'it is necessary', and only 'just', not full compensation.

However, I think that even full compensation may not amount to full reparation understood in a broader sense. A domestic court judgment rendered in violation of the European Convention's provisions may still remain in effect even after a breach of the Convention has been found by the European Court of Human Rights. A 'just' (not full!) compensation may be paid to the victim who, because of criminal conviction, may still remain in prison. This is so because decisions of the European Court do not automatically quash decisions of national courts. In view of this, it may be advisable at this point to think about extending the powers of the European Court in this respect. We need a rule imposing a legal obligation to make provisions for review proceedings aimed at re-opening domestic court decisions in cases when simple compensation leaves the aggrieved person unsatisfied. While at this stage the proposal to give the European Court the power to annul or reverse national decisions may be unacceptable to some States, governments may consider introducing a softer approach which would require States to reopen criminal proceedings in certain situations. There are several European States which have adopted legislation enabling review subsequent to a finding of a violation of the Convention. Because the possibility of review proceedings may be considered as the most appropriate means of advancing the implementation of obligations to comply with the European Convention, this approach may set an example for other members of the Council of Europe. The adoption of this model should particularly be encouraged in the countries of Central and Eastern Europe, many of which have already declared international law to be part of the law of the land. Review procedures will only reinforce the legal authority of the judgments of the European Court of Human Rights throughout Eastern Europe.

Tomuschat: I enjoyed very much the two presentations of this afternoon, but I would like to join Professor Pisillo Mazzeschi in putting a couple of questions. In particular, I have listened very carefully to what was said by Michael Reisman. He talked about the cases before the Interamerican Court, but he did not really answer the question whether *he* finds that under Article 63 of the American Convention the individual has a right, an enforceable right to compensation. The text talks about the obligations of the Court, providing: 'It shall also rule if appropriate, that the consequences, ...'. Now, can we speak of a right of the individual if we compare the two clauses of Article 50 of the European Convention and of Article 63? There are in Article 50 the famous words 'if necessary', and in Article 63 'if appropriate'. This seems to indicate a large measure of discretion of the two courts. In *MacCann*,[1] which is the most glaring case under the European Convention, although the Court found a violation of the right to life, the most important right in the hierarchy of values, it denied any compensation because the victims were terrorists. The *McCann* case has serious implications because the Court, on one hand,

---

[1] *McCann and Others v. United Kingdom*, Judgment of 27 Sep. 1995, Eur. Ct. H. R., Ser. A no. 324.

assessed the facts according to a legal yardstick, on the other, as far as compensation was concerned, according to a moral yardstick. Thus two evaluations ran parallel to one another. It is hard to accept that a breach of the legal rules was found and that nonetheless this breach was left without substantive consequences whatsoever because of the conduct of the victims. I see here an inconsistency. Maybe the Court was not persuaded of its own judgement and wanted to satisfy both sides, adopting therefore a typical judicial attitude, namely to strike a compromise between two contradictory positions. Maybe Mr. Pellonpää can explain to us the background of *McCann*. The fact is that the suspected terrorists were simply gunned down, which makes it, in my eyes, a terrible case.

Now coming to a further point. What I have never understood well in the jurisprudence of the European Court is that the Court, as far as procedural defects are concerned, very often states that it cannot speculate about the potential outcome of the proceeding if procedural rules had been fully observed. I do not agree with that jurisprudence. Even if an important witness, for instance, was not called, the Court essentially dismisses the argument. Although it finds a violation of the European Convention, it says: 'This can have no consequences, because we cannot speculate about the outcome of the proceedings.' This makes almost a mockery of procedural guarantees. National judges can violate them without any consequences for the judgements that were handed down by them. This is a basic inconsistency, and therefore the jurisprudence of the Court should be changed. Of course I see the difficulty because the Court does not feel entitled to quash and set aside a national decision and therefore only grants financial compensation. In those cases, the best remedy would be to order a new trial. That would be the adequate form of reparation. The Court should have the courage to jump across the barriers which it has established itself. In my view, it is not confined to just pronouncing on financial compensation according to Article 50. It could smoothly develop its jurisprudence further as it has already done in the two Greek cases concerning property restitution.

Randelzhofer: You are criticizing the decision of the European Court in the *McCann* case, in which compensation was denied, because those men gunned down were terrorists, and your point of criticism was that the Court brought a moral evaluation into the game. My question is whether being a terrorist really is only a moral characterization or whether it is additionally a legal characterization.

Kooijmans: Mr. Chairman, strangely enough we seem to have strayed this afternoon from the topic of reparation to a more specific form of reparation, namely compensation, without having discussed the question whether compensation is always the only or the most ideal form of reparation.

I fully agree that in individual cases it may seem to be the most logical and satisfactory solution. I would like to bring into the discussion, however, the possible effects of such individual compensation-orders. I will give two completely different examples.

The military regime in Surinam – already referred to by Professor Reisman – started its atrocities in December 1982 by arbitrarily murdering 14 of its opponents (lawyers, trade-unionists, journalists, etc.). The victims' relatives submitted a claim to the UN Human Rights Committee, which found the Government to be in violation of its obligations under the Covenant and recommended financial compensation to the victims' relatives. The military refused to pay that compensation. After a number of years, however, a new, democratically elected government replaced the military. Immediately the question arose: should criminal investigations be started into what had really happened in 1982? I discussed the issue with the Minister of Justice who had been one of my students and I started by saying: 'Well, you can give a good example by paying that compensation which has been recommended by the UN Committee.' His reply was sobering; he said: 'That is exactly what I cannot do, because that would prejudge the question of the criminal investigation. People would say: "How can you pay compensation on the basis of a non-binding recommendation without investigating yourself first the alleged criminal behaviour which entailed the international responsibility of Surinam?" The question whether such criminal investigation should take place, however, is first and foremost a political question. The military still are "a State in the State" and a decision to start an investigation may well lead to the end of the present democratically elected government.'

The second example is from my own country and may have to do with what Professor Pellonpää said this morning, namely that, in the case of a general law, the European Court usually does not order compensation if the application of such a general law in an individual case constitutes a violation of the Convention. About ten years ago a Dutch woman filed a complaint with the UN Human Rights Committee. She maintained that the Dutch Social Security System was discriminatory in the sense of Article 26 of the Covenant. The Committee concluded that she was right and recommended financial compensation. The Committee's finding was accepted by the competent Dutch court. The Dutch Government made a quick calculation of the compensation it might by Court order be obliged to pay to all potential victims of that discriminatory legal provision and came to the conclusion that this would amount to an enormous sum. And then a bizarre thing happened. The Netherlands Government seriously considered the possibility of denouncing the Covenant and to become a party again immediately, but this time making a reservation with regard to Article 26. I have given both examples to show that an individual compensation-order may have far-reaching general effects which in my opinion should be taken into account by the supervisory treaty-bodies.

Tomuschat: Just one observation. When the Federal Republic of Germany ratified the Optional Protocol it made a reservation according to which no communication can be brought under the Optional Protocol invoking Article 26 in connection which a right which is not guaranteed under the Covenant.

Ress: I associate myself with the views expressed by some of the previous speakers. I have always had difficulties to fully understand Article 50 of the European Convention on Human Rights. As I understand this provision, States are under the obligation of reparation for a violation. That is the starting point. States have to repair and reparation is a very broad notion in international law, and it is also applicable to the reparation of breaches of human rights violations. This should be the guiding principle, also for the Court looking at the responsibilities and the obligations of the contracting States. I have never quite understood why the Court has been so reluctant, at least the Strasbourg Court, to give some indications or, if not *directives*, at least recommendations as to how States should behave as to repair fully the consequences of a violation. I was attracted by the practice of the Committee which does not hesitate to give one or the other indication. Whether States follow these indications is quite another problem, but at least the Court ought to provide some guidance for the Committee of Ministers.

Then we come to the problem of consequences of violations. In my view one of the consequences, and one of the obligations for States in cases when a breach for instance of a procedural right has been established, would be the *re-opening* of such a proceeding. I cannot imagine that the Convention has really fulfilled its task in cases as in the *Kremzov* case against Austria,[2] where a man who allegedly committed murder is serving his life sentence in an Austrian prison although the Court has established that during the proceedings the rules of fair trial were violated. The man remains in prison, in the knowledge that the trial was not in conformity with the Convention, but nothing happens. There is no procedure in Austrian law, and it would be the same in Germany, permitting to re-open the case. There is now before our Bundestag a draft bill providing for a re-opening procedure in such cases. I find it overdue to fulfill the obligation of contracting States to make reparation in proceedings which violated the Convention.

---

[2]   *Kremzov v. Austria,* Judgment of 21 Sep. 1993, Eur. Ct. H. R., Ser. A no 268-B.

I have never been convinced, I must say, that the interpretation of the words 'if necessary' in Article 50 really gives the Court an extensive margin of appreciation or discretion. The phrase may even be linked to the evaluation of the facts, that is to the question whether under the domestic legal system in one of the member States reparation is partially or completely possible. If it is only partially possible, then of course just satisfaction is necessary. One could in such a way narrow the interpretation of this rather obscure clause in Article 50. I have always had problems to follow the practice, which is in my view near to arbitrariness, that the Court in one case for non-pecuniary damages awards a rather big sum, in other cases without *any explanation* a rather minor sum. No outsider can guess what the Court had in mind. This kind of reasoning is not satisfactory. Taking into account the behaviour of victims as presumed or established terrorists in the *McCann* case, of course, involves a moral judgment about these activities, but this is not directly linked to the violation in issue, that is the killing of these persons. I would accept such judgment if it was directly linked to the outcome of the case, but as I have understood the decision, this was not the case in relation to the behaviour of the victims in the *McCann* case. Another point is the evaluation of compensation for loss of property rights. Also in this respect a great variety of very general criteria about what could be the just amount in a given case can be found. Judge Martens, in a dissenting opinion, rightly stated that in no domestic court such an ill-defined evaluation would ever take place if it came to the question to what amount an individual who has suffered damages would be entitled. There would be experts, there would be more and precise information, but not such an evaluation according to the rule of the thumb (in German: *'über den Daumen peilen'*). I would rather say that even the word 'just' connected with just satisfaction in my view does not allow such procedural approach.

Cassese: Like previous speakers, I share the remark made by my friend Pisillo Mazzeschi to the effect that we should try to conceptualize and to establish some sort of theoretical framework. However, I would also like to add that probably one of the purposes of this workshop is also to go beyond the existing law and try to suggest new solutions, try to point to new avenues which can be followed in discussing these various problems. In this vein, I would like to ask Michael Reisman a couple of questions, which are based on some imaginary situations. He rightly pointed out that in the various cases he described, the defendant is always a government. I wonder whether, and this is a question to him, there are cases where the State, or the courts involved, the American Court of Human Rights or another international judicial institution, are able to identify the authors of the State delinquency consisting of the carrying out of gross violations of human rights. If so, could we imagine a situation whereby the complainant does not request reparation in the form of monetary compensation, but requests an international court to prosecute the individuals who are responsible for those gross violations of human rights? For instance, if they are State officials, police officers, they might not only be prosecuted, but punished, or if this is not possible, they could be dismissed from office, they could be demoted, there are so many possibilities in lieu of monetary compensation. Or if we think again of monetary compensation, could we imagine a complainant requesting a court to oblige the relevant State, the respondent State, to enjoin his State officials to pay compensation to the victims? In this case, the monetary compensation is paid by the torturers, by the authors of gross violations, to the victim, not by the State. I think that it is immoral that a State (i.e. every citizen, since the money comes from the national treasury) should pay. It is immoral that the whole State should pay for the misbehaviour of, say, ten people who are the torturers, or for a particular section of the police. I don't see why the State should take responsibility for all that, when it could oblige the relevant individuals to pay. So again, there might be new ways of approaching the question of reparation.

I also wonder, and this is my second question, whether there are cases where an international court, for instance the American Court of Human Rights, decides that the respondent government is responsible for gross violations of human rights committed by particular military units (we know that there was, in Buenos Aires for instance, a period of gross violations of human rights. There was a special place in Buenos Aires where marine officers tortured a lot of Argentinians). Now if in this case the court finds that the State is responsible and does not decide upon the issue of reparation, could one of the victims go before a national court and say: I will produce the judgment delivered by the international court, which has found that the whole of that particular military unit was responsible for gross acts of torture; since I know that Mr. X was a member of that particular unit, I would like to ask you, domestic court, to enjoin this particular person to pay compensation to me. This could be a civil suit, but I don't see why again we could not think of a legal weapon, as it were, to be provided to an individual at the domestic level, following a decision by an international court, which might decide for various reasons not to pass upon reparation.

Lastly a remark on the question concerning Article 50. I share the views of the previous speakers. I would go so far as to say that, if what I heard about the Gibraltar case is correct, this is a gross breach by the European Court of Human Rights of Article 51, para. 1, of the European Convention on Human Rights because there it is stated that 'reasons shall be given for the judgment of the court'. If you then read the other provision before and after Article 51, it is clear that this applies to any judgment, to any decision of the Court. Here you have a decision in application of Article 50 where no reason whatsoever, no reasons are given for saying: 'We refuse compensation'. This is a gross deviation from one of the basic principles of our civilized countries, namely that courts must give reasons when they reach a particular decision. So I wonder why in the European Court of Human Rights judges do not point out in dissenting opinions that they do not agree with the majority when it fails to spell out reasons for its rulings.

Malanczuk: I would like to start also from the point of view of general international law, because I am trying to think where we are now. What we have examined under the question of individual reparation claims, and the legal position of individuals in international law, is a set of draft articles established by the International Law Commission in which, as Professor Tomuschat quite rightly has commented, the individual appears only as an object. Thus, the ILC draft is not very relevant to the question which we have been posing. Moreover, it is only a draft and it is relevant only insofar as it codifies customary international law. We have not examined this question with respect to certain consequences preferably being drawn from this draft and applied to other issues. Furthermore, we have examined an international treaty of a general nature and there we have found that there is not much material in it to answer our question. At a minimum, the decisions are not binding (if it comes to a decision in that matter at all) even where a provision is made for reparation. Then we have examined the various regional instruments and treaties that exist, two regional human rights treaties, whereas we have left aside the African treaty, which has a different concept and is also referring to peoples' rights (collective rights), but does not provide for any kind of enforcement mechanism as the two sister conventions do in the Americas and in Europe. But we have found that whatever position the individual has with regard to reparation claims under these two regional conventions, it is based on treaties. This does not mean that this necessarily reflects on the customary law position of the individual, and if it did, it could not reflect anything more than regional custom. Even that I would doubt. Consequently, if we are talking about the legal position of the individual in international law, then we are in reality talking about something which is based upon two regional treaties and determines the individual legal personality of that individual under those treaties. Just to clarify the limitation of the scope of the argument.

Second, as to the procedural aspect, I think with regard to provisions like Article 50 of the European Convention and Article 63 of the American Convention, it is not the old discussion whether objective law necessarily also provides for a subjective right. These are human rights instruments with courts, established to enforce the substance of obligations laid down in the treaties. All of us know that once you establish courts, the judges become creative. Especially under the European Convention, the dynamic nature of the Convention is recognized, and this materializes in the creative role of the judge. Now once the judges apply provisions like Article 50 of the European Convention and award certain types of damages to individual claimants in the first cases that come before them, it is natural in practice and in procedure that this leads to subsequent formulations of requests for appropriate remedies on the same level. This entails the development of a procedural right of the individual arising from the practice of the courts.

A point which I would also like to raise is, from the viewpoint of general international law, terminology. Professor Kooijmans has quite rightly pointed out that we have to be clear that reparation is not the same as compensation and that there are many other forms of remedies listed, for example, in the ILC's draft article 42 where the definition of reparation in para. 1 includes restitution in kind, compensation, satisfaction, assurances and guarantees of non-repetition, etc. Now if you look at the terminology in Article 50 of the European Convention, you find first the term 'partial reparation' and later you find the term 'satisfaction', and this latter term seems to me to be the same as 'reparation', but it is not the same as 'satisfaction' in general international law. In general international law the term 'satisfaction' means, as stipulated in article 45 of the ILC draft articles, something which relates to an infringement of the prestige of States, let me put it that way. So what I am trying to draw your attention to is that terminology is not necessarily consistent, which means also that the concepts are not necessarily consistent between the level of general international law and these regional treaties, and now I come to the more interesting point: What are the differences in concepts and terminology between the two conventions we have really come down to discuss? Is there a difference in the common law approach and the civil law approach mixed with the British approach in the European system? Does 'damage' mean the same? Does 'pecuniary damage' mean the same or does 'non-pecuniary damage' mean the same as 'moral damage'? Michael Reisman has been referring to 'moral damage' in several cases in which no material damage had occurred. That needs investigation, and one would have to examine the type of damage in relationship to the particular type of human right being infringed. So it does not make sense to speak in general terms of human rights violations. We are all thinking of loss of life and imprisonment and these kind of things and we have left, as Professor Ress has quite rightly pointed out, property aside, a right which raises quite a number of different questions with regard to reparation, compensation, etc. Therefore, it is necessary to be more specific in the comparison of what specific human rights are involved and what kind of damages are being addressed: loss of life, mental pain, family loss, etc.

This becomes also very clear if one tries to address the question of the direct or indirect link, namely the question of causality or the question of approximate cause. The ILC report of Arangio-Ruiz, if I remember correctly, was the last one dealing with that issue. It came to the conclusion, after a comparison of the national systems and what has developed into international law, that we cannot do very much with the doctrine of approximate cause. Rather useless, he found. We are speaking about direct, indirect causes and approximate causes without examining the typology of the cases involved while this general principle of cause, approximate cause, does not give you much of an indication as to how to solve the question on the abstract level. To summarize, first of all, so far I think the examination has been fruitful only with regard to two specific regional conventions as to the general theme of the subject. And second, the discussion is not specific enough because it is not comparing specific rights under comparable terminology.

Meron: I have greatly benefited from the papers this morning and this afternoon, and join those who argue that we should try to have a higher degree of conceptualization. I realize it is much easier to make comments on papers than to prepare them. So I apologize for making this suggestion. But I would suggest that at least in the conclusions, several pairs of concepts be addressed and compared. First, reparation-compensation, second gross-individual, third international law-national law, namely compensation under one or the other. With regard to the last pair, following a suggestion made by Peter Malanczuk, compensation for a violation of the duty to respect as compared with compensation for the duty to ensure respect. And finally the dichotomy between treaties and customary law: I think that we really should ask ourselves these sorts of questions. What can we learn from this discussion and these papers about emerging principles of general international law?

Having finished with the general comments, just a few very short ones on points of detail. Michael's extremely interesting paper mentioned the fact that in some cases there has been the tendency to award compensation for pain and suffering of the dead person rather than his family. If my memory does not mislead me, this has its origin already in the *Lusitania* cases where Umpire Parker devoted considerable attention to this aspect.[3] Secondly, comfort women were mentioned in the discussion. The compensation which recently has been offered, very modest compensation, I believe something like $20,000, was not in fact offered by the Japanese Government but by a foundation, which brings me to a subject which I believe requires some

---

[3] Opinion of 1 November 1932, RIAA VII, 32.

reflection. The role of privatization now in various developments pertaining to human rights and enforcement of international law is intriguing. In the United States, but not only in the United States, there has been a tendency to contract out the running of prisons to private companies. This raises many questions with regard to human rights, with regard to abuse of force, with regard to discrimination, with regard to imputability. It is one thing that we will have to confront.

Daniel Thürer mentioned Article 3 of Hague Convention No. IV. Article 3 is very significant for any discussion on compensation because in fact it has been interpreted to confer standing on the victims directly against States. And if we add to that the fact that in the Nuremberg jurisprudence Hague Convention No. IV as a whole has been considered customary law, this is a very significant thing. Finally, regarding Judge Kooijmans' fascinating comment I am under the unfortunate impression that recently another State has sent a notice to the Secretary-General denouncing the Political Covenant, so we may have more practice on that.

Pellonpää: I start with questions and comments by Professor Pisillo Mazzeschi. I fully agree with him and think that the only difference between us was the fact that he was able to articulate the issue in a better way than I was. I fully agree that Article 5(5) entails a right to compensation under domestic law and that as such Article 5 is a provision similar to Articles 6, 7, 8, 9, 10, 11, or all the substantive articles. Article 50 deals with the realization of the responsibility of the State vis-à-vis the individual. I did refer to State responsibility, which was simply unprecise language, as I did not intend to say that Article 50 deals with State responsibility in the sense of general international law. In fact the only reason why I took up the comparison between Article 5(5) and Article 50 is that also Article 5 is included in our background paper.

In many comments I have been, in a way, challenged to defend the European Court of Human Rights, which I am not going to do in every respect. Among other things, I have some difficulties to defend the *McCann* judgment, perhaps partly for reasons which may be surprising. I belonged to those in the European Commission for Human Rights who thought that there was no violation in the *McCann* case. I cannot go into details concerning that. Anyway, I think one need not necessarily speak in terms of a contradiction between legal and moral assessment. You may also see the reference to the nature of the applicants, as an idea based on contributory negligence or mitigation of damages, mitigating them down to zero because of the contributory negligence of the applicants. I assume that Professor Randelzhofer had something similar in mind when he made his remark.

Judge Kooijmans, among other interesting comments, raised the question whether behind the non-payment of compensation in cases where the finding of a violation is based on the general existence of a law is the fear of mass influx of claims. This is a matter of guessing, but I could very well imagine that this has been in the minds of some of the judges of the Court which, as has been rightly pointed out, unfortunately does not always live up to the standards of the very Convention in the reasoning of its judgments. Many speakers touched upon the obligation to reopen proceedings. One may recall that the European Court says nowadays, as a kind of general principle, as it did in the *Papamichalopoulos* case,[4] that a judgment in which the Court finds a breach imposes a legal obligation on the respondent State to put an end to the breach and make reparations for its consequences, in such a way as to restore as far as possible the situation existing before the breach. One may argue that in Article 6 cases this really entails a duty of reopening. This is something the Court has not said so far, however, and I do not think that the entry into force of Protocol No. 11 brings about any fundamental change. Although no radical changes are envisaged, however, the entry into force of the new supervision system may nevertheless provide an opportunity to reconsider also certain practices with regard to various articles of the Convention, including the interpretation and application of Article 50. There is much to do especially concerning the reasoning of the compensation judgments. Whether the Court should take the step and rule that proceedings have to be reopened is not an easy question to answer. Violations of Article 6 may be of a very different nature. There may be very technical violations based on the reason that some document has not been communicated to the applicant in the case and so on. And then there are more fundamental violations of the kind referred to by Professor Ress. To start requiring the State to reopen proceedings in all these cases would be a very delicate step. On the other hand, making distinctions would also bring about the difficulty of drawing a borderline between cases where the reopening is required and where it is not. In my view the correct way is really not to make a radical change, but to envisage, by a protocol or something like that, a duty on the national level to reopen the proceedings. Quite generally I think that increased cooperation between the national and the Strasbourg level is something that the new Court will have to consider increasingly. Today it is already possible, in cases of countries where reopening is provided for, that the Court adjourns the examination of questions under Article 50 pending reopening proceedings, and perhaps the States should be encouraged to make such necessary changes in their domestic law as to make this possible. But I would be very cautious

---

[4] *Papamichalopoulos and Others v. Greece,* Judgment of 31 Oct. 1995 (Art. 50), Ser. A no. 330-B.

of suggesting that the European Court of Human Rights should unreservedly enjoin States to reopen proceedings.

Reisman: Well I must say, Mr. Chairman, I am very grateful for the comments that were made, which certainly will influence the final redaction of the paper. A number of questions and of observations were made and President Cassese raised a number of hypothetical points. I will take them up in the order in which they were presented. Christian Tomuschat said: 'Is there a personal right of individual compensation under Article 63?' I don't know how many of you have heard of Wesley Newcomb Hohfeld, the Dean of Yale Law School who probably put the Law School on the international map with his famous essay called 'Fundamental Legal Conceptions'. He showed that the word 'right' was frequently used by lawyers in a meaningless way. It was meaningful only if you could show that there was a correlative and enforceable duty. In international law, obviously we are reluctant to apply that particular test, since so many things that we like to call rights would rapidly disappear, and so we use the word 'right' in a softer sense. But in the quintessential hard sense, is there a correlative duty that can be enforced against the Court to secure a right of compensation for an individual? The answer is no. On the other hand, a substantial power has been assigned to the Court in the American system with respect to those States that have made the additional declaration accepting jurisdiction, for it includes, under Article 63, the right to fashion reparations and, in particular, to order compensation. That's all you can say with respect to that.

Judge Kooijmans quite correctly observes that I spoke about compensation and not reparation. In the paper I point out that Article 63 of the Convention has three components. It has an injunctive element, i.e., the court can enjoin certain ongoing behaviour that is or would lead to violations. It has a reparative competence. The court can order reparations, and it has a compensatory competence. The jurisprudence begins in 1989. In all of the cases, the Court scrupulously avoided exercise of its reparative competence, with one exception, and then it was really ancillary to compensation, as I will explain in a moment. In all the other cases, when the Commission and in one case the family specifically asked for reparative orders, that would have required significant changes in the technique of public order of the defendant State, the Court refused to take the matter up. It said in each case: 'We have made a declaration on the merits, the preceding phase, and that is satisfactory in our view with respect to reparation.' Now why did the Court do this? Obviously, the Court understood the merits order was ineffective because the defendant government was not rushing to fashion a form of implementation. I think the Court appreciated that further to address the issue of reparation would have taken it into a direct confrontation with the effective elite in each of the States, and that there would be no compliance. So it focused on that section of Article 63 in which compliance was more likely to be forthcoming. When I was in the Commission we were always disappointed with this outcome. Two years away from the experience, reflecting on it, I think the Court probably did the best it could do under difficult circumstances and was probably husbanding its resources and trying to maintain the limited effectiveness it had. The one exception to this practice was in the *Aloeboetoe* case,[5] in which Salamanca tribesmen were murdered by the jungle commando in Surinam. The Court set up a trust which would provide for education of the minor children of the victims. To make this meaningful it had to order the Government to reopen the schools in the village area where those minors lived.

As you know there are instruments that assign only advisory jurisdiction to the International Court, yet the parties to the instruments accept the advisory opinion as binding. It is similarly possible to use a formally recommendatory competence but to agree at the domestic level that the 'recommendation' will be accepted as binding. The Commission sought to persuade a number of governments that had sent signals that they wanted to develop a better relation with the Commission to do this. But nothing came of the initiative. In my view, a strong argument can be made for this. I regret that the Court in the *Isidro-Caballero* case,[6] as I mentioned, rejected the possibility. A strong argument can be made that the decision of an entity like the Commission or its counterpart, the Commission in Europe, in which a government participates in the procedure that follows all the requirements of due process, something more binding than a mere recommendation should be understood. There should be some implied duty of good faith to make an effort to implement. I regret that the Interamerican Court did not share that view.

President Cassese asks: 'Are there cases where the Commission could identify those responsible for the delinquency?' May I say I share completely his sense of frustration that we characterize a State as responsible and hold an entire body politic's revenue, in some cases for years to come, hostage when, in fact, we are dealing with a small group of thugs at the top of a broad-based needle who are entirely responsible for the delinquency. Consider the Iraqi situation in which the Iraqi people are as much victims as were the Kuwaiti people. The Commission did in fact initiate an advisory opinion request No. 14 before the Interamerican Court, in which it asked where there is a clear violation of international law by individuals are they personally responsible?

---

[5] *Aloeboetoe et al.,* Reparations (Art. 63(1) American Convention On Human Rights), Judgment of 10 Sep. 1993, Inter-Am. Ct. H. R. Ser. C no. 15.
[6] *Caballero Delgada and Santana,* Judgment of 8 Dec. 1995, Inter-Am. Ct. H. R. Ser. C. no. 22.

The provocation for that particular request for an advisory opinion was a putative change in the constitution of Peru which would have reinstated the death penalty for a number of activities that formerly were not capital punishment. The American Convention says the death penalty is not prohibited, but you cannot reinstate it or instate it once you become party to the Convention. The Commission had, in effect, tried to issue an injunction against Peru, but President Fujmori indicated he would ignore it. So the Commission tried to put individuals on notice that if they do something that is reprehended by the international community they bear personal responsibility. The Court was not willing to go that far. This is a frustrating problem and should be addressed by us in the future. With respect to specifications of guilty parties in reports of the Interamerican Commission which are published in the annual report to the Assembly of the Organization of the American States, you will frequently find very detailed identifications of the military officers or police officers or units who were responsible for the atrocities that gave rise to the petition. At the end there will be recommendations that the appropriate people be punished.

Judge Cassese also raises the issue of punitive damages. I treat it in my paper. This is an enormous problem for human rights violations. Punitive damages work when you have an identifiable tort feasor, a company or an individual who has done something egregious; that tort feasor is a rational economic maximizer; and you can say that punitive damages are the additional sanction. Rational economic actors will presumably change their behaviour to avoid that deprivation in the future. But can you transpose this technique, which may be used in certain advanced legal systems, to international human rights law against governments? Who are we asking to pay? In asking the government or the State to pay, in effect we are very often taxing the same victims who seek a remedy. The answer to this conundrum, I suggest, is we should be much more specific about identifying the parties actually responsible and not the State as a collectivity. We have a long way to go before we can accomplish that.

Professor Tomuschat and President Cassese ask: 'Is it possible to enforce responsibility for certain human rights violations?' An international human rights convention or a protocol could say that final decisions of the European Court or the Interamerican Court are directly enforceable in any national court of a State party to the convention. There has been great resistance to it since the days of the Permanent Court of International Justice in the *Société Commerciale de Belgique* case.[7]

Referring to Professor Malanczuk, I would like to point out that the Inter-American system is not a common law system. The United States and

---

[7] *Société Commerciale de Belgique*, Judgment, 1939, PCIJ Rep. Ser. A/B no. 78, 160.

Canadian monetary contributions are high, but the degree of influence and shaping of the instruments is quite limited. These are essentially code systems. With respect to the issue of judicial creativity, judges must remember that law making is different from a philosopher dreaming up an appropriate solution or a law professor spouting in a seminar. It is a political activity, for which you must have a political base. There are limits and the astute judge knows exactly how far he or she can go, before there is a kickback.

With respect to the issue of moral damages or emotional damages, the practice of the Interamerican Court since 1989 has assigned three meanings to this. One meaning is, as Professor Meron said, payment for the suffering of the individual who is the victim. And in fact the Interamerican Court specifically cited the *Lusitania* as the authority for this. The second meaning that is assigned is a payment for the suffering of the beneficiaries, the parents, the children, spouses. The third meaning is a sort of aggravated *mala fides* on the part of the defendant government, for example, murders that were essentially racially motivated. With these three meanings, there is a certain flexibility in the American system for going beyond a simple compensation for material injuries.

I would like to comment on Professor Pellonpää's final observation. I think it is very important to distinguish between material and immaterial violations, between technical violations and material violations that really infringe a human right. Because there is so much passion against governments by non-governmental organisations, there is a tendency to slip into a type of reverse chicanery. This can infect human rights bodies, but just squanders their resources and their credibility. The law should be concerned with important things: *de minimis non curat praetor.*

International Obligations to Provide for Reparation Claims?

Riccardo Pisillo-Mazzeschi

I. INTRODUCTION

The problem of the international personality of the individual has been much debated in literature. Its solution often depends on rather different theoretical premises about the nature of international law and about the concept of legal personality in the general theory of law.

However, a more modern and pragmatic approach to this problem may be to examine the data emerging from international practice in the fields in which international law deals with individuals and individual interests. In the past, international law's concern with individuals consisted almost entirely of the treatment of aliens. Today, however, international law tends to deal much more with individual interests and behaviors. In fact, contemporary international law comes more often into direct contact with individuals, since it deals more and more with matters which are domestic and which concern relationships among individuals or between the State and its citizens.

The protection of human rights has assumed great importance amongst these new fields of international law. In fact, as it is well known, there are now numerous international norms, mostly conventional but also customary, which require States to protect fundamental human rights. But does international law establish, corresponding with those international duties of States, only international rights of other States or also international rights of individuals? And, if the last hypothesis is true, are we facing a real structural change in international law?[1]

Until now, studies on the international personality of the individual and the protection of human rights have principally dealt with the *primary* international norms on human rights and the procedural mechanisms open to the individual before the international organs for the protection of human rights. It is now time to start doing research on the *secondary* norms of international

---

[1] See L. Condorelli, *Cours de droit international public*, Université de Genève, Faculté de droit, édition 1990/1991, 22.

A. Randelzhofer and C. Tomuschat (eds.), State Responsibility and the Individual, 149–172.
© 1999 *Kluwer Law International. Printed in Great Britain.*

human rights law and, in particular, on the obligations of reparation for breach of human rights.

There are various international conventional norms on human rights which expressly establish obligations of reparation upon States which have breached such norms. It is common to say that, to those obligations on wrongdoing States, correspond rights in favour of other States. But, can one say nowadays that, to those obligations on wrongdoing States, correspond also true and real *rights of the individual victims* of the breach? And do these possible individual rights directly derive from international rules or, rather, only from domestic rules enacted to implement international rules?

In order to answer these questions it is especially important to examine the obligations of reparation towards the individual. In order to put those obligations in the right context, however, I will also examine the obligations of reparation towards the State. Therefore in my paper I will draw a distinction between the obligation of reparation towards the State established by international law in the framework of inter-State relationships[2], the obligation of reparation towards the individual established by domestic law as implementation of an international obligation[3] and, finally, the obligation of reparation towards the individual directly established by international law[4].

Moreover, in this paper, I will use a broad concept of reparation, since I will speak not only of the traditional 'substantive' reparation (*restitutio in integrum*, compensation, satisfaction and guarantees of non-repetition)[5]; but also of the so-called 'procedural' reparation, the latter consisting of the obligation on the wrongdoing State to provide the individual with effective domestic remedies against the violation.

Finally, in order to verify whether the legal position of the individual in international law is radically changed, I will try to put the research into a historical perspective, by comparing the legal regime of reparation in traditional international law, with particular reference to the protection of aliens[6], with its legal regime in contemporary international law, with particular reference to the protection of human rights[7].

---

[2]   See infra, sec. III.
[3]   See infra, sec. IV.
[4]   See infra, sec. V.
[5]   On 'substantive' reparation, see Arts. 42 (reparation), 43 (restitution in kind), 44 (compensation), 45 (satisfaction), 46 (assurances and guarantees of non-repetition) of the draft articles on State responsibility provisionally adopted by the ILC on first reading, in: Draft Report of the ILC on the Work of its Forty-eighth Session, UN Doc. A/CN.4/L.528/Add.2 of 16 July 1996, 18-20. See also G. Arangio-Ruiz, Preliminary report on State responsibility, Yearbook of the ILC (YILC) 1988 II, Part One, 6-43; id., Second report on State responsibility, YILC 1989 II, Part One, 1-58.
[6]   See infra, sects. III.1, IV.1, V.1.
[7]   See infra, sects. III.2, IV.2, V.2.

II. THE POSITION OF THE INDIVIDUAL IN TRADITIONAL INTERNATIONAL LAW AND IN CONTEMPORARY INTERNATIONAL LAW: FROM THE PROTECTION OF ALIENS TO THE PROTECTION OF HUMAN RIGHTS

One may identify historically two different attitudes in international law regarding the position of the individual: the approach of traditional international law and that of contemporary international law[8].

Traditional international law is concerned with the individual, but as a law that governs relations between sovereign entities (that is to say, inter-state relations) and not as a law that governs relationships between individuals. Therefore individuals are considered as entities entirely subject to the sovereign power of their national State and of the territorial State.

If an individual, for example, is in the territory of one State and has the nationality of another State, he or she is potentially subject to the concurring jurisdiction of both States. Customary international law resolves this potential conflict of jurisdictions by establishing some rights and duties for both States. In particular, the customary rules on the protection of aliens establish that the territorial State must grant certain minimum treatment to the alien, although maintaining sovereign powers over him or her. The national State has the right to demand that the territorial State comply with its duties and, in case of breach of such duties, may start an action for diplomatic protection.

Therefore traditional international law, in its classical approach of inter-State law aimed at preventing and resolving conflicts of sovereignty among States, tends to protect aliens rather than individuals as such. Individuals are taken into consideration only for the purpose of preventing or resolving the various kinds of conflicts of sovereignty that may arise among States with regard to such individuals. In the absence of those conflicts, international law has no interest in intervening with regard to individuals and, in such cases, the legal position of individuals is left to the domestic jurisdiction of States[9].

By contrast, the approach of contemporary international law with respect to the position of the individual is quite different. As I have already noted[10], current international law does not govern only relationships between sovereign entities and matters pertaining to inter-State relationships; rather it tends more and more to govern matters pertaining to inter-individual and domestic relationships[11]. One may consider, for instance, the numerous international conventional rules which govern economic, commercial and social relationships, as well as some quickly developing areas of international law such as

---

[8] See L. Condorelli, *Cours* (note 1), 19-22, 91.
[9] Id., 20, 91.
[10] See supra, sec. I.
[11] See, e.g., B. Conforti, *Diritto internazionale*, 4th ed., 1995, 3.

European Community law, the administrative law of international organizations, international economic law[12], international environmental law and international criminal law.

But the most important example illustrating the new approach of international law with regard to the position of individuals is the area of the international protection of human rights. Contemporary international law has finally become aware of the necessity of protecting, through a series of appropriate rules, not only aliens but also human beings as such, irrespective of any specific State interest and any conflict of sovereignty[13]. The new international law now aims at protecting individuals irrespective of their nationality, and therefore at protecting them also against their own national State.

Thus, as one can see, the legal position of the individual has undergone important changes in passing from the old international law to the new. Keeping in mind this general picture, I will now examine the position of the individual from the more specific point of view of the obligations of reparation. I will deal with reparation for breach of the traditional international rules on the protection of aliens and of the new international rules concerning the protection of human rights.

III. REPARATION TO THE STATE

Let us examine first the *inter-State obligation of reparation*; that is, the obligation imposed by international law on the wrongdoing State to afford reparation in favour of the injured States.

1. Protection of aliens

If we consider the problem of inter-State reparation for breach of the customary rules concerning the protection of aliens, we may formulate the following general principles.

First, there is no doubt that a secondary obligation of reparation exists for the wrongdoing State. There is in fact no agreement in the literature as to whether any wrongful act entails as a consequence an obligation of reparation[14]. With regard to the specific area of the customary rules concerning the

---

[12] See R. Jennings, 'Human Rights and Domestic Law and Courts', in: F. Matscher & H. Petzold (eds.), *Protecting Human Rights: The European Dimension: Studies in Honour of Gérard J. Wiarda*, 1988, 299.

[13] See Condorelli, *Cours* (note 1), 21, 91.

[14] See, e.g., H. Kelsen, 'Unrecht und Unrechtsfolge im Völkerrecht', *Zeitschrift für öffentliches Recht*, 1932, 481. For the theoretical discussion about the consequences of an internationally

protection of aliens, however, all agree that any breach of such rules entails an obligation of reparation.

Second, reparation–from a 'substantive' point of view– may take the forms of *restitutio in integrum*, compensation, satisfaction and guarantees of non-repetition.

Third, in the field of the protection of aliens, there is also an obligation on the wrongdoing State of 'procedural' reparation: that is, the obligation to provide the injured alien with effective domestic remedies against the violation[15].

Fourth, and this is the most important point, one may maintain that, to those obligations of reparation on the territorial State, correspond rights of the national State of the injured alien. In other words, if a State violates the rules concerning the protection of aliens, it commits an internationally wrongful act *towards the national State of the alien* and not towards the alien; the latter State, by exercising diplomatic protection, enforces *its own right* which arises from the injury done to its own citizen.

Moreover, the right to inter-State reparation belongs only to the national State of the alien; that is, to the State that suffered a direct injury to its rights. In fact, generally speaking, traditional international law adopts the so-called principle of 'bilateralism'; that is, the principle according to which a wrongful act creates new legal relationships only between the wrongdoing State and the directly affected State.

Finally, many writers maintain that, in case of breach of the rules governing the protection of aliens, the injured State suffers a material or a moral damage; they therefore reach the more general conclusion that damage is a constitutive element of any internationally wrongful act[16].

---

wrongful act, see, in particular, R. Ago, Third report on State responsibility, UN Doc. A/CN.4/246 and Add.1-3, YILC 1971 II, Part One, 199, para. 30 et seq.; Conforti, *Diritto internazionale* (note 11), 351-354; M. Iovane, *La riparazione nella teoria e nella prassi dell'illecito internazionale*, 1990, 3 et seq., 15 et seq. According to the ILC, any violation of an international obligation entails a duty of reparation. See infra, note 17.

[15] See A.J.P. Tammes, 'The Obligation to Provide Local Remedies', in: *Volkenrechtelijke Opstellen– Aangeboden aan Professor Dr. Gesina H.J. Van Der Molen*, 1962, 152-168; P. Mertens, 'Origines et fondements du droit de recours interne en cas de violation d'une norme de droit international', in: *Institut d'Etudes Européennes, Université Libre de Bruxelles, Les recours des individus devant les instances nationales en cas de violation du droit européen*, 1978, 23 et seq.; Iovane, *La riparazione* (note 14), 236-247.

[16] See, e.g., L. Cavaré, *Droit international public positif*, 3rd ed., vol.II, 1969, 449; A. Décencière-Ferrendière, *La responsabilité internationale des Etats à raison des dommages subis par des étrangers*, 1928, 60; J. Personnaz, *La réparation du préjudice en droit international public*, 1939, 58.

2. Protection of human rights

Can it be said that the developments in contemporary international law concerning the legal position of the individual have also produced important changes with regard to responsibility for breach of human rights? And, in particular, are the general principles on reparation, which were developed in traditional international law especially with regard to the protection of aliens, still valid in contemporary international law and especially in human rights law?

In my opinion, some of the traditional principles remain unchanged while others have changed. First of all, the basic principle has not changed. Under this principle, the internationally wrongful act produces an inter-State obligation of 'substantive' reparation. In fact I would argue that, if the *primary* international rule on human rights imposes upon the State an enforceable obligation, its violation always involves a *secondary* obligation of reparation on the wrongdoing State. My position finds support in the ILC works on State responsibility, from which it is clear that the breach of any international obligation produces an obligation to grant reparation[17]. It is also supported by those writers who have studied the specific topic of responsibility for breach of international human rights[18].

Secondly, I believe that, in the human rights field, too, the obligation of reparation may take the forms of *restitutio in integrum*, compensation, satisfaction and guarantees of non-repetition[19]. Of course this is valid as a

---

[17] See Arts. 1, 36, 42 of the draft articles on State responsibility provisionally adopted by the ILC on first reading (supra note 5).

[18] See F. Lattanzi, *Garanzie dei diritti dell'uomo nel diritto internazionale generale*, 1983, 159 et seqq.; Th. Meron, *Human Rights and Humanitarian Norms As Customary International Law*, 1989, 136 et seqq.; B.G. Ramcharan, *The Concept and Present Status of International Protection of Human Rights: Forty Years After the Universal Declaration*, 1989, 289; M.T. Kamminga, *Inter-State Accountability for Violations of Human Rights*, 1992, 127 et seqq., 171 et seqq.; Th. Van Boven, *Etude concernant le droit à restitution, à indemnisation et à réadaptation des victimes de violations flagrantes des droits de l'homme et des libertés fondamentales*, UN Doc. E/CN.4/Sub.2/1993/8 (2 July 1993); id., *Revised set of basic principles and guidelines on the right to reparation for victims of gross violations of human rights and humanitarian law*, UN Doc. E/CN.4/Sub.2/1996/17 (24 May 1996) (for text, see the annex of this book). On the topic of reparation for breach of international human rights, see also G. Cohen-Jonathan, 'Responsabilité pour atteinte aux droits de l'homme', in: Société Française pour le Droit International (ed.), *La responsabilité dans le système international* (Colloque du Mans), 1991, 101 et seq.; Ph. Frumer, 'La réparation des atteintes aux droits de l'homme internationalement protégés – Quelques données comparatives', *Rev. trim. des droits de l'homme* 7 (1996), 329 et seqq.; L. Joinet, *Question of the impunity of perpetrators of human rights violations (civil and political)*, Revised final report, UN Doc. E/CN.4/Sub.2/1997/20/Rev.1 (2 Oct. 1997).

[19] See Lattanzi, *Garanzie* (note 18), 159 et seqq.; van Boven, *Revised set* (note 18), 3; Joinet, *Question of the impunity* (note 18), 7-8.

matter of principle and leaves open the possibility that specific conventional rules on human rights may establish only specific forms of reparation[20].

Thirdly, I think that there is, also in the human rights field, a 'procedural' obligation of reparation; that is to say, an obligation on the wrongdoing State, owed to other States, to give the injured individual an effective domestic remedy against the violation[21]. This obligation is expressly established in numerous human rights treaties: see, for instance, Article 13 of the European Convention on Human Rights[22]; Article 25 of the American Convention on Human Rights[23]; Article 2(3) of the International Covenant on Civil and Political Rights[24]; Article 6 of the International Convention on the Elimination

---

[20] See, e.g., Art. 50 of the European Convention on Human Rights.

[21] For the moment I am speaking of the *inter-State* obligation to give effective domestic remedies. On the same obligation *towards private individuals* see infra sec. IV.2. On the right to a remedy for violations of human rights, see van Boven, *Revised set* (note 18), 2.

[22] Art. 13 of the European Convention: 'Everyone whose rights and freedoms as set forth in this Convention are violated shall have an effective remedy before a national authority notwithstanding that the violation has been committed by persons acting in an official capacity.'

On Art. 13, see Tammes, *The Obligation* (note 15); Mertens, *Origines* (note 15); P. Mertens, 'Le droit à un recours effectif devant l'autorité nationale compétente dans les conventions internationales relatives à la protection des droits de l'homme', *RBDI* 4 (1968), 446 et seqq.; id., *Le droit de recours effectif devant les instances nationales en cas d'une violation d'un droit de l'homme*, 1973; G. Thune, 'The Right to an Effective Remedy in Domestic Law: Article 13 of the European Convention on Human Rights', in: D. Gomien (ed.), *Broadening the Frontiers of Human Rights: Essays in Honour of Asbjørn Eide*, 1993, 79 et seqq.; W. Strasser, 'The Relationship between Substantive Rights and Procedural Rights Guaranteed by the European Convention on Human Rights', in: Matscher & Petzold (note 12), 595 et seqq.

[23] Art. 25 of the American Convention (right to judicial protection):

'1. Everyone has the right to simple and prompt recourse, or any other effective recourse, to a competent court or tribunal for protection against acts that violate his fundamental rights recognised by the constitution or laws of the state concerned or by this Convention, even though such violation may have been committed by persons acting in the course of their official duties.

2. The State Parties undertake:
(a)   to ensure that any person claiming such remedy shall have his rights determined by the competent authority provided for by the legal system of the state;
(b)   to develop the possibilities of judicial remedy; and
(c)   to ensure that the competent authorities shall enforce such remedies when granted.'

[24] Art. 2(3) of the International Covenant on Civil and Political Rights:

'Each State party to the present Covenant undertakes:
(a)   to ensure that any person whose rights or freedoms as herein recognized are violated shall have an effective remedy, notwithstanding that the violation has been committed by persons acting in an official capacity;
(b)   to ensure that any person claiming such a remedy shall have his right thereto determined by competent judicial, administrative or legislative authorities, or by any other competent authority provided for by the legal system of the State, and to develop the possibilities of judicial remedy;

of All Forms of Racial Discrimination[25]; Article 7(1) of the African Charter on Human and Peoples' Rights[26]. Moreover, in my opinion, this obligation exists not only in conventional international law, but also in customary international law. In fact it is a development, a logical extension, of the same obligation existing in the field of the protection of aliens[27]. In any case, one could also maintain that the obligation for the wrongdoing State to provide remedies under its domestic law for breach of human rights is implicit in those human rights treaties which require national implementation and whose effectiveness depends largely on the availability of domestic remedies[28].

However, there are important differences, as regards the other principles of inter-State reparation, between the traditional international law on the protection of aliens and contemporary international law on human rights.

The first difference concerns the circumstances in which a State is the beneficiary of reparation. For example, in the field of the protection of aliens, because of the so-called principle of 'bilateralism', reparation is due only to the national State of the alien. By contrast, in the field of human rights, the concept of *erga omnes* obligations of conventional law and of customary law has developed. In other words, one can now maintain that a breach of the conventional norms on human rights violates the rights of all States parties and that a breach of the customary norms on human rights violates the rights of all States[29].

(c)   to ensure that the competent authorities shall enforce such remedies when granted.'

[25]   Art. 6 of the International Convention on the Elimination of All Forms of Racial Discrimination: 'States Parties shall assure to everyone within their jurisdiction effective protection and remedies, through the competent national tribunals and other State institutions, against any acts of racial discrimination which violate his human rights and fundamental freedoms contrary to this Convention, as well as the right to seek from such tribunals just and adequate reparation or satisfaction for any damage suffered as a result of such discrimination.'

[26]   Art. 7(1) of the African Charter:

'Every individual shall have the right to have his cause heard. This comprises:
(a)   the right to an appeal to competent national organs against acts violating his fundamental rights as recognized and guaranteed by conventions, laws, regulations and customs in force;
(b)   the right to be presumed innocent until proved guilty by a competent court or tribunal;
(c)   the right to defence, including the right to be defended by counsel of his choice;
(d)   the right to be tried within a reasonable time by an impartial court or tribunal.'

[27]   See, in particular, Tammes, *The obligation* (note 15), 152 et seqq.

[28]   See Meron, *Human Rights* (note 18), 139.

[29]   See Lattanzi, *Garanzie* (note 18), 85, 120 et seqq.; Meron, *Human Rights* (note 18), 188 et seqq.; Kamminga, *Inter-State Accountability* (note 18), 156 et seqq., 163 et seqq.; Ramcharan, *The Concept* (note 18), 289 et seqq. On the topics of 'objective' obligations and '*erga omnes*' obligations concerning human rights, cf. also Cohen-Jonathan, *Responsabilité* (note 18), 109-111 and 127-131.

The second difference concerns the role of damage in the internationally wrongful act. In fact, the traditional theory, which affirmed the connection between damage and responsibility, has declined–owing especially to the new international rules on human rights. In its place, the concept that damage is not a constitutive element of the internationally wrongful act has been established[30].

IV. REPARATION TO THE INDIVIDUAL ESTABLISHED BY DOMESTIC LAW AS IMPLEMENTATION OF AN INTERNATIONAL OBLIGATION

I will now examine whether a breach by a State of the rules concerning the protection of aliens and those concerning the protection of human rights produces a right to reparation *in favour of the injured individual*; that is, a right *within the domestic legal order*, by virtue of the incorporation of an international obligation into the domestic order.

Is it possible that an international rule imposes upon a State a duty to grant to an individual a right to reparation within the domestic legal order (a 'national' or 'domestic' reparation) for the breach of an international obligation on the State itself?

Earlier writers took the view that the international rules, even after they had been incorporated into domestic law, were applicable only to States as between themselves, and could not be used by private individuals. This theory has been abandoned, however, and the principle recognized that international rules, once incorporated in domestic law, are also a source of rights and duties for private individuals. This is true not only when there has been a domestic transformation of international law by the creation of parallel norms of municipal law, but also when there has been a direct adoption of international law in municipal law[31].

However, as is known, in order that the international norm may be invoked by private individuals, it is not enough for it to have been incorporated into municipal law; other conditions are also necessary: the norm must establish a true and binding obligation and not a mere recommendation; it must not

---

[30] See ILC, Commentary on Article 3, YILC 1973 II, 183-184, para. 12. See also Lattanzi, *Garanzie* (note 18), 86 et seq; Meron, *Human Rights* (note 18), 201 et seqq.; A. Tanzi, 'Is Damage a Distinct Condition for the Existence of an Internationally Wrongful Act?', in: M. Spinedi and B. Simma (eds.), *United Nations Codification of State Responsibility*, 1987, 1 et seqq.

[31] See, e.g., Conforti, *Diritto internazionale* (note 11), 287-288.

have a programmatic character[32]; it must establish an obligation requiring the adoption of a particular course of conduct (obligation of conduct) and not an obligation requiring the achievement of a specified result (obligation of result)[33]; it must not need domestic norms or organs or mechanisms for implementation. In short, it must be a self-executing rule[34].

---

[32] But see Conforti, *Diritto internazionale* (note 11), 289; id., 'National Courts and the International Law of Human Rights', in: B. Conforti and F. Francioni (eds.), *Enforcing International Human Rights in Domestic Courts*, 1997, 8-10.

[33] I am now using the distinction between 'obligations of conduct' and 'obligations of result' accepted by the ILC in Arts. 20 and 21 of the draft articles on State responsibility. In the text I suggest that there is a relationship between this distinction and the distinction between self-executing and non self-executing obligations. For the Commentary on Arts. 20 and 21 of the ILC draft articles, see YILC 1977 II, Part Two, 11-30. See also R. Ago, Sixth report on State responsibility, UN Doc. A/CN.4/302 and Add.1-3, YILC 1977 II, Part One, 3-43, paras. 1-46. For a completely different distinction in international law between 'obligations of diligent conduct' (or 'due diligence obligations') and 'obligations of result' (or 'absolute obligations'), see R. Pisillo-Mazzeschi, 'The Due Diligence Rule and the Nature of the International Responsibility of States', *GYIL* 35 (1992), 46 et seqq.; id., '"Due Diligence" e responsabilitá internazionale degli Stati', 1989, in particular 390 et seqq.; id., 'Forms of International Responsibility for Environmental Harm', in: F. Francioni and T. Scovazzi (eds.), *International Responsibility for Environmental Harm*, 1991, 15 et seqq. The latter distinction has recently been applied also by R. Lefeber, *Transboundary Environmental Interference and the Origin of State Liability*, 1996, 61-74 and passim.

[34] In my opinion, the self-executing character of an international rule, or rather the suitability of an international rule to be invoked by private persons in domestic law, depends on various elements. Some elements concern the structure of the obligations established by the rule (binding obligation, non- programmatic obligation, obligation of conduct etc.), while other elements concern the conditions in the domestic legal order in question (direct adoption of international law in domestic law, existence of domestic norms or mechanisms for implementation of the international rule etc.). Therefore the self-executing character of an international rule is a matter pertaining both to international and to national law.

The international literature on self-executing norms is extremely wide-ranging. On the general question see, among others, A.E. Evans, 'Self-Executing Treaties in the United States of America', *BYBIL* 30 (1953), 178; H. Mosler, 'L'application du droit international public par les tribunaux nationaux', in: RC 91 (1957), I, 619; I. Seidl-Hohenveldern, 'Transformation or Adoption of International Law into Municipal Law', *ICLQ* 12 (1963), 88; L. Henkin, *Foreign Affairs and the Constitution*, 1972, 156 et seqq.; L. Condorelli, *Il giudice italiano e i trattati internazionali - Gli accordi* self-executing *e non* self-executing *nell'ottica della giurisprudenza*, 1974; S.M. Schneebaum, 'The Enforceability of Customary Norms of Public International Law', *Brooklyn JIL* 8 (1982), 289; F.G. Jacobs and S. Roberts, *The Effect of Treaties in Domestic Law*, 1987; L. Erades, *Interactions between International and Municipal Law: A Comparative Case Law Study*, 1993, 519 et seqq.

On the more specific question of self-executing human rights norms, see, e.g., O. Schachter, 'The Charter and the Constitution: The Human Rights Provisions in American Law', *Vanderbilt L. Rev.* 4 (1950-51), 643; Q. Wright, 'National Courts and Human Rights: The Fujii Case', *AJIL* 45 (1951), 62; P. Compte, 'The Application of the European Convention on Human Rights in Municipal Law', *Journ. of the Int. Comm. of Jurists* 4 (1962), 94; M. Sørensen, 'Obligations of a State Party to a Treaty as Regards Its Municipal Law', in: A.H. Robertson (ed.), *Human Rights in National and International Law*, 1968, 11; B. Schlüter, 'The Domestic Status of the

At least in theory, therefore, once these conditions have been satisfied, nothing prevents an international norm from imposing upon a State an obligation of reparation towards private individuals. That obligation, once incorporated into domestic law, creates a true right to reparation that the individual can invoke before a municipal court. One should note that this conclusion does not undermine the traditional approach of international law, which tends to deny the international personality of individuals. In fact, according to this conclusion, individuals acquire true rights only within the municipal legal order and only owing to the "indirect" effect of an international rule.

But do such international rules, in the fields of the protection of aliens and of human rights, exist in practice, imposing upon States an obligation to grant individuals *reparation in domestic law*?

1. Protection of aliens

The customary rules concerning the treatment of aliens, and especially those concerning the protection of aliens, do not appear to satisfy the above-mentioned conditions. In fact, the obligation requiring the territorial State to protect aliens appears to be a typical 'obligation of result'. Moreover, the right to obtain reparation for breach of that obligation takes on the shape of a right in favour of the national State of the alien, and not of a right in favour of the alien personally[35]. An individual's right to reparation within the municipal legal order cannot, therefore, derive from those customary rules.

However, a slightly different conclusion can be reached with respect to a group of treaties which can be considered as belonging to the field of the

---

Human Rights Clauses of the United Nations Charter', *California L. Rev.* 61 (1973), 110; C.W. Stotter, 'Self-Executing Treaties and the Human Rights Provisions of the United Nations Charter: A Separation of Powers Problem', *Buffalo L. Rev.* 25 (1976), 773; M.D. Craig, 'The International Covenant on Civil and Political Rights and United States Law: Department of State Proposals for Preserving the Status Quo', *Harvard ILJ* 19 (1978), 845, 855 et seqq.; R. Bilder, 'An Overview of International Human Rights Law', in: H. Hannum (ed.), *Guide to International Human Rights Practice*, 1984, 3, 12 et seqq.; R.B. Lillich, 'The Role of Domestic Courts in Enforcing International Human Rights Law', id., 223 et seqq.; M. Ross, *Die unmittelbare Anwendbarkeit der Europäischen Menschenrechtskonvention - Ein Beitrag zur Lehre der self-executing treaties*, 1984; A. Brudner, 'The Domestic Enforcement of International Covenants on Human Rights: A Theoretical Framework', in: *Univ. Toronto L. J.* 35 (1985), 219, 221 et seqq.; G.E. Longo, 'La jurisprudence la plus récente de la Cour de Cassation italienne en matière d'application de la Convention Européenne des Droits de l'Homme', in: J. O' Reilly (ed.), *Human Rights and Constitutional Law: Essays in Honour of Brian Walsh*, 1992, 85; H.J. Steiner & P. Alston, *International Human Rights in Context – Law, Politics, Morals: Text and Materials*, 1996, 726 et seqq.; Conforti, *National Courts* (note 32), 7 et seqq.

[35] See supra, sec. III.1.

treatment of aliens and which deal more directly with individual interests. Typical examples are the bilateral treaties of friendship and commerce which grant the citizens of one State certain rights with regard to establishing or engaging in a trade or profession in another State. The domestic courts of several States have often held that such treaties are addressed not only to States but also to private individuals and that they are to be considered as self-executing treaties. These courts have therefore entertained legal actions by the citizens of one country seeking to enforce in another country the rights provided for in the treaty[36].

In my opinion, this approach should be endorsed. It means, in practice, that the States parties to those treaties have assumed certain *primary* obligations not only towards other States parties but also towards individuals. This is so even though they have taken up those obligations not in a direct way through the treaty, but indirectly, through the domestic norms implementing the treaty.

But does this mean that the same States parties, in the case of a breach of the primary obligations, have also assumed *secondary* obligations of reparation, not only towards other States parties but also towards individuals?

At first glance, a negative answer seems to derive from the fact that those treaties of friendship and commerce do not usually contain secondary rules regarding responsibility and, in particular, do not expressly provide for a right to reparation in favour of the citizens of the States parties.

However, on closer examination that answer is not entirely convincing: one could perhaps maintain that in those treaties there are implicit rules concerning reparation. In other words, if the individual, by virtue of the self-executing treaty, acquires true and real rights in the domestic legal orders of the States parties, perhaps she or he should also have access to the remedies provided for in those legal orders for breach of those rights. Thus, the individual should also obtain such forms of reparation as are provided for in any single domestic order.

2. Protection of human rights

We have seen that the norms concerning the treatment of aliens usually, although not always, tend to be considered as norms that govern relations only among States, that impose on States mere obligations of result, and that are not self-executing.

---

[36] See Evans, *Self-Executing Treaties* (note 34), 186; Wright, *National Courts* (note 34), 75; Sørensen, *Obligations* (note 34), 22; Stotter, *Self-Executing Treaties* (note 34), 778-9; Steiner & Alston, *International Human Rights* (note 34), 746.

By contrast, the norms concerning human rights govern relations between the State and the individual. It is therefore much more logical that they be interpreted in such a way as to favour their application within the State. In other words, in my opinion, the interpreter should consider such norms, as far as possible, as norms that establish obligations of conduct[37] and are self-executing.

This interpretation should work, in the first place, for those customary rules on human rights that impose negative 'obligations to refrain' on the State (as, for example, norms prohibiting genocide and torture). With respect to torture, one should mention the famous judgment of the United States Court of Appeal for the Second Circuit in the case *Filartiga v. Pena-Irala*[38], where the Court affirmed that the right to be free from torture is a human right which derives from international customary law, that it has become a part of United States domestic law, and that individuals can enforce it before domestic courts. In a similar way, in the case *Rodriguez-Fernandez v. Wilkinson*[39], the District Court of Kansas held that the international customary rule which condemns the practice of arbitrary arrest has created in domestic US law an individual right to be free from that practice[40].

The same arguments are also valid for many conventional rules on human rights which impose negative 'obligations to refrain' on State organs. One may think, for instance, of the norms of the European Convention on Human Rights which establish that 'No one shall be deprived of his life intentionally....' (Article 2(1)); 'No one shall be subjected to torture or to inhuman or degrading treatment or punishment' (Article 3); 'No one shall be held in slavery or servitude' (Article 4(1)); 'No one shall be required to perform forced or compulsory labour' (Article 4(2)).

Finally, the same conclusions are also valid for other conventional rules which impose upon State organs certain positive 'obligations to act' and which may have direct effects. Let us take, for example, Article 5(2) of the European Convention on Human Rights, according to which: 'Everyone who is arrested shall be informed promptly, in a language which he understands, of the reasons for his arrest and of any charge against him'[41].

---

[37] But see R. Ago, Sixth report on State responsibility (note 33), 3 et seqq., para. 22.

[38] 630 F.2d 876 (2d Cir. 1980).

[39] 505 F. Supp. 787 (D. Kan. 1980), aff'd on other grounds sub nom. *Rodriguez-Fernandez v. Wilkinson*, 654 F.2d 1382 (10th Cir. 1981).

[40] See Schneebaum, *The Enforceability* (note 34), 291; Lillich, *The Role* (note 34), 234.

[41] See also Sørensen, *Obligations* (note 34), 24-25.

In conclusion, one should agree with those writers who maintain that the norms of the human rights treaties should, as a rule, be considered as mandatory and self-executing norms[42].

These are considerations of a general character on the primary, customary or conventional norms regarding human rights. More specifically, one should consider that many and important multilateral treaties on human rights contain secondary norms that expressly establish *reparation in domestic law in favour of individual victims* of certain violations of human rights. In particular, many treaties establish both 'substantive' and 'procedural' reparation, the latter consisting of the right to an effective domestic remedy.

Let us examine first the norms which establish 'substantive' reparation and then turn to those which establish 'procedural' reparation. The most important conventional norms providing for *'substantive' reparation* in favour of individuals are Articles 9(5) and 14(6) of the International Covenant on Civil and Political Rights[43], Article 5(5) of the European Convention on Human Rights[44], Article 3 of its Seventh Protocol[45], Article 10 of the American Convention on Human Rights[46], Article 6 of the 1966 Convention on the Elimination of All Forms of Racial Discrimination[47] and Article 14 of the 1984 Convention Against Torture[48].

---

[42] See, e.g., Schachter, *The Charter* (note 34), 643 et seqq.; Conforti, *National Courts* (note 32), 7 et seqq.

[43] Art. 9(5) of the International Covenant: 'Anyone who has been the victim of unlawful arrest or detention shall have an enforceable right to compensation.'

Art. 14(6) of the International Covenant: 'When a person has by a final decision been convicted of a criminal offence and when subsequently his conviction has been reversed or he has been pardoned on the ground that a new or newly discovered fact shows conclusively that there has been a miscarriage of justice, the person who has suffered punishment as a result of such conviction shall be compensated according to law, unless it is proved the non-disclosure of the unknown fact in time is wholly or partly attributable to him.'

[44] Art. 5(5) of the European Convention: 'Everyone who has been the victim of arrest or detention in contravention of the provisions of this Article shall have an enforceable right to compensation.'

[45] Art. 3 of the Seventh Protocol: 'When a person has by a final decision been convicted of a criminal offence and when subsequently his conviction has been reversed, or he has been pardoned, on the ground that a new or newly discovered fact shows conclusively that there has been a miscarriage of justice, the person who has suffered punishment as a result of such conviction shall be compensated according to the law or the practice of the State concerned, unless it is proved that the non-disclosure of the unknown fact in time is wholly or partly attributable to him.'

[46] Art. 10 of the American Convention (right to compensation): 'Every person has the right to be compensated in accordance with the law in the event he has been sentenced by a final judgment through a miscarriage of justice.'

[47] Art. 6 of the Convention on the Elimination of All Forms of Racial Discrimination: 'States Parties shall assure to everyone within their jurisdiction effective protection and remedies, through the competent national tribunals and other State institutions, against any acts of racial discrimination which violate his human rights and fundamental freeedoms contrary to this

The scope of application of these rules differs. Some rules establish reparation only in relation to criminal proceedings. In particular, Article 9(5) of the Civil Covenant and Article 5(5) of the European Convention grant a right to compensation for victims of unlawful arrest or detention; while Article 14(6) of the Civil Covenant, Article 3 of the Seventh Protocol and Article 10 of the American Convention provide for a right to compensation for those convicted by a final judgment through a miscarriage of justice.

Other rules, however, have a wider application. In particular, Article 6 of the Convention on the Elimination of All Forms of Racial Discrimination establishes a right to just and adequate reparation or satisfaction for all those who have suffered damage as a result of racial discrimination; while Article 14 of the Convention Against Torture grants a right to fair and adequate compensation for all victims of acts of torture.

Still, a single problem arises for individual use of all these conventional rules against a State: that is, can we maintain that these rules are self-executing and that injured individuals can therefore claim reparation before the municipal courts of member States? In my opinion, the answer should be in the affirmative. First of all, such a conclusion is derived from a literal interpretation of the above-mentioned norms. See, for instance, Article 5(5) of the European Convention, according to which: 'Everyone who has been the victim of arrest or detention in contravention of the provisions of this Article shall have an enforceable right to compensation'[49].

Moreover, it is clear that it would be completely useless to provide in the treaties for domestic reparation in favour of individuals if those same individuals could not take legal action before domestic courts to obtain such reparation. Finally, I think that States should never be permitted to invoke the lack of domestic norms or mechanisms for granting reparation since the grant of 'substantive' reparation, at least in the form of compensation, does not require any particular domestic norm or mechanism.

Another question to consider is the possible influence of the above-mentioned conventional norms on general international law. Can one maintain

---

Convention, as well as the right to seek from such tribunals just and adequate reparation or satisfaction for any damage suffered as a result of such discrimination.'

[48] Art. 14 of the Convention Against Torture:

'1. Each State Party shall ensure in its legal system that the victim of an act of torture obtains redress and has an enforceable right to fair and adequate compensation, including the means for as full rehabilitation as possible. In the event of the death of the victim as a result of an act of torture, his dependants shall be entitled to compensation.

2. Nothing in this article shall affect any right of the victim or other persons to compensation which may exist under national law.'

[49] See also Sørensen, *Obligations* (note 34), 25.

that these norms reflect, or rather have contributed to the development of, an international customary rule which grants, in favour of individual victims of human rights violations, the right to compensation within the municipal order of the wrongdoing State?

To support such a customary rule one could argue that, in the most important multilateral treaties on human rights, obligations to compensate individuals are established. However, one should note that the above-mentioned conventional rules (which provide expressly for domestic reparation in favour of individuals) have in reality a different content and scope of application, and many of them establish compensation only in some particular areas–particularly the area of criminal proceedings. On the whole, in my opinion, this difference between the various conventional rules does not permit the identification of that uniform practice which is, after all, the basis of international customary law.

Nor can one easily maintain that there are, on this matter, general principles of law recognized by civilized nations, according to Article 38(1)(c) of the ICJ Statute. Yet there are some judgments of municipal courts which seem to move in this direction. For instance, some judgments given in common law countries have established that the violation by judges of fundamental human rights and freedoms protected by the Constitution negates State immunity and requires the State to compensate the injured individual[50]. However, these judgments are for the moment too isolated to create a general principle of law.

I will now examine the problem of the so-called 'procedural' reparation. As I have already suggested[51], aside from the conventional rules which provide for 'substantive' reparation in favour of individuals, there are also many conventional rules which provide for *'procedural' reparation*–that is, the right of the injured individual to obtain an effective remedy before the national authorities. The most important rules in this respect are Article 13 of the European Convention on Human Rights, Article 25 of the American Convention, Article 2(3) of the Civil Covenant, Article 6 of the Racial Discrimination Convention and Article 7(1) of the African Charter.

As you may recall, I have argued that these conventional norms correspond to general international law[52]. But I spoke of these norms in connection with inter-State reparation: in other words, I said that these norms create an obligation on each State party, *owed to the other State parties*, to grant effective domestic remedies. Now we may consider whether these same norms

---

[50] See Privy Council, *Maharaj v. Attorney General of Trinidad and Tobago* (No.2) [1979] A.C. 385; Alberta Provincial Court, *R. v. Germain* (1984) 53 AR 2d 264 (Queen's Bench Division). For a comment on these judgments, see A.A. Olowofoyeku, *Suing Judges: A Study of Judicial Immunity*, 1993, 170-173.

[51] See supra secs. I and III.2.

[52] See supra sec. III.2.

are addressed not only to States but also to private individuals, and whether they are self-executing.

I have no doubt that these norms are addressed also to private individuals; it is enough to refer to the actual wording of the norms. See, for instance, Article 13 of the European Convention, which states:

Everyone whose rights and freedoms as set forth in this Convention are violated shall have an effective remedy before a national authority notwithstanding that the violation has been committed by persons acting in an official capacity.

However, it is more difficult to establish whether these norms are always self-executing[53]. In my opinion, their self-executing character should generally speaking be maintained since their goal is to create a right to a domestic remedy in favour of individuals. However, one should keep in mind that the direct applicability of such norms can be hindered within some States by a lack of adequate tribunals or procedural mechanisms. I therefore think that the self-executing character of such norms also depends on the particular situation in the domestic legal order of any single State.

In any case, I believe that individuals should not lack any protection at the municipal level. In particular, I would maintain that the contracting States, in which such conventional rules are not considered self-executing for lack of adequate domestic mechanisms, must nevertheless grant *compensation* to individuals who cannot use domestic remedies. Such States have in fact violated the obligation undertaken in the treaty to grant those remedies. One should therefore apply, by analogy, the principle developed in European Community law according to which individuals can ask the Member States' courts for compensation for damages resulting from the Member State's failure to implement directives which in themselves do not have direct effect[54].

V. REPARATION TO THE INDIVIDUAL DIRECTLY ESTABLISHED BY INTERNATIONAL LAW

I will now examine whether the violation by a State of the norms concerning the protection of aliens and the protection of human rights produces a right to

---

[53] See, for instance, Mertens, *Le droit à un recours* (note 22), 463, 469, who maintains that Art. 13 of the European Convention is *not* a self-executing norm.

[54] See, in particular, European Court of Justice, judgment of 19 November 1991, Joint Cases C-6/90 and C-9/90, *Francovich v. Italian Republic, Bonifaci and others v. Italian Republic*, E.C.R. 1991, I-5357. For similar and subsequent case-law of the European Court, see M. Balboni, 'La tutela dei singoli dinanzi ai giudici nazionali per violazioni del diritto comunitario da parte degli Stati membri', *Comunicazioni e Studi* 21 (1997), in particular 253, note 147.

reparation *in favour of the injured individual,* a right directly established by international law and *within the framework of the international legal order.*

Here arises the problem of the international personality of individuals. In fact, if one recognizes that international law directly addresses individuals and grants to them rights to reparation that can be enforced within the international order, this conclusion would have a positive effect on the principles of international law concerning the legal personality of individuals[55]. We must therefore consider whether in practice there are, in the field of the protection of aliens and in the human rights field, such rights of individuals to '*international*' reparation.

1. Protection of aliens

I think that the answer should be in the negative, with regard both to customary and conventional rules on the protection of aliens. As I have already noted[56], the customary rules on the protection of aliens establish international obligations on the territorial State towards the national State of the alien, but do not establish any international obligation towards the foreign individual. International practice shows with certainty that only the national State of the alien has an international right to protect its subject; that such a State can decide whether or not to exercise diplomatic protection; that reparation is ultimately due only to such State and not to the individual, so that the State can also decide not to give the individual the compensation obtained.

It is true that some writers have tried to interpret the customary rules on the protection of aliens differently and to envisage also rights and duties of individuals[57]. But such doctrinal theories remain isolated and are not confirmed by international practice. We may perhaps concede that the international rules on the protection of aliens serve not only State interests, but also individual interests[58], however such individual interests do not become true and real international rights.

---

[55] See Condorelli, *Il giudice italiano* (note 34), 82. See also R. Pisillo-Mazzeschi, 'La dottrina pura del diritto di Kelsen e la realtà del diritto internazionale contemporaneo', 4 *Diritto e Cultura* 4 (1994), 43, 58-64; id., 'Die reine Lehre Kelsens und die Realität des heutigen Völkerrechts', in: A. Carrino and G. Winkler (eds.), *Rechtserfahrung und Reine Rechtslehre*, 1995, 129, 145-152.

[56] See supra sects. III.1 and IV.1.

[57] See, e.g., D.P. O'Connell, *International Law*, 2d ed., 1970, vol. 1, 106-112, vol. 2, 941-961. See also, more generally, in favour of the international personality of individuals, the writers cited by Lattanzi, *Garanzie* (note 18), 148-150, notes 146-148.

[58] See Lattanzi, *Garanzie* (note 18), 169-182.

The same conclusion is also valid for the international conventional rules on the treatment and protection of aliens. Such rules usually follow the same traditional inter-State approach and, even in the rare event that they are addressed to private individuals[59], never provide for a true and real right of the individual to reparation *at the international level*. In short, the whole traditional international law on the treatment and protection of aliens leads one to deny the international personality of the individual.

2. Protection of human rights

We must now examine whether the situation is different with respect to the protection of human rights. As I have already noted, the international norms on human rights aim to protect the individual as such[60]. That should lead one to think that the breach of such norms would produce a right to reparation directly in favour of individuals *at the international level*.

In fact, there are in contemporary international law two very interesting examples of norms which seem to establish a right to 'international' reparation in favour of individuals, since they provide for the possibility that an international court might directly require a wrongdoing State to make reparation to the injured individual. These norms are Article 50 of the European Convention on Human Rights and Article 63(1) of the American Convention on Human Rights.

Article 50 of the European Convention states:

> If the Court finds that a decision or a measure taken by a legal authority or any other authority of a High Contracting Party, is completely or partially in conflict with the obligations arising from the present Convention, and if the internal law of the said Party allows only partial reparation to be made for the consequences of this decision or measure, the decision of the Court shall, if necessary, afford *just satisfaction* to the injured party.[61]

---

[59] See supra sec. IV.1.

[60] See supra sec. II.

[61] Italics are mine. On Art. 50 of the European Convention, see M.A. Eissen, 'La Cour européenne des droits de l'homme – De la Convention au règlement', *AFDI* 5 (1959), 618, 635; W. Vis, 'La réparation des violations de la Convention européenne des droits de l'homme (Note sur l'article 50 de la Convention)', in: *La protection internationale des droits de l'homme dans le cadre européen – Travaux du Colloque organisé par la Faculté de Droit et des Sciences Politiques et Economiques de Strasbourg*, 1961, 279; P. Vegleris, 'Modes de redressement des violations de la Convention européenne des droits de l'homme – Esquisse d'une classification', in: *Mélanges offerts à Polys Modinos - Problèmes des droits de l'homme et de l'unification européenne*, 1968, 369; H. Golsong, 'Quelques réflexions à propos du pouvoir de la Cour européenne des droits de l'homme d'accorder une satisfaction équitable (article 50 de la Convention européenne des Droits de l'Homme)', in: *René Cassin Amicorum Discipulorumque Liber*, vol. I, 1969, 89; R. Pelloux, 'Les arrêts de la Cour européenne des droits de l'homme

Some writers maintain that this norm is based on similar norms, found in many arbitration treaties, which had the goal of limiting an arbitral tribunal's power by excluding some forms of reparation, such as *restitutio in integrum*, and by admitting the payment of a sum of money ('just satisfaction') to the creditor State as the only form of reparation[62].

Viewing Article 50 as a continuation of previous conventional practice, scholars initially interpreted this provision in a very traditional way: that is, as a norm establishing only inter-State obligations. They therefore maintained that Article 50 was destined to be applied only in exceptional cases. They also affirmed that the obligation requiring the wrongdoing State to make reparation was not an obligation towards the injured individual, but rather an obligation *towards the other States parties*[63].

---

dans les affaires Stögmuller et Matznetter', *AFDI* 16 (1970), 338; Ch. Vallée, 'Une application de l'article 50 de la Convention européenne des droits de l'homme', *RGDIP* 76 (1972), 1105; A.F. Panzera, 'Il potere della Corte europea dei diritti dell'uomo di accordare un'equa riparazione alla parte lesa', *Riv. dir. eur.* 14 (1974), 317; M. Miele, 'L'art.50 della Convenzione europea sui diritti dell'uomo e le sue prime applicazioni giurisprudenziali', in: *Studi in onore di Manlio Udina*, vol. I, 1975, 539; R. Luzzatto, 'La Corte europea dei diritti dell'uomo e la riparazione delle violazioni della Convenzione', in: id., 423; A. Giardina, 'La mise en oeuvre au niveau national des arrêts et des décisions internationaux', RC 165 (1979), IV, 257; G. Ress, 'Effets des arrêts de la Cour européenne des droits de l'homme en droit interne et pour les tribunaux nationaux', in: *Actes du cinquième colloque international sur la Convention européenne des droits de l'homme (Francfort, 9-12 Avril 1980)*, 1982, 235, 254 et seqq.; M. Gestri, 'Risarcimento del danno per violazioni della Convenzione europea nella giurisprudenza della Corte dei diritti dell'uomo', in: *Foro it.*, 1987, IV, 1; G.M. Ubertazzi, 'L'accertamento della violazione della Convenzione europea come "equa soddisfazione" alla parte lesa', *Riv. int. diritti dell'uomo*, 1988, 75; P. Van Dijk and G.J.H. Van Hoof, *Theory and Practice of the European Convention on Human Rights*, 2nd ed., 1990, 171 et seqq.; J.F. Flauss, 'La "satisfaction équitable" devant les organes de la Convention européenne des droits de l'homme', *Europe*, 1992, 2; J.G. Merrills, *The Development of International Law by the European Court of Human Rights*, 1993, 63 et seqq.; M.E. Mas, 'Right to Compensation under Article 50', in: R.St.J. Macdonald, F. Matscher, H. Petzold (eds.), *The European System for the Protection of Human Rights*, 1993, 775; G. Dannemann, *Schadensersatz bei Verletzung der Europäischen Menschenrechtskonvention – Eine rechtsvergleichende Untersuchung zur Haftung nach Art.50 EMRK*, 1994; J. Sharpe, 'Article 50', in: L.-E. Pettiti, E. Décaux, P.-H. Imbert (eds.), *La Convention européenne des droits de l'homme - Commentaire article par article*, 1995, 809; H.C. Krüger, 'Reflections on Some Aspects of Just Satisfaction under the European Convention on Human Rights', in: *Liber amicorum M.A. Eissen*, 1995; J.F. Flauss, 'La réparation due en cas de violation de la Convention européenne des droits de l'homme', *Journal des tribunaux*, 1996, 8; id., 'La banalisation du contentieux indemnitaire devant la Cour européenne des droits de l'homme', *Rev. trim. des droits de l'homme*, 1996, 93; P. Pirrone, 'Il caso *Papamichalopoulos* dinanzi alla Corte europea dei diritti dell'uomo: *restitutio in integrum* ed equa soddisfazione', *Riv. dir. int.* 80 (1997), 152.

[62] See, e.g., Vis, *La réparation* (note 61), 281-82; Golsong, *Quelques réflexions* (note 61), 92; Luzzatto, *La Corte europea* (note 61), 429-431.

[63] See, for example, Luzzatto, *La Corte europea* (note 61), 437-39.

However, the case-law of the European Court has developed a very different interpretation of Article 50: first, 'just satisfaction' as referred to in the treaty is considered an ordinary means of reparation where the municipal law of a State does not allow total reparation to be made for the consequences of the breach of the Convention; second, the obligation of affording 'just satisfaction' is understood as an obligation *towards the injured individual*. At this juncture, the prevailing doctrine is in agreement with these principles.

Therefore, even if one believes that the original formula of Article 50 was based on some traditional formulas, one must now acknowledge that the introduction of this formula in a very particular system, such as that of the European Convention on Human Rights, has produced entirely new consequences[64]. However, the reparation in favour of the individual is subject to some limitations. First, Article 50 does not encompass all violations of the Convention, but only those cases in which the violation results from a decision or measure taken by a legal authority of the State and the internal law of the State allows only partial reparation to be made for the consequences of this decision or measure.

Second, as I have already noted, Article 50–according to the prevailing interpretation–establishes that the Court may require of the wrongdoing State only the payment of damages, or at least monetary indemnity, and not restitution in kind (such as, for example, the repeal, modification or annulment of the norm or act which resulted in the breach of the Convention)[65]. In substance, therefore, the intervention of the European Court concerning reparation has a subsidiary character. In fact, if *restitutio in integrum* in internal law is possible, it is up to the wrongdoing State to put it into effect; if instead *restitutio* is not possible, the European Court will be able to grant 'just satisfaction' to the individual[66].

Third, Article 50 establishes that the Court affords just satisfaction 'if necessary'. Given that the Court has some discretionary power under Article 50, it is difficult to maintain that the individual has a true and real right to 'just satisfaction' prior to the judgment of the Court. However, the situation is different once the judgment has been delivered. While it is true that the individual, even after a judgment in his or her favour, cannot at the international level force the guilty State to give compensation or indemnity, the application of the European Convention in municipal law creates a right of the individual vis-à-vis the State based on the municipal law of the State itself[67].

---

[64] Cf. Giardina, *La mise en oeuvre* (note 61), 259.

[65] But see, recently, European Court on Human Rights, *Papamichalopoulos et autres c. Grèce*, in: Publications de la Cour européenne des droits de l'homme, sèrie A, vol. 330-B. On this case, cf. Pirrone, Il caso *Papamichalopoulos* (note 61), 152 et seqq.

[66] See, recently, Pirrone, Il caso *Papamichalopoulos* (note 61), 169-170.

[67] Cf. Luzzatto, *La Corte europea* (note 61), 444.

Therefore if a State, found by the European Court to have breached the Convention, refuses to comply with the judgment, there will arise not only a responsibility on the guilty State towards the other States parties, but also a right of the individual to claim 'just satisfaction' before the domestic courts of the guilty State.

Similar considerations apply with regard to Article 63(1) of the American Convention on Human Rights. This norm states:

> If the Court finds that there has been a violation of a right or freedom protected by this convention, the Court shall rule that the injured party be ensured the enjoyment of his right or freedom that was violated. It shall also rule, if appropriate, that the consequences of the measure or situation that constituted the breach of such right or freedom be remedied and that *fair compensation* be paid to the injured party.[68]

Here, too, the individual does not appear to have an actual right to reparation prior to the judgment of the Inter-American Court, even if the wording of Article 63(1) is more favorable to the individual than that of Article 50 of the European Convention. On the other hand, one may also maintain with regard to the American Convention that an individual, having obtained a compensatory judgment, can enforce it before the national courts. This conclusion is reinforced by Article 68 of the Convention which, with regard to enforcing judgments of the Inter-American Court, states:

> 1. The States Parties to the Convention undertake to comply with the judgment of the Court in any case to which they are parties.

> 2. That part of a judgment that stipulates compensatory damages may be executed in the country concerned in accordance with domestic procedure governing the execution of judgments against the state.

Therefore, one can maintain that Article 50 of the European Convention and Article 63 of the American Convention, even with their limitations, constitute an example of 'international' reparation in favour of individuals. In fact, the two norms envisage granting to individuals reparations which are provided for by an international treaty and established by an international court.

Finally, we should also examine, with regard to Article 50 of the European Convention and Article 63 of the American Convention, the problem of the relationship between these two conventional norms and general international law. Can one say that the two conventional norms reflect general international law or that they have contributed to the creation of new customary international law[69]?

---

[68] Italics are mine.

[69] On the relationship between the European Convention on Human Rights and international customary law, see, e.g., P.J. Duffy, 'English Law and the European Convention on Human Rights', in: 29 *ICLQ* 29 (1980), 585, 599-605.

As is well known, some writers maintain that the European Convention and the American Convention entirely correspond to customary international law. But I prefer the prevailing doctrine according to which it is not possible to accept such a global solution and one must instead assess each conventional rule to see whether it corresponds to the customary law existing independently of the Convention. With regard to Article 50 of the European Convention and Article 63 of the American Convention, I think that the answer should be in the negative. These two rules to date remain isolated in the conventional international law of human rights: the European Convention and the American Convention are presently the most advanced examples of the international protection of human rights.

V. CONCLUSION

I think that I can draw some general conclusions from my research. This research has shown that individuals who have been injured by a breach of human rights have a right to reparation ('substantive' and 'procedural' reparation) mostly within municipal legal orders[70] and only rarely, and with many restrictions, within the international legal order[71]. Moreover, even when individuals obtain a right to reparation within the international order (following an international judgment), they have the possibility of actually enforcing that right only through the municipal legal order. To sum up therefore, the best prospects for reparation for individuals continue to be through the incorporation of international law in national law and through the domestic courts.

In other words, what happened in traditional international law continues to happen in contemporary international law, although one should note that the possibilities of using domestic law with regard to human rights are wider than with regard to the protection of aliens[72]. One may therefore conclude that, in passing from the traditional law on the protection of aliens to the new law on the protection of human rights, no real structural change has occurred in international law. The international rules on human rights tend largely to impose on States obligations towards other States concerning the treatment to be granted to individuals subject to their jurisdiction. Those rules thus maintain, on the whole, their character as laws among sovereign entities, or laws which govern inter-State relationships[73]. Within this framework, it is

---

[70] See supra sec. IV.2.

[71] See supra sec. V.2.

[72] See supra sec. IV on the different role of self-executing norms with regard to the protection of aliens and the protection of human rights.

[73] But see, recently, for a somewhat different opinion, A.S. Mullerson, 'Human Rights and the Individual as Subject of International Law: A Soviet View', *EJIL* 1 (1990), 33, 37.

difficult to draw general conclusions in favour of the international personality of the individual.

Moreover, these general conclusions are subject to a reservation. As we have seen, there are some regional conventions on human rights–the European and American Conventions–which adopt a rather peculiar approach and which tend to give a more important role to the individual. They do that both by establishing judicial mechanisms for the settlement of disputes in favour of individuals[74] and by establishing the possibility of an 'international' reparation in favour of individuals for violations, or at least some violations, of human rights.

According to some writers[75], one could speak in such cases of a 'relative' or '*inter partes*' international personality of the individual, that is of a personality limited by the conventional rules and confined to the States parties to the convention. In my opinion, acceptance of the concept of *inter partes* international personality depends on theoretical premises about the very notion of legal personality in the general theory of law. In any case, I think that the concept of *inter partes* personality aptly expresses the fact that the European and American Conventions are very particular conventional systems which have contributed to, and which still contribute to, a process of remarkable change in the international law concerning the condition of the individual.

---

[74] On the importance of those judicial mechanisms with regard to the problem of the international personality of individuals, see, e.g., M. Giuliano, T. Scovazzi & T. Treves, *Diritto internazionale. Parte generale*, 1991, 179-183. We should also consider that the control machinery of the European Convention on Human Rights will be further developed in favour of individuals with the entry into force of the Eleventh Protocol (1994) of the Convention.

[75] Condorelli, *Cours* (note 1), 15-17, 127.

Reparation for Human Rights Violations Committed by the *Apartheid* Regime in South Africa

Lovell Fernandez

I. INTRODUCTION

The first democratic government in South Africa was voted into power in April 1994. This marked the demise of *Apartheid*, a system which was characterised by legally entrenched racial discrimination and severe political repression. The former State security police were merciless in clamping down on political dissidents. The tens of thousands of South Africans who opposed the system were violently murdered, tortured, maimed, abducted and subjected to various forms severely dehumanising ill-treatment. Thousands of people were arrested and detained for long periods, often without trial.

All this affected not only individual lives but also the lives of families and entire communities. In effect, the whole nation was brutalised at the hand of the State. The effects of this ghastly period are still with us today. The new democracy has inherited the plight of thousands of people whose lives and livelihoods have been severely affected under the *Apartheid* past. In recognition of the atrocities perpetrated under the old order, the present Government has pledged itself to nation building and reconciliation. Implicit in this exercise is the principle that those who have suffered gross human rights abuses under *Apartheid* should receive reparation and rehabilitation. Restoring the civil and human dignity of victims is an essential element of national unity and reconciliation.

II. THE LEGAL BASIS FOR REPARATIONS

Under international law there is a well established right which entitles the victims of human rights abuses to compensation for their losses and suffering.[1]

---

[1] Article 8 of the Universal Declaration of Human Rights stipulates as follows: 'Everyone has the right to an effective remedy by the competent national tribunals for acts violating the fundamental rights granted him by the constitution or by law.' Art. 2(3) of the International

A. Randelzhofer and C. Tomuschat (eds.), State Responsibility and the Individual, 173–187.
© 1999 *Kluwer Law International. Printed in Great Britain.*

Over the past three years South Africa has signed a number of major international instruments which place it under obligation to provide victims of human rights abuses with fair and adequate compensation. The duty of the South African State to provide for the victims of gross human rights abuses was reiterated by the Constitutional Court when it held per Didcott J that reparations 'are usually payable by states, and there is no reason to doubt that the postscript envisages our own state shouldering the national responsibility for those. It therefore does not contemplate that the state will go scot free. On the contrary, I believe, an actual commitment on the point is implicit in its terms, a commitment in principle to the assumption by the state of the burden.'[2]

In South Africa, the legal basis for making reparations to the victims of past conflicts is the Promotion of National Unity and Reconciliation Act (hereinafter the 'TRC Act').[3] This law, which was enacted in 1995 amidst fierce opposition from the ranks of the former ruling party, has the following aims:

1. To provide for the investigation and the establishment of as complete a picture as possible of the nature, causes and extent of gross violations of human rights committed within and outside the country during the period from 1 March 1960 to the cut-off date and to establish the fate of the victims;

2. To grant amnesty to persons who make full disclosure of all the relevant facts relating to acts associated with a political objective committed in the course of the conflicts during the stated period;

3. To afford victims an opportunity to relate the violations they suffered;

4. To implement measures aimed at the granting of reparations to, and the rehabilitation and restoration of the human and civil dignity of, victims of violation;

Covenant on Civil and Political Rights (signed by South Africa on 3 October 1994) states: 'Each State Party to the present Covenant undertakes: To ensure that any person whose rights and freedoms as herein recognised are violated shall have an effective remedy, notwithstanding that the violation has been committed by persons acting in an official capacity.' See also the following: Convention against Torture and Other Cruel, Inhuman or Degrading Treatment or Punishment (signed by South Africa on 29 January 1993); Inter-American Convention on Human Rights; Judgement of the Inter-American Court of Human Rights, Series C, No. 4 (1988); Inter-American Commission on Human Rights, Report No. 28/92 (2 October 1992); and Inter-American Commission on Human Rights, Report No. 29/92 (2 October 1992). See generally T. van Boven, Study Concerning the Right to Restitution, Compensation and Rehabilitation of Victims of Gross Violations of Human Rights and Fundamental Freedoms (Report submitted to the UN Commission on Human Rights, 2 July 1993).

[2] *Azapo and Others* v. *The President of the Republic of South Africa and Others*, 1996 (8) BCLR 1015 (CC) at para. 62.

[3] Act No. 34 of 1995.

5. To report to the nation about such violations and victims; and

6. To make recommendations aimed at the prevention of the commission of gross human rights violations.

The Act provides for the establishment of a Truth and Reconciliation Commission, a Committee on Human Rights Violations, a Committee on Amnesty and a Committee on Reparation and Rehabilitation. The Truth and Reconciliation Commission, which was appointed by President Mandela from a list of names nominated by ordinary members of the public, has been at work since 1996 and is scheduled to complete its task by June 1998.

III. THE REPARATION AND REHABILITATION COMMITTEE

In terms of the Act, one of the functions of the TRC is to make recommendations to the President with regard to:

- the policy which should be followed or measures which should be taken with regard to the granting of reparation to victims or the taking of other measures aimed at rehabilitating and restoring the human and civil dignity of victims;
- measures which should be taken to grant urgent interim reparation to victims.[4]

The Reparation and Rehabilitation Committee (hereafter the 'RRC') is the body responsible for formulating the TRC's reparation policy.[5] Pursuant to the Act, the Committee may make recommendations which may include urgent interim measures as to the appropriate reparation to victims.

IV. FORMULATING REPARATION POLICY

A major criticism levelled at the TRC, in particular its RRC, is that it has to date not delivered anything to the victims - this despite its being in existence for more than a year. What annoys people is that nothing has been done for the victims whereas perpetrators who are granted amnesty are released from prison and indemnified from criminal prosecution and civil claims. Added to this is the fact that some people who would have qualified for urgent interim relief have since died. Others are experiencing a severe deterioration in their health or material circumstances. This is particularly disconcerting given the

---

[4] Section 4(f).
[5] Section 23.

fact that the Truth and Reconciliation Commission has repeatedly announced that its work is victim-driven. The chief reason for the delay in making reparation has been the extensive, sluggish and drawn out consultative process which the RRC has adopted. Victims in need of urgent relief find this protracted policy development hard to understand, especially since the funds are available. To be sure, one does not need an elaborate procedure or a host of criteria to be able to tell whether or not someone is in urgent need of medical care or whether or not a person is severely undernourished.

Thorough consultation is a good thing for it makes for wise and informed decision making. However, in the case of RRC it has had the side effect of allowing the emergency needs of some of the victims to pale into background - this to such an extent that only a week ago were the 'Draft Regulations Regarding Urgent Interim Reparation' finalised for promulgation. At the National Consultative Conference which was convened in April 1997, the RRC was criticised by victim groups for consulting widely with other parties and organisations but not sufficiently with the victims themselves.

The National Consultative Conference was called by the RRC to elicit comments on its 'Discussion Document for a Proposed Policy for Urgent Interim Reparation and Final Reparation'.[6] The document sets out the moral and legal basis for reparations, the process of policy development, reparations principles, reparation policy proposals, implementation of reparations and the sources of revenue. I will now address the main elements of the document together with the debate relating to some of them.

V. DEFINITION OF VICTIMS

According to the TRC Act[7] *victims* include
(a) persons who, individually or together with one or more persons, suffered harm in the form of physical or mental injury, emotional suffering, pecuniary loss or a substantial impairment of human rights
  (i)   as a result of a gross violation of human rights; or
  (ii) as a result of an act associated with a political objective for which amnesty has been granted;
(b) persons who, individually or together with one or more persons, suffered harm in the form of physical or mental injury, emotional suffering, pecuniary loss or a substantial impairment of human rights, as a result of such a person intervening to assist persons contemplated in paragraph (a) who

---

[6]   Truth and Reconciliation Commission: National Consultation 1997/04/02 (prepared by G. Wildschut and W. Orr).
[7]   Section 1(1).

were in distress or to prevent victimisation of such persons; and such relatives or dependants of victims as may be described.

Relatives and dependants are defined in the Final Draft Regulations which await to be gazetted. Relatives of victims are defined as
(i) a parent of, or somebody who acted as a parent for a victim;
(ii) a grandparent of a victim;
(iii)a person married to the victim under any law, custom or belief; and
(iv)a child of a victim, irrespective of whether such child was born in or out of wedlock or was adopted.[8]

The dependants of victims include
(i) a relative or other relation of a victim who is of necessity dependent on the victim for his or her livelihood;
(ii) a child of a victim, irrespective of whether he or she was born in or out of wedlock or was adopted, including a child of the spouse of a victim, who is of necessity dependent on the victim for his or her livelihood; and
(iii)any person to whom a victim has a legal duty to support.[9]

A concern that has been raised by victim support groups is that there are many victims who have not heard about the TRC or who, for various reasons, have not been able to appear before the Commission to make a statement. This applies particularly to people living in remote and barely accessible rural areas which, in practice, suffered most under *Apartheid*. One cannot therefore, at this stage, speak of a closed list of victims. The RRC has acknowledged that it will have to address the needs of 'on-going victims'. It has therefore decided to create a 'window of opportunity' for such people. However, the RRC has intimated that a fixed timespan will have to be stipulated within which such victims should come forward.
To be sure, this would be of no avail to unknowing victims if public education on the purpose of the TRC is not extended to the remotest areas. Radio stations could play a crucial role in reaching rural victims. It has also been contended that TRC staff whose contract period with the Commission has expired, should be re-employed to help access the outstanding victims.

---

[8] Regulation 1 (2)(a) of the 'Promotion of National Unity and Reconciliation Act, 1995' (Act No. 34 of 1995): Measures to Provide Urgent Interim Reparation to Victims (ungazetted Government Notice, 1997).
[9] Ibid. Section 1(2)(b).

VI. PRINCIPLES OF REPARATION

1. Categories of Reparation

The development of reparation policy took into account the following categories of reparation:[10]

Redress, which refers to the right to fair and adequate compensation;

Restitution, which is the right to be reinstated, as far as possible, in the situation that existed for the beneficiary prior to the violation (*restitutio in integrum*);

Rehabilitation, which is the right to the provision of medical and psychological care and fulfilment of significant personal and community needs;

Restoration of dignity, which could include symbolic forms of reparation; and

Reassurance of non-repetition, which refers to the enactment of legislative and administrative measures which contribute to the maintenance of a stable society and the prevention of the re-occurrence of human rights violations.

2. Quantum of Reparation

The RRC has decided, as a matter of policy, that victims will not be subjected to a means test and that each primary victim will receive the same quantum of reparation.

This policy decision has elicited a great deal of criticism from victim support groups. The RRC's rationale for not imposing a means test on the victims is that the viability of a means testing and the administration thereof would cost more money than would be saved by excluding certain categories of person. 'The data gathered by the RRC suggest that the proportion of relatively wealthy victims that would be excluded as a result of means testing is extremely small in relation to the victims that would qualify for reparation. Therefore the saving that would be made by excluding certain victims on the ground of wealth would not offset the costs which would have to be incurred in administering and verifying a means test'.[11]

Whilst this argument is theoretically sound, in practice it is bound to unleash a negative public sentiment. The fact of the matter is that it is relatively wealthy people who are able to access the means to state their

---

[10] Wildschut & Orr (supra note 6), at 10.

[11] Ibid. at 12.

claims before the TRC. As noted above, there are victims who have not been able to come before the commission, invariably because they lack the means.

The fact that all primary victims will receive an equal quantum of reparations, regardless of the number of times they have suffered gross human rights violations, is bound to cause even more dissatisfaction. The argument enunciated by the RRC is that 'it is impossible to devise a set of criteria which provide for varying amounts of reparation to be paid to victims according to their degree of suffering without producing unfair or arbitrary results'.[12] Another argument put forward by the RRC is that 'certain individuals can withstand horrendous long term torture and remain relatively healthy and functional, while other individuals may be permanently debilitated as a result of a single act of violence'.[13] The reasoning here is that one would be penalising those who were able to cope with torture.

This is a matter that the RRC and indeed the TRC will find hard to justify morally to a widow whose politically activist husband was killed by the police or the child whose parents were shot and killed at a public protest meeting against *Apartheid* policies. Although it may be hard to assess the actual degree of suffering that people have undergone, it should not be an insurmountable hurdle to determine their present degree of need as a result of the gross human rights violations that they have suffered.

Delegates at the National Consultative Forum referred to above grudgingly accepted the rationale underlying the payment of the same quantum of final reparation. However, several speakers criticised the RRC for not having explained to the affected victim population the reasoning behind the decision. It was emphasised that it is absolutely essential for the RRC to launch a massive campaign aimed at educating the public on this matter if it wants to avoid tension in communities.

VII. PHASES OF REPARATION POLICY

The RRC has divided its reparation policy into two categories namely, Urgent Interim Reparation and Final Reparation. The former refers to the delivery of short-term reparative measures to victims in urgent need who cannot wait for an implementing structure for delivering final reparation. Urgent interim reparation should take place until final reparation is made. Final reparation speaks for itself; it means just that. Those victims who received urgent interim reparation will receive priority in the making of final reparation. Beneficiaries

---

[12] Ibid.
[13] Ibid.

of urgent interim reparation will not in any way be prejudiced in the quantity and quality of final relief granted.

1. Implementation Mechanism for Urgent Interim Reparation

Draft regulations, to be promulgated soon, have now been formulated to provide urgent interim reparation to the victims of gross violations of human rights. The regulations make provision for the creation of a panel which will execute the orders of the RRC in respect of the action necessary to aid the victims. The panel, which shall be constituted by the Minister of Justice, shall consist of six people, namely an accounting person as chairperson; an officer from the Department of Justice; an officer from the Department of Health; an officer from the Department of Welfare; and an officer from any other Department of State as the Minister of Justice may consider expedient. The panel may co-opt other persons so that NGOs may also become involved in its work. However, the co-opted person will not participate in the actual decision making.

When the RRC receives an application for reparation, it must ensure the following:[14]

- the applicant is a victim as defined in the Act;
- the applicant is alive at the time the application is considered;
- the applicant is in urgent need of medical, emotional, educational, symbolic, legal or administrative assistance or intervention; and
- it will cause undue hardship or it will be unjust or unreasonable if the applicant should await the implementation of a system of final reparation before he or she may receive reparation or rehabilitation.

Once these criteria are met, the RRC shall order that the victim receive assistance with regard to:

- emotional support, including counselling, therapy and victim-offender mediation in order to restore the emotional quality of life affected as a result of gross human rights violation;
- medical assistance to enable him or her to deal with, and if possible, improve a potentially life-threatening medical condition that occurred as a result of the gross human rights violation;
- education or training for a victim who has been physically or mentally disabled as a result of the gross violation of his or her human rights in order to restore his or her human dignity or physical or mental well-being; or
- symbolic, legal, administrative assistance, including the issuing of death certificates, the obtaining of declarations of death and the exhumation,

---

[14] Regulation 3(1) the 'Promotion of National Unity and Reconciliation Act' (note 8).

reburial and erection of headstones in respect of persons killed or who died as a result of the gross violation of human rights in the past in order to restore his or her human dignity or physical or emotional well-being.[15]

Once the RRC issues any of these written orders to the Panel, the Panel shall without delay execute the order of the Committee by

- taking the necessary steps to facilitate access for a victim to the appropriate services as ordered by the Committee; and
- arranging for payments from the Fund in respect of any service to which the victim has been referred; or
- arranging for payments from the Fund to or on behalf of the victim where the Committee ordered that an amount of money be paid to the victim.[16]

The benefits for the individual victims will be a referral to appropriate services, depending on type of need. In instances where free services are not available, financial assistance may be awarded in order to access and/or pay for services deemed necessary to meet specific identified urgent needs. Each victim will be entitled to a maximum of R2,000 in order to meet these costs.[17]

The regulations also provide that no award of reparation shall be ceded or assigned by the victim; attached under a court judgement or execution order; or form part of the victim's estate should it be sequestrated.[18]

2. Implementing Mechanism for Final Reparation

At present there is no implementation structure in place. However, in its policy document,[19] the RRC sets out an implementation programme involving the Office of the President, a Board of Trustees, a National Reparation Office and the nine Provincial Reparation Offices.

The President shall establish the National Reparation Office, appoint a Board of Trustees for the President's Fund and administer the President 's Fund. The RRC recommends that members of the Board, who would be honorary, should be drawn from the corporate sector, government, NGOs, faith communities and victims. The duty of the Board would be to report to the President on income and expenditure of funds and on the status of the President's Fund.

The National Reparation Office shall be established in the office of the President and it shall comprise members of the relevant government depart-

---

[15] Ibid., Regulation 3(2).

[16] Regulation 4(1).

[17] 'Proposed Reparation and Rehabilitation Policies (Urgent Interim Reparation and Final Reparation)' (Truth and Reconciliation Commission 1997/09/09), 9.

[18] Regulation 5.

[19] See supra note 6.

ments. The Office will cease its operations once final reparation grants have been paid out and all applications from communities have been entertained. This is a three- to five-year programme.

The functions of the *National Reparation Office* shall be to

- Establish regional offices and give directives pertaining to the implementation of all RRC policy recommendations;
- Implement and administer the Individual Benefits Policy;
- Receive and refer victims to appropriate regional offices;
- Finalise, regulate and administer possible interventions for the Symbolic Reparation recommendations;
- Monitor and lobby for issues pertaining to emotional, medical, educational and material interventions;
- Report to the Office of the President on the process of implementation;
- Report to the Board of Trustees on financial matters;
- Receive monthly reports from provincial offices; and
- Receive community applications in all the categories of possible reparations.

The RRC envisages the Provincial Reparation Offices to be established in existing government structures with linkage to existing Social Welfare offices. These offices will exist until each victim has been accessed and signed up. The function of the Offices will be to

- Implement policy matters as determined by the National Reparation Office;
- Receive names and information about victims and communities from the National Office;
- Contact victims, prioritising those in urgent need, explaining how to access reparation awards and explain the various ways in which the Individual Benefits Policy could be used;
- Disburse money;
- Liase with financial institutions and other professional human rights bodies to provide financial management and other services as well as individual counselling;
- Consult with communities who make applications for symbolic reparations;
- Arrange activities of healing/mourning/reconciliation in the region; and
- Report on all provincial activities and the progress of implementation on a monthly basis.

VIII. FINAL REPARATION BENEFITS

Each victim will receive a maximum individual grant of R23,023 (D-Mark 8,923 or US $4,898). This sum is based on a benchmark amount of R21,700, which is the median annual household income in South Africa in 1997.[20] The poverty datum line of R15,600 per annum was rejected as a benchmark as this would condemn victims to a life close to poverty rather than enabling them to live in dignity. The monetary package to which each victim will be entitled will be based on an easily administered formula, which differentiates according to three criteria:

1. An acknowledgement of the suffering caused by the violation;
2. An amount to facilitate access to services. Rural people, who in practice access services with difficulty, will receive a premium on their grant which is on the assumption that services in the rural areas are 30 per cent more expensive than in urban areas;
3. An amount to subsidise daily living costs, which is based on the number of dependants and/or relatives up to a maximum of nine people. Again, people in rural areas will receive more because the cost of living in rural areas is 15 per cent more expensive than in urban areas.[21]

Each portion of the formula is weighted as follows: 1 = 50 per cent; 2 = 25 per cent; and 3 = 25 per cent of the total individual reparation grant. The annual individual reparation grant will be calculated for each beneficiary and paid as 50 per cent of the total every 6 months. The annual payments will continue for a period of six years.

IX. ADMINISTRATION: THE PRESIDENT'S FUND

The grants will be administered and funded through the President's Fund, which was established in terms of the TRC Act.[22] The Fund has been accruing resources through international and local donations, parliamentary appropriations and earned interest on these funds. With an estimated 22,000 victims, the provisional total cost of implementing the reparations policy will be R2.864.400,000 (D-Mark 1.102.325,000), which represents 0,5 per cent of the country's national budget.[23] The costs could be considerably higher given the fact that not all victims have made statements before the TRC.

---

[20] Information obtained from Mr. Lindley Moloi on 17 September 1997. See 'Proposed Reparation and Rehabilitation Policies' (note 17), at 15.

[21] Ibid. at 16.

[22] Section 42. The Act (Section 47) states as from the date on which the Truth and Reconciliation Commission is dissolved, all the Fund's assets shall be transferred to the Disaster Relief Fund.

[23] 'Proposed Reparation and Rehabilitation Policies' (note 17), at 16.

X. SYMBOLIC REPARATION, COMMUNITY REHABILITATION AND INSTITUTIONAL REFORM

One of the cornerstones of the *Apartheid* system was the ruthless policy of 'divide and rule'. In pursuance of this policy the entire nation was classified into racial categories and sub-categories. With 87 per cent of the country's land declared habitable only by white people, over 3½ million black people were forcibly removed and relocated under the Group Areas laws to places where it was difficult to eke out a living. Community life was destroyed, schools were closed done and whatever social amenities existed in black communities were summarily brought to an abrupt end. The Group Areas legislation was undergirded by related legislation which forcibly kept families apart, practically forcing black men working in urban areas to live for decades without their families. Wives lived apart from their husbands and children apart from their fathers.

All this resulted in massive social psychological dislocation. Added to this were the draconian state security laws which drove thousands of people into exile where they lived for many years away from their dear ones. This caused complex physical and emotional needs. Many of the people and whole communities affected by these measures are still suffering both the physical and mental anguish that accompanied their experiences. The huge crime rate presently sweeping the country is directly related to laws which forced children to grow up in abnormal homes and communities. Today thousands of young people are illiterate, unemployable and live in poverty. Many of the deponents who have appeared before the TRC exhibit the adverse effects of post traumatic stress symptoms.

The TRC has consequently formulated the following community rehabilitation programmes which are based on the needs expressed by the victims themselves in their statements. In fact, over 90 per cent of the deponents asked for a range of services which can be purchased if money is available, for example, education, medical care, housing etc.[24]

1) Symbolic Reparation: The following services are planned for the individual beneficiaries:

Death certificates will be issued to people who have not received death certificates for their relatives. Mechanisms to facilitate the declaration of death will be established and implemented in those cases where the family requests an official declaration of death. Exhumations, reburials and solemn ceremonies are envisaged. In a number of cases the need has become evident for the

---

[24] Ibid. at 15.

erection of tombstones and headstones.[25] The costs would be met from the individual reparation grant.

The TRC is recommending that mechanisms be put in place to expunge the criminal records of the victims who received criminal sentences for their political activities. Another recommendation is that mechanisms be implemented to facilitate the resolution of outstanding legal matters which are directly related to reported violations.

For the benefit of the community, streets and community facilities will be renamed to reflect, remember and honour individuals or events in particular communities. The TRC is also proposing the building of monuments and memorials to commemorate the conflicts and/or victories of the past. It recommends that the specific needs of communities regarding remembering and/or celebrating should be honoured through culturally appropriate ceremonies.

National symbolic benefits will include the renaming of public facilities in honour of individuals or past events. The necessary mechanisms should be put in place by the appropriate Ministries.[26]

2) Health Care:[27] A national demobilisation programme is planned to demilitarise young people and to assist them to resolve conflicts without resorting to violence. Many of them hardened by their past exposure to and involvement in political violence. Educational institutions and sporting bodies will be drawn into the programme, which will consist of social, therapeutic and political processes and interventions appropriate for the area in which they are being implemented.

The TRC is recommending the implementation of a multi-disciplinary programme to address the stress, trauma and unemployment resulting from the dislocation and displacement of people from their homes because of past political conflicts. This programme calls for the involvement of the relevant Ministries and Departments of Health, Housing and Welfare. Equally necessary is the need for multi-disciplinary teams to cater for the emotional and physical needs of victims and survivors of human rights violations.. The TRC is recommending that the Department of Health set up easily accessible treatment centres and that it should also take into account cultural and personal preferences.

Perpetrators and their families need to be integrated into normal community life. This is essential to create a society in which human rights abuses do not recur. The TRC is recommending that individual and family rehabilitative

---

[25] Ibid. at 18.

[26] Ibid. at 19.

[27] Ibid. at 20-21.

systems need to be instituted to assist individuals and families to come to terms with their violent past and learn ways of resolving conflict non-violently.[28]

Providing community based mental health care to victims and their families is being proposed as one of the central features of community rehabilitation. The TRC is recommending that the public needs to be educated about mental health in order to dispel prevailing negative perceptions of mental therapy. This campaign should include educating the public on the link between mental health and conflicts of the past. However, mental health care should not be regarded in isolation, but should be linked to skills training and socio-economic development projects such as the current *Masakhane* (Xhosa word meaning 'let us build each other') project. Also proposed is the establishment of self-sustaining community based survivor support groups with trained facilitators from the community. The TRC further recommends that special-ised Trauma Counselling Services which could also be used to train health care workers in order to improve their skills in the area of family-based therapy.[29]

In order to compensate lost educational opportunities as a result of human rights abuses, the TRC is suggesting the establishment of Community Colleges and Youth Centres which could help to re-integrate the affected youth into society. Rebuilding of schools, particularly in rural and disadvan-taged areas, should be prioritised. Remedial and emotional support should be included in mainstream educational programmes. The TRC specifically recommends that educational facilities should provide skill-based training courses in order to respond to the needs of mature students, to help them find employment.[30]

Another proposal is that specific attention should be given to establishing housing projects in communities where gross violations of human rights led to mass destruction of property and/or displacement. The Ministry of Housing is suggested as the appropriate authority to put the mechanism in place.[31]

3) Institutional Reform: In its Final Report the TRC will make recommenda-tions around institutional, legislative and administrative measures designed to prevent the recurrence of human rights abuses in the future.[32] Of particular importance is the need to establish public confidence in the administration of justice, for under the *Apartheid* era, with a few notable exceptions, the judges,

---

[28] Ibid. at 21.
[29] Ibid.
[30] Ibid. 22.
[31] Ibid.
[32] Ibid.

magistrates, Attorneys-General, prosecutors and court personnel were devoid of a human rights ethos. The judiciary was almost exclusively comprised of white people who had no inkling of the woes suffered by black people, the main clients of the criminal justice system. Our most formidable task is to reconcile the citizen with the State, which has wronged its subjects and downtrodden their dignity. What is called for now is justice with a human face. The accused should no longer be seen as an object of the proceedings, but as a participant with procedural rights and guarantees.

At present, the Department of Justice is planning to implement a comprehensive re-education programme for the judiciary and the prosecutorial service. The former South African Police Force, which is now called the South African Police Services (emphasis on service), is also undergoing training in human rights law. Efforts are already underway to make the courts user-friendly and service-orientated. There is also a massive drive to make justice more accessible to the public.

XI. CONCLUSION

The South African Government has accepted that it is morally obliged to carry the debts of its predecessors and is thus responsible for reparation. The financial costs of making reparation are enormous for a country such as South Africa. At present the State does not have the resources to meet this obligation. The economy is under enormous strain. Realistically speaking, where this money will come from is not certain. Most of it will have to be generated from within the country. The fact of the matter is that expectations have been created and have to be met.

At the same time we need to recognise that there are thousands of other people who under *Apartheid* have suffered what would ordinarily be regarded as gross human rights violations but who do not qualify for reparation under the Truth and Reconciliation Act. They, too, are bearing the sequelae of *Apartheid*. It is therefore important that reparations not only be limited to those who qualify under the law, but reparation in kind be made to whole communities. Many of the actual victims of human rights abuses were not persecuted as individuals but as representatives of communities and organisations. To emphasise the needs of the victim at the expense of the community could therefore create divisiveness. It is therefore essential that reparation to the victims should be accompanied by concrete reparations to the communities as well, for example, by building schools, houses, clinics and recreational facilities.

Discussion (Part 3)

Czaplinski: Just three short remarks, two concerning the text of Professor Mazzeschi and one referring indirectly to the presentation by Professor Fernandez.

First I had the impression that you paid a lot of attention to the concept of direct applicability of human rights treaties as a factor decisive for the system of reparation for violations of human rights in general and treaties in particular. I would like to say that it is a fact that the States in which violations of human rights treaties take place usually deny the applicability of these treaties. Direct applicability is more a problem of constitutional law than of international law. So it cannot, in my opinion, be taken as a decisive factor establishing reparation. The other problem is the problem of reparation towards other States for violation of human rights treaties. It corresponds with the presentation of Christian Tomuschat yesterday and the concept of injured state. The problem is that all the human rights treaties in my opinion establish self-contained régimes (in the meaning that measures provided for by all human rights instruments can be applied exclusively by and in respect of parties to those instruments; a similar solution has been formulated by the ICJ in the *Nicaragua* judgment of 1986).[1] So one cannot generalize. One cannot say in general that there is a duty to reparation for violations of human rights treaties towards third States. It might be established eventually if there is any practice in the field, for instance the practice of the Security Council. But such action takes place exclusively in cases of mass violations, and not in every case of a violation of human rights treaties. These actions depend upon politics. Let us take into account the intervention of Vietnam in Cambodia in the seventies. There certainly were mass violations of human rights in Cambodia, but there was no unanimity as to the evaluation of the legality of the action by Vietnam. So that is what Peter Malanczuk said. If we want to establish the duty of reparation for human rights violations we must look not to treaties, but to general customary law. And I cannot state on the basis of

---

[1]   ICJ Reports 1986, 14, at 134.

A. Randelzhofer and C. Tomuschat (eds.), State Responsibility and the Individual, 189–212.
© 1999 *Kluwer Law International. Printed in Great Britain.*

today's general practice in general international law that there is such a duty of reparation.

My third remark. Professor Fernandez made a very interesting presentation, dealing with issues which are unknown to people, at least in Central Europe. We are confronted with similar problems, of course not on that scale, but also with problems of responsibility for violations of human rights and, as I could understand, the system of South Africa is based on national law mostly. We have got in our political practice a number of judicial decisions dealing with reparation for injuries suffered under the communist régime based directly upon international law. We have, for instance, decisions of supreme courts and constitutional courts referring to the illegality of judicial decisions passed under the martial law in the early eighties, based directly on some provisions of the human rights covenants, e.g. on the retroactivity principle. So just to add to your presentation that the same claims can be based directly upon international law.

Stein: I have a small remark to make to both of this morning's speakers. I completely agree with Professor Mazzeschi's conclusion that apart from clear and self-executing conventional norms there is no direct claim for reparation for individuals under international law. But if a foreign State is responsible for the violation of human rights, the home State of the victims does have such a claim. This is the traditional rule in international law, and all the more important is that whatever the home State of the victims then receives as compensation is passed on to the victims whose rights were violated. And I have in mind those lump-sum agreements where the money somewhere disappeared and the victims never saw a dime. The question is whether we could think of an international law basis for a claim of the individual against his or her State to participate in that compensation that has been paid by the responsible State. And here again, of course, if we have a clear self-executing norm, it will be no problem, but that's probably rather rare. I doubt whether pertinent clauses in lump-sum agreements are directly applicable or self-executing. These are obligations between the States which agreed on that lump-sum payment. But maybe there is a general idea that might apply in that context. We certainly cannot transpose the European Court's *Francovich* decision to international law in general. European law is a 'self-contained régime' in some way, so we cannot take that decision and say: 'OK, this is a development in international law which is the basis of a new claim for the individual.' But one, if not the main, rationale behind that *Francovich* decision is the old idea of *effet utile*. Can we not say that the idea or doctrine of *effet utile* is a more general one, and that here the development of international human rights instruments has changed something on the international law level. Under traditional international law and the law of aliens, it was maybe the objective and purpose of all those rules that the State as the owner, patron and guardian of its nationals should receive compensation and that it was free to pass it on or not, since the State was the only player at that time. But since we have the international human rights guarantees, and because the *effet utile* of those instruments may be a different one, we may have to place more emphasis on the individual, so that we could say that there is a sort of general rule, a general principle to the effect that if there is a violation of human rights and if compensation is paid, that under the aspect of *effet utile* there is an international-law duty of the State which receives the lump-sum compensation to pass it on. This is my first remark.

The second, very short one is on Professor Fernandez's very interesting, almost moving presentation. I was struck by the fact – when he described that in the amnesty field the offence has to be a political one – how closely the criteria that he named are the same that we have in international extradition when dealing with a political offence. It struck me that in the field of international extradition, there is at least a tendency to reduce the scope of political offences, but I understand perfectly well that here we need all those criteria: motive, context, proportionality; but they are exactly the criteria that we use in international extradition for the political offence exception to extradition.

Randelzhofer: I will come back to one problem you mentioned in your report, Professor Fernandez. You told us that it was decided to allocate the same quantum of compensation to every victim, irrespective of what had happened to him, and you told us that human rights groups are strongly against that solution, and if I understood you correctly, you, too, are against this solution. I understand that criticism totally as far as the degree of violation of human rights is concerned. It does not seem to be very sound to give the same sum of compensation to a person who has experienced two days of imprisonment and to a person who has experienced two years of imprisonment. Insofar, I completely understand your criticism. I have problems when you and the human rights groups criticize this solution as far as the fortune of the victims is concerned. Because I think the compensation has to be proportional to the degree of the violation of human rights and I think one cannot say that a prosperous man having suffered torture or one year of imprisonment has suffered less than a poor man. Therefore I think, as to this point, I cannot agree with the criticism you have expressed.

A short additional remark to Wladyslaw Czaplinski. He stated that in his view the human rights treaties are self-contained régimes. I have considerable doubt whether that is the common view, and I must say I think it is a dangerous view. Imagine a State party having only ratified the International Covenant on Civil and Political Rights, not having accepted Article 41, not having accepted the Optional Protocol. Then the only remedy against violations would be the soft procedure of Article 40, the system of reports. I think that will not be very sound and, as I see it, it is not the predominant view in legal writings either.

Kooijmans: I am very grateful that Professor Mazzeschi expanded his theme to State claims; I found his comparison with the law of aliens very instructive. I came to the conclusion, however, that the differences between the law of aliens régime and the human rights régime are greater than the similarities. In the first place, the law of aliens is part of customary law, whereas human rights law to a great extent is treaty law, which means that claims can only be brought by virtue of conventional provisions. Damages, therefore, can only be claimed if that is foreseen by such conventions. Let me give an example.

A number of years ago several countries were approached by NGOs to bring a claim under the Genocide Convention against Cambodia before the International Court of Justice. If these countries had responded positively, what kind of reparation could they have claimed? In the case between *Bosnia and Herzegovina* and *Yugoslavia,* which is before the Court at present, it is quite clear that Bosnia is directly injured by the alleged violations of the Genocide Convention by Yugoslavia and that it can claim compensation. Its own nationals have been the victims and consequently the same calculation method can be used as under the law of aliens, namely that the damage sustained by the individual is taken as the basis for the calculation of the compensation due to the injured State. What, however, is the basis for compensation in the case of a State-to-State claim where the claiming State is not directly injured by the violation? If, e.g., the Netherlands had brought a claim against Cambodia, could it have asked for more than satisfaction, which could take the form of a declaratory judgment and assurances of non-repetition? The Genocide Convention does not contain a provision comparable to Article 9, para. 5, of the Covenant on Civil and Political Rights which states that anyone who has been the victim of unlawful arrest or detention shall have an enforceable right to compensation. Such compensation, not being part of general international law, therefore cannot be part of the State claim. So, if a State brings a claim under the Genocide Convention, it does so out of concern about what happened and in the expectation that there will be an order of non-repetition, but for the victims themselves and their relatives it can do frightfully little.

My second remark concerns Professor Fernandez' fascinating exposé about the situation in South Africa. I was struck by the fact that great attention is given to the psychological and medical assistance of the victims. When I was

Special Rapporteur on Torture appointed by the UN Human Rights Commission, I saw many torture victims; what always struck me was that the mental effects of torture in the long run were often far more important than the physical ones. This makes clear that there is no genuine reparation if such long-term effects are not taken into account. My question is: is there any experience under the European or American Convention in this respect? Are such long-term effects taken into account for the calculation of the compensation due?

Danilenko: I have a couple of remarks with respect to the very interesting presentation of Professor Mazzeschi. I agree that there is an international obligation to provide for national reparation claims at least on the basis of treaties. However, I have doubts about your analysis of the self-executing nature of international obligations in this area, in particular Article 5(5) of the European Convention. One may wonder whether it is appropriate to approach the question of the self-executing nature of Article 5(5) in the abstract. The self-executing or non-self-executing nature of international treaty rules is not an international law question. It is a domestic law question. In order to determine whether a particular treaty rule is self-executing or not, we need to look to the relevant domestic standards developed in different countries. Monistic countries have different standards and different definitions of self-executing or directly applicable treaties. We also have to keep in mind that in dualistic countries this question does not arise at all.

But if we try to determine whether Article 5 of the European Convention could be self-executing in a monistic country, I would argue that there are serious doubts that this provision may be considered as self-executing. The words 'enforceable right' are, of course, very nice, but we have a big problem with respect to the proclaimed right to compensation. What kind of compensation are we talking about? Is it full or just? I think a judge in a monistic country faced with the problem of applying this particular clause would encounter serious difficulties in finding out what the exact standard is. If we take Article 5 in conjunction with Article 50 of the European Convention we would see that there is a reference to national law. But national law may provide for only partial reparation. This means that under the European Convention different national laws may provide for different standards. As we have discovered yesterday, international standards that have been developed by the European Court are, to some extent at least, arbitrary. Standards applied by the European Court differ in different situations. There is a general obligation to compensate, but what is the exact standard of compensation?

I think at this stage national laws define the exact amount of compensation. Of course, it might be nice to have a clause in the Europan Convention defining the exact standard to be applied. However, at this juncture Article 5(5) does not really provide a domestic judge with any clear guidance. It follows that judges would probably consider this treaty clause to be non-self-executing.

With respect to Professor Fernandez's fascinating report, I have two questions. The first question relates to the standard of proof. You mentioned that a person would come to the Truth Commission to tell her or his story and then this person would be referred to the Reparation Commission. Now, what is the standard of proof? Is there any shifting of burden of proof? Please give us some additional information on this.

The second question concerns the nature of the proceedings before the Truth Commission with respect to judges. If we take Eastern Europe I think there is a tendency to deal with each judge individually. Now, in South Africa there may be judges who used to hand down very tough decisions with respect to dissidents. They may therefore be removed from office for past human rights violations. However, the procedures you described deal with judges as a collective body. It appears that there is collective responsibility for all judges irrespective of their prior conduct. Is it true that these procedures are based on the notion of collective responsibility?

Thürer: Let me join the previous speakers in saying how impressed I was by both presentations. I would just like to add some examples to the theme we are discussing.

One example concerns the possible enforcement of violations of international human rights law and humanitarian law through civil procedures. We mentioned yesterday the Alien Tort Statute of the United States[2]. It might be interesting to note that in a New York District Court cases are pending which could be of far-reaching importance. I am referring to a class action against Swiss banks in which it is alleged that treaties and customary international law prohibiting genocide, war crimes, crimes against peace, slavery and forced labor were violated by Swiss banks during and in the aftermath of the Second World War. Perhaps the Court will deal with highly interesting questions of international law such as the problem as to whether the principles mentioned were already part of general international law at that time; whether they are applicable to private law entities or only directly vis-à-vis States; whether the acts stated really violated these principles, and whether evidence can be brought that the relevant acts had in fact been committed.

Secondly, I am astonished that two very important reports to the Human Rights Commission have not been mentioned so far. First the report delivered by Professor van Boven concerning guidelines and basic principles on the

---

[2]   28 U.S.C. § 1350 (1996).

right to compensation for victims of gross violations of human rights and humanitarian law, and second the report of Judge Joinet concerning impunity. It might be that one day the principles enunciated in these reports evolve into a sort of 'soft law' which would have the capacity to influence and shape the interpretation of national law, especially constitutional provisions concerning the right to life. Let me just give an example for that. In Swiss law, I think as in many legal systems of Europe, there is no claim for compensation against state authorities except when a title is granted in liability law. We had a case in the Federal Supreme Court in Switzerland[3] where a young lady was killed by police forces at a demonstration. Her mother, who was economically dependent on her daughter, was not granted compensation on the grounds that title was not provided for in the liability law of the State. One could imagine that international 'soft law' might one day contribute to the interpretation of constitutional guarantees, in the present case the right to life, in such a way that title could be deduced directly from the constitutional guarantee and not only from statute law. My third example concerns a piece of news I have just read in the paper, so I do not know if my information is quite correct. According to this article there is a law pending in the Knesset in Israel concerning the handling of suits arising from security force activities in Judea, Samaria and in the Gaza strip, a law which, if adopted by the Knesset, could provide for exemptions from liability and compensation. It would provide that compensation be granted for humanitarian reasons only and not as a title of law; that the sums of compensation would be lower compared to the existing standard, and that rules of evidence would be altered so that it would be harder to establish negligence on the part of the security force. Here the question arises whether this law, if adopted, would be compatible with the Fourth Geneva Convention of 12 August 1949, the customary international law behind this Convention, the principles of customary international law embodied in Protocol I of 10 June 1977 Additional to the Geneva Conventions of 12 August 1949, and with Article 3 (as well as the preamble) of the Hague Convention No. IV of 18 October 1907 concerning the Laws and Customs of War on Land. The last remark I wanted to make is that, so far, we have only dealt with treaty law and customary international law. An important question seems to me to be whether basic principles of compensation are not or could not one day become part of the general principles of law as in the third category of sources of law traditionally recognized in international law.

Hilger: Mr. Chairman, I liked the lecture by Professor Mazzeschi tremendously. In its clarity and logic of presentation, it was in the best tradition of the

---

[3] *Hunziker* case, decided in 1923, BGE 49 II 497 et seqq., quoted in: P. Saladin, *Grundrechte im Wandel*, 3rd ed. 1982, at 199.

Italian school of international law. When Professor Mazzeschi said that many of his remarks were directed to the younger generation here present I recalled that many years ago in Göttingen I wrote my thesis on the same issue of whether the classical law of aliens – that rights and obligations exist only between States and the individual just provides the case but has no rights whatsoever – has not been changed by the development in human rights. But I would still say I do not agree with Judge Kooijmans. Probably, I think, and I agree with Professor Mazzeschi, that the right and classical approach to the rights of aliens and the right to present claims out of human rights violations are still very close and from the one school of thought you can enter into the second area of rights and obligations. I would mention that the International Law Commission has taken up the subject of diplomatic protection, has appointed a rapporteur, and, in the next five years, will deal with that issue. It will be very interesting to see what is said then and brought together. I think in my view still, as I said, the two fields are very close to one another.

As for the second presentation by Professor Fernandez, it gave me also great satisfaction, having worked over many, many years in Geneva and in New York on resolutions against *apartheid* in the Human Rights Commission, in the Third Committee, in the International Labour Organization, to see that the *apartheid* régime has been overcome and in a very good way without bloodshed. I was also struck by what Professor Fernandez said on the efforts of the Truth Commission in South Africa and on the problems they are facing. Here again as a practitioner, I would say these problems are very similar to what we are discussing right now in the Federal Government. You know that the Federal Republic has paid huge sums over the years for the victims of Nazi atrocities, but still there are those which one might call the double victims, first of nazism and then of communism, who haven't received much or have received nearly nothing. Just one example. The Federal Parliament has attributed 80 million DM to be distributed amongst victims in the smaller states of Central and Eastern Europe, i.e. Hungary, Slovakia, Romania, Bulgaria and the States in the former Yugoslavia. We would like to find a way to make payments directly to the victims and we are in contact with the International Committee of the Red Cross and the International Tracing Agency in Arolsen to identify the victims in cooperation with the National Red Cross Societies in these countries. But once it is established that a person was in a concentration camp or in a ghetto, the idea is also here to pay just one sum and not to enter into further differentiation as to how long he was imprisoned, as to whether his economic situation is not such that he should not receive any compensation. So the idea under this programme is to pay about D-Mark 1,000 to 1,500 per case. I noted with great interest that also in South Africa similar considerations are relied upon although they may produce results which will not be satisfactory inasmuch as somebody spent only six months in such a camp and another one many, many years. The great dividing line which is still valid in the Federal Republic of Germany, but we will see whether it can be maintained given various claims before national courts, is that forced labour as such during the Second World War does not entitle the victims to compensation under the current system. The case is very well known to Professor Randelzhofer and others. The dividing line is heavily contested from abroad and also within the Federal Republic by the parties of the left wing of the political spectrum, but we will see. In any case, I was struck by the similarities between the situation we are facing right now and the problems which the Truth Commissions in South Africa has to cope with.

Verhoeven: Just a few questions to our colleague Mazzeschi, who is apparently considering that there is a right to compensation only under Article 5(5), as far as the European Convention is concerned, and under Article 10, as far as the American Convention is concerned. I have serious difficulties in accepting that. It is a fact that Article 5 [resp. Article 10] is the only provision referring explicitly to an enforceable right to compensation. But this does not imply at all, in my view, that no compensation is due when other articles of the Convention are breached. Who could seriously suggest that an individual who was tortured is not entitled to compensation just because there is no such mention in Article 3 of the Convention? This would be ridiculous! In my view, there is a right to compensation in each case the Convention is violated. In fact, the only problem is to know why Article 5 is the only one referring explicitly to compensation. I have no answer. But the answer could not be that any compensation is excluded everywhere else. It is true also that Article 50 of the European Convention is not clear. But no firm conclusion can be deduced from that. If I am not mistaken, Article 50 basically reproduces provisions which were quite usual in the conciliation and arbitration treaties concluded after the First World War to facilitate the settlement of inter-State disputes. At that time, their meaning was quite obvious. This is not the case as far as Article 50 is now concerned, taking especially into account the way it is applied in Strasbourg. Still, it is impossible to draw any conclusion regarding the right to compensation just from the term 'if necessary'.

I also disagree with the view that the duty to compensate has a purely conventional basis, i.e. that it is on the basis of the will of the contracting parties only, as expressed in the European or American Convention, that there exists a right to be compensated. Even if there is no proof of a customary rule, it is still a general principle of law that any victim of a wrongful act is entitled to get adequate reparation. I know of no court, under any system of law, which has ever denied that. The existence of a wrongful act can be disputed, not the right to reparation in case it is established. In such a context, it is quite understandable that the victim brings a claim before a national court, knowing that he or she normally has no access to an international body. Pisillo Mazzeschi told us that no right can be claimed if the treaty is not self-executing. Maybe. But many national courts accept claims introduced by victims who enjoy no right, strictly speaking. This is also part of the *Francovich* judgment of the EC Court. To succeed, it is sufficient that the claimant show the special interest needed to ask the Court to sanction the violation by the State of its obligations, even if there is no individual right strictly corresponding to it. Such a sanction can be the duty to compensate the victims of the breach. Theoretically, some will possibly prefer that such a compensation be claimed by States under international law. I am not sure that such a view is really well-founded. But, in any case, this remains hypothetical. For the time being, resort to national bodies is – and will probably remain for decades – the only possibility to get effective reparation, under national law.

Wühler: What I want to speak about briefly is an experience in another country which is somehow quite comparable to what is going on in South Africa at the moment but which is in many respects also quite different. One of the major differences between the two cases is that the events in South Africa are very visible and highly exposed, both inside the country and internationally. Whereas the efforts made in the country I am speaking of are largely unknown, around the world generally and even in the international legal community. I am speaking about Malawi. As you all know, Malawi had one of the longest-standing dictatorships not only in Africa but in modern times generally. The régime of Dr. Hastings Banda was there for over 30 years. What happened in Malawi in 1994 after an election that resulted in, I think what Mr. Hilger referred to yesterday, the change to the better and democracy, was that first Malawi drafted a Constitution. Second, as part of that Constitution it created, with a view to providing redress, domestically a national compensation tribunal with a very far-reaching mandate, and I would just like to read that one section of the Constitution which says: 'There shall be a national compensation tribunal which shall entertain claims with respect to alleged criminal and civil liability of the Government of Malawi', which was basically at the time of Hastings Banda. Now I will not speak about criminal liability. Civil liability basically means that claims arising out of violations of human rights – and there were gross and numerous human rights violations in Malawi during that former régime – could be brought before that national compensation tribunal. The composition of this tribunal, and again, this is laid down in the Constitution itself, forsees one chairman who is a judge, assisted by two other persons, one of which is an accountant who is supposed to fulfill two functions: he is to supervise the accounts of the national compensation fund and he is to advise the tribunal as to the quantum of compensation payable with respect to any claim coming before the tribunal. The other one is a member of the bar who would act as legal representative for any party claiming compensation in front of the tribunal and who is not represented by legal counsel. This is the setup of the tribunal. I followed its work a little bit in the beginning when it was established. However, I have lost touch over the last year. I know that they expected several thousands of claims. The reason I know about it is because the chairman came to Geneva to our Commission, since he had heard about our body and he was trying to look around and see how one deals with what he thought was an enormous number of claims. For his standard and for his resources, that certainly was the case. He was a little bit surprised when he saw our number of claims, but certainly for his standard he had a huge task in front of himself. Why I am mentioning this here is: First it is, in my view, a very interesting development in yet a domestic sphere and it goes on completely unnoticed by the international community. The Malawi experience is in my view quite comparable in a number of respects to what is going on in South Africa.

Zemanek: Thank you very much. I originally intended to make two points, but previous speakers provoked me in making two additional points. The first point I want to raise is a problem that puzzles me since yesterday. How can one determine fairly the amount of financial compensation for moral damage, or emotional damage, or non-pecuniary damage, with global validity? Somebody in the discussion, I think it was the speaker, said the Human Rights Committee should become bolder and indicate an amount. Then Michael Reisman told us about the compensation practice in the Americas and put the figure at US $20,000 and I asked myself: Why 20,000, why not 10,000 or 15,000? This discussion highlights the problem in an even more disturbing fashion: Usually it would seem that one could fix such an amount in a society which has a set of common values. Now we have been told that even in one society it is extremely difficult to decide the question. How should it then be possible to do it on the global level, i.e. how should the Human Rights Committee determine such an amount? I have no answer, I am raising the question. But this is, to my mind, an important question if we talk about financial compensation for immaterial damage.

The second point I wanted to make concerns Professor Mazzeschi's report. It is rather an addition. He argues that incorporation of human rights conventions into domestic law should give a right to reparation. In Austria, this raises a problem with the competence of the courts. Violations of human rights fall within the competence of the Constitutional Court. The Constitutional Court has the capacity to rescind laws or other general orders but it does not have the competence to revoke an individual administrative act. If the violation is caused by an individual administrative act, the Constitutional Court may establish the violation of human rights, but it has no means of revoking the act or of according compensation. For that, the plaintiff must institute proceedings in a different tribunal, which is cumbersome. But any attempt at change would meet with the opposition of constitutional lawyers because it would change the whole balance of courts in Austria since the revocation of individual administrative acts falls within the competence of the Administrative Court. Thus we have to take the organisation of the judiciary in a specific country into account when talking about compensation.

That brings me to one of the other points provoked by an earlier speaker, and that was Joe Verhoeven. If he postulates that there is a general international right to compensation, I would ask how that could be enforced and where?

My last remark is provoked by Professor Czaplinski. I agree with Professor Randelzhofer's observation concerning the self-contained régime and I beg to differ with Professor Czaplinski and Judge Kooijmans. First of all I think that the term or the concept is ill-conceived. There is no such thing as a self-contained régime. If you consider the case in which the International Court of Justice invented the concept, the *Tehran* hostage case,[4] what the Court stated does not even apply to diplomatic law. It applies certainly to diplomatic inviolability, but nothing prevents a State from suspending a treaty as countermeasure against a violation of diplomatic law. Diplomatic law is not a self-contained régime and the International Law Commission very wisely avoided the term when it talked about exceptions to the law of contermeasures. It simply said that diplomatic personnel and premises are not an object of countermeasures. I do not think that human rights conventions are a self-contained régime. That would mean that in case of a violation no other means than those provided by the subsystem itself were applicable. If a human rights convention does not provide for effective means of enforcement, a ratifying State would only subscribe to the title of the convention and could for the rest do what it wants. As I said yesterday, I am fully aware that the concept of *erga omnes* obligations and their enforcement is not yet fully discussed. It needs refinement, but in my opinion it is the only means of securing compliance with such conventions unless you establish collective enforcement, in other words, unless you give competence to an international organisation to enforce them. But if that is not done, and it seems a very remote possibility, the right of an individual State to enforce *erga omnes* obligations is the only means of opposing the famous defence of intervention. And do not forget that at least

---

[4]   ICJ Reports 1980, 3, at 40.

we in Europe have in the conclusions of the Moscow meeting of the CSCE the first official statement by the former Soviet Union that they agree that human rights are the concern of all States and do not belong to the exclusive domestic competence of the State. If we are going to live up to that, the only way is individual enforcement of *erga omnes* obligations. Therefore I think this is a very dangerous notion to say that human rights treaties are self-contained régimes.

Tomuschat: I fully agree with what was just said. One only needs to look into yearbooks of international law reflecting national practice, Swiss international practice, French international practice, e.g. The European Council at each of its meetings makes statements on human rights issues in foreign countries. This abundant practice shows that there is no exclusive character of the mechanisms under the human rights treaties.

But let me make another point. Professor Pisillo Mazzeschi's presentation was very impressive. Yet I would recommend not to use the terminology coined by the International Law Commission on obligations of result and obligations of conduct. This classification has created a conceptual chaos. Some years ago I looked into the issue myself and found the rules suggested by the ILC hardly understandable. Fortunately I can say that this part of the draft articles on State responsibility was drawn up without my participation.

As far as the self-executing character of Articles 9, para. 5, and 14, para. 6, of the International Covenant on Civil and Political Rights is concerned, I agree with Gennady Danilenko in the sense that this is exclusively a matter of domestic law. Whether a person can invoke a treaty within his national legal system is entirely dependent on the constitutional order of the country concerned. In the United Kingdom, for instance, international treaties are almost never made part of the law of the land, and therefore the question simply does not arise there. Thus, it cannot be an issue of international law whether a treaty provision is suitable for application to individuals. The problem emerges only in countries which incorporate the treaty as such into the national legal system.

On the other hand, I would like to contradict Gennady Danilenko's contention that the jurisprudence of the European Court of Human Rights in Strasbourg is arbitrary. I would say that it is a little bit chaotic. The Court has established different categories through a process of empirical intuition. The criteria characterizing the different groups of cases are not quite clear. One does not yet see the light at the end of the tunnel, but speaking of arbitrariness would seem to be somewhat too harsh. One should be a bit more cautious in evaluating the jurisprudence. I myself found, in a study to appear soon, that there are some messy cases where the Court really missed the right solution.

But I still think that on the whole the judges have a good instinctive feeling of what is right and just and equitable. Maybe in a few years we shall be provided with a complete picture of the different categories of cases. This is how law in action and judge-made law works.

As far as the presentation by Professor Fernandez is concerned, I would like to make some reference to my own experience in Guatemala, where I am currently heading the national truth commission (Historical Clarification Commission). I would like to raise two points only. First: We are competent to deal with human rights violations which are related to the armed conflict. On the other hand, an amnesty law was adopted which provides an amnesty for acts closely related to the armed conflict. In terms of textual basis, this is almost the same formula. But the interpretation must and will be totally different. It is the task of the Commission to give a comprehensive picture of what happened in Guatemala for 36 years. Consequently, our mandate must be interpreted in a broad fashion in the sense that all acts which were politically motivated are subject to our investigation. The political motivation is the main criterion, not so much the armed conflict. Just to give an example: to disappear a person cannot be deemed an element of an armed conflict, it is part of a political power struggle fought out with methods inconsistent with the rule of law. On the other hand, the amnesty law which grants amnesty for acts closely related to armed conflict means what? Well, the answer will probably go along the following lines: Persons, i.e. combatants who did not always respect humanitarian law while in armed conflict should enjoy the benefits of amnesty, but not those who engaged in murder and kidnapping. Thus, essentially the same words will be interpreted in largely different ways.

One of the great difficulties the Commission is confronted with stems from its duty to make recommendations at the end of its work. It is said in the instruments which underlie our work that the recommendations should also provide for reparation. This is a terribly difficult task. During the armed conflict up to 200,000 people were killed. How are we going to frame recommendations which, on the one hand, will do justice to the victims but which, on the other, are commensurate with the limited economic capacity of a poor country? Obviously, we shall not choose the easy way of making generous recommendations which in practice would not be capable of being implemented for lack of available ressources. The actual dilemma will emerge at the final stage of our work when we have taken stock of all the losses entailed by the armed conflict. It was very helpful for me to learn that South Africa has engaged in a dialogue with the victims, aiming to learn what they expect of the Government as reparation. In Guatemala we should do the same, talk to people and ask them about their ideas how reparation could be effected in the best manner conceivable.

Meron: Before coming to my main point I would like to agree with Karl Zemanek's view on self-contained régimes. I have never been persuaded by the logical cogency of that concept. When we have a provision in a treaty obliging us to limit ourselves to one particular avenue of recourse, of course it is binding. But beyond that it really makes no sense especially with regard to those international agreements which have very weak enforcement mechanisms.

My main point has a sort of overlap with ideas already expressed by Daniel Thürer and Joe Verhoeven. I think that we are taking an excessively narrow view of the whole subject of human rights: Very often, we have the very same substantive or material norm described as part of the human rights law, civil rights, or constitutional norms or even labour norms. Take the example given yesterday by Judge Kooijmans which came up under the Covenant on Civil and Political Rights (Article 26), but pertained to the Economic Covenant, labour rights, welfare rights and compensation rights. We ought to look at the core of the material norm that we are talking about without worrying too much about labels. The fact that human rights conventions are not very generous on provisions for compensation may reflect the fact that at the present stage of international development, States are not ready to give too much competence to human rights bodies. But if there is a certain norm which has become a widely accepted primary norm, and if we see that in fact violations of that norm are addressed fairly effectively by most of the national legal systems, what is the legal analysis that we ought to use? Let's take for example egregious discrimination against women. In the United States, the Political Covenant would not at all be effective because of reservations dealing with the non-self-executing nature of the Covenant. But women could sue and often obtain very significant relief under American civil rights laws. What I think that we ought to look at is some kind of emerging general principles of law. Karl Zemanek asked a very pertinent question. If so, he said, how do you enforce such principles? And that's of course a very good question, but if we discussed it, we could ask it with regard to very many other aspects of human rights. But I would not like to escape entirely this problem of enforcement. If there is some kind of tribunal of arbitration or commission with broad competence over the subject, it might take into account general principles of law. So I'm suggesting that we broaden the perspective on the subject, otherwise our discussions will result in very pessimistic conclusions on the whole topic.

Fleck: Since I am the last one on the list, let me first volunteer to express a vote of thanks for two tremendous presentations today and a fascinating debate, indeed. If I might echo one of the remarks made yesterday by Judge

Kooijmans, this of course is again food for thought for at least another week. I should like to ask three questions. The first one I would address to both speakers and the second and third to each of the speakers individually, if I may. Firstly, it intrigues me after the presentation on the South African situation whether one can really consider claims for reparation being based on international law or not. Here of course Article 9(5) of the International Covenant on Civil and Political Rights is at stake. If we could answer this question in an affirmative way, it would have not only theoretical but also practical policy consequences and the result could be adapted to other situations which are not yet settled, unlike the South African case.

My second question is related to the tremendous amount of mental effects, health effects and financial burdens in the South African case. Would you believe that appropriate redress can be provided at all at national level, to what extent is international assistance essential if the notion of reparation shall be meaningful?

And lastly, since Professor Pisillo Mazzeschi did not mention reparation for war crimes and war victims, I would like to expand a bit what was suggested by Professor Thürer with reference to the van Boven report. Are the international covenants, e.g. the Convention Against Torture, applicable to these types of events? This is a very difficult question, because in referring to armed conflicts today we cannot refer to international wars. But even in international armed conflicts the question is open whether Article 91 of the First Additional Protocol to the Geneva Conventions has any practical meaning. I think this aspect could be expanded for the publication of the book you are planning to prepare. Maybe some proposals *de lege ferenda* could be worked out to carry this issue further.

Fernandez: Perhaps I should start with Professor Randelzhofer. You pointed out, and I think to some extent you are right, that one cannot punish a rich person who has suffered torture by giving him less than a poor person. The mental anguish and the physical suffering that he or she has sustained is just as much if not even worse than that suffered by another person. I am not against rich people getting money, far from that. I think everybody is entitled to some kind of compensation. The only problem I have is that in practice, and I think that has been verified also by the practices in Geneva, the educated people, the people who have the means, are usually those people who are first to access because they know about these things and the poor person is the one who invariably does not know about it or may know about it but does not have the means to access. And the criticism that has been coming from human rights groups in South Africa is that you might find that because those in the means have the ability to access those funds more readily than the others they are thereby taking a bigger slice of the cake. But I agree entirely with you that one should not discriminate on the basis of wealth.

Coming to Professor Danilenko, you asked a question concerning the standard of proof. Now when somebody goes to the Truth Commission, to the amnesty committee, and confesses that he or she has perpetrated a certain act, one of the requirements is that that person must make full disclosure, partial disclosure is not enough. But if afterwards the amnesty committee decides that they are not going to give that person amnesty and that they are going to pass that information on to the Attorney General to make a decision on whether or not he is going to prosecute, the evidence that was tendered at the committee cannot be used against that very person if the Attorney General decides to prosecute that person. It cannot be used. The other thing that I need to point out is that once amnesty has been given, the act perpetrated by the person is totally expunged, in other words that person cannot be brought before the court and sued for damages. That person cannot be prosecuted although that person has admitted to having committed the act. In other words, he is neither attainable by way of civil law nor by way of criminal law. And this is something that has caused quite a lot of bitterness because the victims say: Look, this person has admitted to it, but why can I not get reparations? Why can I not sue the person for damage? But this, as I have pointed out, is a product of the negotiated political process. We don't have here the concept of victor's justice or *Siegerjustiz* like Nuremberg or Tokyo. This was part of the deal between the ANC and the Government. It is in the Constitution and it is accepted now that no prosecutions will take place and the victims will not be able to bring a claim for damages.

Now the important thing to bear in mind is that first of all we do not have the capacity in South Africa to successfully process a charge against an officer of the State who operated under the *apartheid* régime. Because it is in the nature of things that when you live under an oppressive régime and you give a police officer *carte blanche* powers with respect to how he deals with the ordinary person, it is going to be very difficult – and this is the experience we were also taught from Argentina – to prove beyond a reasonable doubt that that person did perpetrate a gross human rights violation. Coupled with the fact that in South Africa we do not have the capacity to sustain charges in that large number, we have a high fluctuation with our prosecutorial service, our prosecutors are overstressed. The average experience of the South African prosecutor is six months. There is a high turnover there. The courts lack the personnel and the infrastructure to be able to prosecute these people. And the other important thing is that rather than to procecute one person, what we insist on is truth. Imprisonment is not essential. It is truth that is required, because thereby you can have a greater horizontal satisfaction.

Take the example of a police officer who has been responsible for the death of 30 other people, has tortured 40 other people. If I were to bring a charge against him that process, that court procedure would operate only in respect of me and that police officer. But if that person tells the truth, then he satisfies a large number of people because for them what is important is to know what happened to their loved one, or to a relative. That is the most important thing to them, to know where his remains are, that sort of thing, they can go and fetch that person and bury him.

Now with regard to the nature of the proceedings against judges, the legal profession has been called upon by the Truth Commission to come before it and to explain to it, not with the intention of a witchhunt, not with the intention of prosecuting anybody, but to explain why things went as they did, why the legal profession could not take a stand against some of the most vicious discriminatory laws, why judges for example did not stand up and say: these laws run against the grain of a democratic legal society, why in their judgments they could not also just refer to the fact that they found this totally unacceptable. The judges will go forward. They are at the moment consulting amongst themselves. I do not know how they will handle the challenge, but there will be some kind of a presentation made on behalf of the judiciary, not to the intention of singling out any culprit but just to commit themselves to the Constitution, to a bill of rights and to say why they think they went wrong in the past. The legal profession will be called upon somehow to make that commitment, which is important also for the way the ordinary public sees the courts, the law and its institutions in the future.

Professor Zemanek's remarks with regard to the arbitrary nature of compensation: I also do not know. Professor Ress said yesterday you just make it according to the rule of thumb ('Pi mal Daumen'). Hereto, the basic consideration was that the kind of intervention that should be made must be such that it substantially elevates the quality of life of the victim and it was felt that the amount of 23,000 Rand a year would do that. Whether that is going to be the case, I do not know. For some of the people that will not be enough. Most of the people, over 90% of the people that testified before the Truth Commission, have said that what they want is not so much the money, what they want is, first of all, to reestablish their good name, and furthermore, some amenities. They want schools, they want clinics, they want technicians, those things that would empower them and make them have a decent life. Now there is a serious problem because, under the *apartheid* regime there existed many laws which violated human rights across the board. If you think for example of the pass laws and the group laws. The victims of those laws are not covered by the Act. Yet those people suffered as well. And if you grant reparation to one person, you must know that other people might have had more problems under those laws. Redress should not cause tension. Many of the people who are regarded as victims did not act on their own or out of self-enlightened interest. They acted on behalf of organizations and communities. So they were persecuted on behalf of the community. Thus the community itself is also a victim. Consequently, the suggestion has been put forward that in compensating the victim, that person should not be looked at in isolation; rather, help should be provided generally, empowering a community by building schools, and thereby let it feel that something is being done for it.

Pisillo Mazzeschi: I was a little bit overwhelmed by the many comments because everyone in the room took the floor and made a comment on my paper.

Professor Czaplinski wonders why the problem of direct applicability is so important in my paper. Well, in my view it is very important from the perspective of the rights of individuals. I admit that I am very much taken by my dualist education and so I tend to give great importance to the problem of direct applicability. But I do not agree with some colleagues, like Professor Tomuschat, who said that the problem of the self-executing character of a rule is only a matter of domestic law. A similar remark was made by Professor Danilenko. I think on the contrary that it is a problem of international law and of constitutional law, a mixed problem. International law has something to say about the general criteria for establishing the existence of self-executing rules. On the other hand, it matters also whether there are domestic organs or implementation procedures; thus, answers also depend on constitutional law. But I would not say that we are facing only a problem of constitutional law.

The second point concerns inter-State reparation and third States. This is also a difficult problem. In my paper I did not want to deal very much with inter-State reparation, which was a little bit outside of my topic. I only mentioned the *erga omnes* obligations in human rights, saying that there are *erga omnes* obligations of conventional and customary international law. I agree that most human rights derive from treaty law, but some human rights are also rooted in customary international law. If a violation of these primary rules occurs, there should also be reparation. I did not want to imply that there are many rules of customary international law on human rights, neither that for the breach of any single human rights norm reparation is owed to the victim. And again, I would distinguish among inter-State reparation, namely individual domestic reparation in implementation of international law and a kind of international reparation for individuals.

Professor Stein basically agrees with my report. What he said about some claims of individuals to reparation also in the traditional law on the protection of aliens is interesting. He also said, if I remember well, that self-executing treaties are more unusual than I would like them to be. Well, I agree that States and domestic courts tend to deny very often the self-executing character of treaties. But I think that this tendency should be rejected and that our task is to persuade the interpreters and judges that they should have a more open mind about self-executing treaties.

Another point raised by Professor Stein was about the difficulty of reconciling the law of the European Convention and European Community law with general international law. This is also an interesting problem. Is European law a self-contained régime? I agree with Professor Zemanek and Professor Meron, who do not like the idea of self-contained régimes for human rights treaties; and I also tend, as a generalist of international law, to think that European Convention law and European Community law are a part of international law. I also think that a progressive court could apply a principle of Community law, like the *Francovich* principle, to international law.

Judge Kooijmans raises some important points about inter-State claims. He said that there is more difference between customary law on protection of aliens and human rights law than I said in my paper. Well, we can agree or not on this statement according to one's perspective. Since I was departing from the point of view of the international rules concerning more directly the position of the individual, it was interesting for me, in a historical perspective, to compare the protection of aliens with the protection of human rights. I tend to believe, like Mr. Hilger, that there are many similarities between those fields of international law. But of course there are also some important differences and perhaps my concern about the traditional law on the protection of aliens went somewhat too far.

Then there is the problem of reparation towards third States: What are the rights of a State which is not a direct victim of a breach of human rights? A discussion of this topic would take hours. In short, I think third States could claim satisfaction and guarantees of non-repetition. Could we also think about a kind of compensation for third States under the framework of an international organization? Such kind of coordination among all the State claims to compensation can be a possible development of international law. However, everyone knows the difficulties of the problem of the relationship between *erga omnes* obligations and self-help reactions by third States. I tend to think that we cannot admit strong reactions, like reprisals, by third States. But if we speak only of reparation, I do not see why a non-directly injured State cannot ask for compensation for the breach of *erga omnes* obligations. But this rather constitutes progressive development of international law than it reflects present international law.

Professor Danilenko said he conceives reparation for breach of human rights only on the basis of treaties. I partly agree and partly disagree, because what kind of reparation is he speaking about? If we speak about domestic reparation in implementation of an international obligation, especially the 'substantive' reparation, I agree with him also in my paper. But the situation is perhaps different with regard to the 'procedural' reparation, i.e. the right to have effective domestic remedies. I think that in this case there are so many similar treaty rules like Article 13 of the European Convention, that we might try to infer from these rules a general norm of international law. Professor Danilenko also said that there are many different standards or amounts of compensation. I agree with that, but in my paper I was not too much concerned about the amount of compensation. From my point of view the right to compensation, or rather the principle itself of reparation, is important.

Professor Thürer did not make comments on my report. All the same I found his idea about the relevance of general principles of law concerning reparation very interesting. In my paper I made a short reference to general principles of law and my conclusion was that we should be cautious about trying to find a general principle of law concerning domestic reparation. And then of course there is another problem: Do general principles of law really exist in contemporary international law? Everyone has different ideas about that.

Professor Zemanek spoke about incorporation of international law in Austria. His observations about the difficulties within the Austrian legal system were very interesting. Here again we come to the problem of self-executing rules. If there is a treaty ratified by Austria and there is a self-executing rule which has been incorporated into Austrian domestic law, and the rule asks for reparation to individuals, I think that Austria has a duty to comply with it. So, I see here again a problem concerning the self-executing or non self-executing character of an international rule and a problem of identifying the best means of domestic implementation of the rule.

Professor Tomuschat spoke of the distinction between obligations of conduct and obligations of result. This topic is very intriguing for me because a few years ago I wrote a book on due diligence and State responsibility, where I tried to develop a distinction between obligations of due diligence and obligations of result which was very different from the distinction which the International Law Commission was developing at that time, between obligations of conduct and obligations of result (articles 20 and 21 of the draft on State responsibility). Therefore there are two ways of thinking about obligations of result. One is illustrated by civil systems of law, for instance French law, and the other has been developed by Professor Ago and the ILC. In my view, the ILC distinction between obligations of conduct and obligations of result is not a very convincing distinction. But it can be useful sometimes. It just came to my mind in preparing my paper that, if we accept the latter distinction, we may have repercussions also on the problem of the self-executing character of a rule. In fact, if a certain rule establishes an obligation of result, it is difficult to think that it is a self-executing rule. In other words, there is, in my view, a link, which can be interesting, between the distinction obligations of conduct/obligations of results and the problem of self-executing rules.

Professor Tomuschat said, like some others, that the self-executing character of rules concerns only domestic law. He gives the example of the legal system of the United Kingdom. Well, I know that in the United Kingdom there is no process of incorporation of international treaty law in national law and that they use the method of transforming international treaties into domestic law. Then, of course, the problem of self-executing international rules does not arise. But on the other hand in the United Kingdom there is the principle that customary international law is part of the law of the land; and therefore, at least for customary international law, the problem arises whether a rule is self-executing or not. In other terms, the problem of self-executing rules is mainly, but not exclusively, a problem of treaty law. There are also customary rules of international law which are not self-executing. Think of the rule of the breadth of the territorial sea. According to general international law each State can have 12 miles of territorial sea; but starting from where? Each State has to draw a map, taking into account the straight baselines method, and so on. Therefore one may conclude that the rule of 12 miles is not a self-executing rule, since it needs domestic implementation procedures. And that works also for the English legal system. In short, I think that the problem of self-executing rules is important not only for certain dualistic systems (such as the Italian one) which use the method of direct incorporation of international law within domestic law; but also, sometimes, for other domestic legal systems (such as the English one), whenever they use a method of direct incorporation of international law.

Now I come to Professor Meron's remarks. First of all Professor Meron is against self-contained régimes in human rights law; and I agree. Second, Professor Meron invites us not to take a narrow view of the whole subject of reparation for breach of human rights. On that, it is really difficult to reply. If I have understood well, he says that if there is a primary rule on human rights and a violation of that rule, there is also a right to reparation. I agree with that; but again I think we are speaking of traditional international law and traditional inter-State reparation. If a State violates any binding rule of international human rights law (treaty or customary law), a right of reparation arises in favour of the other States parties of the treaty or in favour of all States. But in my paper the problem was a different one: Does a right to reparation arise in favour of the individual? Is it a domestic right or an international right? In this case I would not be really prepared to maintain that a right of individuals to reparation arises from any breach of any international rule on human rights. But maybe I am too conservative.

Mr. Fleck asked me a difficult question concerning the applicability in time of war of the 1984 Convention Against Torture and of some remedies therein provided for; but I am afraid I am not sure about the answer, since I am not an expert of international humanitarian law.

At last I shall try to reply to Professor Verhoeven. Here I am very sorry but I have not understood some of the critical remarks he made. With regard to Article 5 of the European Convention, I did not say in my report that this is the only norm on reparation. On the contrary, I cited in my paper other norms on reparation. For instance there is Article 50 of the Convention. But, again, the two norms work at different levels. Article 50 establishes international reparation for the benefit of States and now, according to the case law of the European Court, also international reparation for the individual. But we cannot find many rules similar to Article 50. Instead, Article 5 is a completely different norm, because it establishes an obligation of the State parties to provide domestic compensation to the individual, that is a compensation within the domestic legal system and before the domestic courts. There are many other human rights treaties which have a rule similar to Article 5. But does that mean that Article 5 corresponds to general international law? I do not think so, as I said in my report. Can we reach a more general conclusion on the basis of the general principles of law? In other words, can we say that in domestic legal orders reparation is usually provided for in case of a breach of any human right? It is difficult to reach such a conclusion. Moreover, can we say that there is an international customary rule which provides for reparation for any breach of any human rights? Well, it depends again on what kind of reparation we are talking about: inter-State reparation or domestic reparation to individuals or international reparation to individuals? Maybe I am too affectionate to distinctions, like lawyers sometimes are; but if we do not make these distinctions we risk to create a bit of confusion. Finally, I come to Art. 50 of the European Convention. I said in my paper that Article 50 is only a conventional rule. Yes, I firmly believe that Article 50 and Article 63 of the American Convention are at present two unique rules because they are the only rules according to which an international court makes a judgment granting reparation to an individual. Are there other treaties which contain such rules? I do not think so. I would like to conclude my remarks by saying that maybe I was not able in my report to explain some of my ideas clearly. I hope that when Professor Verhoeven reads my paper our dissent will disappear.

The United Nations Compensation Commission

Norbert Wühler

I. Introduction[*]

The United Nations Compensation Commission (the 'UNCC') was established in 1991 as a subsidiary organ of the United Nations Security Council to process claims and pay compensation for losses resulting from Iraq's unlawful invasion and occupation of Kuwait. Iraq's legal responsibility and liability for such losses was confirmed in Security Council resolution 687 (1991) which stated that 'Iraq ... is liable under international law for any direct loss, damage, including environmental damage and the depletion of natural resources, or injury to foreign Governments, nationals and corporations, as a result of the unlawful invasion and occupation of Kuwait'.[1] By its resolution 692 (1991), the Security Council created the UN Compensation Fund and the UN Compensation Commission.[2] The Commission's headquarters was established at the UN offices in Geneva.

While not all aspects of the UNCC's activities are relevant to the topic of this colloquium, the considerable part of the Commission's work that deals with claims by individuals for the compensation of what in many instances are human rights violations, fits squarely under its theme.[3]

---

[*] The views expressed in this chapter do not necessarily represent those of the United Nations Compensation Commission.

[1] UN Security Council resolution 687 (1991), 8 Apr. 1991. Three days later Iraq accepted the terms of that resolution.

[2] UN Security Council resolution 692 (1991), 20 May 1991. The Fund and the Commission were created in accordance with a report that the UN Secretary-General had submitted to the Council; UN Doc. S/22559, 2 May 1991.

[3] On the Commission and its background, see, for instance, C. Alzamora, 'Reflections on the UN Compensation Commission', *Arbitration International* 9 (1993), 349; D.J. Bederman, 'The United Nations Compensation Commission and the Tradition of International Claims Settlement', *New York University Journal of International Law and Politics* 27 (1994), 1; K.-H. Böckstiegel, 'Internationale Streiterledigung vor neuen Herausforderungen', in: U. Beyerlin, M. Bothe, R. Hofmann & E.-U. Petersmann (eds.), *Recht zwischen Umbruch und Bewahrung*,

A. Randelzhofer and C. Tomuschat (eds.), *State Responsibility and the Individual*, 213–229.
© 1999 *Kluwer Law International. Printed in Great Britain.*

The inclusion of the UNCC into this colloquium was particularly timely. While the focus of the Commission's activities is shifting away from the claims of the individuals to the corporate and government claims, and while this has increased the attention that, in particular, members and representatives of this latter part of the 'claimant community' pay to the work of the Commission, one should not forget that the vast majority of the claims before the Commission have been claims of individuals. Their inclusion in this claims program remains one of its most important features, and this colloquium provides an opportunity to recall what contribution this part of the UNCC's work has made to the legal position of the individual under international law. After all, the priority that the Commission has accorded to the individual claims, both in processing and in payment, was prompted by humanitarian considerations. It was the needs of the individuals, as well as the human rights nature of the individuals' rights, the violation of which gave rise to their claims, that resulted in the priority treatment of those claims.

II. THE ORGANIZATION OF THE UNCC

1) The Governing Council

The UNCC is organized into three main components. The Governing Council is the principal policy-making organ of the Commission. Its membership is the same as that of the Security Council at any given time. It establishes the criteria for the compensability of claims, the rules and procedures that govern the processing of the claims, the guidelines regarding the administration and financing of the Compensation Fund and the procedures for the payment of

---

1995, 671; P. d'Argent, 'Le Fonds et la Commission de Compensation des Nations Unies', *Revue Belge de Droit International* 25 (1992), 485; M. Frigessi di Rattalma, *Nazioni Unite e Danni Derivanti dalla Guerra del Golfo*, 1995; International Law Institute, *Gulf War Claims Reporter*, since 1992; W. Kälin (ed.), *Human Rights in Times of Occupation: The Case of Kuwait*, 1994; R.B. Lillich (ed.), *The United Nations Compensation Commission*, 1995; F.H. Paolillo, 'Nature et Caractéristiques de la Procédure devant la Commission d'Indemnisation des Nations Unies', in: R.-J. Dupuy (ed.), *The Development of the Role of the Security Council*, 1992, 287; B. Stern, 'Un système hybride: la procédure de règlement pour la réparation des dommages résultant de l'occupation illicite du Koweit par l'Irak', *McGill Law Journal* 37 (1992), 625; G. Townsend, 'The Iraq Claims Process: A Progress Report on the United Nations Compensation Commission and U.S. Remedies', *Loyola of Los Angeles International and Comparative Law Journal* 17 (1995), 973; United Nations (Department of Public Information), *The United Nations and the Iraq-Kuwait Conflict, 1990-1996*, 1996; and N. Wühler, 'Ansprüche gegen Irak vor der United Nations Compensation Commission', *Beilage zum Betriebs-Berater* 12 (1996), 23. Texts of Commissioner panel reports and Governing Council decisions are published in: E. Lauterpacht (ed.), *International Law Reports* 109 (1998), and ILM. The Commission maintains a web-site on the internet that is regularly updated (http://www.uncc.ch).

compensation. Most importantly, the Governing Council has to approve the reports and recommendations that the panels of Commissioners make on groups of claims. These decisions on compensation awards are final and not subject to appeal or review.[4]

2) The Commissioners

Commissioners verify and evaluate the claims, determine the amount of losses and recommend compensation awards to the Governing Council for its approval. Candidates are proposed by the Executive Secretary of the Commission to the United Nations Secretary-General, nominated by the Secretary-General and appointed by the Governing Council. Commissioners work in three-member panels and are assigned groups of claims for review in instalments. They do not work full-time for the Commission. Thus far thirteen panels of Commissioners have been established, three of which have concluded their work.[5] Four additional panels are expected to be established by the end of 1998.

3) The Secretariat

The secretariat of the Commission services the Governing Council and the panels of Commissioners, providing legal, technical and administrative support. It also administers the Compensation Fund. The secretariat is headed by an Executive Secretary who is appointed by the UN Secretary-General. It is comprised of over 200 staff members, the majority of whom are lawyers and legal support staff. In addition, there are accountants, loss adjusters, statisticians, computer specialists and financial and administrative staff. To assist the secretariat in preparing the claims for submission to the panels of Commissioners, and to assist the panels in the verification, valuation and quantification of the claims, the Commission often retains outside experts, particularly accountants and loss adjusters.

---

[4] By Sep. 1998, the Governing Council had adopted 56 decisions, including 25 approving Commissioner panel reports.

[5] The Commissioners appointed to date represent 38 different nationalities.

III. The Jurisdiction of the UNCC

1) Who is eligible to claim?

Paragraph 16 of Security Council resolution 687 (1991) provides that Iraq is liable for loss, damage and injury of individuals, corporations and governments. These three are thus the categories of claimants that are entitled to claim before the Commission. While the claims of individuals and corporations are submitted through the respective governments, it is clear that the claims are those of the individuals and the corporations. The submission through governments is dictated by the huge number of claimants, the direct contact with whom would be impossible to manage for the Commission. The standing of the individuals and corporations is otherwise not in question, and their legal position as the owners of the claims not doubtful.[6]

Some of the aspects of the Commission's treatment of eligibility, standing and submission of claims by individuals are particularly interesting in the context of this colloquium. Governments may submit claims on behalf of their nationals and of other persons resident in their territory.[7] In the latter category, the Commission has accepted that governments submit claims on behalf of, *inter alia*, permanent residents, refugees and asylum seekers. In the case of governments existing in the territory of a former federal State, one such government may submit claims on behalf of nationals and corporations of another such government, if both governments agree.[8]

In a provision that is in this form unprecedented, the Rules foresaw that an appropriate person, authority or body should be appointed to submit claims on behalf of persons who were not in a position to have their claims submitted by a government.[9] The United Nations Development Programme (UNDP), the United Nations High Commissioner for Refugees (UNHCR), and the United Nations Relief and Works Agency for Palestine Refugees in the Near East

---

[6]   This is apparent from a number of procedural features. First, in the definitions section of the Commission's Provisional Rules for Claims Procedure (the 'Rules')(UN Doc. S/AC.26/1992/10, 26 June 1992), a claimant is described as 'any individual, corporation ... that files a claim with the Commission' (Art. 1, para. 12). Second, governments submit claims on behalf of the individuals and corporations (Art. 5). Third, procedural orders or other communications from the Commission are addressed to the individuals and corporations. And fourth, awards are made in respect of the individual claims within each instalment of claims that is reviewed and decided by a panel of Commissioners (Arts. 37 and 38).

[7]   Art. 5, para. 1, lit. a of the Rules.

[8]   Art. 5, para. 1, lit. a of the Rules. This facility was used in the case of claims from States that were previously part of the former Yugoslavia and the Soviet Union.

[9]   Art. 5, para. 2. It was anticipated, and turned out to be the case, that many Palestinians would be in such a situation.

(UNRWA) have been so appointed and have each submitted large numbers of claims, mostly on behalf of Palestinians.

Two further rules with respect to the Commission's jurisdiction *ratione personae* are worth noting. Iraqi nationals are not eligible to submit claims unless such a claimant also possesses the *bona fide* nationality of another State.[10] And claims by members of the Allied Coalition Armed Forces, as a consequence of their involvement in coalition military operations against Iraq, are excluded, except if they are for loss or injury that is otherwise compensable before the Commission, if the claimant has been a prisoner of war, and if the loss or injury resulted from mistreatment in violation of international humanitarian law (including the Geneva Conventions of 1949).[11]

In certain circumstances claims could be submitted by family members. While child, parent and spouse were generally defined as such eligible family members[12], a panel of Commissioners provided further clarification of what may constitute a family in a claims program in which over 90 countries, with many different legal and cultural backgrounds are participating.[13] The panel also concluded that the age of children or their marital status should not affect the eligibility for compensation. It further found that, in conformity with general principles of private international law, where national laws accord a claimant legal rights similar to those accorded to a biological parent or child (such as in the case of adopted children, foster parents, wards and guardians), the claimant will be treated as a biological parent or child before the Commission.[14] And the same panel finally decided that, exceptionally, claims could be brought by a third person on behalf of an injured person when the injured person was in no position to bring a claim him or herself.[15]

A last issue arose in connection with the standing of claimants where the government concerned refused to put forward a claim that a claimant wanted

---

[10] Governing Council decision 1, para. 17 (UN Doc. S/AC.26/1991/1, 2 Aug. 1991). The category 'A' panel of Commissioners has laid down criteria for the existence of such a *bona fide* dual nationality; see first 'A' panel report, paras. 27 et seq. (UN Doc. S/AC.26/1994/2, 21 Oct. 1994). The same criteria have subsequently been applied by other panels of Commissioners.

[11] Governing Council decision 11 (UN Doc. S/AC.26/1992/11, 26 June 1992).

[12] Governing Council decision 1, para. 13 (UN Doc. S/AC.26/1991/1, 2 Aug. 1991).

[13] In death claims, where the deceased had more than one legally recognized wife, the panel considered that each wife and the children born from that union constituted a separate family unit for the purpose of compensation entitlement. First 'B' panel report, at 19 (UN Doc. S/AC.1994/1, 26 May 1994).

[14] Ibid., at 18.

[15] Ibid., at 19. However, the compensation was awarded to the injured person. The situation was different when a claim for injury was submitted by the executor of the estate of a deceased person who had suffered an injury. Unless there was a link between the death and the injury, the panel found that an executor of an estate was not eligible to claim for an injury suffered by the deceased, since the right to claim belongs only to the injured person him or herself.

to submit. This goes to the question of whether the individual has a right to compensation that he or she can pursue on their own. In the case of a human rights violation, absent a forum or institution that is provided specifically by treaty or otherwise, there is currently no general system under international law to which individuals can have recourse in such a case. Where such a forum or institution is provided, it depends on its jurisdictional grant whether the individual claimant has direct access should a government refuse to submit the claim. Corporate claimants could avail themselves of this possibility before the UNCC.[16] The same possibility was not offered to individual claimants. The reason was not, however, that the Commission did not acknowledge such a right for individuals, but rather that the large number of individual claims made it impossible, for practical reasons, to open up the system for what would have become an unmanageable number of direct contacts with claimants.

2) What losses are compensable?

The types of 'loss, damage or injury' that Security Council resolution 687 (1991) states to be compensable have been defined in considerable detail in subsequent decisions of the Commission's Governing Council. Several of the six categories of claims that were created have been reserved for particular loss types. In addition, two of the claim categories are for fixed amounts, whereas in the other four the amount of compensation depends on the evidence provided. Lastly, in view of the large number of claims and out of humanitarian considerations, the processing of the individual claims was expedited and these urgent claims were given priority, also in payment, over the corporate and government claims, marking a significant step in the evolution of international claims practice and post-conflict peace building.

  The expedited categories of individual claims are[17]: 'A' claims for departure from Kuwait or Iraq (925,000); 'B' claims for serious personal injury or death of a family member (6,000); and 'C' claims for individual losses up to US$100,000 (1,620,000).

  The larger and more complex claims categories are[18]: 'D' claims for individual losses over US$100,000 (11,000); 'E' corporate claims (6,000); and 'F' government claims, including claims for environmental damage[19] (300).

---

[16] Art. 5, para.3 of the Rules. In practice, this has happened in only a very few cases.

[17] The number of claims received by the Commission is identified in parentheses for each category (figures have been rounded).

[18] The losses that are compensable in these categories of claims are enumerated in Governing Council decision 7 (UN Doc. S/AC.26/1991/7/Rev.1, 17 March 1992). Further criteria for the compensability in particular of business losses are contained in Governing Council decision 9

This paper concentrates on the claims made by individuals in categories 'A', 'B' and 'C', many of which arose out of situations that constituted human rights violations.[20] The Commission has fulfilled its humanitarian mandate and has nearly completed the processing of these urgent claims.[21] To a considerable extent, the very large numbers in which these smaller individual claims were submitted determined not only the ceilings for the compensation amounts allowed for these categories but also the methods by which the claims were processed and the compensation determined.[22] A brief overview is given below for each of these three categories.

(S/AC.26/1992/9, 6 March 1992) and decision 15 (S/AC.26/1992/15, 4 Jan. 1992). Significantly, costs of the Allied Coalition Forces, including those of military operations against Iraq, are not compensable; see Governing Council decision 19 (S/AC.26/Dec.19, 24 March 1994).

[19] For a discussion of the complex legal issues that will have to be addressed in the review of the environmental claims, see 'Report of the Working Group of Experts on Liability and Compensation for Environmental Damage Arising from Military Activities' (UN Doc. UNEP/Env.Law/3/Inf.1, 15 Oct. 1996).

[20] The work on the category 'D', 'E' and 'F' claims has only fully started in the last two years. Considering their number, volume and complexity, the review and evaluation of those claims will require considerable effort. Last year the Commission developed a work programme that aims at completing the processing of all claims (with the possible exception of environmental claims) by mid-2003. Because many of the 'D', 'E' and 'F' claims are complex and seek large amounts of compensation, and because the Rules require that they each be reviewed individually, the Commission can apply expedited procedures for these claims only to a limited extent. Nevertheless, the evident similarity of loss types and issues across significant numbers of claims allows the Commission to employ a precedent setting procedure whereby it attempts to resolve common legal issues and decide upon common valuation methods with the first instalment of such claims. Once relevant precedents are established, Commissioner panels may then apply those precedents in their review of subsequent instalments, thus limiting their task to the verification and valuation of the claims, and to the calculation of the allowable compensation. This procedure is also particularly relevant for the determination of those corporate and government claims that fall outside the Commission's jurisdiction. Losses that are not 'direct' and those that result only from the trade embargo against Iraq are not compensable; on the directness requirement, see N. Wühler, 'Causation and Directness of Loss as Elements of Compensability Before the United Nations Compensation Commission', in: Lillich, supra note 3, at 207. A third jurisdictional limitation excludes claims with respect to debts or obligations of Iraq that existed prior to its invasion of Kuwait. The scope of this last limitation has recently been defined more precisely by one of the Commissioner panels dealing with corporate claims; see 'Report and recommendations made by the Panel of Commissioners concerning the first instalment of "E2" claims' (UN Doc. S/AC.26/1998/7, 3 July 1998). For an overview of the Commission's treatment of 'E' and 'F' claims and the results so far, see V. Heiskanen and R. O'Brien, 'UN Compensation Commission Panel Sets Precedents on Government Claims', *AJIL* 92 (1998), 339.

[21] One last instalment of approximately 70,000 'C' claims remains to be processed.

[22] As the category 'C' panel of Commissioners concluded, 'with such a large number of "urgent" claims to be reviewed in a relatively short period of time, the methods used to process them necessarily must depart from traditional approaches to claims adjustment or arbitration. Reflecting these observations and the Governing Council's directive, the Panel has concluded that it is neither appropriate nor feasible ... to review individually each element of loss for each

IV. The Individual Claims

1) Category 'A' claims (departure)

Category 'A' claims are individual departure claims submitted by those who had to leave Iraq or Kuwait between the date of the invasion of Kuwait, 2 August 1990, and the date upon which the occupation came to an end, 2 March 1991. Compensation for such claims was set at the fixed sum of US$2,500 for individual claimants and US$5,000 for families. If a claimant filed claims only in category 'A', he or she was eligible to receive US$4,000 for an individual and US$8,000 for a family. These are notional amounts, intended to provide limited financial relief for the consequences of the forced departure of what were, in most cases, foreign workers and their families. Considering the large number of claims filed in this category, this turned out to be the only practical approach.

The Commission received over 925,000 'A' claims. More than one third of these were verified by a computer comparison of claims data against departure data consisting of nearly five million entries, on paper and in computerized format, that the secretariat collected from governments and international organizations concerning the departure of people from Iraq or Kuwait during the relevant period.[23] The remainder of the 'A' claims were processed through sampling, resulting in awards for approximately 500,000 further claims.[24] The

---

"C" claim ... [M]ost claims necessarily will be processed under methodologies designed to resolve massive numbers in a fair and expeditious manner. In developing such an approach, the Panel has weighed the interests of Iraq as well as those of the claimants and the humanitarian concerns underlying category "C".' First 'C' panel report, at 39 (UN Doc. S/AC.26/1994/3, 21 Dec. 1994). And further, 'the Panel has sought to create a mass claims processing system that treats claimants, as well as the responsible party, Iraq, as fairly as possible, within the bounds of the Rules, Decisions and guidelines established by the Security Council and the Governing Council. The Panel also has been influenced by the humanitarian nature of its work in this regard. Where information was available, the Panel has taken into account the socio-economic backgrounds of claimant populations from particular countries and the scope of the relevant national claims programmes'. First 'C' panel report, at 43. The majority of the methods used to deal with the massive number of individual claims fall within the concept of 'mass claims processing'. For a general discussion of mass processing techniques, see, for instance, F. McGovern, 'Resolving Mature Mass Tort Litigation', *Boston University Law Review* 69 (1989), 659, and id., 'Looking to the Future of Mass Torts: A Comment on Schuck and Siliciano', *Cornell Law Review* 80 (1995), 101.
[23] The first 'A' panel report (UN Doc. S/AC.26/1994/2, 21 Oct. 1994) describes this computer 'matching'. See also C. Gibson, 'Using Computers to Evaluate Arbitral Claims: The Experience of the United Nations Compensation Commission', *Arbitration International* 13 (1997), 167.
[24] The sampling methodologies applied are described in the fourth 'A' panel report (UN Doc. S/AC.26/1995/4, 12 Oct. 1995). That report also contains a detailed review of the use of comparable methods in similar mass claims situations and institutions, both at the national and international levels. The panel summarized the rationale for their use as follows: 'Faced with

successful 'A' claimants have been awarded a total compensation of US$3.2 billion.

2) Category 'B' claims (injury or death)

Category 'B' claims are individual claims submitted by those who suffered serious personal injury or whose spouse, child or parent died as a result of Iraq's invasion and occupation of Kuwait. Category 'B' claimants were eligible to receive fixed sums of US$2,500 for individuals and up to US$10,000 for families. These are interim payments in cases where claimants sought compensation in the other individual claims categories 'C' or 'D' for actual losses in connection with the same injury or death.

The types of injuries that would entitle someone to compensation were defined in relative detail by the Governing Council.[25] Where it deemed necessary, the panel of Commissioners obtained the advice of a medical expert to assist in the review of the death and injury claims. The Commission has resolved all of the more than 6,000 'B' claims that were submitted to it. Nearly 4,000 of these claims have been awarded a total compensation amount of US$13.4 million.

3) Category 'C' claims (damages up to US$100,000)

Category 'C' claims are individual claims for damages up to US$100,000 and cover the following types of losses: damages arising from departure from Iraq or Kuwait; hostage taking or other forced detention; personal injury; death of a family member; loss of personal property; loss of bank accounts; loss of income, unpaid salaries or support; real property losses; and individual business losses.

The Commission received approximately 420,000 'C' claims. In addition, Egypt submitted a consolidated claim on behalf of over 900,000 Egyptian

---

situations of mass claims and other situations where a large number of cases involving common issues of law and fact arise, courts, tribunals and commissions have adopted methodologies, including that of sampling, recognizing that the traditional method of individualized adjudication if applied to such cases would not be appropriate as it would result in unacceptable delays and substantially increase the burden of costs for such claimants and more so for the respondents. The legal principle involved may be stated as follows: in situations involving mass claims or analogous situations raising common factual and legal issues, it is permissible in the interest of effective justice to apply methodologies and procedures which provide for an examination and determination of a representative sample of these claims'; see first 'A' panel report, para. 9 (UN Doc. S/AC.26/1994/2, 21 Oct. 1994).

[25] Governing Council decision 3 (UN Doc. S/AC.26/1991/3, 23 Oct. 1991).

workers in Iraq who were seeking compensation for the non-transfer of funds they had deposited in Iraqi banks to beneficiaries in Egypt.[26]

Different from those in categories 'A' and 'B', claimants in category 'C' do not receive a pre-determined fixed sum, but rather are entitled to compensation to the extent and in the amount that can be established for the individual claim. This did not require— and indeed it would have been totally impractical—that the 420,000 claims would each be examined one-by-one. The Rules foresaw that groups of claims would be reviewed together and that techniques such as computer-assisted processing and sampling would be employed.[27] As it turned out, a variety of techniques were used for the various loss types, including sampling, statistical analysis, regression modelling and individual review.[28] All these processes had to rely heavily on computer support. A large database as well as specially designed software applications were indispensable tools.[29]

In this way the Commission has, to date, managed to complete the processing of 350,000 of the 420,000 'C' claims by dispensing 'rough justice' that neither spends excessive time and resources on a claim-by-claim review nor simply assigns a flat sum to the different claims.[30] For certain claims, such as those for mental pain and anguish which are permissible in connection with some of the loss types, the Governing Council has laid down maximum ceilings above which no compensation may be awarded. These ceilings vary according to the different loss types.[31] To assist them in the application of

---

[26] The report of the Commissioner panel appointed specifically to deal with the Egyptian workers' claims contains detailed conclusions on what constitute 'direct' losses that are compensable and what constitute pre-existing debts and obligations of Iraq that are outside the Commission's jurisdiction. The panel found that approximately 225,000 of the claims in this group were within the Commission's jurisdiction; Egyptian Workers' Claims panel report (UN Doc. S/AC.26/1997/3, 2 Oct. 1997).

[27] Arts. 37(a) and (b) of the Rules.

[28] Most instructive on how the category 'C' panel used these various techniques are the first, second and sixth panel reports (UN Docs. S/AC.26/1994/3, 21 Dec. 1994; S/AC.26/1996/1, 30 May 1996; and S/AC.26/1998/6, 2 July 1998).

[29] See also C. Gibson, 'Mass Claims Processing: Techniques for Processing Over 400,000 Claims for Individual Loss at the United Nations Compensation Commission', in: Lillich, supra note 3, 155.

[30] The UNCC thus appears to have found a workable middle ground, at least for category 'C' types of claims, that did not seem feasible, for instance, to the Truth and Reconciliation Commission in the context of reparations for human rights violations committed by the apartheid regime in South Africa. See the statement of that Commission's Reparation and Rehabilitation Committee that 'it is impossible to devise a set of criteria which provide for varying amounts of reparation to be paid to victims according to their degree of suffering without producing unfair or arbitrary results'; Discussion Document for a Proposed Policy for Urgent Interim Reparation and Final Reparation, Truth and Reconciliation Commission: National Consultation 1997/04/02 (prepared by Glenda Wildschut and Wendy Orr), 12.

[31] Governing Council decision 8 (UN Doc. S/AC.26/1992/8, 27 Jan. 1992).

these criteria, the 'C' panel sought the advice of a group of psychiatric experts who were especially experienced in disaster psychiatry and in the treatment of torture victims.[32] The panel also sought expert advice from a specialist in international labour law with respect to claims for salary losses[33] and it had, in the development of its claims processing approaches, the benefit of a specialist in the trial of mass torts.[34]

So far, a total compensation amount of US$2.9 billion has been awarded to the successful claimants in category 'C', including US$85 million for 225,000 of the claims of the Egyptian workers that were found to be compensable.

While individual claims for damages above US$100,000 can be brought under category 'D' for loss types that are, for the most part, the same as those covered by category 'C', the evidentiary standard is stricter in category 'D' since the amounts claimed in that category are higher. Whereas 'D' claims must be supported by 'documentary and other appropriate evidence sufficient to demonstrate the circumstances and amount of the loss claimed',[35] it is sufficient for 'C' claims that the documents and other evidence are 'the reasonable minimum that is appropriate under the particular circumstances of the case'.[36] Again, humanitarian considerations are reflected in the process for the smaller claims of individuals for whom it was difficult or impossible to keep or obtain documentary evidence that could have served to support subsequent claims when they were fleeing in hurried circumstances or had their homes looted.

V. THE APPLICABLE LAW AT THE UNCC

Considering the UNCC's genesis, its organizational setting as a subsidiary organ of the UN Security Council and the specificity of its mandate, it is not surprising that the 'applicable law' rule which governs its work is focussed on this very framework. The relevant Article 31 of the Rules provides:

> In considering the claims, Commissioners will apply Security Council resolution 687 (1991) and other relevant Security Council resolutions, the criteria established by the Governing Council for particular categories of claims, and any pertinent decisions of the Governing Council. In addition, where necessary, Commissioners shall apply other relevant rules of international law.

---

[32] See the Expert Report on Mental Pain and Anguish in Annex VI to the first 'C' panel report (UN Doc. S/AC.26/1994/3, 21 Dec. 1994).
[33] See first 'C' panel report, Annex VII.
[34] Ibid., at 40.
[35] Art. 35(3) of the Rules.
[36] Art. 35(2)(c) of the Rules. For smaller claims such as those below US$20,000, even a 'lesser degree of documentary evidence ordinarily will be sufficient'.

Building on the initial legal basis of paragraph 16 of Security Council resolution 687, the Commission's Governing Council has provided extensive guidance, both for the procedural aspects of the review of the claims,[37] as well as on the substantive rules governing the compensability of the claims and the various loss types.[38] In its first decision, the Governing Council expanded on the central requirement of the 'directness' of loss for the claims by individuals in categories 'A', 'B' and 'C'. Such direct loss, which must be as a result of Iraq's invasion and occupation of Kuwait, includes any loss suffered as a result of:

(a) military operations or threat of military action by either side during the period 2 August 1990 to 2 March 1991;
(b) departure from or inability to leave Iraq or Kuwait (or a decision not to return) during that period;
(c) actions by officials, employees or agents of the Government of Iraq or its controlled entities during that period in connection with the invasion or occupation;
(d) the breakdown of civil order in Kuwait or Iraq during that period; or
(e) hostage-taking or other illegal detention.[39]

Commissioner panels have generally found a sufficient basis in resolution 687 and the Governing Council decisions for their determinations on the claims and their recommendations on compensation. There have been instances, however, where they relied on what the Rules refer to as 'other relevant rules of international law'.[40] And in the criteria for the compensation

---

[37] For an in-depth analysis of the Commission's Rules, see M.F. Raboin, 'The Provisional Rules for Claims Procedure of the United Nations Compensation Commission: A Practical Approach to Mass Claims Processing', in: Lillich, supra note 3, 119.

[38] As of Sep. 1998, the Governing Council had rendered 56 decisions, almost half of which provided such guidance, with the remainder approving or otherwise relating to Commissioner panel reports.

[39] Governing Council decision 1, para. 18 (UN Doc. S/AC.26/1991/1, 2 Aug. 1991). The same criteria were later declared applicable to the larger individual claims and for the corporate and government claims; Governing Council decision 7 (S/AC.26/1991/7/Rev.1, 17 March 1992).

[40] Cf., for instance, the statement that 'international law and jurisprudence ... recognize the principle that interest should be paid', first 'A' panel report, at 21 (UN Doc. S/AC.26/1994/2, 21 Oct. 1994); the definition of family 'in conformity with general principles of private international law'; first 'B' panel report, at 18 (S/AC.26/1994/1, 26 May 1994); and several references by the 'C' panel to general principles of law; see first 'C' panel report, at 28, 30 and 192 (S/AC.26/1994/3, 21 Dec. 1994). With respect to evidentiary requirements, one panel concluded that '[t]he rule of *actori incumbit probatio* is recognized and applied in both municipal and international law, though with more flexibility in international law'. See first 'D' panel report, para. 69 (S/AC.26/1998/1, 3 Feb. 1998) (referring to M. Kazazi, *Burden of Proof and Related Issues: A Study on Evidence Before International Tribunals*, 1996, 116). Another panel found that the Governing Council's decision to hold Iraq liable for, *inter alia*, direct loss, damage or injury suffered as a result of '[m]ilitary operations or threat of military action *by either side*' during the relevant period was in accordance with the general principles of international law; Report of the panel reviewing the Well Blowout Control ('WBC') claim, para. 86 (S/AC.26/1996/5/Annex, 18 Dec. 1996). The same panel referred to 'general principles

of business losses, the Governing Council itself referred in several places to general principles, particularly of contract law.[41]

VI. PAYMENT AND THE COMPENSATION FUND

Payments of compensation are made from a special fund that receives a percentage of the proceeds derived from the sale of Iraqi oil. Since the value of approved awards exceeds the resources available in the Compensation Fund, the Governing Council devised a payment mechanism for the allocation of available funds to successful claimants that gives priority treatment across categories to the three urgent categories of claims and gives equal treatment to similarly situated claims within each category. Only when each successful claimant in categories 'A', 'B' and 'C' has been paid up to US$2,500 in awarded compensation will payments commence for claims in other categories.[42] Ultimately, however, category 'B' claims were paid in full for humanitarian considerations. Accordingly only successful category 'A' and category 'C' claimants are receiving the US$2,500 partial payment. Payment is made when sufficient resources have accumulated in the Fund to pay up to US$2,500 to all the successful claimants in the claims instalments concerned.

The payment of compensation awards is made through the governments that originally submitted the claims.[43] Any government that receives compensation payments is responsible for the distribution of compensation to successful claimants. The government must submit reports within certain time periods to the Governing Council, describing its payment distribution mechanisms and detailing the amount and date of payment to each successful claimant. Money that is not distributed by governments to successful claimants within twelve months must be returned to the Commission. Through the reports from the governments, the Commission can monitor the distribution of compensation to successful claimants. If the Governing Council determines that a government does not fulfill its reporting obligations in a satisfactory manner, it can suspend compensation payments to the government concerned.

---

of international law relating to mitigation of damages'; ibid., para. 54. One of the government claims panels relied on general principles of international law when it selected a date for purposes of currency conversion; first 'F' panel report, para. 100 (S/AC.26/1997/6, 18 Dec. 1997). And a corporate claims panel '[applied] the principle of article 31 of the Vienna Convention' on the Law of Treaties from which it '[took] guidance ... [i]n interpreting Security Council resolution 687 (1991)'; first 'E2' panel report, paras. 54, 64 (S/AC.26/1998/7, 3 July 1998).

[41] Governing Council decision 9, paras. 8, 9 and 11 (UN Doc. S/AC.26/1992/9, 6 March 1992).

[42] Governing Council decision 17 (UN Doc. S/AC.26/Dec.17, 24 March 1994).

[43] Governing Council decision 18 (UN Doc. S/AC.26/Dec.18, 24 March 1994).

Payments are dependent upon the availability of resources in the Compensation Fund. As stipulated by Security Council resolution 705 (1991), thirty percent of the revenue from the sale of Iraqi oil is deposited in the Fund and put toward the payment of compensation, as well as toward the operating costs of the Commission. The level of Iraq's contribution to the Fund has been an item of considerable debate and continues to be so the longer the trade embargo against Iraq stays in place. It is said that where a State has to pay compensation, its payment capacity should be taken into account, and that one should make those who have committed the wrongful acts pay themselves rather than "tax" the State and penalize the population as a whole. This is not the place to examine whether in the case of Iraq another mechanism could or should have been implemented. And in the interests of the Iraqi people who suffer greatly from the effects of the embargo one must hope that the conditions for its lifting are met as soon as possible. As far as Iraq's payment capacity is concerned, however, this was in fact taken into account when the level of its contribution to the Fund was determined.[44]

The Compensation Fund receives its income pursuant to the 'oil-for-food' mechanism that authorizes Iraq to sell petroleum and petroleum products, up to a ceiling amount per authorized time period. Under this mechanism, the revenue derived from the oil sales is used to meet the humanitarian needs of the Iraqi population, to cover the expenses of the United Nations Special Commission on Iraq (UNSCOM) that deals with weapons inspections, and to provide income for the Compensation Fund.[45]

As of September 1998, the Commission had resolved almost 2.5 million out of the nearly 2.6 million claims it received, including nearly all of the claims

---

[44] In accordance with para. 19 of Security Council resolution 687 (1991), the percentage was to take into account 'the requirements of the people of Iraq, Iraq's payment capacity as assessed in conjunction with the international financial institutions taking into consideration external debt service, and the needs of the Iraqi economy'. When the Secretary-General suggested the figure of 30 percent to the Security Council, he considered the probable levels of future oil export revenues of Iraq, the amounts of military spending and arms imports in the past, the service of Iraq's foreign debt and the needs for reconstruction and development in the country. See Report of the Secretary-General pursuant to para. 19 of resolution 687 (UN Doc. S/22559, 2 May 1991), para. 13, and Note of the Secretary-General pursuant to paragraph 13 of his report of 2 May 1991 (UN Doc. S/22661, 30 May 1991). Interestingly, prior to the invasion, Iraq's military spending corresponded to approximately 30 percent of its oil revenues which is the level at which the contribution was eventually fixed.

[45] Since Dec. 1996, the Fund has received on average around US$100 million each month. The latest extension of the 'oil-for-food' mechanism, which came into effect in May 1998 with the Secretary-General's approval of the new plan submitted by Iraq for the distribution of humanitarian supplies to the Iraqi people, raised the total value of oil that Iraq is allowed to sell every six months from US$2 billion to US$5.2 billion. Consequently, the Commission expects the amount of money that the Compensation Fund receives each month to increase, thereby enabling the more frequent payment of awards to successful claimants.

in the three urgent categories of individual claims that were given priority for humanitarian reasons.[46] The total compensation awarded to individual claimants in categories 'A', 'B' and 'C' is over US$6 billion, and the total amount of compensation paid to successful claims in these categories is, to date, close to US$2 billion.

VII. OUTLOOK

With its program for individual claims practically completed, one may ask whether the UNCC has so far fulfilled its mandate, and how its experience compares with that of other institutions. Such an assessment is, of course, influenced by the understanding one has of the Commission's character and of what role and function it is to perform within the framework in which it was created and in which it operates.

Some authors have questioned the Security Council's authority to establish the UNCC in the first place and to structure its process in the way in which it has been done. In particular, the level foreseen for Iraq's participation in the proceedings has been criticized as violating principles of fairness and due process.[47] Others have shown that the Security Council acted within its powers when it created the Commission and established its framework.[48] And several of the UNCC's panels of Commissioners have confirmed that the Security Council acted under Chapter VII of the United Nations Charter when it determined 'that compensation in accordance with international law should be provided to foreign Governments, nationals and corporations for any direct loss, damage or injury sustained by them as a result of Iraq's unlawful

---

[46] As stated above, the Commission's work programme foresees that the processing of the remaining, mostly larger, claims in categories 'D', 'E' and 'F' will be completed by mid-2003.

[47] B. Graefrath, 'Iraqi Reparations and the Security Council', *Zeitschrift für ausländisches öffentliches Recht und Völkerrecht* 55 (1995), 1; P. Malanczuk, 'International Business and New Rules of State Responsibility? The Law Applied by the United Nations (Security Council) Compensation Commission for Claims Against Iraq', in: K.-H. Böckstiegel (ed.), *Perspectives of Air Law, Space Law and International Business Law for the Next Century*, 1995, 117; M.E. Schneider, 'How Fair and Efficient is the United Nations Compensation Commission System?', *Journal of International Arbitration* 15 (1998), 15.

[48] D. Caron, 'The Legitimacy of the Collective Authority of the Security Council', *AJIL* 87 (1993), 552; J. Carver, 'Dispute Resolution or Administrative Tribunal: A Question of Due Process', in: Lillich, supra note 3, 69; M. Herdegen, 'Der Sicherheitsrat und die autoritative Konkretisierung des VII. Kapitels der UN-Charta', in: Beyerlin, supra note 3, 103. For a broad construction of the Security Council's powers in the process of reconstruction and reconciliation after the end of armed hostilities, see also B. Fassbender, *UN Security Council Reform and the Right of Veto: A Constitutional Perspective*, 1998, at 212-214.

invasion and occupation of Kuwait, in order to restore international peace and security'.[49]

In its report on the situation of human rights in Kuwait under Iraqi occupation, the Special Rapporteur of the Commission on Human Rights found that, during Iraq's occupation of Kuwait, Iraq committed numerous human rights violations that 'amount[ed] to grave breaches in the sense of the Geneva Conventions', and that Iraq was internationally responsible for such violations of human rights.[50] The Special Rapporteur recalled that the Security Council had explicitly recognized the applicability of these principles in the case of Iraq[51], and he concluded that

[t]he establishment of the [Compensation F]und ensures that compensation will be paid for material damage caused to public and private property in Kuwait. This means that there will be compensation for important aspects of the violation of economic, social and cultural rights and the corresponding guarantees of international humanitarian law, namely the dismantling, pillaging and destruction of health-care, educational, research and cultural institutions and facilities.[52]

In a study concerning the right to restitution, compensation and rehabilitation for victims of gross violations of human rights and fundamental freedoms, the Special Rapporteur of the Sub-Commission on Prevention of Discrimination and Protection of Minorities of the Commission on Human Rights concluded that when the Security Council reaffirmed Iraq's liability, it based itself more on traditional concepts of international law and not so much on international human rights law.[53] Nevertheless, he found that 'significant trends and elements can be discerned in the overall context' of the right to compensation for human rights violations and that certain of the criteria elaborated by the UNCC's Governing Council 'may provide helpful guidance

---

[49] Report of the WBC claim panel, para. 68 (UN Doc. S/AC.26/1996/5/Annex, 18 Dec. 1996); see also, for instance, first 'F1' panel report, para. 48 (S/AC.26/1997/6, 18 Dec. 1997).

[50] Para. 252 of the Report (the 'Kälin report') (UN Doc. E/CN.4/1992/26, 16 Jan. 1992). The acts to which the Special Rapporteur referred in particular included summary and arbitrary executions, widespread and systematic acts of torture, deportation of large numbers of civilians to Iraq, the use of third-country nationals as 'human shields', and the extensive destruction of important parts of the infrastructure of Kuwait, including health-care and educational facilities.

[51] UN Security Council resolutions 670 (1990), 25 Sep. 1990, and 674 (1990), 29 Oct. 1990.

[52] Ibid., para. 259. Various other UN reports that document the damage and dislocation caused in Kuwait during the invasion and occupation by Iraq are referred to in the first 'D' panel report, paras. 22 et seq. (UN Doc. S/AC.26/1998/1, 3 Feb. 1998); see the 'Ahtisaari report' and the two 'Farah reports'.

[53] Para. 95 of the Final Report submitted by the Special Rapporteur (the 'van Boven report') (UN Doc. E/CN.4/Sub.2/1993/8, 2 July 1993), and para.105: 'It is in the nature of the task and mandate of the Security Council that the creation of the Compensation Fund and the criteria for the processing of the claims are governed by State interests. The legal framework is set out in the law relating to reparation claims on the part of foreign subjects rather than in modern international human rights law'.

in developing criteria concerning the right to reparation for victims of gross violations of human rights'.[54] Notwithstanding the different emphasis that these reports may place on certain aspects of the UNCC's compensation scheme, there is agreement that the Commission and its process have a firm foundation in international law.

What is novel about the Commission is thus not the legal basis for Iraq's liability or the criteria for compensation, but rather the fact that the international community has placed a compensation scheme within the United Nations framework in which almost one hundred States participate, and that it has created a system that can handle as many as 2.6 million claims.[55] While this kind of response to mass violations of human rights may not always be feasible[56], the system is, in the case of the individual claims before the UNCC, serving its purpose and brings, albeit limited, financial relief to those who were most directly affected by Iraq's invasion and occupation of Kuwait. Some fear that the Commission could, in future, by awarding large amounts of compensation for corporate and government claims with only limited Iraqi participation in the process, move towards a system that would be more like 'victor's justice'[57]. However, there is no indication that such a development might occur, and, based on its practice to date, there is every expectation that the UNCC will continue to meet its challenge and balance the legitimate rights to compensation of those who suffered losses, with the interest of Iraq not to have to pay for more than what was a direct result of its invasion and occupation of Kuwait.

---

[54] Ibid., para. 105.

[55] Cf. J.R. Crook, 'The United Nations Compensation Commission: A New Structure to Enforce State Responsibility', *AJIL* 87 (1993), 144; C. Whelton, 'The United Nations Compensation Commission and International Claims Law: A Fresh Approach', *Ottawa Law Review* 25 (1993), 607.

[56] But see the Commission for Real Property Claims pursuant to Annex VII of the Dayton Peace Agreement that uses mass processing techniques, in many respects similar to those applied by the UNCC for its individual claims, to deal with hundreds of thousands of claims of displaced persons and refugees from Bosnia-Herzegovina. For the work of that Commission, see H. van Houtte, 'The Property Claims Commission in Bosnia-Herzegovina: A New Path to Restore Real Estate Rights in Post-War Societies?', in: K. Wellens (ed.), *International Law, Theory and Practice*, 1998, 549. See also, at the domestic level, the Truth and Reconciliation Commission of South Africa, the Truth and Justice Commission of Haiti, and the National Compensation Tribunal of Malawi.

[57] For a comparison of the UNCC with the reparations system after the First World War, see, for instance, E.J. Garmise, 'The Iraqi Claims Process and the Ghost of Versailles', *New York University Law Review* 67 (1992), 840, and C.P.R. Romano, 'Woe to the Vanquished? A comparison of the Reparations Process after World War I (1914-18) and the Gulf War (1990-91)', *Austrian Review of International and European Law* 2 (1997), 362. See also A.A. Levy, 'The Persian Gulf War Cease-Fire Agreement Compared with the Japanese Peace Treaty in Terms of Reparations and Reconstruction', *Dickinson Journal of International Law* 10 (1992), 541.

The Legal Position of the Individual under Present International Law

Albrecht Randelzhofer

I. INTRODUCTION

During this colloquium we have been listening to a series of reports dealing with the specific question whether and to what extent there exist individual reparation claims as a consequence of human rights violations. At first sight, the title of my presentation seems to address a different matter. And indeed, during yesterday's discussion one participant expressed the view that the title of the colloquium and the sub-heading define different topics. Others were of the opinion that, although these are different topics, they are yet linked to each other. They qualified the problem of individual reparation claims entailed by human rights violations to be an aspect, an important aspect, of the much broader problem of the legal position of the individual under international law. That is exactly the idea of the organizers of this colloquium. The existence or non-existence of individual reparation claims is related to the problem whether and to what extent the individual is a subject of public international law. On the other hand, this problem is not confined to the specific topic of our colloquium but has a much broader ambit. Perhaps it was a mistake to type the sub-heading in the same bold face as the main title. That could have suggested an intention to deal with both topics on a basis of parity. But a second look at the program makes clear that this has never been our intention. Seven eminent speakers have dealt with the topic of individual reparation claims, an important but nevertheless restricted topic, and I alone, focusing on the much broader topic of the position of the individual under international law, should do that in the same comprehensive fashion? Nobody will expect that from me.

It thus should be clear that I am dealing with the broader topic as an annex to the specific topic of the colloquium. The aim of my presentation is to give an answer to the question whether the results of our colloquium give rise to a new evaluation of the legal position of the individual under current international law. For that purpose, it is necessary to provide an overview of the legal position of the individual under international law, its development and its present stage.

A. Randelzhofer and C. Tomuschat (eds.), State Responsibility and the Individual, 231–242.

II. AN ASSESSMENT OF RECENT DEVELOPMENTS

1) Until the beginning of this century the quality of the individual as a subject of public international law was not even raised as a question. Sovereign States were the almost exclusive subjects, accompanied by only very few international organisations and some peculiar entities such as, for example, the Pope or the Order of the Knights of Malta.

It is worth mentioning that the then leading treatise of public international law in Germany by von Liszt and Fleischmann, in its twelfth and last edition published in 1925, does not refer to the individual as a possible subject of public international law at all. This is no proof of a peculiar old-fashioned way of thinking of German scholars but corresponds to the line of similar treatises of public international law of that epoch in other countries.

Other eminent authors of the same time do address the issue whether the individual is a subject of public international law. However, they come to the conclusion that the treaties and the customary law seeming to establish rights and duties of individuals really entitle or oblige States only. An example for this view is provided by the third edition of Anzilotti's treatise on public international law published in 1927 (German edition of 1929)[1].

2) Today it is generally accepted that the individual is indeed a subject of public international law. This transformation of the position of the individual is one of the most remarkable developments in contemporary international law[2]. Nevertheless, this position remains highly controversial as far as details are concerned[3]. Verdross in his famous textbook on international law says: 'The manifold controversies as to the position of the individual in international law have their origin in most cases not in substantive contrasts, but in unclarified terms.'[4] I dare to say that our discussion proves to some extent, too, that the statement of Verdross is still valid.

a) Already the term 'subject of public international law' is understood in different ways.

The so-called sociological school in France, represented especially by Duguit and Scelle, not only regarded the human being and its protection as the object of the whole legal order, including international law, but even considered the individual to be its exclusive subject. States had only the function of

---

[1]   D. Anzilotti, *Lehrbuch des Völkerrechts*, 1929, 98.

[2]   This is rightly stressed by S. Oda, 'The Individual in International Law', in: M. Sørensen (ed.), *Manual of Public International Law*, 1968, 471.

[3]   See K.-J. Partsch, 'Individuals in International Law', in: R. Bernhardt (ed.), *Encyclopedia of Public International Law* (EPIL), vol. II, 1995, 958.

[4]   A. Verdross, *Völkerrecht*, 5th ed., 1964, 216.

providing a legal machinery to regulate the rights and duties of collectivities or individuals[5].

It was stressed by Sir Humphrey Waldock that

> to express the matter in that way is to abandon law for philosophy. For law is an artificial system which has its own concepts and principles, and anyone invoking the law will find himself confronted by these concepts and principles. Neither international nor municipal law treats the state merely as a convenient piece of machinery; and in international law it may make all the difference in the world to the individual that it is normally his state, not himself, who is the bearer of international rights and duties.[6]

Similar to this criticism is Berber's statement to the effect that this reasoning results in confusing the bearers of rights and obligations of international law with the final beneficiaries of law[7].

There is no need to determine the notion of subject of law within public international law otherwise than in any other legal order. This means that in public international law, too, a subject of law is whoever bears rights and obligations directly under this branch of the law.

b) This is today by far the predominant view. But another controversy centers on whether in addition to the bearing of rights it is necessary that such rights can be enforced by individuals on the international level. Many contemporary writers answer this question in the affirmative[8]. On the other hand it is noteworthy that authors who are the chief advocates of the view that the individual is a subject of international law, as for example H. Lauterpacht, do not insist on this additional requirement. In fact, this requirement blurs the distinction between the bearing of rights and the capacity to exercise those rights oneself[9].

In the judgment of December 15, 1933, in the *Peter Pazmany* case, the Permanent Court of International Justice said: 'It is scarcely necessary to point

---

[5]   See, e.g., L. Duguit, *Traité de droit constitutionnel*, 2nd ed., 1921, 319; G. Scelle, *Manuel élémentaire de droit international public*, 1943, 16 et seq., 408 et seq.

[6]   H. Waldock, 'General Course on Public International Law', *Recueil des Cours* 106 (1962-II), 1, 192.

[7]   F. Berber, *Lehrbuch des Völkerrechts*, vol. 1, 2nd ed., 1975, 170.

[8]   Cf., e.g., H. Kelsen, *Principles of International Law*, 1952, 143 et seq.; H. Mosler, 'The International Society as a Legal Community', *Recueil des Cours* 140 (1973-III), 70; A. Verdross & B. Simma, *Universelles Völkerrecht*, 3rd ed., 1984, 256; I. Brownlie, *Principles of Public International Law*, 4th ed., 1990, 58; V. Epping, 'Völkerrechtssubjekte', in: K. Ipsen et al., *Völkerrecht*, 3rd ed. 1990, 52, 76.

[9]   This distinction is maintained for example by H. Lauterpacht, 'The Subjects of the Law of Nations', L.Q.R. 63 (1947), 438, 455, and L.Q.R. 64 (1948), 97; id., *International Law and Human Rights*, 1950, 27; Ch. Rousseau, *Droit International Public*, vol. II, 1974, 696; C.A. Nørgaard, *The Individual in International Law*, 1962, 32; M. Grassi, *Die Rechtsstellung des Individuums im Völkerrecht*, 1955, 89; D.P. O'Connell, *International Law*, vol. 1, 2nd ed., 1970, 108.

out that the capacity to possess civil rights does not necessarily imply the capacity to exercise those rights oneself.'[10] Although speaking explicitly of 'civil rights', the Court, as it emerges from a close reading of its judgment, is of the opinion that this proposition is not confined to civil law, but typical of any legal order.

So we have to distinguish:

(i) Whoever is a bearer of rights or duties under international law is a subject of international law.

(ii) It is not, additionally, necessary that the bearer of a right also have the capacity to exercise this right himself.

On the other hand, I agree with the view that if in today's international law an individual has standing before an international court or tribunal or before another international institution, the conclusion may be drawn that he has a right. It is still correct to say as it was stated in Roman law: *Ubi actio, ibi ius.* But the reverse–*ubi ius, ibi actio*–is not necessarily correct. It would be too high a hurdle to acknowledge rights of the individual only in cases in which he has the capacity to exercise the right himself.

(iii) An even higher hurdle was established yesterday by Michael Reisman. Being asked whether there exist rights of the individual under the American Convention on Human Rights, he answered in the negative. His argument was that the decisions of the Court are not enforceable.

In my view, that goes too far. To recognize the individual as a subject of international law only if he is bearer of rights, has standing before an international court *and* if the decision of the court is enforceable against a State would set the individual as a possible subject of international law too wide apart from the other subjects of international law.

3) As it has been pointed out, the individual is a subject of international law as far as he holds rights or bears obligations under public international law.

a) As far as customary law is concerned, at first sight the protection of aliens in foreign state territory could give rise to the assumption that the individual is a subject of international law inasmuch as the law obliges States to treat aliens within their territory according to the so-called minimum standard. But the law on the protection of aliens is fundamentally different from human rights[11]. It stems from an era of public international law when the individual was totally mediatized by the State. The individual was in fact protected by

---

[10] PCIJ Series A/B, No. 61, *Appeal from a Judgment of the Hungaro-Czechoslovak Mixed Arbitral Tribunal*, 231.

[11] This difference is correctly emphasised by Verdross & Simma (supra note 8), at 797, but blurred by L. Henkin, 'Human Rights', in: EPIL, vol. II, 1995, 887.

the relevant rules, but the individual was and is not the holder of a corresponding right. As it was stated by the Permanent International Court of
Justice in the *Mavrommatis* case, if the minimum standard is breached it is not
the individual who is violated in his rights but the State of nationality of the
victim[12]. The State is the holder of the relevant rights. The individual is not
protected as such but only as the national of another State. The State is
entitled, though not obliged, to seek remedy for this violation of law by means
of diplomatic protection.

Up to now I do not see any right of the individual under public international
law being granted by customary law.

b) But meanwhile, under treaty law, the individual is at least holder of rights
in public international law.

i) It was not clear from the beginning whether rights could be conferred upon
an individual by an international treaty or if such a treaty obliges only the
States parties to create such rights in their municipal law.

In its advisory opinion of March 3, 1928 concerning the *Jurisdiction of the
Courts of Danzig*, the Permanent Court of International Justice said: 'It cannot
be disputed that the very object of an international agreement, according to the
intention of the contracting parties, may be the adoption by the parties of some
definite rules creating individual rights and obligations ...'.[13] Since then it is
commonly accepted also in legal writings that the individual may become a
subject of public international law by virtue of such treaties.

ii) It is especially the realm of human rights in which rights are granted to the
individual by international treaties. But this by no means is tantamount to
saying that all the treaties protecting human rights directly grant rights to
individuals.

The protection of human rights by public international law did not start with
conventions aiming at a comprehensive protection of human rights, but with
specific agreements intending to protect especially endangered categories of
individuals against gross violations. The following agreements, in particular,
should be mentioned in this connection: the Agreement on Slavery of
September 25, 1926, amended by the Protocol of December 7, 1953; the
agreements of May 18, 1904 and May 4, 1910 against the trade in white
women and girls; the conventions of September 30, 1921 and October 11,
1933 against the trade in women and girls. All these treaties aim at the
protection of individuals, but they do not grant rights to individuals. If a State

---

[12] PCIJ Series A, No. 2, *The Mavrommatis Palestine Concessions* (Jurisdiction), 12.
[13] PCIJ Series B, No. 15, 17 et seq.

party violates these treaties, it is not rights of individuals that are violated but only rights of the other States parties.

iii) The protection of human rights has reached another level after World War II. Whilst the Covenant of the League of Nations remained silent about human rights, the Charter of the United Nations in its preamble reaffirms the faith of the peoples of the United Nations 'in fundamental human rights, in the dignity and worth of the human person'. Article 1, para. 3, of the Charter states as a purpose of the United Nations 'promoting and encouraging respect for human rights and for fundamental freedoms for all ...'. According to Article 55 of the Charter, the United Nations shall promote 'universal respect for, and obser- vance of human rights and fundamental freedoms for all ...'. Article 56 says that 'all Members pledge themselves to take joint and separate action in co- operation with the organization for the achievement of the purposes set forth in Article 55'.

Irrespective of the great importance the Charter attaches to human rights, already the wording makes clear that, in and by itself, it does not grant rights to the individual. The Universal Declaration of Human Rights of December 10, 1948 could, as to its wording, confer rights on the individual. But being a resolution of the General Assembly, the Declaration as such does not constitute binding law. Some authors[14] are of the opinion that the contents of the Universal Declaration has meanwhile become customary law, as States have referred to it in numerous official statements.

In my opinion this conclusion is not convincing because reference to the Universal Declaration by States does not necessarily mean its acceptance as existing law. In most cases such a reference means the acceptance of the aims of the United Nations. Had the States accepted the contents of the Universal Declaration as binding customary law, it would hardly be understandable why in the universal multilateral conventions on human rights they have remained considerably below the normative level of the Universal Declaration.

One of the relevant multilateral conventions is the International Covenant on Economic, Social and Cultural Rights of December 19, 1966. This Covenant does not contain rights of the individual. Its Article 2 makes clear that the rights mentioned in the Covenant shall be achieved by measures to be taken by the States parties. According to this article, a State must fulfil its obligations 'to a maximum of its available resources, with a view to achieving progressively the full realization of the rights recognized'. That shows that the

---

[14] See, e.g., Verdross & Simma (supra note 8), 822 et seqq.

Covenant is of a 'promotional' character and does not confer rights upon individuals[15].

On the other hand, the International Covenant on Civil and Political Rights of December 19, 1966 contains directly applicable law, comprising not only rights of the State parties, but also rights of the individual[16]. Article 2 of the Covenant states that each State party is obliged to grant the rights contained in this Covenant to all persons within its territory. Additional proof of the existence of rights of the individual is provided by the fact that there is an Optional Protocol to the Covenant of the same day giving the individual the opportunity to bring an alleged violation of its rights under the Covenant before the Human Rights Committee.

The Convention on the Elimination of All Forms of Racial Discrimination of March 7, 1966[17] in its Article 5 establishes a specific right of equality before the law to be enjoyed by the individual. According to Article 14 of the Convention, each State party may at any time declare that it recognizes the competence of the Committee on the Elimination of All Forms of Racial Discrimination to review allegations of individuals to be violated in their right of equality before the law.

The European Convention on Human Rights of November 4, 1950 granted rights to the individual even before the International Covenant on Civil and Political Rights. Article 1 provides that the Contracting Parties 'shall secure to everyone ... the rights ...'. 'Everyone' comprises also individuals, which becomes very clear in the French version: 'Les Hautes Parties Contractantes reconnaissent à toute personne (!) ... les droits et libertés ...'. That means that individuals are bearers of the rights contained in the European Convention on Human Rights[18]. There is not only an obligation of the State parties to grant such rights by municipal law. According to Article 25, the individual is entitled to bring a violation of his or her rights before the European Commission of Human Rights. Article 25 requires a special acceptance by the States parties for that procedure. Meanwhile all of the States parties have made such a declaration of acceptance[19].

---

[15] Partsch, 'Individuals in International Law' (supra note 3), at 957, 961; K. Zemanek, 'The Legal Foundations of the International System', *Recueil des Cours* 266 (1997), 114 et seq.; Verdross & Simma (supra note 8), 834; K. Hailbronner, 'Der Staat und der einzelne als Völkerrechtssubjekte', in: W. Graf Vitzthum (ed.), *Völkerrecht*, 1997, 181, 243.

[16] See, e.g., M. Nowak, *U.N. Covenant on Civil and Political Rights: CCPR Commentary*, 1993, Introduction, paras. 14, 16 (against Partsch, supra note 3, at 961 et seq.).

[17] For text, see I. Brownlie, *Basic Documents in International Law*, 4th ed., 1995, 310.

[18] J.A. Frowein in: J.A. Frowein & W. Peukert, *Europäische Menschenrechtskonvention - EMRK-Kommentar*, 2nd ed., 1996, 17.

[19] After the entry into force of Protocol No. 11 to the European Convention on Nov. 1, 1998, the individual right of petition to the new permanent European Court of Human Rights is laid

The American Convention of Human Rights of November 22, 1969 has almost the same wording as the European Convention. It contains rights of the individual, too. The individual can likewise bring a violation of his or her rights before the American Commission of Human Rights (Article 44). Contrary to the European Convention on Human Rights (as it stood until November 1, 1998) no special acceptance is required for this procedure. Article 44 is applicable upon ratification of the Convention as such.

African States concluded the Banjul Charter on Human Rights and Rights of the Peoples on June 27, 1982[20]. This instrument also contains rights of the individual whose violation can be denounced by the individual before the African Commission of Human Rights (Article 55). But the Commission brings such complaints to the attention of the Assembly of the Heads of States or Governments only if a complaint seems to prove a series of serious or massive violations of human rights (Article 58).

c) Undoubtedly, the realm of human rights is the most apparent example of rights of the individual in today's public international law. But there are also many other examples. It is especially worth mentioning that a considerable time before the development of the international protection of human rights, legal regimes of the most diverse nature granting rights under international law to individuals had emerged. The position of the individual as a subject of international law did not develop on the basis of a comprehensive theoretical concept, but in an eclectic manner as a response to practical demands of specific situations.

i) The first treaty giving individuals standing before an international court to defend their rights was–or should have been–the Convention on an International Prize Court of October 18, 1907[21]. Individuals of neutral or enemy status were to have access to the court with regard to actions involving their property. Because of lack of ratification, however, this convention never entered into force.

ii) Only two months later, on December 20, 1907, Costa Rica, El Salvador, Guatemala, Honduras and Nicaragua concluded a treaty establishing the Central American Court of Justice[22]. This treaty entered into force in 1908 and the court acted until 1918. The jurisdiction of the court was extremely broad

---

down in Art. 34 of the Convention, and a special acceptance by States parties is not any longer necessary.

[20] For text, see ILM 21 (1982), 59.

[21] See U. Scheuner, 'International Prize Court', in: EPIL, vol. II, 1995, 1346-1348.

[22] For text, see G.F. de Martens (ed.), *Nouveau Recueil Général*, 3ème série, vol. III, 105.

and allowed States, individuals (!) and domestic institutions to appear as parties. It was 'a revolutionary development'[23] that individuals could bring complaints against a Central American republic (other than their own) for the violation of treaties or conventions and other cases of an international character. Local remedies had to be exhausted or a denial of justice be shown. Of the ten cases which came before the Court, five involved individuals though not one of these was successful.

iii) According to Article 296 of the Peace Treaty of Versailles of June 28, 1919, individuals were entitled to bring their claims before mixed arbitral tribunals.

iv) The Convention of May 15, 1922, concluded between Germany and Poland relating to the protection of minorities[24], established an Arbitral Tribunal which had to decide on cases dealing with nationality, right of residence and all sorts of vested rights. Individuals were entitled to bring cases against their own State and against the foreign State before the court.

v) The Geneva Convention of August 12, 1949 relative to the Treatment of Prisoners of War contains rights of the individual. That is made clear by Article 7 of this Convention stating that prisoners of war may in no circumstances renounce the 'rights secured to them(!)' by the Convention. According to Article 78, para 2, of the Convention, prisoners of war have the 'unrestricted right to apply to the representatives of the Protecting Powers' and to present complaints to them.

The Geneva Convention of August 12, 1949 regarding the Protection of Civil Persons in Time of War also contains rights of the individual, as is shown by Articles 30, 52 and 101. Protected persons have the right to apply to the Protecting Powers and to the International Committee of the Red Cross.

vi) The Agreement on the Settlement of Investment Disputes of March 18, 1965[25] grants individuals standing before the International Center for the Settlement of Investment Disputes established by this agreement. Some authors[26] see this as a further example of the position of individuals in international law. But that evaluation depends on the question whether

---

[23] See H.M. Hill, 'Central American Court of Justice', in: EPIL, vol. I, 1992, 552.
[24] For text, see *Nouveau Recueil Général*, 3ème série (supra note 22), vol. XVI, 645.
[25] For text, see UNTS vol. 575, 159.
[26] See, e.g., P. Malanczuk, *Akehurst's Modern Introduction to International Law*, 7th ed., 1997, 101.

investment treaties between States and individuals are part of public international law, a question still highly controversial today.

vii) Under the Canada-United States Free Trade Agreement (FTA) of 1988[27] private parties have access to binational panels which can reach binding decisions in certain cases, for example in disputes concerning investment, anti-dumping and countervailing measures (Article 1904 FTA).

viii) Listening to Dr. Wühler's lecture today[28], we have learned that the United Nations Compensation Commission was created by Security Resolution 692 of May 20th, 1991 in accordance with Security Resolution 687[29]. Individuals who have suffered from the unlawful invasion and occupation of Kuwait by Iraq have standing before this Commission concerning their claims.

ix) The Permanent Court of Arbitration in the Hague on July 6, 1993 modified its procedure to encourage access of 'Parties of which only one is a State'. But under these new 'Optional Rules of Procedure of the PCA'[30] non-State parties are entitled to engage in arbitration (Article 1) only with the consent of the other side. Here again, it must be stressed that this is an example of rights of the individual under international law in asmuch as treaties between an individual and a State are deemed to constitute international law.

This list is not exhaustive. One will be certainly able to find more examples.

d) The question whether the individual is a subject of public international law is not confined to the question whether he is holder of rights under international law. The question also comprises the problem whether the individual is bearer of obligations under international law.

This problem is dealt with especially in the laws of armed conflict. States are obliged to punish their own nationals for having committed war crimes; they are entitled to punish foreign nationals for having perpetrated such crimes. It is still disputed whether the basis for such a punishment is municipal law or public international law[31].

---

[27] For text, see ILM 27 (1988), 281.

[28] See N. Wühler, 'The United Nations Compensation Commission', supra at 213 et seq.

[29] See K.-H. Böckstiegel, 'Der Aggressor wird haftbar gemacht. Die Entschädigungskommission der Vereinten Nationen (UNCC) für Ansprüche gegen Irak', *Vereinte Nationen* 1997, 89 et seqq.

[30] International Bureau of the Permanent Court of Arbitration (ed.), *Permanent Court of Arbitration Optional Rules for Arbitrating Disputes between Two Parties of which only one is a State*, 1993.

[31] Cf. F. Berber, *Lehrbuch des Völkerrechts*, 2nd ed., vol. II, 1969, 241 et seq.; K. Ipsen, 'Völkerrechtliche Verantwortlichkeit und Völkerstrafrecht', in: Ipsen et al., *Völkerrecht* (supra note 8), 488, 531-543.

Article 1 of Hague Convention IV of 1907, Article 49 of Geneva Convention I, Article 50 of Geneva Convention II, Article 129 of Geneva Convention III and Article 146 of Geneva Convention IV, which enjoin the State parties to make the commitments of the conventions binding for their nationals through municipal law, point to the view that the Conventions themselves do not contain obligations of the individual[32].

The opinion that the Nuremberg and Tokyo Trials have created customary law to the effect that the individual is a bearer of obligations under the laws of war is questionable[33], given the fact that up to now the efforts to corroborate this view by corresponding treaty law have not been successful.

The Yugoslavia and Rwanda Tribunals were created by Security Council resolutions[34] on the basis of the assumption that the individual is directly obliged by international law. Nevertheless it must be pointed out that the relevant Security Council resolutions describe only roughly the crimes the tribunals are dealing with and that nothing specific is said about the available penalties.

Whether the project of the ILC to establish a permanent International Criminal Court will come to a successful end remains to be seen[35]. The Code of Crimes, too, does not contain rules as exact and comprehensive as penal codes in municipal law. After all it remains doubtful whether individuals are bearers of obligations under public international law.

III. CONCLUSIONS

Trying to draw a conclusion from this survey, I want to make the following eight points:

---

[32] As far as Hague Convention IV and the annexed Regulations respecting the Laws and Customs of War on Land are concerned, it is by far the prevailing view in literature that they do not give rights to the individual. See, e.g., K. Strupp, *Das Internationale Landkriegsrecht*, 1914, 29; D. Kube, *Private Kriegsschäden in der völkerrechtlichen Praxis. Ein Beitrag zur Staatenverantwortlichkeit im Kriege*, 1971, 40 et seq.; A. Randelzhofer & O. Dörr, *Entschädigung für Zwangsarbeit?*, 1994, 23 et seqq. This view is shared by national courts; see, e.g., *Tel Oren v. Libyan Arab Republic*, 726 F.2d 774 (816) (D.C. Col 1984); *Handel v. Artukovic*, 601 F.Supp. 1421 (D.C.Col. 1985); *Goldstar (Panama) S.A. v. United States*, 967 F.2d 965 (968-969) (Fourth Circuit 1992).

[33] Partsch, 'Individuals in International Law' (supra note 3), 960.

[34] UN Security Council Res. 827 of 25 May 1993 and 955 of 8 Nov. 1994.

[35] Meanwhile the Rome Statute of the International Criminal Court has been adopted by a diplomatic conference of plenipotentiaries on July 17, 1998.

1) It is commonly accepted today that rights and obligations of the individual can be created by international agreement, thus making the individual a subject of international law.

2) Such agreements exist especially within the realm of protection of human rights.

3) Other examples deal with the regulation of rather specific problems and are often of a transitory nature.

4) Obligations of the individual may be viewed in agreements of the laws of war. But this view is still disputed.

5) Under customary international law there is no rule granting rights directly to the individual.

6) Individual reparation claims entailed by human rights violations improve the legal position of the individual in quantity but not in quality.

7) The role of the individual in public international law has not changed in substance. Whether and to what extent the individual is a subject of international law still depends on the corresponding will of States.

8) The predominant role of States in international law still exists, though not totally unchallenged. International law still is predominantly an inter-State system. There is no need, at present, for a new definition of international law.

I admit that, as it was said during this colloquium, a 'tendency of privatization' (that was the expression Michael Reisman used in the discussion) can be seen in today's international law, that there are developments under way. But tendencies and developments are not yet results. Perhaps they will materialize one day. Then the time has come to newly define international law.

Discussion (Part 4)

Malanczuk: I would like to start with a comment on the very interesting presentation by my old friend Norbert Wühler. Mr. Chairman, I have to disclose, perhaps at the beginning, that I am legal counsel of Iraq before the UNCC and that I have represented Iraq together with Lalive and Partners before the Commission on the issue of the right to legal defence and on the so-called 'Well Blowout' claim, which is for firefighting costs, one of the big claims. My intention is not to act as legal counsel in this forum, my intention is to speak as a student of international law and so I will limit myself to certain aspects which I think are of interest for putting the model of the Commission into perspective for the question which relevance it has for our topic and for future forums of compensation.

The first point is that I have serious doubts as to the legal basis of this whole enterprise. This is not to disqualify the professionalism of the Secretariat in any way which has acted in a prudent manner towards all sides involved and developed a scheme which is highly sophisticated and expresses the high legal qualification of many persons in the Secretariat, often gained in long experience with the Iran-US Claims Tribunal. But it is a matter of principle that I feel I have to raise in three respects. The first respect is that the activism of the Security Council after the end of the Cold War has manifested itself in many areas where the question of the limits of the power of the Security Council under Chapter VII of the UN Charter has come into the forefront. It is not only the creation of the United Nations Compensation Commission, as you are aware. This issue has played a role in the manner in which the Yugoslavia Tribunal has been set up. In the *Tadic* case[1] the appeals chamber has addressed this extensively, but amongst scholars it still is a matter of debate.

Having said that, let me be somewhat more concrete as to the UNCC legal basis. It is true that Iraq has recognized in principle its liability under Security Council Resolution 687, but Iraq has never consented to the specific scheme

---

[1]   *The Prosecutor v. Dusko Tadic*, 2 Oct. 1995, Judgment of the ICTY Appeals Chamber, Case No. IT-94-1-AR72, ILR 105, 419.

A. Randelzhofer and C. Tomuschat (eds.), State Responsibility and the Individual, 243–250.
© 1999 *Kluwer Law International. Printed in Great Britain.*

of administering this clause. There is a lack of consent of the defendant State to this particular mode of operation. It has on the contrary continuously protested against it. Now the Security Council has done two things. First, it has abandoned the usual forms of settling war damages which we know in history. The UNCC scheme is a unique and unprecedented case. The Council has assumed the judicial function in replacing the usual forms of dispute settlement or settlement of claims after wars. The Security Council has assumed the judicial function by placing its powers in a subsidiary body which mirrors exactly the composition of the Council and retains the ultimate political control of the outcome of this *quasi* administrative, *quasi* judicial process.

Second, the Security Council has also assumed law-making functions by changing the rules of State responsibility in many respects, through UNCC Governing Council decisions. I submit that the Security Council is not entrusted with law-making functions under Chapter VII of the United Nations Charter in the framework of Article 39. Therefore, the applicable law provision which Dr. Wühler has mentioned is also significant, because international law is only a subsidiary source of the decision-making of the Council. The real sources, the primary sources, are resolutions of the Governing Council, *de facto* resolutions of the Security Council. I could go into many areas where the rules in substance have been changed from the traditional ones of State responsibility.

Next point: The procedure is an administrative procedure and substitutes the usual forms of settlement of disputes between States (which rest upon consent in one form or another). Under the UNCC Iraq has no formal legal standing of a substantial sort. There is no right to defence. The Secretariat in its original drafting of the procedural rules of the UNCC had provided that Iraq should be more involved. That provision has not been accepted due to political pressure which members of the Security Council felt was necessary to impose upon Iraq, *inter alia* because of the interlink with the disarmament issue. One has to see this whole process in connection with this disarmament issue, the chemical, biological and nuclear weapons in Iraq. In effect, it means that a fundamental principle of law is being violated here–namely the right to proper defence and the guarantee of due process of law. It is true that with the mass of these claims (2.6 million claims) it would have been impossible to impose a scheme like the existing Iran-US Claims Tribunal which was supposed to last only two years and, as we know, still exists for certain reasons. However, I submit to you that the right of Iraq to defence has been curtailed to an extent that it is ineffective in cases of a larger nature where corporations and governments have filed huge and complex cases. These cases require proper presentation of pleadings, briefings, hearings, and legal and expert defence from both sides, for a panel to be able to arrive at something even close to the truth and to be able to distinguish between inflated claims, fraudulent claims, unsubstantiated claims and so forth.

That goes down right to the accounting of the matters. It is also insufficient to have only accountants on one side even if they are supervised by a neutral Secretariat. In the Egyptian-workers claim, which Norbert has mentioned, Böckstiegel introduced a hearing and has given opportunity for defence, but these are *de facto* elements and they are not structural within the whole process of the UNCC. So there is a problem and we will have to see whether a change in the rules will be made or at least in practice to provide for a proper opportunity for Iraq in the large corporate claims and in the government claims to defend itself and allow the panels to arrive at the truth. It is true that one can look at the mass claims for poor workers and needy individuals in a different way because there is also a principle of justice that compensation should be paid swiftly in the sense that relief can actually be offered to those persons, meaning that other standards may have to be applied to the 'lower' categories of cases which are already settled. But even there we would have to enter into the justification of the statistical modeling and sampling techniques which the Commission has taken over from American mass tort claims in deciding in such a situation. That may be an appropriate approach to deal with such a situation but I submit it is only appropriate if there is also defence. In American mass tort claims there is always a defence lawyer even in mass cases.

Now sanctions. Also yesterday the question was raised by Professor Tomuschat to which extent one can let the population of a state bleed for damages if the claim is made in full. Here we know from several international organizations like UNICEF and the Food and Agriculture Organization that the civilian population has been suffering extremely under the sanctions régime. There are figures mentioned like 500,000 children who have died due to the effects of the sanctions. We all know that these figures may be inflated and that whether they are directly related to the sanctions may often be questionable. Whatever the true figure may be, certainly there is a problem. One could also say that the effects might be attributable to the Government, that the Government is responsible for not providing for the conditions to feed its own population properly, to provide for clean water and so forth, and that it should comply with the sanctions régime. But then there is a problem for us as international lawyers which we have to recognize, namely that international law, if this is the law, is still a primitive legal system in the sense that it engages the collective responsibility of a whole population for an internationally wrongful act of its government, and that is something we would have to think about, whether that is the correct solution. Maybe it is inevitable, because it is a primitive legal system.

Finally, some remarks on the very interesting questions which Professor Zemanek has raised, namely: Are we in a position at all to find criteria to determine an amount of compensation with global validity? Two ideas came to my mind which I have not fully thought through but I would like to share them with you, my colleagues. The first thought is: would it not be possible, if one took an economic perspective on the matter, to make a linkage to living standards indexes as provided for example by the World Bank? One could say these would be the criteria as far as the financial side is concerned. Of course one would have to make some accommodation for a universally operating body, of course not in the regional framework of the European Convention, but at least these indexes might give some indication as to different scales. The problem of course is the validity of the criteria which the World Bank itself is applying or those of the International Monetary Fund. But these differentiations exist, so there are certain scales. The second point arising: Is it really only an economic criterion that we have to take into account, or is it not also a cultural-sociological criterion which we have to consider measuring such matters?

I would also like to mention that the issue of the capacity to pay has become very clear to me due to the experience I had in Ethiopia where, for two years on behalf of the Dutch Government, I was training some officers of the transitional Government for international tasks. There have been massive human rights violations by the Mengistu régime, which had been backed by the Soviet Union and by Eastern Germany. The Soviet Union had been supplying the arms to bomb the villages and East Germany had been supplying the security forces for torture practices. Now, the Ethiopian Government itself would hardly be in a position to pay compensation. Neither can it be held responsible, unless one would say it is an insurrectional régime that came into power, thereby having to assume retroactive responsibility. But that rule applies only in favour of aliens. As we heard from Professor Fernandez, in developing countries the primary concern is not so much monetary compensation, but people are rather desirous of obtaining economic conditions and services under which they can survive in the first place. Now this is again the issue which my colleague Dr. Fleck has raised, namely whether international assistance can be of any relevance in that. In South Africa, we have heard that only some of the Scandinavian countries have offered a relatively insignificant amount for assistance. But I think it is entirely unrealistic to expect that any substantial financial amount would be available from the international community, or from the World Bank or from the International Monetary Fund to provide for any kind of compensation funds of this nature.

Kooijmans: I would like to make two comments on Professor Randelzhofer's highly interesting presentation.

My first comment has to do with the customary law character of human rights. I fully agree with Professor Randelzhofer that not every word of the Universal Declaration of Human Rights has become customary law. I would like to point out, however, that already in 1968 the international community stated in the Declaration of Tehran that the Universal Declaration constitutes an obligation for all States. That statement may be seen as an expression by the international community of an *opinio iuris sive necessitatis*, which is one component element of customary law. The other component element, State practice, in my opinion is not reflected in the Yearbooks of Amnesty International with the endless list of human rights violations. This State behaviour could be interpreted as a consistent denial of the customary law character of human rights but is not relevant as State practice. The State practice which is relevant is the constant denial of human rights violations by States which are accused of such violations; such denials constitute State conduct which is a confirmation of the norm and is in support of the *opinio iuris*. This means that a great part of human rights law is customary law. This is not even denied by countries which have not ratified the two Covenants on human rights, such as China or Indonesia.

My second remark concerns the individual as a bearer of international rights. It is often said that the individual as bearer of rights under international law, has a (restricted) legal personality, but that this personality is derivative. He or she has this personality because his or her State has consented to grant him or her this personality, e.g. by ratifying a human rights convention. His legal personality is dependent upon State consent. On the other hand there is general agreement that a number of human rights issues are linked to the obligations *erga omnes*: the prohibition of genocide, of slavery, of racial discrimination etc. and that such obligations exist independently of State consent. That raises the question: if a State, each State, is the bearer of the obligation not to perpetrate massive human rights violations, who is the bearer of the corresponding right? From a procedural point of view it can be said that all other States are entitled to compliance with that obligation and therefore qualify as injured States in the sense of the ILC draft articles on State responsibility if that obligation is breached. But is there also a corresponding right of those in whose interest that prohibition is given: the individual? That would mean that there is a differentiated concept of the bearer of rights: from the procedural point of view all other States, from a substantive point of view the individual. That is why I mentioned yesterday the example of the *East Timor* case where the peoples are called the bearers of the right in the case of an *erga omnes* obligation. This reasoning leads us to a highly interesting conclusion. Since we have seen that *erga omnes* obligations exist independently of State consent, the corresponding rights exist also independently of State consent. That means that the bearer of these rights, the individual, has an international legal status that cannot be dependent upon state consent either. The individual's status in international law, therefore, would not be derivative but original.

Wühler: I will not comment on the question of the power of the Security Council to set up the particular system of the UNCC. Maybe it would be interesting if you could see me agree with a position that would basically take away my employer, at least legally, but I will not comment on this. I would like to address the second aspect of that remark by Peter which is that, Iraq having recognized its liability in principle under international law, has not recognized the UNCC and the scheme around it. That is not correct. One has to be very careful in identifying what Iraq accepts and what it recognizes and what it does not. At least before the Commission–and it makes regular statements before the Governing Council at each session of the Governing Council of the Commission–Iraq continues to recognize its liability in principle as it was stated in Resolution 687, and it continues to recognize the UNCC in principle.What it does not accept, what it takes issue with is the level of its participation and the possibilities to participate procedurally in the proceedings of the Commission. But it does not, at least not in front of the Commission, deny its recognition of the scheme as such in principle.

A more technical point. I found it very interesting that there are various possibilities as far as the calculation or the assessment of amounts of compensation in those various types of losses is concerned. I found it also interesting to think of differentiations in general terms, e.g. scales, indexing, etc., by countries or regions of the world measured at World Bank data and similar statistics. Of course we did not have enough time, and it is a very technical subject, but in a way I am very pleased for this comment, because what the Commission has done with the statistical models I have mentioned, the statistical regression analysis for present property claims, for example, is precisely that. I cannot explain to you all the technical details, but what has gone partly into these models is precisely the wealth situation of the different categories of claimants, because you have claimants from Bangladesh and you have claimants from the United States that obviously had a very different wealth and property situation in Iraq or Kuwait and as far as their purchasing power and their standard of living was concerned. That was not the only one, but it was a very important parameter that went into the statistical models that were used.

Randelzhofer: Judge Kooijmans has picked up a provocative point of my statements. Perhaps I have formulated too harshly. I was especially interested in the problem whether under customary international law there is a right of the individual, and this is especially what I still doubt. I would agree in reconsidering the whole ambit of my statement that one will have to admit that in so far as the Universal Declaration contains obligations and rights of the States, it has developed into customary law. Therefore I agree with you that the foreign ministers discussing the problem of human rights in China, being aware that China is not a contracting party of human rights conventions, do not interfere in the internal affairs of China. As far as the rights of the individual are concerned, I still doubt whether one can say that the Universal Declaration has become customary law. Insofar I am of the same opinion as Professor Pisillo Mazzeschi, that the nature of public international law has not yet fundamentally changed. We are under way, but I think we will have to wait and see what will be the final outcome.

Tomuschat: Dear friends, we are now reaching the last stage of our proceedings. At meetings in France at the end of an academic conference a prominent participant stands up as the great magician, presenting general conclusions. Everyone then wonders a little bit and asks himself: Is that really the result of our conference? But the 'grand prestidigitateur' firmly says: This is indeed the result, and everyone has to believe it. Our debate was so sophisticated, so well-balanced and rich in substance that it would hardly be possible to sum it up in a few minutes. Such an effort could not do justice to what we have been placing under reconnaissance in two days. We have looked into theory, and here I should mention in particular the presentations by Pisillo Mazzeschi, Randelzhofer and the present speaker. But we have also looked into what can be found empirically, we have assembled the relevant factual data in order to gain a clear and faithful picture. In this connection, I should mention Eckart Klein, Michael Reisman, Pellonpää, Wühler and Fernandez. In another paper, which supplements the proceedings of this colloquium, Bardo Fassbender describes the way the reunited Germany has dealt with human rights violations suffered in East Germany during the time of Soviet occupation and the existence of a separate East German State, the GDR. On that basis we have tried to make ends meet, or more correctly: to make the map and the terrain meet. In this attempt, I dare say that we have been successful. From both ends we worked, from the theoretical platform, on one hand, but trying also to explore the real ground. It is almost natural, then, that views were wide apart. As an advocate of the classical school I would mention Professor Stein who said: 'It is quite clear that the individual still has no right to reparation against the State.' This statement was contradicted by a progressive extremist, Joe

Verhoeven, who observed: 'It is quite clear. Of course in every case of a breach of human rights obligations, the individual must have a right to reparation.' These are really contradictory viewpoints. But we must not feel torn apart by the extremes since a large measure of middleground was mapped by those terrible liberals who say: 'Yes, this is right, but on the other hand ...' I wish to refer especially to Michael Reisman who disagreed with me, not putting his views in crystal-clear conceptual terms, but saying that so much is growing and that therefore my scepticism did not truly meet the actual situation as it has been shaped by international practice.

Lastly, let me just say as a general conclusion that I agree to a great extent with Judge Kooijmans. My central thesis is exactly the same as his, namely that one can derive from the draft code, from the concept of international crimes under Article 19 of the draft articles on State responsibility and from *ius cogens* and *erga omnes* obligations a direct legal status of the individual under international law. These four concepts are more or less identical although they operate in different contexts. From them legal positions of the individual can be derived which are not dependent on the will of any State. Yet States do not like these constructs. They wish to remain the masters of international law. The concept of an individual acting independently on the international level is to them more a nuisance than an achievement as became manifest in the *Francovich* case under the law of the European Communities which did not meet with an unreserved welcome by all the governments of the member States.

Rehabilitation and Compensation of Victims of Human Rights Violations Suffered in East Germany (1945–1990)

Bardo Fassbender

I. INTRODUCTION

The systematic violation of human rights by the Government of the German Democratic Republic (GDR) and the communist party behind it, in particular the right to freedom of opinion and expression, the right to freedom of thought, conscience and religion, and the right to freedom of peaceful assembly and association, was a major reason for the revolution which took place in East Germany in the fall of 1989 and for the eventual reunification of Germany a year later. The fall of the communist regime was accelerated by a mass flight of East Germans in August and September 1989 who escaped from the GDR via Hungary, Czechoslovakia and Poland, thus claiming a right, promised by the Universal Declaration of Human Rights and the International Covenant on Civil and Political Rights, they had been denied since the foundation of the GDR in 1949 – the right to leave any country, including one's own.[1]

However, the question how to deal with these human rights violations in the reunified Germany turned out to be a divisive issue. Those who called for a remedy as comprehensive as possible were opposed by others who recommended 'to leave the past alone', and also by open or secret supporters of the vanished regime. When it was realized that billions of dollars would be needed to create living conditions in East Germany comparable to those in the

---

[1] See Art. 13, no. 2, of the Universal Declaration, and Art. 12, para. 2, of the Covenant. The Covenant was signed by the GDR on March 3, 1973 and ratified on Nov. 2, 1973 (Gesetzblatt der DDR 1974 II, 57). It became binding on the GDR on March 23, 1976 (Gesetzblatt der DDR 1976 II, 108). However, the Covenant was not confirmed by the *Volkskammer* (Parliament) by way of legislation in accordance with Art. 51 of the GDR Constitution (as amended 1974); see Entscheidungen des Bundesgerichtshofs in Strafsachen, vol. 39, at 1, 16-17 (1994) ('*Schüsse an der Berliner Mauer*' case). It was the official view of the GDR that the Covenant was not part of the domestic law of East Germany and could not be directly invoked by GDR citizens. See B. Graefrath, *Menschenrechte und internationale Kooperation*, 1988, 55 et seq., and S. Mampel, *Die sozialistische Verfassung der Deutschen Demokratischen Republik*, 3d ed. 1997, 937.

A. Randelzhofer and C. Tomuschat (eds.), State Responsibility and the Individual, 251–279.

Western parts of the country, the financial capacity of the Federal Republic became an important aspect of the debate. Until today, public discussion is dominated by the problem of a restitution of property, whereas comparatively little attention has been paid to a reparation of violations of other, and arguably more fundamental, human rights like the right to life and liberty, the right to freedom from inhumane or degrading treatment or punishment, or the right to a fair trial.

Germany had faced a similar problem once before, after World War II, when the victims of the Nazi regime claimed rehabilitation and compensation for the outrageous wrongs committed against them between 1933 and 1945 in Germany and territories occupied by Germany. However, the complex legislation enacted to make good this injustice[2] did not play an important role in the public discussion of 1989-90 and the following years. It seems that, more than fifty years after the end of World War II, this legislation is largely forgotten. Also, had the new laws simply copied the old, parliament could have been misunderstood as taking sides in the difficult controversy of the historical uniqueness of the Nazi atrocities.

II. THE LEGAL RESPONSIBILITY OF THE FEDERAL REPUBLIC OF GERMANY FOR HUMAN RIGHTS VIOLATIONS IN EAST GERMANY

In view of the political controversy about the kind and range of reparation for human rights violations committed in the territory which today is called East Germany[3] first in the time of Soviet military occupation (1945-1949) and then during the existence of the GDR (1949-1990), it is not astonishing that the Federal Government, learned authors and courts in Germany supported a legal construction of State responsibility which would leave room for political manoeuvre and compromise.

The line of reasoning is simple. As regards measures taken by the Soviet Military Government or, with its explicit or just tacit approval, German

---

[2] For a comprehensive official account, see Federal Ministry of Finance & W. Schwarz (eds.), *Die Wiedergutmachung nationalsozialistischen Unrechts durch die Bundesrepublik Deutschland*, 6 vols., 1974-1987 (vol. 7 forthcoming). For recent summaries, see W. Schwarz, 'Zur Einführung: Das Recht der Wiedergutmachung und seine Geschichte', *Juristische Schulung* 1986, 433 et seqq., W. Tappert, 'Die Wiedergutmachung von Staatsunrecht im 20. Jahrhundert', *Die Friedens-Warte* 70 (1995), 211, 220-231, and L. Wiegand, 'Kriegsfolgengesetzgebung in der Bundesrepublik Deutschland', *Archiv für Sozialgeschichte* 35 (1995), 71, 72-77. The reparation of judicial injustice is dealt with by R. Vogl, *Stückwerk und Verdrängung: Wiedergutmachung nationalsozialistischen Strafjustizunrechts in Deutschland*, 1997.

[3] In the past, the term generally designated the Eastern provinces of Germany (Pomerania, Silesia, East Prussia) which were placed under Polish and Soviet administration by the Potsdam Agreement of 1945 and finally ceded by Germany in 1990.

authorities before the proclamation of the GDR on October 7, 1949, they are declared acts of a foreign State not attributable to the Federal Republic. With regard to measures taken afterwards by GDR authorities, it is similarly argued that the Federal Republic cannot be held responsible for them because the exercise of governmental authority of the Federal Republic was *de facto* and *de jure* limited to the West German territory, and the GDR Government was not a government constituted under the 1949 Constitution of the Federal Republic (the 'Basic Law'). A responsibility according to the international law of State succession has also been denied.[4] The Federal Republic is said to have been entitled to reject the concept of a 'general succession' (*Universalsukzession*) and instead to accept only 'certain' (i.e., almost all) rights and 'certain' (i.e., very few) obligations of the extinct GDR. These obligations do not include commitments of the GDR arising from governmental tortious acts.[5] This construction has also led to an impairment of the legal position of victims of GDR injustice who had fled to West Germany, for as long as the GDR existed they could claim diplomatic protection of the Federal Republic in their efforts to obtain reparation.

It is a different question whether, after reunification, the Federal Republic's own constitution called for an annulment of at least certain GDR measures or a reparation for human rights violations, regardless of their legality under East German law. In principle, this question was answered in the negative. The argument goes as follows: In East Germany, the Basic Law entered into force only after reunification on October 3, 1990. The human rights guarantees of the Basic Law have no retroactive effect. Therefore, they are not applicable to measures taken by the Soviet occupation power or GDR authorities before reunification, and no reparation claims can arise because of an incompatibility of such measures with the provisions of the Basic Law. Consequently, the Federal Constitutional Court decided that the legislature has a particularly broad leeway when dealing with a possible reparation of damage caused by such measures.[6] Only in very exceptional cases may the German *ordre public*

---

[4]   Such responsibility could only arise with respect to violations of GDR law or international law because otherwise there is no obligation which could possibly devolve on the Federal Republic as a successor State. For the liability of a State under customary international law for human rights violations, and the entitlement of a German citizen to claim reparation for such a violation by Germany before German courts, see Michael Trassl, *Die Wiedergutmachung von Menschenrechtsverletzungen im Völkerrecht*, 1994, 53-105, 125-141 (summaries at 104 and 140).

[5]   For a concise statement of that position, see the joint letter of the Federal Ministries of Justice and the Interior, Dec. 3, 1992, reprinted in: *Deutsch-Deutsche Rechtszeitschrift* 1993, 115. See also S. Leutheusser-Schnarrenberger, Federal Minister of Justice, 'Das Zweite Gesetz zur Bereinigung von SED-Unrecht', loc. cit. at 162, 163.

[6]   See Entscheidungen des Bundesverfassungsgerichts (hereinafter BVerfGE) vol. 84, at 90, 126 (1991) (*Bodenreform*). See also J. Isensee, 'Rechtsstaat – Vorgabe und Aufgabe der Einung

require that an East German measure is denied legal effect. The Court went back to its jurisprudence regarding the reparation of war damages and violations of rights by the National Socialist regime, where it had similarly left it to legislative discretion to provide for reparation according to the financial capacity of the State.[7] A respective obligation of the legislature may only stem from the constitutional definition of Germany as a social State (*Sozialstaatsprinzip*, Article 20, para. 1, of the Basic Law) and the constitutional right to be treated equally by the State (Article 3). The former principle may require to mitigate extreme hardships suffered because of human rights violations in East Germany, while the latter right prevents the legislature from discriminating against certain groups of citizens, i.e., if one group has been granted a claim for compensation, another group with similar traits may not arbitrarily be denied such a claim.[8] However, as far as our issue is concerned, both rules have not effected a restriction of the freedom of the legislature.

This reasoning, consistent and in line with the way the Federal Republic dealt domestically with Hitler's legacy, can hardly be challenged from a legal point of view. After 1949, the Federal Republic insisted that, as a 'new' and democratic Germany, it could not be held responsible for violations of rights committed by the Nazi regime in the same way as if it had committed them itself, although as a legal person it asserted to be identical with the *Reich* founded in 1867-1871. It was only with regard to violations suffered by foreigners that it had to accept full responsibility in accordance with international law.[9] If a constitutional change was deemed sufficient to deny claims

---

Deutschlands', in: J. Isensee & P. Kirchhof (eds.), *Handbuch des Staatsrechts der Bundesrepublik Deutschland*, vol. IX, 1997, 3, 87-90; H.-J. Papier, 'Vergangenheitsbewältigung: Abwicklung, Ahndung, Entschädigung', loc. cit. at 587, 606-608.

[7] See BVerfGE vol. 27 (1970), 253, 270, 283-286 (*Besatzungsschäden*), and vol. 41 (1976), 126, 150-154 (*Reparationsschäden*). See also Basic Law Art. 135a, para. 1, and G. Ress, 'Grundlagen und Entwicklung der innerdeutschen Beziehungen', in: *Handbuch des Staatsrechts* (supra note 6), vol. I, 1987, at 449, 541 et seq. In spite of this legal construction, the Federal Republic granted German victims of Nazi injustice and their dependants substantial compensation, regardless of whether they resided in the Federal Republic or not. It is estimated that a total of D-Mark 90 to 100 billion (90,000 to 100,000 million) has been redistributed to victims since 1947, 80 percent of which have gone to victims living abroad. See W. Schwarz, 'Zur Einführung' (supra note 2), at 433, 437.

[8] Art. 26 of the International Covenant on Civil and Political Rights has never been mentioned in this context. The Human Rights Committee has held that if a State party repairs a violation of rights by a restitution of property or monetary compensation, it has to extend these benefits to all victims, without discriminating against any group or person (irrespective of whether the violation occurred before the entry-into-force of the Covenant and the Optional Protocol, and notwithstanding the fact that the right to property, as such, is not protected under the Covenant). See *Alina Simunek et al. v. the Czech Republic*, Communication No. 516/1992, Views adopted by the Human Rights Committee on 19 July 1995, paras. 4.3-4.5, 11.3, UN Doc. CCPR/C/57/1.

[9] See Art. 5, paras. 2 and 3, and Appendix A of the London Agreement on German External Debts of Feb. 27, 1953; Bundesgesetzblatt (hereinafter BGBl.) 1953 II, 333, 340, 473. Annex

based on events that had taken place under the 'old order', then all the more the extinction of a State which seceded from, or tried to secede from, Germany as a whole. Germany could also refer to a rule of international law supported, as the ninth edition of Oppenheim's treatise puts it, by 'good authority', saying that a State does not become liable for unliquidated damages for the torts or delicts of the extinct State which it has absorbed.[10] That the Basic Law does not require the Federal Republic to repair acts which were lawful under the law of the GDR as well as international law, is also an opinion not open to serious doubt.

And yet, one feels somewhat uneasy about the resolvedness with which the reunited Germany draws a dividing line between itself and the East German State. The way it now treats the GDR government as a foreign power contrasts sharply with previous efforts, in particular of the Constitutional Court, to emphasize a 'special legal proximity' of the Federal Republic and the GDR. This proximity was said to arise from the fact that both States were parts of a still existing all-German State with a single people.[11] 'The German Democratic Republic', the Court ruled in the case concerning the 1972 Basic Treaty between the two German States, 'belongs to Germany; in its relationship with the Federal Republic of Germany it cannot be regarded as a foreign State'.[12] In a way, the former West German *Alleinvertretungsanspruch* (the claim to be the only legitimate representative of Germany as a whole) is now continued: Between 1945 and 1990, the 'true' Germany, a Germany responsible for its acts, resided only in the West. One could also say that now, eventually, the GDR, which since the sixties claimed to be a completely independent State, is taken at its word. In consequence, the East Germans including those who had fled to the West between 1949 and 1990 lost their debtor in 1990.

One could certainly be less critical of this policy if the legislature had used its more or less unrestrained freedom to deal with East German human rights violations in a more generous way. Instead, it limited reparation to a few

---

VIII of the agreement (id. at 463) was interpreted as excluding the compensation of individual victims of Nazi injustice from the moratorium provided for in Art. 5. See H. Rumpf, 'Die deutschen Reparationen nach dem Zweiten Weltkrieg', in: B. Willms (ed.), *Handbuch zur Deutschen Nation*, vol. 1, 1986, 333, 345-346 (with a list of German compensation payments to foreign States at 358-359).

[10] See R. Jennings & A. Watts (eds.), *Oppenheim's International Law*, 9th ed., 1992, vol. 1, pt. 1, 218. See also A. Verdross & B. Simma, *Universelles Völkerrecht*, 3d ed., 1984, 633 et seq. To me, it seems that a successor State which has taken over all the assets of its predecessor, is at least obliged to repair grave violations of human rights committed by the latter. See also I. Seidl-Hohenveldern, Book Review, *Zeitschrift für öffentliches Recht* 53 (1998), 129, 131 (the Federal Republic is liable to render compensation for measures of expropriation which violated international law on grounds of unjustified enrichment).

[11] See BVerfGE vol. 36 (1973), 1, 15-17 *(Grundlagenvertrag)*.

[12] See id. at 17.

narrowly defined categories of wrongs, and what it granted the victims was rather little again.

III. REHABILITATION OF VICTIMS OF INJUSTICE IN EAST GERMANY AND THE COMPENSATION OF THEIR LOSSES

1. The Unification Treaty

The law concerning the rehabilitation and compensation of victims of injustice in East Germany is fairly complicated. Earlier statutory law promulgated shortly before reunification by the first freely elected GDR parliament was superseded by agreements concluded between the two German States and later by all-German legislation. This legislation often refers to statutes enacted in West Germany for the benefit of other groups of persons, in particular victims of World War II.

In Article 17 of the Treaty Between the Federal Republic of Germany and the GDR on the Establishment of the Unity of Germany (Unification Treaty) of August 31, 1990[13] the parties stipulated the following:

> The High Contracting Parties confirm their intention promptly to create a statutory basis for a rehabilitation of all persons which have become victims of politically motivated criminal prosecution or any other judicial decision inconsistent with the rule of law or the constitution. Rehabilitation of these victims of the SED regime of injustice (*SED-Unrechts-Regime*) shall entail compensation which is *angemessen* (appropriate or adequate).[14]

The provision is an exception to the rule laid down in Article 18 of the treaty, according to which the decisions of GDR courts were to remain in force.[15]

A second exception can be found in Article 18, paragraph 2, which accorded someone convicted by a GDR criminal court an individual right to seek cassation of the respective decision.[16] The device of cassation, imported

---

[13] *Vertrag zwischen der Bundesrepublik Deutschland und der Deutschen Demokratischen Republik über die Herstellung der Einheit Deutschlands (Einigungsvertrag)*, BGBl. 1990 II, 889. For the history and background of the treaty, see, e.g., P.E. Quint, *The Imperfect Union: Constitutional Structures of German Unification*, 1992, 103-123.

[14] Translations of the agreements between the two German governments and German statutes quoted in this article are provided by the author. The abbreviation SED stands for *Sozialistische Einheitspartei Deutschlands* (Socialist Unity Party of Germany), which was the ruling communist party in the GDR.

[15] For a criticism of that scheme of rule and exception, see F. Haft, 'Die "Bereinigung" des SED-Unrechts', *Deutsch-Deutsche Rechts-Zeitschrift* 1994, 258, 259.

[16] The Code of Criminal Procedure was amended accordingly. See Unification Treaty attachment I, ch. III(A), para. III(14)(h).

from Soviet law, had ordinarily been used in the GDR as a method of exercising party control over the judiciary, by allowing the Attorney General or the President of the Supreme Court to petition for a change in a judgment even after it had become final.[17] After the GDR Code of Criminal Procedure had been liberalized in June 1990, cassation operated in favor of the defendant only.[18] While until the effective date of the Unification Treaty cassation required that the challenged decision had gravely violated GDR law, or that the sentence was grossly wrong, the Treaty introduced as a second ground the 'incompatibility of a decision with the standards of the rule of law (*rechts-staatliche Maßstäbe*)'.[19] This was clearly necessary because in order to do justice to the political victims of the communist regime the previous procedure had to rely on an interpretation of GDR statutes 'quite unlike anything that the courts of the old regime would actually have done'.[20]

The method of cassation was only applicable to final and non-appealable decisions of GDR criminal courts. For convictions which still remained to be enforced at the moment of reunification, it was stipulated that there would be no enforcement if, on request by the person convicted or the State prosecutor, a court decided that the conviction did not conform to the principles of the rule of law, or that the penalty was not appropriate.[21]

According to Article 19 of the Unification Treaty, administrative acts of the GDR would remain in effect, unless they were inconsistent with the treaty itself or 'with principles of the rule of law'.

From the wording of Article 17 of the Unification Treaty as quoted above it appears that, apart from the special case of cassation, final regulation of the issue of rehabilitation was left to the future all-German parliament because the views of the two sides diverged. As Professor Peter Quint put it, 'the GDR sought broad coverage and substantial compensation while the negotiators of the Federal Republic, conscious of the soaring costs of unification, sought a more modest solution'.[22] Even the general standard of financial compensation

---

[17] See sec. 312, para. 1, of the Code of Criminal Procedure of the GDR (as amended Dec. 19, 1974), Gesetzblatt der DDR 1975 I, 61, 98. Para. 2 constitutes a special rule for decisions of district courts (*Kreisgerichte*).

[18] See sec. 311, para. 2, cl. 1, of the Code of Criminal Procedure of the GDR (as amended June 29, 1990), Gesetzblatt der DDR 1990 I, 526, 537.

[19] See Unification Treaty attachment I, ch. III(A), para. III(14)(h)(hh) (inserted by Art. 4 of the Agreement on the Implementation and Interpretation of the Unification Treaty of Sep. 18, 1990; see BGBl. 1990 II, 885, 934, 1239, 1243).

[20] See Quint (supra note 13), at 217. For a detailed analysis of the rules of cassation, see M. Amelung et al., *Rehabilitierung und Kassation: Beseitigung von Justizunrecht in der DDR*, 1991, 139-201.

[21] See Unification Treaty, attachment I, ch. III(A), para. III(14)(d).

[22] Quint (supra note 13), at 219.

remained ambiguous because the German word 'angemessen' can mean 'appropriate' as well as 'adequate'.

2. The 1990 GDR Rehabilitation Law

However, the members of the East German Parliament (the *Volkskammer*), which had been freely elected for the first time in the history of the GDR on March 18, 1990, were anxious to shape the future all-German legislation. Shortly after the Unification Treaty had been signed, they enacted a comprehensive 'Rehabilitation Law'.[23] The law sought to rehabilitate all persons 'prosecuted, discriminated against, or otherwise seriously disturbed in the enjoyment of their rights, contrary to the fundamental and human rights guaranteed by the Constitution' (preamble). At the beginning of the part on criminal rehabilitation, the law set out that 'individuals will be rehabilitated who were sentenced because of an act by which they exercised constitutional political rights'. Thus, a bill of rights was taken as a yardstick for rehabilitation which, though included in the GDR Constitutions of 1949, 1968 and 1974, had never been judicially enforceable but instead had often been ignored by statutory law. In the preamble, rehabilitation was defined as an act by which a person is freed from 'the stigma of criminal prosecution or other discrimination'.[24] In other words, the State officially declares that its previous judicial or administrative decision was wrong and shall no longer have any legal effect. The law granted those persons rehabilitation who had been unconstitutionally convicted by a criminal court, as well as those who had been victims of politically motivated administrative decisions or disadvantages in employment. It also provided for rehabilitation of persons arbitrarily arrested by 'the Allied Powers of Occupation or their agencies' (sec. 18, para. 1). Section 3 of the law, dealing with rehabilitation for criminal prosecution, specifically mentioned persons convicted because they had opposed the communist regime for political reasons in word and writing, peaceful demonstrations or associations, or had left the GDR or had tried to do so, or had contacted governmental agencies, organizations or private persons outside the GDR. Section 21 particularly described as victims of administrative injustice those who, for political reasons, were deprived of their property or GDR citizenship, or forced to leave their homes in the vicinity of the border

---

[23] See *Rehabilitierungsgesetz* of Sep. 6, 1990, entered into force Sep. 18, 1990; Gesetzblatt der DDR 1990 I, 1459. Reprinted in: W. Pfister & W. Mütze (eds.), *Rehabilitierungsrecht: Kommentar*, 1994, part E 10.1. For a detailed discussion of the rules of criminal rehabilitation, see Amelung et al. (supra note 20), 33-138.

[24] See also sec. 2, para. 1: 'Rehabilitation has as its object a political and moral satisfaction (*Genugtuung*) of the person concerned.'

separating East Germany from West Germany or West Berlin, or subjected to treatment in psychiatric hospitals.

However, this statute 'was too sweeping for the government of the Federal Republic, whose taxpayers would be paying most of the bills'.[25] Accordingly, in an agreement of September 18, 1990 amending and supplementing the Unification Treaty, the two governments agreed that only the sections of the statute providing for rehabilitation for criminal prosecution and incarceration in mental hospitals would remain in force in the united Germany.[26] The all-German parliament would have to decide how to deal with administrative discrimination and discrimination in employment, as well as with arbitrary detention of persons by the Soviet Occupation Power.

What were the legal consequences of rehabilitation for criminal prosecution according to that amended statute? The most important consequence was the revocation of the judgment. This revocation would 'eliminate the legal effects of the judgment' (sec. 4). Any execution of a punishment must be ended, and the respective entries in the register of convictions be deleted (sec. 5). According to section 6, a later law would deal with the issue of reimbursement for fines and fees paid by the convicted. Section 7 determined that in case of detention rehabilitation gives rise to a right to social benefits as a compensation for a loss of health and financial or other disadvantages. For the kind and extent of benefits, the law referred to the law of the Federal Republic on assistance for persons detained for political reasons outside of the Federal Republic of Germany.[27]

3. The 1992 Law on Rehabilitation and Compensation for Criminal Prosecution

It took more than two years until the all-German parliament, the *Bundestag*, was able to agree on a new 'Law on the Rehabilitation and Compensation of

---

[25] See Quint (supra note 13), at 220.
[26] See *Vereinbarung zur Durchführung und Auslegung des Einigungsvertrages*, BGBl. 1990 II, 1239, Art. 3, no. 6a. The GDR law entered into force on Sep. 18, 1990, its amendment, agreed upon by the two German governments on the same day, became effective with reunification on Oct. 3, 1990. Accordingly, there was a short period in which the rules of the GDR law on compensation for administrative and employment discrimination were in force. However, rehabilitation decisions made before Oct. 3, 1990 have not become known. See W. Pfister, 'Die Aufhebung von Willkürurteilen', in: J. Weber & M. Piazolo (eds.), *Eine Diktatur vor Gericht: Aufarbeitung von SED-Unrecht durch die Justiz*, 1995, 181, 184.
[27] See *Gesetz über Hilfsmassnahmen für Personen, die aus politischen Gründen ausserhalb der Bundesrepublik Deutschland in Gewahrsam genommen wurden (Häftlingshilfegesetz)*, as amended Dec. 19, 1986 and Dec. 22, 1989, BGBl. 1987 I, 513, 1989 I, 2398, 2401. For the version presently being in force, see BGBl. 1993 I, 839, 1994 I, 1214.

Victims of Measures of Criminal Prosecution Taken Contrary to the Rule of Law'.[28] The law, enacted as part of the (first) 'Statute for the Correction of SED Injustice',[29] repealed the amended GDR law of 1990, according to which applications for rehabilitation had been dealt with in the meantime.[30] It also abolished the alternative procedure of cassation[31] which had followed different rules and had been taken care of by different panels of judges.

Section 1 of the statute provides that a criminal conviction by a German court in East Germany, between May 8, 1945, the day of the unconditional surrender of the German armed forces, and October 2, 1990, the day before reunification, will be declared a violation of the principle of rule of law and annulled (this declaration and the annulment together constitute the rehabilitation) to the extent that it is 'inconsistent with the essential principles of a free order [based on] the rule of law'[32]. In particular, this requirement – much more narrowly formulated than Article 17 of the Unification Treaty – will be met if the conviction served the purpose of political persecution, or if the penalty was grossly disproportionate to the offense.[33] By listing, in a non-exhaustive way, a number of offenses under the GDR Constitution and Criminal Code,

---

[28] See *Gesetz über die Rehabilitierung und Entschädigung von Opfern rechtsstaatswidriger Strafverfolgungsmaßnahmen im Beitrittsgebiet (Strafrechtliches Rehabilitierungsgesetz)* of Oct. 29, 1992, entered into force Nov. 4, 1992; BGBl. 1992 I, 1814. The statute was amended by Art. 2 of the law of June 8, 1994 (BGBl. 1994 I, 1214), Art. 6 of the law of June 23, 1994 (BGBl. 1994 I, 1311, 1320), Art. 1 of the law of Dec. 15, 1995 (BGBl. 1995 I, 1782), and Art. 3 of the law of July 1, 1997 (BGBl. 1997 I, 1609, 1611). A consolidated version was published in BGBl. 1997 I, 1614. For a quasi-official interpretation, see L.-W. Keck et al., 'Das Strafrechtliche Rehabilitierungsgesetz im Überblick', *Deutsch-Deutsche Rechts-Zeitschrift* 1993, 2 et seqq.; for a section by section analysis, see M. Bruns et al., *Strafrechtliches Rehabilitierungsgesetz: Kommentar*, 1993, and J. Herzler (ed.), *Strafrechtliches Rehabilitierungsgesetz: Potsdamer Kommentar*, 1993.

[29] *Erstes Gesetz zur Bereinigung von SED-Unrecht (Erstes SED-Unrechtsbereinigungsgesetz)*, Oct. 29, 1992, BGBl. 1992 I, 1814. See supra note 14.

[30] See also sec. 1, para. 6, of the 1992 Rehabilitation Law (supra note 28), according to which an application under the law is inadmissible if after Oct. 2, 1990 a court has conclusively decided about an application for rehabilitation or cassation based on the same facts and circumstances. However, a new application is admissible if the applicant can demonstrate that the former application would have been successful under the 1992 law.

[31] See supra text accompanying note 16 et seqq.

[32] Translation by Quint (supra note 13), at 220 et seq. For the meaning of the notion of *Rechtsstaat* in the context of reparation of GDR injustice, see C. Starck, 'Der Rechtsstaat und die Aufarbeitung der vor-rechtsstaatlichen Vergangenheit', in: *Veröffentlichungen der Vereinigung der Deutschen Staatsrechtslehrer* no. 51, 1992, at 11-20.

[33] Thus, the point of reference for rehabilitation was shifted. While under the GDR law it was the exercise of political rights, i.e. an activity of the individual, it is now the political persecution of an individual by the State. See Keck et al. (supra note 28), at 3 et seq. The GDR law resembled postwar legislation providing for the annulment of certain penal judgments passed between 1933 and 1945. This legislation had also referred to the motivation of the convicted person. See Tappert (supra note 2), at 222 et seq.

a statutory presumption was established that such convictions had been politically motivated. The listed offenses include: Transfer of nonsecret information to foreign States or organizations (*landesverräterische Nachrichtenübermittlung*, sec. 99 of the Criminal Code),[34] rendering assistance to persons trying to flee the GDR or to stay abroad (*staatsfeindlicher Menschenhandel*, sec. 105), agitation inimical to the State (*staatsfeindliche Hetze*, sec. 106), contacting organizations or persons opposing the public order of the GDR (*ungesetzliche Verbindungsaufnahme*, sec. 219), illegal crossing of the border (*ungesetzlicher Grenzübertritt*, sec. 213), boycott agitation (*Boykotthetze*) against democratic institutions and organizations (Art. 6, para. 2, of the 1949 GDR Constitution), refusal to serve in the armed forces (*Wehrdienstentziehung and Wehrdienstverweigerung*, sec. 256 of the Criminal Code), and treason and espionage (secs. 96-98, 100, 108) if committed for the Federal Republic of Germany or one of its allies. Another offense often misused to punish persons who wanted to leave the GDR was the so-called disturbance of the work of the government (*Beeinträchtigung staatlicher oder gesellschaftlicher Tätigkeit*, sec. 214).[35] Today it is estimated that between 1949 and 1990 GDR criminal courts convicted as many as 200,000 men, women and young persons for political reasons.[36]

Section 2 (as amended in 1994)[37] declares that the law analogously applies to administrative or judicial decisions imposing a deprivation of liberty, in particular decisions to lock up persons in mental hospitals for the purpose of

---

[34] For illustrative examples of convictions for that offense, see Katharina Gelinsky, 'Karlsruhe billigt Verurteilung wegen Rechtsbeugung', in: *Frankfurter Allgemeine Zeitung*, April 23, 1998, at 4. The *Stadtgericht* (Municipal Court) of Berlin gave a couple a prison sentence of more than two years for having given a copy of its application for permission to leave the GDR to the Office of the Permanent Representative of the Federal Republic of Germany in East Berlin. Another person was convicted to two years of imprisonment for having consulted the same office about ways to obtain a permission to leave East Germany.

[35] For an analysis of the political misuse of the administration of criminal justice in the GDR, see, e.g., Pfister (supra note 26), at 186-196 (with an overview of rehabilitation cases); K.W. Fricke, *Politik und Justiz in der DDR: Zur Geschichte der politischen Verfolgung 1945-1968*, 2d ed. 1990; W. Schuller, *Geschichte des politischen Strafrechts der DDR bis 1968*, 1980; Landesjustizverwaltungen der Länder Berlin, Brandenburg, Mecklenburg-Vorpommern, Sachsen, Sachsen-Anhalt und Thüringen (eds.), *Politische Strafjustiz in der früheren DDR, dargestellt an ausgewählten Einzelschicksalen*, 1997; G.M. Kraut, *Rechtsbeugung? Die Justiz der DDR auf dem Prüfstand des Rechtsstaates*, 1997, 150-226; F. Werkentin, *Politische Strafjustiz in der Ära Ulbricht*, 1995; R. Beckert, *Die erste und letzte Instanz: Schau- und Geheimprozesse vor dem Obersten Gericht der DDR*, 1995. See also the material assembled by a *Bundestag* commission of inquiry: *Materialien der Enquête-Kommission 'Aufarbeitung von Geschichte und Folgen der SED-Diktatur in Deutschland' (12. Wahlperiode des Deutschen Bundestages)*, vol. 4: *Justiz und Polizei im SED-Staat*, 1995.

[36] See K.W. Fricke, 'Gefängnisregime und politische Verfolgung unter totalitärer Herrschaft', *Deutschland Archiv* 31 (1998), 650, 651.

[37] See Art. 6, no. 1, of the *Zweites SED-Unrechtsbereinigungsgesetz* (supra note 63).

political persecution or for other 'irrelevant' (i.e. non-medical) reasons. Life under conditions similar to imprisonment, and forced labour under such conditions are considered as imprisonment.

Sections 3 to 6 and 16 to 25 deal with the legal consequences of a rehabilitation. The enforcement of the respective judgment must be ended (sec. 4), the annulled decision is deleted from the federal register of convictions (sec. 5, para. 3), and fines and fees paid by the convicted, including the costs of the original trial, are refunded (sec. 6).[38] If the conviction included a confiscation of property, restitution would take place (or not take place) according to the 'Statute concerning the Settlement of Open Property Questions' ('Property Statute')[39] and the 'Statute concerning Special Investments in the GDR' ('Investment Statute')[40].

According to section 16 et seqq., a rehabilitated person who suffered disadvantages from imprisonment[41] has a right to special social benefits. First, such a person, or his or her heirs, will receive D-Mark 300 (i.e. approximately US $170) for each month of imprisonment.[42] An additional D-Mark 250 (US $140) will be paid to those who resided in the GDR until November 9, 1989, the day the Berlin Wall was opened (sec. 17). 'The additional amount represents compensation for the stigmatization to which political convicts who remained in the GDR were often subjected; they confronted a harder fate than those whose freedom was purchased by the Federal Republic or who otherwise succeeded in reaching the West after their imprisonment.'[43] The Federal Government had proposed an additional amount of only D-Mark 150 (US $85) per month, but critics pointed to the fact that persons wrongfully imprisoned

---

[38] For two GDR marks originally paid, a person is refunded one D-Mark. This is the same exchange rate as it was applied to claims and liabilities (with the exception of wages, salaries, grants, pension, rents and leases, where the rate was one to one) when the West German currency was introduced into the GDR on July 1, 1990. See Treaty Establishing a Monetary, Economic and Social Union ('State Treaty') of May 18, 1990, Art. 10(5), BGBl. 1990 II, 537, 538. For an English version, see ILM 29 (1990), 1108, 1126.

[39] *Gesetz zur Regelung offener Vermögensfragen (Vermögensgesetz)* (see infra note 88). The 1992 Rehabilitation Law referred to the version of July 14, 1992, BGBl. 1992 I, 1257.

[40] *Gesetz über besondere Investitionen in der DDR (Investitionsgesetz)*, see infra note 89.

[41] For a description of the fate of political prisoners in GDR jails, see K.W. Fricke, *Zur Menschen- und Grundrechtssituation politischer Gefangener in der DDR*, 2d ed. 1988; Gedenkstätte für die Opfer politischer Gewalt Moritzplatz Magdeburg (ed.), *'Die Vergangenheit lässt uns nicht los ...' Haftbedingungen politischer Gefangener in der SBZ/DDR und deren gesundheitliche Folgen*, 1997.

[42] For orientation, the legislature had looked at the amount fixed for victims of the Nazi regime. According to sec. 45 of the *Bundesgesetz zur Entschädigung für Opfer der nationalsozialistischen Verfolgung (Bundesentschädigungsgesetz)* (Federal Compensation Law) (BGBl. 1956 I, 562, 570) they had received D-Mark 150 (US $85) for each month of imprisonment. See Keck et al. (supra note 28), at 3, 7.

[43] Quint (supra note 13), at 223.

in the Federal Republic (i.e., before October 3, 1990, in West Germany) receive compensation of D-Mark 600 (US $340) per month.[44] The total amount of D-Mark 550 (US $310), which the *Bundestag* eventually determined, still remains lower than that.[45] Also, only a few of the entitled would receive immediate payment. In view of the difficult budgetary situation, payment could be deferred until December 31, 1999.[46]

Formerly imprisoned individuals who today are in particular economic distress may receive additional financial assistance (see sects. 18 and 19), but it is largely left to the discretion of the respective agencies whether and to which extent such assistance is provided.[47] Persons whose health has been impaired because of imprisonment are entitled to benefits according to the provisions of the Federal Statute concerning Care for War Victims (sec. 21).[48] These benefits may include reimbursement for medical expenses, grants supporting the education of childen, and a disablement pension.[49] The time of imprisonment and a subsequent time of inability to work or unemployment is taken into account in the computation of pensions.[50] If a person died in

---

[44] See sec. 7, para. 3, of the *Gesetz über die Entschädigung für Strafverfolgungsmassnahmen* (Law on Compensation for Measures of Criminal Prosecution and Penalties) of March 8, 1971, BGBl. 1971 I, 157, 158, as amended May 24, 1988, BGBl. 1988 I, 638 (D-Mark 20 for each day of imprisonment).

[45] On the other hand, victims receive considerably more than according to sec. 7, para. 2, of the 1990 GDR Rehabilitation Law which referred to the West German *Häftlingshilfegesetz* (see supra note 27). Secs. 9a-9c of that law provided for a *Eingliederungshilfe* (integration assistance) of D-Mark 80 (US $45) per month of imprisonment, and there was no such financial assistance for an imprisonment suffered before Jan. 1, 1947.

[46] See sec. 1 of the *Verordnung über die Gewährung der Kapitalentschädigung nach dem Strafrechtlichen Rehabilitierungsgesetz* (Ministerial Order on the Granting of Compensation by Capital Payment according to the Criminal Rehabilitation Law), March 19, 1993, BGBl. 1993 I, 362. Sec. 2 establishes the order in which payment is made. Persons aged 70 or more are first considered. According to the Federal Minister of Justice, approximately D-Mark 400 million were paid to former political prisoners until July 31, 1994. The Federal Government anticipates a total amount of D-Mark 2 billion (2,000 million). See S. Leutheusser-Schnarrenberger, 'Bewältigung der rechtlichen Probleme der Wiedervereinigung', *Deutsch-Deutsche Rechts-Zeitschrift* 1994, 290, 291.

[47] Benefits according to sec. 18 are granted by the 'Foundation for Former Political Prisoners' established by sec. 15 of the *Häftlingshilfegesetz* (supra note 27). See also *Richtlinien für die Gewährung von Unterstützungsleistungen nach §18 des Strafrechtlichen Rehabilitationsgesetzes* (Guidelines for Payments According to Section 18 of the Criminal Rehabilitation Law), Jan. 26, 1993, Bundesanzeiger 1993 No. 143, p. 7141, reprinted in: Pfister & Mütze (supra note 23), part A 58.

[48] See *Gesetz über die Versorgung der Opfer des Krieges (Bundesversorgungsgesetz)* of Dec. 20, 1950, BGBl. 1950, 791, as amended, BGBl. 1982 I, 21.

[49] For a catalogue of benefits, see secs. 9 and 25b of the *Bundesversorgungsgesetz*.

[50] See *Sozialgesetzbuch, Sechstes Buch: Gesetzliche Rentenversicherung* (Federal Public Welfare Code, Book 6: Social National Pension Insurance) of Dec. 18, 1989, sec. 250, para. 1, no. 5a; BGBl. 1989 I, 2261, as amended July 25, 1991, BGBl. 1991 I, 1606, 1620.

consequence of an impairment of his or her health that occurred because of imprisonment, surviving dependants can claim benefits under the same War Victims statute (sec. 22). The same applies if a death penalty, imposed by a decision meeting the requirements of section 1, was executed.[51]

The capital payment (sec. 17), but not the benefits provided for in sections 21 and 22, can also be claimed by persons imprisoned in East Germany 'in connection with the establishment or maintenance of the communist tyranny' without having been sentenced by a German court (sec. 25, para. 2, no. 2). Thus, persons imprisoned by the Soviet Occupation Power (in particular in consequence of trials before Soviet military tribunals)[52] can receive financial compensation although they cannot apply for rehabilitation under the statute. While the original 1990 GDR Rehabilitation Law had included this group of people,[53] the Federal Government argued that rules of international law prevented Germany from granting rehabilitation for acts of a foreign State.[54] In 1992, the Russian 'Law on Rehabilitation of Victims of Political Repression' was amended to include persons sentenced by Soviet courts outside the Soviet Union.[55] It has been criticized that so far decisions under that law have only been made according to the record (which often is missing, incomplete

---

[51] According to latest figures, German courts in the Soviet Zone of Occupation (1945-49) inflicted capital punishment in 142 cases; in 47 cases the death penalty was executed. After 1949, GDR courts imposed the death penalty 230 times; the penalty was executed in 159 cases. The death penalty was abolished in East Germany in 1987. See Peter Jochen Winters, 'DDR-Juristen wegen Totschlags und Rechtsbeugung verurteilt', *Frankfurter Allgemeine Zeitung*, July 3, 1998, at 2.

[52] For figures of the persons imprisoned in Soviet internment camps in East Germany between 1945 and 1990, see statement of the Federal Government of June 15, 1992 in reply to an interpellation of Mr. R. Schwanitz, member of the *Bundestag*; Bundestagsdrucksache no. 12/2864, at 7 et seq. (according to Soviet sources, 123,000 Germans were imprisoned, 43,000 of which died during the time of imprisonment. 45,000 are listed as having been released, and 13,000 as deported to the Soviet Union).

[53] See supra text following note 24.

[54] See the draft law of Nov. 15, 1991: *Entwurf eines Ersten Gesetzes zur Bereinigung von SED-Unrecht, Einzelbegründung zu § 25 Abs. 2 (Nr. 5) Strafrechtliches Rehabilitierungsgesetz*; Bundestagsdrucksache 12/1608, at 29, reprinted in: Pfister & Mütze (supra note 23), part D 10.1, 46.

[55] See Tappert (supra note 2), at 233-36, and W. Seiffert, 'Das russische Rehabilitationsgesetz und seine Auswirkungen auf deutsche Staatsangehörige', *Recht in Ost und West* 42 (1998), 26-29. For a German translation of the law (as amended), see *Recht in Ost und West* 42 (1998), 36-40. According to the Russian Judge Advocate General, Jurij Djomin, 13,000 applications for rehabilitation filed by foreigners (11,000 of which were filed by Germans) have been decided since 1992. About 7,100 Germans have been rehabilitated. In comparison, the number of Germans convicted by Soviet military courts is estimated at 200,000. The Russian law is unclear about persons imprisoned and expropriated without judicial proceedings (the so-called *administrativ Verfolgten* or 'persons persecuted by administrative measures'). See Markus Wehner, 'Djomin: Die Bundesregierung hat keinen Einfluß ausgeübt', *Frankfurter Allgemeine Zeitung*, July 7, 1998, 4.

or only consisting of a confession obtained by coercion); neither the victim nor witnesses are heard. In view of this procedure it is indeed questionable to make restitution of property expropriated in East Germany between 1945 and 1949 dependent on a Russian rehabilitation decision.[56]

An application for rehabilitation under the German 1992 statute can not only be filed by the victim, but also by his or her spouse, certain close relatives, and persons having a legitimate interest in the rehabilitation. The State prosecutor is entitled to make an application if the victim does not disagree (sec. 7). Originally, the deadline for applications was December 31, 1994. The respective period has been prolonged twice; the deadline is now December 31, 1999.[57]

Two other points are worth mentioning. First, according to section 16, para. 2, of the 1992 Rehabilitation Law benefits for disadvantages suffered from imprisonment are not granted if the convicted person 'violated the principles of humanity or the rule of law, or misused his position to his own advantage or to the disadvantage of another, in a serious manner'. The first exception is modelled on similar provisions in other statutes for the benefit of refugees and expellees and political prisoners.[58] To concretize the phrase 'principles of humanity', courts have relied on international human rights instruments, in particular the Universal Declaration of Human Rights, the International Covenant on Civil and Political Rights, and the European Convention for the Protection of Human Rights and Fundamental Freedoms.[59] The provision mainly aimed at convicts who in jail spied on other inmates and delivered information to the GDR 'State security service' (*Staatssicherheitsdienst*), or, tragically, obtained an abridgment of their sentence by promising that they would work for the secret police after having been released from prison.

Second, section 9, para. 2, of the 1992 Rehabilitation Law prohibits a person who has been a judge or State prosecutor in the GDR from hearing rehabilitation cases unless he or she has passed all screening processes and has received a new judicial appointment. At any rate, not more than one former GDR judge or prosecutor may sit on a three-judge rehabilitation panel.

---

[56] See infra text accompanying note 110.

[57] Until April 1994, approximately 100,000 rehabilitation cases had been decided; 19,000 applications were still pending. See Leutheusser-Schnarrenberger (supra note 46), at 291.

[58] See *Gesetz über die Angelegenheiten der Vertriebenen und Flüchtlinge (Bundesvertriebenengesetz)* of May 19, 1953 (BGBl. 1953 I, 201, 204), secs. 3 and 11, no. 1; sec. 3, para. 2, as amended Jan. 2, 1993 (BGBl. 1993 I, 830, 831), and sec. 2, para. 1, no. 2 of the *Häftlingshilfegesetz* (supra note 27).

[59] See Mütze, Comment on sec. 16, para. 2, of the 1992 Rehabilitation Law, in: Pfister/Mütze (supra note 23), part B 10, 14 et seq.

On the same day the Criminal Rehabilitation Law was enacted, the *Bundestag* unanimously adopted a 'statement in defence of the honour of the victims of the communist tyranny':[60]

> The German *Bundestag* acknowledges the hard fate of the victims and their families who have suffered from the injustice of the communist tyranny.
>
> The men and women who suffered under communist despotism in many ways experienced injustice or arbitrariness. They were deprived of their freedom and kept imprisoned in conditions violating human dignity. Many died in prisons falling far short of humane conditions. They were tortured, tormented and killed. In their professional lives, they were disadvantaged, harassed, and discriminated against. They were deported. In disregard for elementary principles of humanity, they were turned out of their towns and villages, of house and home. Their property and assets were hurt.
>
> The German Parliament bowes before all the victims of communist injustice. It shows its profound respect and gratefulness to all those whose sacrifice helped reuniting in freedom the divided Germany after more than forty years.

As much as the *Bundestag* must be commended for having spoken these clear words, one cannot help feeling that they were meant to make up for a law which would repair only little of the listed wrongs.

4. The 1994 Administrative Rehabilitation Law

The 1992 law described in the preceding section excluded administrative discrimination in the GDR as well as discrimination in employment for political reasons – two forms of discrimination which the original 1990 GDR Rehabilitation Law had sought to regulate,[61] and which indeed were encountered by many more East Germans than measures of criminal prosecution. Covering a wide range of possible cases and injuries of greatly varying intensity, typical cases included, as Professor Quint wrote, 'dismissal from employment in retaliation for filing an application to leave the GDR, or exclusion from an advanced high school (*Oberschule*) on political grounds with the resulting inability to attend university and pursue a professional career. In many of these cases the problems of proof, as well as the difficulties of measuring the ultimate consequences of the claimed discrimination, were daunting. Moreover, it would be impossible to undo the effects of these

---

[60] *Ehrenerklärung für die Opfer der kommunistischen Gewaltherrschaft*, June 17, 1992; Verhandlungen des Deutschen Bundestags, 12. Wahlperiode, Stenographische Berichte, vol. 162, 97. Sitzung, 7953, reprinted in: Pfister & Mütze (supra note 23), sec. D 10.2. On June 5, 1998, the Bundestag adopted a 'Law on the Establishment of a Foundation for a Critical Reappraisal of the SED Dictatorship' (*Gesetz über die Errichtung einer Stiftung zur Aufarbeitung der SED-Diktatur*); BGBl. 1998 I, 1226. *Inter alia*, the foundation shall 'support the counselling of, and care for, victims of the Soviet Occupation Power and the SED dictatorship' (sec. 2, para. 2, no. 2).

[61] See supra text following note 258.

discriminations, and many asserted that any attempts to provide real compensation for their effects would be quixotic and beyond the resources of the treasury of the Federal Republic'.[62]

After a long and intense debate, the *Bundestag*, almost four years after reunification, finally passed the 'Second Statute for the Correction of SED Injustice'.[63] As an umbrella law, it included two statutes, the Administrative Rehabilitation Law[64] and the Employment Rehabilitation Law[65].

Section 1 of the Administrative Rehabilitation Law provides that an administrative decision of a German public authority, agency or body, made between May 8, 1945 and October 2, 1990, which has led to a health defect, a property loss or a disadvantage in employment, can be revoked at the victim's request, 'if it is absolutely inconsistent with leading principles of a State based on the rule of law, and its consequences directly continue into the present in an onerous and unacceptable manner'.[66] Section 2 further explains: 'Absolutely inconsistent with leading principles of a State based on the rule of law are measures which have seriously violated principles of justice, legal security, or proportionality, and have either served the purpose of political persecution or constituted arbitrary action in the individual case.' As an example of such measures, section 3 mentions the compulsory resettlement of persons living close to the western border of the GDR. The law does not apply to administrative decisions in tax matters, which were dealt with in separate regulations,[67] nor to acts of expropriation carried out by German authorities

---

[62] See Quint (supra note 13), at 224.

[63] *Zweites Gesetz zur Bereinigung von SED-Unrecht (Zweites SED-Unrechtsbereinigungsgesetz)*, June 23, 1994, BGBl. 1994 I, 1311. For the first statute, see supra note 29.

[64] The full title is *Gesetz über die Aufhebung rechtsstaatswidriger Verwaltungsentscheidungen im Beitrittsgebiet und die daran anknüpfenden Folgeansprüche (Verwaltungsrechtliches Rehabilitierungsgesetz)* (Law on the revocation of administrative decisions in the area [East Germany] inconsistent with the rule of law and claims following therefrom (Administrative Rehabilitation Law)). The statute was amended by Art. 1, para. 2, of the law of Dec. 15, 1995 (BGBl. 1995 I, 1782), and again by Art. 2 of the law of July 1, 1997 (BGBl. 1997 I, 1609). A consolidated version was published in BGBl. 1997 I, 1621. For a systematic analysis, see Klaus Wimmer, *Verwaltungsrechtliches Rehabilitierungsgesetz: Kommentar*, 1995.

[65] The full title is *Gesetz über den Ausgleich beruflicher Benachteiligungen für Opfer politischer Verfolgung im Beitrittsgebiet (Berufliches Rehabilitierungsgesetz)* (Law on the compensation of victims of political persecution in the area [East Germany] for employment disadvantages (Employment Rehabilitation Law)). The statute was first amended by Art. 1, para. 3, of the law of Dec. 15, 1995 (BGBl. 1995 I, 1782), and again by Art. 1 of the law of July 1, 1997 (BGBl. 1997 I, 1609). A consolidated version was published in BGBl. 1997 I, 1626.

[66] Cf. sec. 21 of the original 1990 GDR Rehabilitation Law (supra note 23): 'Persons will be rehabilitated who suffered considerable disadvantages because of administrative measures which violated or inadmissibly restricted basic rights guaranteed in the constitution, and were meant to accomplish political goals.'

[67] See the draft law of May 19, 1993: *Entwurf eines Zweiten Gesetzes zur Bereinigung von SED-Unrecht, Einzelbegründung zu § 1 Abs. 1 (Nr. 8) Verwaltungsrechtliches Rehabili-*

between 1945 and the proclamation of the GDR in 1949, which are attributed to the Soviet Occupation Power (sec. 1, para. 1, second and third sentence).[68] On the other hand, the law analogously applies to acts of the ruling communist party, the *Sozialistische Einheitspartei Deutschlands* (SED), and other parties and organizations controlled by it (sec. 1, para. 6).

Similar to what the 1992 Law on rehabilitation for criminal prosecution says, persons whose health has been impaired because of an administrative act are entitled to benefits according to the provisions of the Federal Statute concerning Care for War Victims (sec. 3). If the victim died in consequence of an impairment of his or her health, surviving dependants can claim benefits under the same statute (sec. 4). In case the administrative measure included confiscation of property, the victim can claim restitution in accordance with the 'Property Statute'[69] and related statutes (sec. 7). For employment discrimination in consequence of the administrative measure, section 8 refers to the Employment Rehabilitation Law.[70] All these claims are excluded if the victim 'violated the principles of humanity or the rule of law, or misused his position to his own advantage or to the disadvantage of another, in a serious manner' (sec. 2, para. 2).[71]

An application for rehabilitation under the law can be filed by the victim or, after his or her death, by anyone having a legal interest in the rehabilitation of the victim (sec. 9). Originally, an application had to be filed before December 31, 1995; the period was later extended twice, so that the relevant date is now December 31, 1999.

It is true that the law, by requiring an extraordinarily severe form of injustice before rehabilitation will be triggered, promised few tangible benefits to the politically oppressed of the former GDR.[72] It is also true that it deviated from the Unification Treaty which defined those entitled to rehabilitation and compensation as 'victims of a ... judicial decision inconsistent with the rule of law or the constitution'[73] without further qualifications. However, the restriction introduced by the law was what the legislature had intended. When submitting the bill to parliament, the Federal Government declared:

---

tierungsgesetz; Bundestagsdrucksache 12/4994, at 22, reprinted in: Pfister/Mütze (supra note 23), part D 20.1, 19.

[68] For a further exclusion of claims, see sec. 2, para. 3.

[69] See supra note 88.

[70] See infra text following note 78.

[71] See supra text accompanying note 58 et seq.

[72] See the critique by Quint (supra note 13), at 224. See also H. Kaschkat, 'Die Haftung für DDR-Unrecht und der Entwurf des 2. SED-Unrechtsbereinigungsgesetzes', *Deutschland Archiv* 26 (1993), 598, 601.

[73] See supra text accompanying note 14.

So many measures of injustice have been discovered that not all of them can be covered by this law. It is impossible to make good forty years of GDR injustice. In addition, the economic situation of the new *Länder* requires such self-restraint. It must be the primary goal further to support the economic upturn in East Germany; governmental manpower and financial means must primarily serve that task. Therefore, as far as rehabilitation is concerned, all that can be done is to take up and, if possible, make good grave violations of leading principles of the *Rechtsstaat*... . In the interest of legal security, and for financial reasons, only the most blatant violations of the rule of law will be taken up.[74]

Even before the enactment of the law, it was criticized that the legislature's objective not to overstrain the State budget could not only have been achieved by such narrowly defined tests of eligibility but also by a distinction between rehabilitation as such (a formal statement that an administrative measure was inconsistent with rule of law-principles) and compensation, in a way that someone was entitled to only the first and not the second.[75] It was argued that if such a distinction had been made, the conditions of rehabilitation could have been less strict, and a far greater number of people would have enjoyed some moral satisfaction. In 1997, the legislature finally half-heartedly responded to this criticism by inserting a new section 1a into the law. It set out that an addressee of an administrative measure (or, after his or her death anybody having a legitimate interest in the rehabilitation of the deceased) can apply for a statement saying that the measure was inconsistent with principles of the rule of law, even if there was no violation of health or property, or an employment discrimination (see sec. 1), provided that the measure 'is absolutely inconsistent with leading principles of a State based on the rule of law and led to a serious disparagement of the person concerned in his or her personal sphere'.[76] No further claims can be based on such a statement.[77]

---

[74] See the draft law of May 19, 1993 (supra note 67), *Begründung Allgemeiner Teil*, at 16, 18. Reprinted in: Pfister/Mütze (supra note 23), part D 20.1, 11, 14.

[75] See, e.g., G. Saathoff et al., 'Kritik am Entwurf der Bundesregierung für ein 2. SED-Unrechtsbereinigungsgesetz', *Deutschland Archiv* 26 (1993), 603, 607.

[76] See *Gesetz zur Verbesserung rehabilitierungsrechtlicher Vorschriften für Opfer der politischen Verfolgung in der ehemaligen DDR*, July 1, 1997, Art. 2, no. 1, BGBl. 1997 I, 1609, 1610. For a short explanation of the law, see Gerlinde Bürger, 'Gesetz zur Verbesserung ...', *Deutsch-Deutsche Rechts-Zeitschrift* 1997, 342.

[77] In July 1998, the Humboldt University in Berlin, which was located in the Soviet sector of the city, declared as 'immoral and void' the acts of the period 1945-1990 by which it had deprived former students of their academic titles because they had politically opposed the communist regime or illegally left East Germany. See M. Vec, 'Aberkennung aberkannt', in: *Frankfurter Allgemeine Zeitung*, July 11, 1998, 42.

5. The 1994 Employment Rehabilitation Law

This law[78], which like the Administrative Rehabilitation Law was passed as part of the 'Second Statute for the Correction of SED Injustice',[79] is perhaps the most disappointing of the three rehabilitation laws. Its provisions are far from keeping the promise of its title, even if it only speaks of *Ausgleich*, which in German legal terminology is less than full or adequate compensation (*Entschädigung*). Instead, the law only applies to an extremely narrowly defined group of politically persecuted persons, and gives them little more than some benefits regarding pension payments.

When submitting the bill, the Federal Government explained:

> Compared to those classes of persons especially supported by the communist system, and also the West Germans, the majority of the GDR population experienced disadvantages in education and employment. In the GDR, there was no free choice of profession. The entire education system, in particular higher education, was orientated to the anticipated labor requirements, and subjected to intense, ideologically motivated regulation. Therefore, it was the fate of a large part of the East German population not to receive the desired education or professional training, or not to have the desired occupation. Success in professional life did often not depend on individual qualification or performance. Again and again, people encountered limits set not by their own abilities but the political system. ... Such general East German fate cannot lead to claims for compensation ...[80]

In section 1 of the law, the group of 'politically persecuted persons', which may receive compensation under the statute, is defined as those people who in the time between May 8, 1945 and October 2, 1990, because of an act of political persecution, in particular imprisonment, could, at least temporarily, not follow the profession they had practised before, they had learned or provably aspired to. In the same words as those used by the other two rehabilitation laws, compensation is excluded if the person in question 'violated the principles of humanity or the rule of law, or misused his position to his own advantage or to the disadvantage of another, in a serious manner' (sec. 4).[81] Section 5 limits claims based on political discrimination in employment and education to those set out in the statute under discussion.

In sections 6 and 7, the statute grants some financial assistance in re-education or further education in the claimant's area of specialization. This, and only this assistance can also be claimed by former students who for political reasons were not admitted to high school or an institution of higher

---

[78] See supra note 65. For analysis, see W.-J. Lehmann et al., 'Das Zweite Gesetz zur Bereinigung von SED-Unrecht (Teil 1)', *Neue Justiz* 1994, 350 et seqq.

[79] See supra note 63.

[80] See the draft law of May 19, 1993 (supra note 67), *Begründung Allgemeiner Teil, II. Leitlinien der beruflichen Rehabilitierung*, at 18. Reprinted in: Pfister/Mütze (supra note 23), part D 30.1, p. 14.

[81] See supra text accompanying notes 58 et seq. and 71.

education (sec. 3). According to section 8, persecuted persons whose present economic situation is particularly bad, and who probably in the future will have an income lower than that necessary to cover the basic cost of living (as defined by social welfare legislation), are entitled to a monthly payment in addition to normal social welfare benefits. However, persons who left the GDR before October 2, 1990 can only receive this payment if their persecution (normally imprisonment) lasted longer than three years (sec. 2, sec. 8, para. 1). Originally, the amount was D-Mark 150 (US $85), and payments were only made until the claimant would receive a pension. In July 1997, the amount was doubled, and payments of D-Mark 200 (US $115) per month extended to pensioners.[82]

In its central part (secs. 10-16), the statute attempts to adjust pension payments so that they would resemble the payments that would have been received if the individual had not been subjected to political discrimination. In other words, the law treats the individual as if he or she had regularly made contributions to the public pension insurance fund during the time of political persecution at a level of those made at the time by an average worker or employee in the respective profession. It does not matter whether somebody would have been particularly capable and successful or not. In retrospect, everybody is treated like the average worker in the respective field; and it is indeed hard to see how the law could have justly differentiated in that respect. No provision is made for the recovery of a position from which an individual was excluded, or a payment of lost wages, or a preferential treatment with regard to employment in the public service. It is true that thus 'substantial compensation for employment discrimination is deferred until retirement, and limited by the period of time that the claimant receives a pension'.[83]

According to the original wording of section 20, an application for an official statement declaring that someone was entitled to compensation under the statute had to be filed before December 31, 1995. As in the case of the Administrative Rehabilitation Law, the period was twice prolonged, and is now going to end on December 31, 1999.[84] Even after the death of a victim his surviving dependants can ask for such a statement.

---

[82] See law of July 1, 1997 (supra note 76), Art. 1, no. 3.

[83] See Quint (supra note 13), at 226.

[84] Applications for the compensation itself must now be filed before December 31, 2000 or, in case of the monthly payment supplementing the pension, within half a year after pension payment has begun.

6. Restitution of Property and Compensation for Loss of Property

The systematic expropriations which took place in East Germany during the time of Soviet military occupation and after the GDR had been established can be regarded as a human rights violation in and by itself, therefore to be considered in this paper. In addition, for property losses suffered because of political persecution, the criminal and the administrative rehabilitation statute both refer to the legislation regarding the restitution of property. For these reasons, it seems necessary briefly to describe this legislation. A comprehensive discussion of the many intricate problems in this area, which keep a flourishing branch of legal scholarship and practice occupied, is not intended.[85]

Article 41, para. 1, of the Unification Treaty incorporated the 'Joint Declaration on the Regulation of Open Property Questions' of the Governments of the Federal Republic and the GDR of June 15, 1990.[86] An additional paragraph dealt with property to be used for investment. Article 41 was given constitutional rank by Article 4, paragraph 5, of the Unification Treaty, which inserted a new Article 143 in the Basic Law: 'Article 41 of the Unification Treaty and rules enacted for its implementation are constitutional even in so far as they provide that measures of expropriation in the area described in Article 3 of that treaty (i.e. East Germany) are not to be repaired.' The Unification Treaty[87] also put into force two laws passed by the GDR *Volkskammer* shortly before reunification, namely the 'Property Statute'[88] and the 'Investment Statute'.[89] In 1992, the latter was repealed and replaced by the 'Investment Preference Statute'.[90]

---

[85] For an instructive overview, see Quint (supra note 13), at 124 et seqq.

[86] *Gemeinsame Erklärung der Regierungen der Bundesrepublik Deutschland und der Deutschen Demokratischen Republik zur Regelung offener Vermögensfragen;* Bulletin des Presse- und Informationsamtes der Bundesregierung no. 77, June 19, 1990, 661; attachment III of the Unification Treaty, BGBl. 1990 II, 1237.

[87] See Unification Treaty (supra note 13), attachment II, ch. III(B), para. I(4) and (5).

[88] *Gesetz zur Regelung offener Vermögensfragen,* Gesetzblatt der DDR 1990 I, 1899. The statute, adopted by the GDR Volkskammer on Sep. 23, 1990, was put into force by the Unification Treaty (supra note 13), attachment II, ch. III(B), para. I(5), and later repeatedly amended. On Aug. 4, 1997, a consolidated version was published in BGBl. 1997 I, 1974. For an extensive loose-leaf collection of legislative acts and judicial decisions concerning the restitution of property in East Germany, see A. Brandt & H.-D. Kittke, *Rechtsprechung und Gesetzgebung zur Regelung offener Vermögensfragen (RGV),* 1993-98. For a systematic explanation of the Property Statute, see W. Fricke & K. Märker, *Enteignetes Vermögen in der Ex-DDR,* 1996.

[89] *Gesetz über besondere Investitionen in der Deutschen Demokratischen Republik,* Gesetzblatt der DDR 1990 I, 1867. The statute, adopted by the GDR Volkskammer, was put into force together with the Property Statute by the Unification Treaty (supra note 13), attachment II, ch.

The Joint Declaration of 1990 embodied two equally controversial decisions which were retained by later legislation. The first was that expropriations 'on the basis of occupation law or occupation authority' – that is, the expropriations of 1945-49 – are not to be undone.[91] This meant that the bulk of land and industrial property expropriated in East Germany between 1945 and the moment of reunification would not be returned to the former owners.[92] The official reasoning for this decision (and the justification for the implied departure from the constitutional principle of equal treatment)[93] was that the 'inviolability' of the 1945-49 expropriations had been 'a non-negotiable precondition' for the consent of both the Soviet and the GDR Government to the unification of Germany.[94] It is debatable whether this contention is true.[95] It seems that the Federal Government was actually rather yielding to what appeared to be the position of a majority of GDR citizens (and future voters in the reunited country), who, quite in line with the communist propaganda of forty years, believed in the land reform as a 'historical achievement' and abhorred the idea of a 'return of the Junkers'. In addition, the Federal

---

III(B), para. I(4). It was amended by Art. 2 of the law of March 22, 1991, BGBl. 1991 I, 766, 774.

[90] *Gesetz über den Vorrang für Investitionen bei Rückübertragungsansprüchen nach dem Vermögensgesetz (Investitionsvorranggesetz)*, July 14, 1992, BGBl. 1992 I, 1257, 1268, 1993 I, 1811. After further amendments, a consolidated version was published on Aug. 4, 1997 in BGBl. 1997 I, 1996.

[91] Joint Declaration (supra note 86), no. 1. See also sec. 1, para. 8 a), of the Property Statute (supra note 88). For an extensive analysis and critique of this decision, the legislation implementing it and the Constitutional Court rulings upholding it, see G. Biehler, *Die Bodenkonfiskationen in der Sowjetischen Besatzungszone Deutschlands 1945 nach Wiederherstellung der gesamtdeutschen Rechtsordnung 1990*, 1994; W. Graf Vitzthum & W. März, *Restitutionsausschluss: Berliner Liste 3, Verfahrensbeteiligung, Entschädigungs- und Ausgleichsleistungsgesetz*, 1995; J. Wagner, *Rückgabe und Entschädigung von konfisziertem Grundeigentum: Aktuelle Verfassungsrechtsfragen der Bodenreform in der SBZ*, 1995.

[92] The Soviet Military Government expropriated essentially all large business enterprises of the East. The so-called *Bodenreform* or land reform resulted in an expropriation of approximately 35 percent of the agricultural land in the Soviet zone. See Quint (supra note 13), at 125, and the *Bodenreform-Urteil* (supra note 6), at 96-102. For further statistical information about expropriations in the Soviet Zone of Occupation and the GDR, see Fricke & Märker (supra note 88), at 9-23, and Leutheusser-Schnarrenberger (supra note 46), at 293.

[93] Art. 3 of the Basic Law; see supra text following note 7.

[94] See *Bodenreform-Urteil* (supra note 6), at 109 et seq., and the decision of the Constitutional Court of April 18, 1996; BVerfGE vol. 94 (1997), at 12, 29 et seq.

[95] For the arguments of those who hold that there was no such precondition, see the decision of April 18, 1996 (supra note 94), at 23-25. The Court itself cautiously concluded that it was the responsibility of the Federal Government to determine whether indeed reunification depended on the consent of the Federal Republic to an exclusion of a restitution of the respective property, and that, making this determination, the Government had broad discretionary powers. The assessment of the situation by the Government could not be regarded as a 'violation of duty'. See id. at 35 et seq.

Government hoped to finance at least a substantial part of the cost of unification by selling 'socialist property' which would come under its control.

In contrast, the Declaration set out that, as a rule, real property expropriated
by the GDR, or placed under State administration, must be restituted. The
Property Statute specified that the expropriation must have been effected
without compensation or with a compensation lower than that GDR citizens
were entitled to claim (sec. 1, para. 1). At the same time, it provided for a
restitution of all property assets, not just real property.

However, the Declaration and Article 41, para. 2, of the Unification Treaty
provided for a number of exceptions. According to the first, and most
important, a former owner can be denied a return of real property if that
property is needed for urgent investment uses that would yield general
economic benefits in East Germany. This exception is the subject of the
investment statutes referred to above. Secondly, the Declaration excluded the
return of property if such return is practically impossible because, for instance,
pieces of land have been merged to build a large apartment complex.[96]
Thirdly, a return does not take place if property has been acquired *bona fide*
(*in redlicher Weise*).[97] The Property Statute introduced further exceptions
from restitution for business property.[98] In all these cases, a claim to some
monetary compensation arises which remains far below the actual trade value
of the property.[99] Of particular importance in that respect is section 7 of the
Compensation Law which provides for a progressive reduction of compensation payments exceeding the amount of D-Mark 10,000 (US $5,700). If the
amount exceeds D-Mark 30,000 (US $17,100), there is a reduction by fifty
percent; if the amount exceeds three million D-Mark (US $1,710,000), the
payment is reduced by ninety-five percent. Compensation is not rendered by
cash payments but by an allocation of transferable bonds which fall due only
in 2004. Before that date, they also do not yield interest.

It was only in September 1994 that the German Parliament reluctantly
passed the 'Equalization Payments Law' providing for a compensation of
individuals[100] for expropriations of the 1945-49 period.[101] Parliament thus

---

[96] See also secs. 4 and 5 of the Property Statute (supra note 88) (as amended).

[97] See sec. 4, paras. 2 and 3 of the Property Statute (supra note 88). From these provisions it
follows that the condition is usually met whenever the transaction was legal under GDR law.

[98] See secs. 4 and 6 of the Property Statute (supra note 88).

[99] See sec. 16 of the Investment Preference Statute (supra note 90), sec. 9 of the Property
Statute (supra note 88), and the *Gesetz über die Entschädigung nach dem Gesetz zur Regelung
offener Vermögensfragen (Entschädigungsgesetz)* (Compensation Law) of Sep. 27, 1994; BGBl.
1994 I, 2624, 1995 I, 110. For an analysis of the latter statute, see H.-J. Rodenbach & O.
Löffler, *Entschädigungen und Ausgleichsleistungen für Vermögensverluste in der ehemaligen
DDR und der SBZ*, 1995, 65-109.

[100] In contrast, compensation according to the Compensation Law (supra note 99) can be
claimed by natural and juridical persons alike.

reacted to a controversial judgment of the German Federal Constitutional Court of April 23, 1991, which had upheld the provision of the Unification Treaty that the 1945-49 expropriations would remain permanent, but had also declared that the constitutional principle of equality (Article 3 of the Basic Law) required some degree of compensation of the former owners.[102] As explained above, a restitution of real property is excluded even if it is presently owned by the Federal Republic, a State (*Land*) or a municipality. In contrast, movable property is to be returned as long as it is not connected to real property, or has been acquired 'in an honest manner', or constitutes cultural property meant for public exhibition.[103] In principle, compensation is granted according to the Compensation Law, but further restrictions and exceptions apply.[104] In particular, so-called reparation losses arising from a removal or destruction of economic goods by the Soviet Occupation Power are not compensated for. As regards farmland and forests presently owned by the State, former owners are entitled to repurchase a limited expanse at favorable prices, but a present lessee of the property, including a former collective farm,[105] has a prior right of purchase.[106]

Claims under the Equalization Payments Law are generally barred if the expropriated person or his or her heir, or an expropriated corporation 'violated the principles of humanity or the rule of law, or misused his position to his own advantage or to the disadvantage of another, in a serious manner, or substantially supported the national socialist or the communist system' in East Germany.[107]

According to section 1, para. 7, of the Property Statute, the statute also applies to a restitution of property 'in the context of an annulment of criminal or administrative law decisions inconsistent with principles of the rule of law, which has been effected in accordance with other provisions'. These 'other provisions' are the 1992 Criminal Rehabilitation Law[108] and the 1994

---

[101] *Gesetz über staatliche Ausgleichsleistungen für Enteignungen auf besatzungsrechtlicher oder besatzungshoheitlicher Grundlage, die nicht mehr rückgängig gemacht werden können (Ausgleichsleistungsgesetz)* (Equalization Payments Law), Sep. 27, 1994, BGBl. 1994 I, 2624, 2628. See generally M. Schmidt-Preuss, *Neue Juristische Wochenschrift* 1994, 3249-3256; B. Zimmermann, 'Wiedergutmachung zwischen materieller Gerechtigkeit und politischem Kompromiss', *Deutsch-Deutsche Rechts-Zeitschrift* 1994, 359-362; Rodenbach & Löffler (supra note 99), at 111-154; and Quint (supra note 13), at 141-144.

[102] See the *Bodenreform* judgment (supra note 6), at 90, 128-31. The judgment was confirmed by a decision of April 18, 1996; BVerfGE vol. 94 (1997), at 12 et seqq.

[103] See sec. 5 of the Equalization Payments Law (supra note 101).

[104] See secs. 1, para. 3, and 2, paras. 2-7, of the Equalization Payments Law (supra note 101).

[105] *Landwirtschaftliche Produktionsgenossenschaft (LPG)*.

[106] See sec. 3 of the Equalization Payments Law (supra note 101).

[107] See sec. 1, para. 4, of the Equalization Payments Law.

[108] See supra note 28.

Administrative Rehabilitation Law,[109] as well as the Russian Rehabilitation Law.[110] From this it follows that a person rehabilitated under one of these laws can claim the restitution of his or her property according to the provisions of the Property Statute. If restitution is excluded by these provisions, the person must be content with receiving compensation according to the 1994 Compensation Law.[111] As far as expropriated property is concerned, a victim of a politically motivated criminal judgment or administrative measure is thus not treated differently from any other person expropriated in East Germany. However, someone sentenced by a Soviet military tribunal in the years 1945 to 1949 who is rehabilitated in Russia can claim restitution or compensation under the Property Statute and the Compensation Statute and not just a payment according to the Equalization Payments Law.

IV. CONCLUSION

Assessing human rights violations in East Germany, the legislation and judicial practice of the united Germany generally referred to internationally recognized standards. The Federal Republic did not simply retroactively apply its norms to what had happened in the East of the divided country between 1945 and 1990. It did not do so in the field of criminal prosecution, where it meticulously sought to observe the guarantee of *nulla poena sine lege* (Article 103, para. 2, of the Basic Law).[112] When the Federal Republic had to decide which judicial and administrative decisions of the GDR it would set aside because they had violated, or continued to violate, fundamental rights and freedoms, it similarly applied standards reflecting an international consensus rather than West German law pure and simple. The 1992 Law on Rehabilita-

---

[109] See supra note 64.

[110] See supra text accompanying note 55. For an official statement of the Federal Ministry of Justice of Oct. 14, 1996 on a recognition of Russian rehabilitation decisions for the purpose of a restitution of property, see *Deutsch-Deutsche Rechts-Zeitschrift* 1997, 49. See also K. Märker, 'Restitution besatzungsrechtlich enteigneten Vermögens bei russischer Rehabilitierung', *Zeitschrift für offene Vermögensfragen* 1997, 4-8, and B. Hoffmeister, 'Die letzte Chance für Eigentümer – Rückgabe des aufgrund Besatzungsrechts enteigneten Vermögens nach Rehabilitierung durch die Russische Föderation', id. at 76-78. While Germany attributes to the Soviet Union expropriations initiated or executed in East Germany by German authorities during the time of Soviet occupation, and therefore has excluded them from the scope of the Administrative Rehabilitation Law (see supra text accompanying note 68), the Russian Federation regards such expropriations as German measures to be repealed by German authorities. Thus, at present victims can seek rehabilitation neither in Germany nor in Russia.

[111] See supra note 99.

[112] See, in particular, the decision of the Federal Constitutional Court of Oct. 24, 1996 (*Killing of Refugees at the Border Between East and West Germany*), BVerfGE vol. 95 (1997), 96, 130-135.

tion and Compensation for Criminal Prosecution, for instance, refers to 'essential principles of a free order [based on] the rule of law'.[113] Thus, one may say that the legal evaluation of the East German past followed broader, and therefore possibly more objective, principles. On the other hand, this internationalization of the controlling standards meant that a substantially higher number of GDR judicial and administrative decisions would remain effective than would have been the case if the higher standard of protection of the (West) German constitution had been applied.

While thus international law, and constitutional principles common to Western-type constitutional States, have to a certain extent governed the question whether there has been a violation of human rights, neither the German Government nor the legislative bodies considered themselves bound by any rules of international law when they provided for measures of rehabilitation and financial compensation. The only accepted legal standard in that regard was the German Constitution. This confirms the view that under customary international law a State is entitled to repair the damage which its own citizens have sustained on the part of its authorities or another State, but is not obliged to do so.[114]

Considering the respective legislative decisions after reunification, one cannot help thinking of the phrase 'too little, too late'. The West German political rhetoric, which for more than forty years denounced the East German regime as illegitimate and assured the East Germans of the solidarity of their 'brothers and sisters in the West', was not to be taken at face value. The German legislation on the rehabilitation and compensation of victims of human rights violations in East Germany since 1945 is the result of an attitude, prevailing in the East and the West of the reunited country, that it is less important and urgent to care for the victims of the past than to rebuild an economy for the future. Government and political parties were rather outspoken on this point. After the unification, it took the *Bundestag* two years to enact a new Criminal Rehabilitation Law, and four years had to pass before rehabilitation for administrative and employment discrimination was made possible. Different from the way one had dealt with the decisions of Nazi courts in the American and the British Zone of Occupation and, eventually, the whole of Germany,[115] no general annulment of judgments was provided

---

[113] See supra text accompanying note 32.

[114] See Christian Tomuschat's contribution to this volume, supra at 1. See also A. Scheffler, *Die Bewältigung hoheitlich begangenen Unrechts durch fremde Zivilgerichte*, 1997, 201, 205-206, 219-220.

[115] See Vogl (supra note 2), at 77-79, 104-117. After a long controversy, the *Bundestag* adopted on May 28, 1998 a law (*Gesetz zur Aufhebung nationalsozialistischer Unrechtsurteile in der Strafrechtspflege*, Bundestagsdrucksache no. 13/10848, BGBl. 1998 I, 2501) by which all convictions and sentences were annulled which 'were imposed after January 30, 1933 [the day

for. Instead, victims had to seek a case-by-case review. A limited financial compensation was only given to political prisoners. No provision was made for a repeal of decisions of civil and labour courts which violated human rights. Rehabilitation for administrative discrimination can only be requested for a measure 'absolutely inconsistent with leading principles of a State based on the rule of law', and the consequences of the measure must 'directly continue into the present in an onerous and unacceptable manner'. Persons who suffered a disadvantage in education and employment can receive some financial assistance in re-education or further education, provided they are not too old or sick, and their pension payments are adjusted to resemble those they would have received without the political discrimination.

In comparison, the financial compensation which was granted the victims of the Nazi regime exceeded in almost all respects that given to those who suffered under the communist system.[116] The comprehensive reparation of Nazi injustice was an outcome of several factors, all of them missing in the case of GDR injustice.[117] The victims were well organized, they were massively supported by the Occupying Powers, their concerns were recognized by a postwar political elite which had already been active in the Weimar Republic and was then pushed aside or even persecuted by the Nazis. Further, the reparation of Nazi injustice constituted an important part of the postwar German foreign policy; it directly served the reintegration of West Germany into the international community. In this situation, the complete bankruptcy of West Germany after World War II was no obstacle for a comprehensive and generous reparation policy. Conversely, the lack of such a policy after the fall of the East German State cannot be adequately explained with a lack of money.

Restitution of expropriated property was granted only with the greatest reluctance. An expropriation was regarded as valid if the former owner had received some compensation under GDR law even if the amount came close to nothing. If expropriated property was acquired by another East German, it will generally stay with that person. If the property was regarded as necessary for rebuilding the economy, the State could sell it to some investor. And even if someone was actually entitled to a restoration of his or her property rights, it was effected slowly and unwillingly by the local authorities of the eastern *Länder*. As to the expropriations of the years 1945 to 1949, it was a German political decision not to repair them. By cloaking this decision with pseudo-

---

Hitler was appointed Chancellor] for political, military, racial, religious or philosophical (*weltanschaulich*) reasons in order to establish or maintain the Nazi tyranny, and which violated elementary concepts of justice (*elementare Gedanken der Gerechtigkeit*)' (sec. 1).

[116] See Tappert (supra note 2), at 228-231.

[117] See Tappert (supra note 2), at 243-246.

legal reasons, law has been done a disservice. By excluding the respective property from restitution, the legal system of the Federal Republic of Germany has gone against one of its own fundamental principles. Respect for private property must be universal, and requires not to distinguish between politically welcome and unwelcome property. The long-term consequences of this decision for the attitude of the German society towards private property may be severer than the present political class is aware of.

Finally, one must deplore the overly complicated nature of the legislation reviewed in this paper. In this respect, nothing has been learned from the experience of the postwar laws in favor of the victims of the Nazi regime which were of a similarly diffuse character. Even a trained lawyer encounters many difficulties in understanding the various laws and their relationship, and so do apparently the authorities entrusted with their administration. Laws meant at least partially to repair governmental wrong of the kind committed by the communist regime in East Germany must be readily comprehensible by those for whom they were made – the victims. Otherwise, their main beneficiary will be the legal community.

Documentary Annex

**Document 1: Basic Principles and Guidelines on the Right to Repara-
tion for Victims of [Gross] Violations of Human Rights and International Humanitarian Law** (UN Doc. E/CN.4/1997/104, 16 January 1997)

COMMISSION ON HUMAN RIGHTS
Fifty-third session
Item 8 of the provisional agenda

QUESTION OF THE HUMAN RIGHTS OF ALL PERSONS SUBJECTED TO ANY
FORM OF DETENTION OR IMPRISONMENT

Note by the Secretary-General

1.   At its forty-eighth session, the Sub-Commission, in its resolution
1996/28 of 29 August 1996, decided to transmit the revised draft basic
principles and guidelines on the right to reparation for victims of gross
violations of human rights and humanitarian law prepared by the former
Special Rapporteur of the Sub-Commission, Mr. Theo van Boven
(E/CN.4/Sub.2/1996/17), to the Commission on Human Rights for its
consideration together with the comments of the sessional working group of
the Sub-Commission on the administration of justice and the question of
compensation (E/CN.4/Sub.2/1996/16, paras. 10-32), and the comments of the
Sub-Commission during its forty-eighth session (see E/CN.4/Sub.2/1996/
SR.25-29 and 35).

2.   The Sub-Commission also requested Mr. van Boven to prepare, without
financial implications, a note taking into account the comments and observations of the working group and the Sub-Commission referred to above, in
order to facilitate the examination by the Commission on Human Rights of the
draft revised basic principles and guidelines.

A. Randelzhofer and C. Tomuschat (eds.), State Responsibility and the Individual, 281–287.
© 1999 *Kluwer Law International. Printed in Great Britain.*

3.   In pursuance of this resolution, the Secretary-General is transmitting to the Commission on Human Rights the revised draft basic principles and guidelines on the right to reparation for victims of gross violations of human rights and humanitarian law prepared by Mr. Theo van Boven (E/CN.4/Sub.2/1996/17) and the report of the sessional working group of the Sub-Commission on the administration of justice and the question of compensation (E/CN.4/Sub.2/1996/16).

4.   The note prepared by Mr. van Boven is contained in the annex to the present document.

ANNEX

Note prepared by the former Special Rapporteur of the Sub-Commission, Mr. Theo van Boven, in accordance with paragraph 2 of Sub-Commission resolution 1996/28

[13 January 1997]

1.   The former Special Rapporteur carefully examined the comments and observations made by members of the sessional working group of the Sub-Commission on the administration of justice and the question of compensation and by other participants in these proceedings, as reflected in the report of the working group (E/CN.4/Sub.2/1996/16, paras. 10-32), as well as a number of suggestions he received from individual members of the Sub-Commission. On that basis he has reviewed the draft revised basic principles and guidelines he previously submitted to the Sub-Commission (E/CN.4/Sub.2/1996/17).

2.   As a result, with a view to facilitate the work of the Commission on Human Rights, the former Special Rapporteur now submits in the appendix hereto the draft revised basic principles and guidelines in a partly adapted version. Wherever wording is suggested as additions to or changes of the revised basic principles and guidelines, such wording is presented in italics. Where wording is put in square brackets, the former Special Rapporteur suggests that such wording be deleted. He hopes that this method will serve a helpful purpose and he is confident that the Commission on Human Rights will be able to deal fruitfully and expeditiously with this important matter.

<u>Appendix</u>

BASIC PRINCIPLES AND GUIDELINES ON THE RIGHT TO REPARATION FOR
VICTIMS OF [GROSS] VIOLATIONS OF HUMAN RIGHTS AND *INTERNATIONAL*
HUMANITARIAN LAW

<u>The duty to respect and to ensure respect for human rights and *international*
humanitarian law</u>

1.   Under international law every State has the duty to respect and to ensure
respect for human rights and *international* humanitarian law.

<u>Scope of the obligation to respect and to ensure respect for human rights and
international humanitarian law</u>

2.   The obligation to respect and to ensure respect for human rights and
international humanitarian law includes the duty: to prevent violations, to
investigate violations, to take appropriate action against the violators, and to
afford remedies and reparation to victims. Particular attention must be paid to
the prevention of gross violations of human rights *and international humanitarian law* and to the duty to prosecute and punish perpetrators of crimes
under international law.

<u>Applicable norms</u>

3.   The human rights and humanitarian norms which every State has the
duty to respect and to ensure respect for, are defined by international law and
must be incorporated and in any event made effective in national law. In the
event international and national norms differ, the State shall ensure that the
norm providing the higher degree of protection *will be made* applicable.

<u>Right to a remedy</u>

4.   Every State shall ensure that adequate legal or other appropriate
remedies are available to any person claiming that his or her *human* rights
have been violated. The right to a remedy against violations of human rights
and humanitarian norms includes the right to access to national and *any
available* international procedures for their protection.

5.   The legal system of every state shall provide for prompt and effective
disciplinary, administrative, civil and criminal procedures so as to ensure

readily accessible and adequate redress, and protection from intimidation and retaliation.

Every State shall provide for universal jurisdiction over gross violations of human rights and *international* humanitarian law which constitute crimes under international law.

Reparation

6.   Reparation may be claimed individually and where appropriate collectively, by the direct victims *of violations of human rights and international humanitarian law*, the immediate family, dependants or other persons or groups of persons *closely* connected with the direct victims.

7.   [In accordance with international law,] States have the duty to adopt special measures, where necessary, to permit expeditious and fully effective reparations. Reparation shall render justice by removing or redressing the consequences of the wrongful acts and by preventing and deterring violations. Reparations shall be proportionate to the gravity of the violations and the resulting damage and shall include restitution, compensation, rehabilitation, satisfaction and guarantees of non-repetition.

8.   Every State shall make known, through public and private mechanisms, [both at home and where necessary abroad,] the available procedures for reparations.

9.   Statutes of limitations shall not apply in respect of periods during which no effective remedies exist for violations of human rights *or international* humanitarian law. Civil claims relating to reparations for gross violations of human rights and *international* humanitarian law shall not be subject to statutes of limitations.

10.   Every State shall make readily available to competent authorities all information in its possession relevant to the determination of claims for reparation.

11.   Decisions relating to reparations for victims of violations of human rights *or international* humanitarian law shall be implemented in a diligent and prompt manner.

Forms of reparation

Reparations, *to be provided in accordance with the law of every State,* may take any one or more of the forms mentioned below, which are not exhaustive, viz:

12.   Restitution shall be provided to re-establish the situation that existed prior to the violations of human rights *or international* humanitarian law. Restitution requires, inter alia, restoration of liberty, family life, citizenship, return to one's place of residence, *and restoration of* employment *or* property.

13.   Compensation shall be provided for any economically assessable damage resulting from violations of human rights *or international* humanitarian law, such as:
(a)   Physical or mental harm, including pain, suffering and emotional distress;
(b)   Lost opportunities including education;
(c)   Material damages and loss of earnings, including loss of earning potential;
(d)   Harm to reputation or dignity;
(e)   Costs required for legal or expert assistance, *medicines and medical services.*

14.   Rehabilitation shall be provided and will include medical and psychological care as well as legal and social services.

15.   Satisfaction and guarantees of non-repetition shall be provided, including, as necessary:
(a)   Cessation of continuing violations;
(b)   Verification of the facts and full and public disclosure of the truth;
(c)   An official declaration or a judicial decision restoring the dignity, reputation and legal rights of the victim and/or of persons closely connected with the victim;
(d)   Apology, including public acknowledgement of the facts and acceptance of responsibility;
(e)   Judicial or administrative sanctions against persons responsible for the violations;
(f)   Commemorations and paying tribute to the victims;
(g)   Inclusion in human rights training and in history *or school* textbooks of an accurate account of the violations committed in the field of human rights and *international* humanitarian law;

(h)   Preventing the recurrence of violations by such means as:
  (i)   Ensuring effective civilian control of military and security forces;
  (ii)   Restricting the jurisdiction of military tribunals only to specifically military offences committed by members of the armed forces;
  (iii) Strengthening the independence of the judiciary;
  (iv)   Protecting *persons* in the legal profession and human rights defenders;
  (v)   *Conducting and strengthening*, on a priority *and continued* basis, human rights training to all sectors of society, in particular to military and security forces and to law enforcement officials.

Document 2: The right to restitution, compensation and rehabilitation for victims of grave violations of human rights and fundamental freedoms. Resolution 1998/43 of the United Nations Commission on Human Rights, 17 April 1998 (adopted without a vote)

The Commission on Human Rights,

Guided by the Charter of the United Nations, the Universal Declaration of Human Rights, the International Covenants on Human Rights, other relevant human rights instruments and the Vienna Declaration and Programme of Action,

Reaffirming that, pursuant to internationally proclaimed human rights principles, victims of grave violations of human rights should receive, in appropriate cases, restitution, compensation and rehabilitation,

Reiterating the importance of addressing the question of restitution, compensation and rehabilitation for victims of grave violations of human rights and fundamental freedoms in a systematic and thorough way at the national and international levels,

Recalling its resolution 1996/35 of 19 April 1996, in which it regarded the basic principles and guidelines proposed by the former Special Rapporteur of the Sub-Commission on Prevention of Discrimination and Protection of Minorities, Mr. Theo van Boven, as a useful basis for giving priority attention to the question of restitution, compensation and rehabilitation,

<u>Taking note with appreciation</u> of the report of the Secretary-General (E/CN.4/1998/34) submitted in compliance with Commission resolution 1997/29 of 11 April 1997,

<u>Noting with interest</u> the positive experience of countries that have established policies and adopted legislation on restitution, compensation and rehabilitation for victims of grave violations of human rights,

1. <u>Calls once more</u> upon the international community to give due attention to the right to restitution, compensation and rehabilitation for victims of grave violations of human rights;

2. <u>Requests</u> the Chairman of the Commission to appoint an expert to prepare a revised version of the basic principles and guidelines elaborated by Mr. van Boven, taking into account the views and comments provided by States and intergovernmental and non-governmental organizations, and to submit it to the Commission at its fifty-fifth session, with a view to its adoption by the General Assembly;

3. <u>Requests</u> the Secretary-General to invite States that have not yet done so, as well as intergovernmental and non-governmental organizations, to submit their views and comments on the basic principles and guidelines prepared by Mr. van Boven as soon as possible, and by no later than 31 October 1998, and to make that information available to the independent expert;

4. <u>Decides</u> to continue its consideration of this matter at its fifty-fifth session under the agenda item entitled 'Question of the human rights of all persons subjected to any form of detention or imprisonment'.

Participants of the International Colloquium, Berlin, 26–28 September 1998

Rudolf Bernhardt, Professor of Law, former Director of the Max Planck Institute for Comparative Public Law and International Law, Heidelberg; former Judge at the European Court of Human Rights

Antonio Cassese, Professor of Law, University of Rome; President of the International Criminal Tribunal for the Former Yugoslavia, The Hague

Wladislaw Czaplinski, Professor of European Law, University of Danzig

Gennady Danilenko, Institute of State and Law, Academy of Science, Moscow

Bardo Fassbender, Assistant Professor of Law, Humboldt University, Berlin

Lovell Fernandez, Professor of Public and Adjective Law, University of the Western Cape, Bellville

Dieter Fleck, First Counsellor, Legal Department, Federal Ministry of Defence, Bonn

Reinhard Hilger, Head, Department of Public International Law, Federal Ministry of Foreign Affairs, Bonn

Eckart Klein, Professor of Constitutional Law, Public International Law and European Law, University of Potsdam; Member of the Human Rights Committee under the International Covenant on Civil and Political Rights

Pieter H. Kooijmans, Professor of Law, University of Leyden; Judge at the International Court of Justice

Peter Malanczuk, Professor of Law, University of Amsterdam

A. Randelzhofer and C. Tomuschat (eds.), State Responsibility and the Individual, 289–290.
© 1999 *Kluwer Law International. Printed in Great Britain.*

Riccardo Pisillo Mazzeschi, Professor of Public International Law, University of Siena

Theodor Meron, Professor of Law, New York University

Matti Pellonpää, Associate Professor of International Law, University of Helsinki; Judge at the European Court of Human Rights

Albrecht Randelzhofer, Professor of Constitutional Law, Administrative Law, Public International Law and European Law, Free University, Berlin

W. Michael Reisman, Hohfeld Professor of Jurisprudence, Yale Law School, New Haven, Connecticut

Georg Ress, Professor of Law, Co-Director of the Institute of European Studies, University of the Saarland, Saarbrücken; Judge at the European Court of Human Rights

Gerd Seidel, Professor of Public Law, Humboldt University, Berlin

Torsten Stein, Professor of Law, Co-Director of the Institute of European Studies, University of the Saarland, Saarbrücken

Daniel Thürer, Professor of Law, University of Zurich

Christian Tomuschat, Professor of Public Law, Director of the Institute of International and European Law, Humboldt University, Berlin

Joe Verhoeven, Professor of Law, Catholic University, Leuven

Norbert Wühler, Chief, Legal Services Branch, United Nations Compensation Commission, Geneva

Karl Zemanek, Professor of Law, Director of the Institute of Public International Law and International Relations, University of Vienna

Index of Cases

A. Randelzhofer and C. Tomuschat (eds.), State Responsibility and the Individual, 291–296.
© 1999 *Kluwer Law International. Printed in Great Britain.*

European Court of Justice

Interamerican Court of Human Rights

Human Rights Committee

Commission on Human Rights - Special Rapporteurs